John Herman Randall, Jr.

Naturalism
and
Historical
Understanding

Essays on the Philosophy of
JOHN HERMAN RANDALL, Jr.

Edited by
JOHN P. ANTON

STATE UNIVERSITY OF NEW YORK PRESS

Printed in the United States of America

Editor's Preface

Most of the papers which appear in this volume were presented to Professor John H. Randall, Jr., on the occasion of his sixty-fifth birthday anniversary, February 14, 1964. With the exception of three which arrived at a later date, the papers were written for this special event. Warm statements and appreciative essays were written for the occasion by Josephine Waters Bennett, Herbert A. Deane, Carlo Diano, John R. Everett, C. A. Fritz, Jr., Joseph Katz, Corliss Lamont, Evelyn Shirk, and Charles E. Trinkhaus, Jr. *Festschrift* papers were also contributed by E. A. Burtt, W. E. Hocking, C. H. Kahn, S. Lamprecht, M. Lipman, R. McKeon, and J. J. Walsh.

The special character of this volume, which was designed as a series of critical discussions of the work and thought of John H. Randall, Jr., did not permit the inclusion of all the excellent essays initially among the set of papers presented to Dr. Randall on that memorable occasion. The editor wishes to express his gratitude for these contributions, and to beg the forgiveness of their authors for being prevented by circumstances from including their essays in this volume. The editor also wishes to express his deep appreciation for the "Anniversary Meditation" written by Herbert Schneider for that special event. Its lyrical and personal tone, its profundity of thought, and its character as philosophical poetry made the message so nearly sacred that it seemed only appropriate to the editor to accede to the author's wish to withhold it from publication. The editor wishes also to acknowledge his indebtedness to Columbia University Press for permission to reprint here a part of the first chapter of Professor Justus Buchler's recent book, *Metaphysics of Natural Complexes* (pp. 30-51); an earlier version of this part of the book was one of the papers presented to Professor Randall on his sixty-fifth birthday anniversary.

The committee that planned the event to celebrate Randall's sixty-fifth anniversary consisted of John P. Anton, Horace L. Friess, J. Glenn Gray, James Gutmann, George L. Kline, and H. Standish Thayer. Without the generous help and valuable suggestions of the members of this committee, the editor of this volume could never have brought his task to fruition.

I am grateful to the Committee of Allocation of Research Funds of the Graduate School, State University of New York at Buffalo, for its generous support through two grants in 1963 and 1964 to undertake the editorial and bibliographical work for this volume. Special thanks must go to Dr. Henry Woodburn, formerly Dean of the Graduate School, for his practical wisdom, and for his interest in this work. To the University of Buffalo Foundation and its able Director, Dr. William J. O'Connor, I owe special gratitude for generous services and advice. The constant encouragement and help which my friends and colleagues Professors Rollo Handy and Marvin Farber have given me from the inception to the completion of my tasks I shall probably never be able to repay. The kind consideration given to this project by Dr. Chandler McC. Brooks, Chairman of the Publications Committee of the State University of New York Press, and by Professor John Sirjimaki, when it was first submitted in manuscript form to the Committee, must also be acknowledged here with gratitude. When all is said and done, this volume is more the work of devoted friends and scholars than of any single person—least of all, the editor.

With regard to the bibliography of Randall's published works, I wish to make the following acknowledgments: I am grateful to Dr. James Gutmann and Dr. Corliss Lamont for their valuable suggestions and for bringing to my attention a number of items otherwise unknown to me. Mrs. John H. Randall, Jr., generously made available her invaluable collection and has given helpful suggestions for the completion of the bibliography. Mr. Milo Vannucci, through his professional competence and advice, has contributed significantly to the final preparation of the bibliography. My friend and student, Mr. J. Stanley Yake, has done much to assist in the preparation of the manuscript, and Miss Carol Breitenbach's secretarial abilities have been of incalculable value throughout this undertaking.

J. P. A.

Buffalo, N.Y.
January 3, 1967

Table of Contents

JOHN P. ANTON
State University of New York at Buffalo

John Herman Randall, Jr.

A Biographical Sketch

Among the great teachers of philosophy in America, there is surely none who stands in less need of introduction than John H. Randall, Jr. One of our century's most distinguished historians of philosophy, and a philosopher in his own right, he is well known both in this country and abroad for his contributions, at once scholarly and exciting, to the study of Greek philosophy, to the interpretation of Aristotle, and to the exploration of the Aristotelian tradition in the Renaissance and the origins of modern scientific thought. To generations of American college and university students, he is the man who above all others rendered the development of the modern Western mind both perspicuous and enchanting. To American philosophers and in American philosophy, his voice has been among the most eloquent in the defence and elaboration of that profoundly civil, natural, and wise philosophy he learned—or first began to learn—from his own two greatest teachers, Frederick J. E. Woodbridge and John Dewey. It can be said in truth that Randall never touched a subject-matter without making it luminous and intelligible, and in his almost fifty years of inspired teaching and writing he has scorned no inquiry, no idea, no vision ever ardently pursued by men anywhere. The measure of our intellectual indebtedness to him will not be soon taken.

He was born on February 14, 1899, in Grand Rapids, Michigan. His interest in philosophy dates from his days as a student at Columbia College, when, as a sophomore, his "philosophical and historical imagination was stirred" by Frederick J. E. Woodbridge. Among his other teachers at Columbia College, from which he graduated Phi Beta Kappa in 1918, were John Erskine, Felix Adler, Charles A. Beard, and James Harvey Robinson. The following year (1919) he earned his Master of Arts with a thesis on the "Neokantian Social Philosophy in Germany and France: The Critical Method Applied to the Philosophy of Control." In 1920, while still a graduate student, he was made a lecturer in philosophy in the University Extension, and in July of 1921 was raised to the rank of instructor. One year later (1922), upon submitting and successfully defending a dissertation on "The Problem of Group Responsibility to Society: an Interpretation of the History of American Labor," he was awarded his doctorate by Columbia University. But the happiest event in that year was the winning of Miss Mercedes Irene Moritz to be his wife.

Though his publishing career began in 1919 with an article, "Instrumentalism and Mythology," published in the *Journal of Philosophy*, the first book-length venture in which he engaged was the cooperative volume, *An Introduction to Reflective Thinking*, his collaborators being two men who were to be his friends and colleagues at Columbia for many years to come, James Gutmann and Herbert Schneider. This work, to which Professor Randall contributed several chapters, appeared in 1923, and in the following year (1924) he published in two volumes and under the title of *The Western Mind: Its Origins and Development* the book that two years later (1926) in a revised and expanded version was to become his famous *The Making of the Modern Mind*. Revised again in 1940, this book has remained continuously in print since its initial appearance, and has found an appreciative and grateful readership far beyond the confines of philosophy and history. He was promoted to the rank of assistant professor in 1925, and in 1929 published his second book, *Our Changing Civilization: How Science and Machine Are Reconstructing Modern Life*. A German translation of this work appeared in 1932. His promotion to the rank of associate professor came in 1931, and in 1935 he attained the rank of full professor. Thus a career already rich in creative thinking, teaching, and writing reached a first culmination. In 1945, he was elected to the vice-presidency of the American Philosophical Association, Eastern Division, and in 1947, in recognition of his distinguished service in his field of learning, Columbia University awarded him its coveted Butler Medal. The following year he spent as a visiting professor at the University of Washington in Seattle.

A high water mark in both his professional and personal life came on January 1, 1951, when he was appointed to the Frederick J. E. Woodbridge Professorship of the History of Philosophy, and so became the first occupant of the chair created in memory of his beloved teacher. In 1954, he was elected to the presidency of the newly-founded Renaissance Society of America, a post in which he served till 1957. In 1955, he delivered the Mead-Swing Lectures at Oberlin College, published in 1958 as *The Role of Knowledge in Western Religion*. He became president of the American Philosophical Association, Eastern Division, in 1956. In the summer of 1958, at the meeting of the Twelfth International Congress of Philosophy in Venice and Padua, he and his friend Carlo Diano became respectively the American and Italian fathers of the Columbia-Padua Institute (Istituto Columbiano-Padovano), a society devoted to the study of the Aristotelian tradition in the Veneto, sponsored in Italy by the University of Padua and in the United States by Columbia University. His *Nature and Historical Experience*—one of the several influential contributions to the formulation of a naturalistic metaphysics made by the students of Woodbridge—appeared in the same year (1958), and two years later (1961) his *School of Padua and the Emergence of Modern Science* was published by the Institute in Padua. This small but important work consisted of three essays revised and expanded from earlier versions, and called attention once again to Professor Randall's original but now widely accepted thesis that modern science is to a significant degree Aristotelian (and Paduan) in its origins.

In 1961, Professor Randall delivered two distinguished series of lectures: the Matchette Lectures at Wesleyan University, and the Merrick Lectures at Ohio Wesleyan University. The Matchette Lectures, which bore the title "How Philosophy Uses Its Past," were published in 1963 under the same title. On the occasion of the Merrick Lectures on the theme "The Intellectual Challenge of Religious Pluralism," the honorary degree of Doctor of Literature was conferred on him by Ohio Wesleyan University. During these years—indeed, all through the years in which he taught the history of philosophy at Columbia—Professor Randall was at work on his *magnum opus: The Career of Philosophy*, the first volume of which appeared in 1962, and the second in 1965. The third and final volume of this monumental history of Western thought from the Middle Ages to the present is now in preparation. To the generations of students in his History of Philosophy whom he delighted with his insights, his rich and irrepressible Socratic humor, and his oratorical grace and power, he could make no greater gift. It was both fitting and (one likes to think) inevitable that in 1964 the Society of Older Graduates of Columbia should present him its "Great Teachers Award," with the following aptly and beautifully worded citation:

JOHN HERMAN RANDALL, JR.

Frederick J. E. Woodbridge Professor of Philosophy

Generations of grateful students have learned from you the love of wisdom which philosophy and its history cherish. Your books, in which nature and history are analyzed, but never trivialized and marred, have spurred the quest of scholars, enriching countless minds. Your career in philosophy has been marked by high honors and offices in learned societies and academic institutions at home and abroad. The brilliance of your scholarship, anticipated in your undergraduate achievements, has added to the radiance of Alma Mater's

light. As fellow alumni, we bring to you, worthy successor of the great
teacher whose name is attached to the chair you fill, grateful acknowl-
edgement of the lasting debt all Columbia men may share in contem-
plation of your distinguished life.[1]

He has been awarded the 1966 Ralph Waldo Emerson Award by the
Phi Beta Kappa Senate for his book, *The Career of Philosophy: From the
German Enlightenment to the Age of Darwin*. In recommending the
work for the honor, the awards committee commented: "This is a work
of maturest scholarship, rich in erudition and acumen, lively but free of
idiosyncracies and free too of pedantry. It will remain our standard comprehensive history of philosophy for years to come."

Now in his last year of teaching at the University he has served so
well and devotedly all his life, John Herman Randall remains what he
has always been: a great teacher, a consummate human being, and a
ready friend to all those who are inflamed by the same love of philosophy
and history that have been his since his first encounter with Dean Woodbridge. In January of this year he will go to that other country and city
where nothing is alien to him, and where he has long been a denizen in
spirit—to Italy and Padua—there to be made a doctor by the University
of Padua, and so to enter the company of the great Paduan doctors of the
Renaissance whose image he has done so much to rescue and brighten in
the present. It is hard indeed to imagine a place in which John Herman
Randall would be an alien, provided only that there are men who love
ideas there.

---

[1] Kindly sent to the editor by Mr. Roger Shelley, Assistant to the Director of the
Columbia University News Office.

PART ONE

PHILOSOPHICAL TRADITIONS

JACQUES BARZUN
Columbia University

Ideas Just in Time

The long continuity of Western civilization and the growth—perhaps the overgrowth—of the historical sense during the last hundred and fifty years have conspired to put among our chief intellectual concerns the history of ideas. Both civilization and history are forms of self-consciousness, and it is congenial to the self-conscious to trace their own descent, whether by descent is meant pride of ancestry or manifest decline. In either sense one readily catches the ear of the twentieth century by talking about ideas.

But there are two ways of talking about ideas, which divide mankind as effectively as most definitions of human types. One way is to describe and interlink ideas by their contents analytically considered. In this kind of history the great thinkers resemble a troupe of performers on the trapeze, who hang each from his predecessor's feet, except when, from time to time, one flings himself across a void to catch an unoccupied bar swinging at a distance. In this kind of history the adequacy of the idea to its subject—and, one might add, the beauty and daring of the feats of strength —provide the reader's pleasure. The student is brought to understand ideas from within and by the light of their declared purpose. The chief qualities needed for this kind of historiography are subtlety and thoroughness in perceiving abstract relations and interpreting words.

The second kind of history treats ideas as objects of culture. The connections of ideas so considered are not solely with other ideas, all equally pure and professional, but with persons, events, emotions, and the muddy, unexamined ideas of the many. The great ideas are, in this view, looked at from outside, and only in a special way from within. The undeclared intention, the possibly illogical or ulterior motive, become important to the chronicler, so that there is no telling beforehand what trivial or momentous fact of a different order from the intellectual may find itself caught up and given a role in the narrative. This type of history appeals to the more robust spirits, who can stand, and indeed who prefer, their explanations filled with the miscellany of existence. The subtlety here required is not less than in the analytic game, but it addresses itself to events and emotions more than to words and concepts; it is not so geometrical and cannot be thorough, but partakes rather of the finesse of poetic imagination. Both kinds of history (when written and not merely conceived) are precious possessions, and it would be convenient if they were distinguished by name: the first, or acrobatic kind, might be properly called "intellectual history"; the second, or worldly kind, might be called "the history of ideas."

Being something of a worker in the second kind, I may be permitted to put on record a word or two about one of the contemporary masters of the genre, whose works shaped not only my own nascent interest in it but also the minds of thousands of other students during the last forty years. It was in the first instance *The Making of the Modern Mind* that opened to us in our youth the panorama of ideas-in-time. The ordinary book or course of lectures on the history of philosophy may, it is true, employ biographical tidbits to introduce each new figure in the parade of thought, but its use of time is merely a convenience to mark simple succession: it is empty time, in which Kant follows Hume who follows Berkeley and Locke by a kind of parthenogenesis. There is virtually no collateral branching, and certainly no miscegenation with barbarians and illiterates, as in the coarse but comprehensive history of ideas.

Time, in the latter kind of history, is not a category but a plural existence: it is *the times,* full, overcrowded, a hodgepodge. That is what permits the historian I call worldly to describe the making of the modern mind, yours and mine, as against the distilled essence of Kant's or Comte's. Such an historian faces the enormous task of selection, the ever-present duty of gauging relevance. Up to a point he can be analytical, for he too must understand ideas and how they evolve, but his success lies a good way beyond analysis: he must know history not merely like a philosopher but like a common, or garden, historian; he must possess the instinct for reconstructing the conditions in which ideas are born, live, and die; and he must exercise the tact that will keep him from overdoing any such analogy. He falls into the error of too much zeal the moment he shows ideas as products, the moment he substitutes surrounding conditions for thinking minds. Again, he must bring clarity, trace patterns, assign influences; but he betrays his calling as soon as he discerns and promotes a grand design.

I have been describing—and, as I believe, praising—the mind and the work of John Herman Randall. When I say "the work" I mean both the annunciatory *Making of the Modern Mind* and the body of studies, exploring or definitive, that have followed it. To those of us who found our first ideas about ideas under the spur of that early book of his, the miracle of its publication will always remain vivid. To be sure, the Columbia tradition inaugurated by James Harvey Robinson, and its sequel, the influential course in Contemporary Civilization, help to explain the precocious mastery of our young teachers Irwin Edman, Herbert Schneider, and John Randall. Even their legend was instructive—and they had become legendary within five years. A freshman reading Edman's *Human Traits* in the fall knew that the book was by the youngest instructor on the staff. In the spring, when he had Randall's book, the word went round college halls that it was by a fellow graduated the previous June—the swiftest flowering of ideas on record.

What was impressive about Randall's textbook was not alone its extraordinary mass of solid fact and perfectly lucid organization and exposition. After all, competent textbooks answer precisely to these specifications. No, the great surprise was the mysterious absence of the textbook smell; or to put it positively, the excellence, the delight came from the *movement* of ideas, the suspense (not to say the element of plot) in the story. And when one came to reflect one saw that the pervasive cause was the sense of history as action. We read, for example, that "throughout the long eighteenth-century attack upon the old regime, there had been no serious attempt at intellectual defense of the existing order." Well, why not? The next sentence resolves our suspense: "Those who upheld it either considered it strong enough to stand by itself without any apology, or else, being in control, resorted to the readiest weapon of the entrenched conservative, force and suppression." The slowest wit can learn from these remarks the meaning of "man thinking": it is that man thinks for, against, within, a state of fact. A few lines later the impression is confirmed. When during and after the French Revolution the conservative case was finally made out, "this philosophy was largely apologetic, and its main lines were determined by the nature of the attack to which it was the answer."

But are there not thinkers who do not make out a case, or who stand aside from the main stream? To be sure there are, but their isolation is seldom more than apparent, they are never known to push against a void, the mark of time is always upon them: Spinoza uses geometrical form, and Kierkegaard has Hegel on the brain. A few eccentrics apart, the central figures, great and small, produce their ideas not only in the thick of time but *just in time*; by which I mean that their ideas fit; they are received because they correspond and are wanted. In short, ideas in history are always being born at the right minute; though it is of course always possible that contrary examples do not occur because they do not survive.

At any rate, this self-confirming operation has one important consequence for the historian of ideas, a consequence which serves as a caution and which reading Randall at the impressionable time of life made indelible. It is this: because ideas arise from a situation and have an aim, one cannot truthfully represent them as fitting all possible situations and having all deducible aims. They are in fact limited to something less than the universality implied in abstract statements. Of Voltaire's Anglophile ideas, for instance, Randall tells us that they rested on "no conception whatever" that Parliamentary rule was "based on a long historical development of self-government." Voltaire always thought liberties "could be much more efficiently attained at the hands of an enlightened despot like Frederick." This is the Voltairean, as against the unconditioned, meaning of freedom.

This observation points to the chief danger of the purely intellectual historian: he squeezes all he can out of the words of his author, whether the author poured so much meaning into them or not. Reason, Freedom, Nature, is to the pure analyst ever one and the same and never less than what his text allows him to conceive, whether one century or another, one man or another, uses the term. Only a context of words, not of persons or events, narrows it down from an absolute. Into this noble error the receptive student of Randall can never fall. Even a student who is weak on inference is protected by large-type captions that force him to remain within the historical reality: *The Natural No Longer The Reasonable*— after which he is better equipped to grapple with the Romantic Movement.

To say all this is to say that despite trifling causes of irritation here and there such as any large synthesis must contain (I for one cannot even now condone the sneering reference to Frazer's marvelous *Golden Bough* as "third-hand misinformation"), *The Making of the Modern Mind* is a book of that rare kind which can lay the foundations for another man's intellectual career. After studying it and teaching from it, one was ready for the series of articles, lectures, and books, short and long, which exhibited the deepening and enlarging of Randall's thought. It was always historical thought, as well as philosophy; always history of ideas, as well as analysis and criticism. I wish I had the space here to turn analyst for a moment and try my hand upon Randall's view of history, stretching from the article in the symposium published by the Social Science Research Council to the recent volume of Matchette Lectures on *How Philosophy Uses Its Past*. But the historian's philosophy of history is a great field, which my present cursory remarks cannot decently introduce. I content my self with a last illustration showing that, from his brilliant beginnings to his impressive maturity, Randall's mind has not abandoned the historical mode. It was only seven years ago that he published his marvelously concise and illuminating *Aristotle*. What does the author promise us on setting out, and present in the sequel as the *raison d'être* of the universal philosopher? This simple conclusion:

> Aristotle aimed to understand Greece: he never forgot that aim. He did
> not aim to understand something else—the Heavenly Beauty in the sky,
> the moral order in the universe, the divine creator of the world—any of
> those things which men would like to find in the world, but which so far
> as the evidence goes, are not there. Aristotle tried to understand the world
> of Greece that *was* there.

Again, and always, ideas are for a purpose, and the history of ideas
is a recital of that purpose—a purpose shifting with time, but anchored
in things that are indubitably *there*.

JOHN P. ANTON

State University of New York at Buffalo

Randall's Interpretation of Greek Philosophy

I

It was in the academic year 1949-50 that I attended Professor Randall's exciting and inspired lectures on the General History of Philosophy. The auditorium was frequently filled to capacity with legitimate students, naturalists from Columbia proper and "seminarians" from the Union at Riverside, and also with a substantial number of visitors many of us would bring along to witness for themselves the cause of our intellectual enthusiasm. That many of these visitors turned out to be permanent "illegitimates" is another matter. I still remember that nine o'clock Monday morning class when Professor Randall moved on from the Sophistic movement to lecture on Plato, and I first heard him elaborate carefully on a certain key notion, lest we would fail, as many of us did, to capture the importance of the message.

If I single out this particular instance, it is only because of what it has come to mean to me for my own probings in the world of Plato, and for understanding the sort of philosophical thinking the lecturer himself has been doing throughout his long and distinguished career. Since I am quoting from memory, I am prepared to take the blame for any inaccuracies. I recall Randall saying:

> Plato has no closed system, no definitive doctrine. He has no passion for literal truth. What concerns him most is not the mere understanding of facts but their imaginative ideal possibilities and implications for the life of *theoria*. Plato brings forth the fruits of philosophy rather than systematic reflection on philosophy itself.

That Randall was teaching us and telling us, I have no doubt now any more than I did then. It may well be that he was reiterating what sound advice his sage teacher Frederick J. E. Woodbridge had given him. But Randall did more than share his insights. He found a ripe occasion to issue an admonition. He was alerting us to the ever-present temptation of trying to turn Plato's philosophical talking into a Platonism, of sorts.

Many of us found it most difficult to resist such sound advice. His insights proved to be even more irresistible. Thus what initially dawned as a faint suggestion grew as the years went by into an aspiring working idea. Thus it occurred to me that it might be rewarding to try to say about Randall's philosophy the very same things he said about Plato, to find out how true it would be to say that he understands and does philosophy much in the way in which he told us Plato did. At the end, the quest took on the more inclusive shape of an examination of Randall's treatment of Greek philosophy, its development and attainments.

It would be a Herculean task to try to explore down to its last detail the immense world of assimilated facts from the history of ideas, philosophical traditions, and cultural developments Randall has discussed in his writings. The scope and depth of this man's learning is simply breathtaking. Admirable and overwhelming though it is, it can never be called a collection of facts. Nor is the critical dimension it exhibits the result of a mere passion for literal truth. Randall, like the Plato he taught us, never becomes blindly attached to the facts of his unusual historical learning. That Plato had more use for drama and less use for history than Randall, goes without saying. But no matter how different they may be in that respect, both knew what to do with their respective domains of fact. To stop with Randall's erudite mastery of the history of philosophical and cultural traditions, including his critical interpretations of their cumulative reconstructions, would be to admire the scholar but miss the philosopher. The latter emerges forcefully, fruitfully, and clearly when we begin to see what Randall does with his immense knowledge of facts, the uses to which he ultimately puts them, the novel and best philosophical possibilities he finds in them, and the significance they come to possess. In this respect, at least, Randall is doing what he found best in Plato. If only in this sense of philosophy as *technē*, he is admirably close to Plato.[1] Somehow it is most tempting to say at this point that what Randall the historian of philosophy has so eloquently said about Plato is strikingly autobiographical of Randall the philosopher.

II

Randall is more than an admirer of the great philosophers of Greece. He has repeatedly stated that philosophy, after its long modern odyssey, "with many a wound and many a scar," is returning to the naturalism of Greek thought.[2] To assess the meaning of this statement and probe into the depth of Randall's interpretation and evaluation of Greek philosophy and its contribution to Western thought, is the purpose of this paper. It should be pointed out at the very beginning that an adequate treatment of Randall's reaction to the Greeks deserves the length of a full volume. His insights into the cultural and intellectual roots of Western man have far-reaching consequences for understanding Greek philosophy itself and for the critical and creative work that lies ahead for generations to come.

It is impossible to read his analyses of the classical thinkers Plato and Aristotle without a growing realization that he is at once conversing with the Greeks, revealing unsuspected aspects, details, possibilities, and developments, as well as learning from their wisdom, to erect upon this heritage a philosophical monument of his own. If we, as a professional philosophical public in this country, try to remember from time to time that there is a way of doing philosophy which is characteristically American, we would in that measure hardly fail to notice how Randall has deepened and extended this tradition, with the aid of critically reconstructed ideas whose historical antecedents go back to what he found best in Greek philosophy. In fact, Randall has come to show that the scope of American naturalistic philosophy has come of age by "learning from experience" so as to claim a vitality and universality such as the Greeks once exhibited, but without the limitations of some of their unavoidable assumptions.[3]

Any careful examination of Randall's treatment of Greek philosophy —what he thinks philosophy did for the Greeks, how in his view subsequent movements absorbed and understood it, what he has found there of lasting significance, how he criticizes and illumines it, what he singles out as its limitations, these and other issues—leads back to Randall's own philosophy. Thus, in the course of carrying out this task, even within the limits of a brief essay, we cannot avoid coming to grips with his own theory of history, his philosophy of experience, his broader cultural functionalism, and his evolutionary experimentalism. We hope to show that Randall's interest in the Greeks is neither an accident nor a convenience. In fact, he has been more than an enthusiastic advocate of the study of the classical tradition; he has repeatedly stated philosophical arguments for the necessity of understanding the Greeks. The argument is an essential part of his conception of the historical character of experience, and embedded in it.

In a recent work, Randall wrote the following: "Since the eighteenth century all our philosophies have been philosophies of experience; they have been forged as critical instruments with which to reconstruct the intellectual past."[4] This past, this subject-matter which underwent reconstruction in modern times, is primarily the classic tradition; it is therefore presupposed. If so, it follows that these philosophies of experience, including Randall's own, demand a knowledge of that tradition for the proper appraisal of what they are, how they function, and what they mean. Thus:

We must study the classic tradition, and come to feel its intellectual power, even when we are anxious to go beyond it. Else we shall find ourselves denying what it saw, instead of placing those insights in our broader context. To go beyond is to see more, not to see less. To embrace a philosophy of criticism with no inkling of what it is criticizing, is to run the danger of the myopia into which these latter days some of us have been tempted to fall.[5]

The implications of the warning go even further. If I understand Randall correctly, he is prepared to insist that a philosophy of experience that excludes what is presupposed in its subject-matter will ultimately fail to attain its very goals: it will fall short of "self-knowledge" and of offering an adequate philosophy of the nature of experience itself. His esteem for such thinkers as Woodbridge, Dewey, and Whitehead, for instance, is partly explained on the grounds of their working with classic tradition while formulating their respective theories of experience.

Randall himself has a philosophy of experience and is a philosopher of experience. What he has said of others holds true in his own case. His approach is one of forging "critical instruments to reconstruct the intellectual past." His deepest *philosophical* concern has always been that of reconstructing the inherited philosophies of experience in order that he may achieve one which meets the demands of *adequacy*. In this respect, Randall is at the forefront of contemporary philosophy; and though he works with the classic tradition, his views are continuous with it only in the sense that the Greeks are rendered significantly amenable to the critical expectations of the modern philosophies of experience. As we shall see, this framework of experience is fundamental to Randall's notion of "significance" in his theory of history. That he is a historian of philosophy can be best understood as part of his being a philosopher of experience. But that Randall is also Greek, though with an important qualification, can be said only to the extent that his philosophy of experience allows.

Randall is a superb example of how to study the classic tradition clearheadedly, a prototype of how to learn the past and learn from it. Unlike Dewey, for instance, who went to the Greeks but frequently failed to reach them, Randall's historical scholarship enabled him to distinguish between the Greeks themselves and the layers of philosophical traditions in which their thought became embedded. Randall has read them and has used them. By using them he criticized and "reconstructed" them. But he has done so wide-awake, fully aware of the uses of the classic philosophical past in an already reconstructed and critically extended different tradition: the naturalistic philosophy of experience. Unless we understand what Randall has done with the latter we will inevitably miss the significance of his analyses of the former. But before we turn to his theory of experience we must pause to consider how he formulated his approach to the nature and goals of Greek thought when he wrote *The Making of the Modern Mind*. The earlier comparative contrasts were made against the background of the emergence of modern science and in conjunction with the problems of social, economic, and religious reconstructions since the end of the Middle Ages. The diagnostic statements were at once bold and clear:

> Our science tells us how to do an infinitely greater number of things, it picks apart the cog-wheels of nature; but it is not wise, it does not discriminate what is worth doing, and before the greatest problem of all, what meaning can man give to his life in this vast world it gives a despairing "Nescio," if not an "I don't care." [6]

Yet Greek science, though lacking in efficiency and impressive applications, possessed decided superiority in its ethical concern. It had wisdom:

> Athenian science was primarily interested in living. It was biological, not mathematical; hence it was most wise in the study of man and his works, and least successful in the sticks and stones that failed to interest it. Aristotle's ethics and politics are a marvel, his physics is rightly subject for ridicule. . . . What the Greeks wanted to know was not how things originated, but what they could do. . . . To know man was not physiology, it was the good life. [7]

When human affairs are allowed to move in ways that polarize our resources in opposite directions, ethics and physics tend to become mutually exclusive and terminate in serious loss and failure: "With ethics alone, man may love the good, but never find it; with physics alone he may gain the whole world, and lose his own soul." [8]

Randall had no doubt then, any more than he has now, what was the most urgent problem for modern man and what road philosophy should follow to meet the occasion. What is still needed above all is a science of values, and the framework within which it can be formulated and work out the details is no other than that of a naturalistic philosophy of human experience. When he wrote in 1935 that "our modern naturalisms are as yet programs rather than achievement," [9] it was this very *desideratum* which gave the statement its sense of poignant urgency. Randall has already written a whole volume to illumine historically and document the issue. In his own words:

> The philosophies of human experience—all the heirs of Hegel, from dialectical materialism to Dewey—subject values to the same scientific methods of criticism and testing as other beliefs; and thus offer the hope of using all we have learned of scientific procedure to erect at last *a science of values* comparable to the science that was the glory of Greek thought. [10]

Having thus chosen the Greeks, and fortified with the confidence that comes from a painstaking assimilation of the cumulative record of Western man, Randall proceeded to meet the challenge he clearly saw before him: "We must develop a philosophy of nature adequate to human experience, and a philosophy of scientific method adequate to the task before it." [11] It is against this background that Randall worked out his philosophy of experience; and in the light of the implications of his findings he revisited the Greeks and sought to restate their place in our present.

III

Randall has formulated a pluralistic view of experience, where experience is always an "encountering," a co-operation between man's activities and other activities in his world: an active interaction or transaction. This approach, highly critical of the intellectualisms which result from a restricting of experience to the cognitive, led him to reject the passive intellectualism of the Greek pure *nous,* as well as that of the modern empiricists. But it has also alerted him to ways of utilizing the philosophical insights of those ancient and modern philosophers who explored the active character of experience: the Greeks, Plato and Aristotle, who saw it as *technē*—the active manipulation of human and natural materials—and the moderns, Kant, James, Dewey, and Heidegger, who analyzed the active character of experience "from the inside." [12] In Randall's view, the active character of experience is pluralistic at least in two senses: First, it involves in our diverse transactions a plurality of factors in specific contexts and situations; and second, as a situational transaction experience functions in different ways, religiously, artistically, linguistically, cognitively, ethically, and so on. It is important to note here that Randall's central point is that the most fruitful approach to experience is best done in terms of functions, not types. [13] Given Randall's objective relativism in his approach to nature and experience, there is a definite sense in which experience is inescapably *historical*.

In avoiding the pitfalls attending the hypostatization of abstractions of human nature, Randall has come to assert that "human nature is not 'constant' and 'original,' but fundamentally historical in character; human nature is an historical nature, like the seed's career. . . . Human ways of acting are the 'substratum' or τὸ ὑποκείμενον of any history: they are what persists, is acted upon, and modified in that history." [14] All experience has an inevitable historical character; it is such that makes historical knowledge possible. [15] Not all knowledge is strictly historical knowledge, but to understand fully any knowledge involves viewing it historically; for all knowing as a way of acting functions historically. The same holds for all other ways of acting. Randall himself has contributed fresh insights into the way in which historical knowledge itself becomes better understood when viewed historically. All these considerations lead us to see the basic role the historical character of experience has played in his philosophy, how he has come to place all "history" in experience, and why he has put all experience in historical perspective. His objective and functional relativism obtains equally in his theories of experience, nature, and history, and most importantly, of human nature.

When he turns to discovering a key to untangle the patterns of historical change—itself a type of historical continuity, he finds it in what he calls "philosophical traditions." It is against this background of the historical character of experience and his analysis of philosophical traditions that we hope to discuss his treatment of Greek philosophy. In any event, a philosophical tradition "is a kind of toolbox, a set of instruments a philosopher has at his disposal in working on his own problems." [16] As we shall see, this is precisely what Randall himself does with the Greeks and how he learns from the Greeks. Philosophic traditions constitute a type of historical continuity. They exhibit "careers," i.e., what they become in the hands of those who work with them in their efforts to face their own intellectual and cultural problems. Such traditions usually start as achievements of some "philosophical statesman." [17] Their function lies in what they do not only for the philosophical statesman but also in the contributive role they play in the historical experience of those thinkers who choose to work with them.

Randall's active and adaptational view of experience as manipulative and experimental response to problematic confrontations in "present" and novel situations assigns primal importance to the task of reconstructing useful traditions, to viewing them critically in order to determine both their limitations and advantages. [18] Once again, Randall comes to show that since philosophical experience, like all experience, never starts with "pure" experience, the philosopher must come to grips with the traditions with which his ideas are continuous and through which he hopes to solve his problems. It is the history of a tradition that best reveals "what it can and what it cannot fruitfully accomplish" when we are confronted with fresh problems and novel experiences. As expected, Randall at once uses and selects from traditions; especially the classical tradition, of which he has remained a steady admirer and a most penetrating critic. He states characteristically:

> In the West these traditions have for the most part started with the pioneer Greeks. But the traditions the Western world inherited from the Greek thinkers and schools have been carried on, worked with, applied to new cultural conflicts and problems, as men's intellectual and social experience

has altered, and reconstructed again and again as a result of how they have been modified and added to in facing new problems. Whenever philosophic thinking has been vital, and not merely inherited, such traditions have been transformed. But certain of their features persist, and enable us to identify them as later stages of the same tradition. Much like the career of a man, we may say they exhibit a continuing identity of personality.[19]

Randall has repeatedly emphasized two fundamental beliefs of the classical tradition: (a) The world is intelligible and valuable; and (b) thinking and valuing are themselves natural events. *Technē*, another fundamental feature, was mentioned before. His assessment of its limitations pointed out the following: (a) The Greek attainments were those of a *single* culture, a fact which explains why the thinkers of that tradition did not reflect on the conflict of cultures. Limited in this respect, their wisdom stands in need of critical enrichment before it can be made relevant to our present problems. (b) The Greeks were creating a *single* science and thus came up with a philosophy of knowledge whose intellectual formulations lack the requisite power to explain how one science leads to another, a problem that modern science must face and answer satisfactorily. Evidently, Randall's criticism stems from his critical naturalism and the demand to provide for continuity in the light of the pluralistic character of experience, be this a plurality of cultures or a plurality of sciences. The problem of "the one and the many" which the Greeks sought to solve has emerged with a fresh meaning for us and awaits radical answers. The Greeks sought their own unities, but we must establish continuities for our plural yet conflicting cultures and plural yet separate sciences. It is this very objective that defines naturalism as a programmatic philosophy. However, it is important to remember that whereas the Greeks were successful in their quest for unity we are still groping for ours. It is this difference that leads me to say that, with the first "limitation," Randall has pushed his criticism a bit too far. One could make a good case for the proposition that even here the Greeks suggest the way toward the solution. Recent historical accounts of the Greeks give ample evidence that they too were faced *ab initio* with a variety of conflicting and inherited cultures before they *effected* the unifications. Even their *single* ethos has been questioned, at least in some quarters. Despite the amazing unifications of the Greeks, the pluralistic character of their culture was never completely overcome.[20]

The upshot of Randall's analysis is that the Greeks became intoxicated with the discovery of intelligibility and came to claim more than what intelligence as a tool could ensure. For Randall, the classical tradition did not confine itself to just reading the universe in a manner agreeable to its own mode of thinking and living. The Greeks went so far as to read this very manner into the universe, thus turning their intellectual and structural notions, which are but "proper objects of knowledge," into features of nature's intelligible structure. This classical tradition, based on a faith in the isomorphism between experience intellectualized and nature cognized, Randall, the critic, telescoped from the vantage point of an experimental and pluralistic conception of experience. His analysis of historical traditions is basically a reconstructive tool. The purpose of its use is not so much to cut to size what he sees in the heaven of philosophical constellations, as to see each tradition for what it is and preserve all that he finds vital and relevant. Actually, his analysis went deeper than the questioning of the classical claim of the isomorphism between cognitive experience and the intelligible structure of nature. He extended his analysis and became equally, if not more, critical of the modern idealistic conceptions of experience that tended to swallow nature completely within the schemes of *conceptualized* experience. Here the moderns differ from the Greeks, who cannot be said to be guilty of the modern *hubris;* however enamored with their ideals, the Greeks always managed to keep nature intact.

Randall's is fundamentally a philosophy of experience. His calling our attention to the need for a reconstruction of the classical tradition, to effect an enlarged Aristotelianism, is best understood in the light of what experience means for him. Some of his central points are: (a) What we know is experience, and consequently the proper objects of knowlege are always in experience. (b) Nature is intelligible because we know it as experience, we encounter it in active transactions. (c) The specific schemes of intelligibility within experience for knowing what has been discerned in it, are neither exhaustive of experience nor isomorphic with the "intelligibility of nature." (d) Our own schemes are themselves dynamic, changing, situational, determinate, objectively relative, selective, cumulative, historico-cultural. (e) "Nature" becomes for us what intelligible experience makes possible; and, hence, far from asserting that the logos of nature is the logos of man, Randall insists that the former is at least what the experimental and cumulative character of experience reveals when it functions best. (f) Critical thinking, sharpened with the aid of the best available tools and enriched through the cumulative gains of the intellectual past, grows increasingly closer to nature, and can be properly said to approximate the logos of the system of processes that the universe might be. (g) "Nature rendered intelligible" ultimately means experience clarified critically and operating experimentally. At least this much can be safely claimed: The intelligibility of nature is a function of man's experience, just as the changing interpretations of nature are a function of the history of the diverse conceptions of human intelligence. It should be noted that for Randall "intelligence" means far more than its traditional identification with intellectual cognizing. In reconstructing its meaning to preserve it in his own experimental and naturalistic philosophy of experience, he has learned from the traditional sins of omission and commission as well as those of the present. For Randall, it means understanding all that falls within experience: poetry and the aesthetic transaction, self-sacrifice and religious adoration, indeed, knowing itself. Since all these facts occur in experience, "they have definite implications for the character of the nature that sustains them." [21]

The objective of Randall's philosophical reconstruction has been that of putting all human activities back into their proper setting: human experience. As an attainment, it should be seen as the culminating result, built piece by piece, by means of those broad and specific criticisms that constitute the core of the amazingly complex modern philosophical tradition which he calls *the philosophies of experience*. The net result was not only that mechanical science, and eventually all science and all knowing, gradually were placed within experience; even the whole classical tradition itself has come to find its home in it. It is this latter accomplishment that Randall refers to as an "enlarged Aristotelianism." The key expression "within experience" no longer suffers from the limitations of British epistemology and Kantian *a priorism*. It points to a broader biological and social context, and one in which all search for, and schemes of, intelligibility find their place. Aside from Darwinism and Dewey's social instrumentalism, the other tradition with which we worked to arrive here was the classical one, Aristotelianism in particular, a tradition rendered "flexible enough to deal with those problems of changing cultures and shifting schemes of science which were originally outside its scope." [22] Thus, it has again become clear, that Randall went well prepared to the classical tradition because of what it could do for him. He found it flexible and capable of being critically deepened, broadened, and reconstructed in the light of novel and complex problems; and though not initially designed for such problems, it proved to be the very ally which the experimental naturalism of experience needed. Here is where we have arrived:

> Today we possess at last a science that, insisting on the reality and importance of all man's experiences and enterprises, has the concepts through which it hopes to make them intelligible, and a philosophy that can embrace in one natural world, accessible to thought in all its parts and amenable to the operations of intelligence in all its processes, all the realities to which human experience points: symphonies as well as atoms, personality as well as reflex action, religious consecration as well as the laws of motion. [23]

Yet all this is still a program; it points to work that lies ahead. In the meantime we cannot say for sure how much nearer we have come to our initial goal of bringing about our *own* science of values. The Greeks still seem ahead of us in this respect.

IV

Randall states: "Greek culture is not part of *the* past, except as a body of records and documents, to which archeology is daily making startling additions, but *our* past. There can be no other significant past. And our past is not buried in *the* past: it is living in the present." [24]

Unlike so many contemporary philosophers who decided that the best thing for philosophy was to start with a clean slate and willful indifference toward the *dead* past, Randall boldly declared that "we must start with tradition, and we must end with tradition criticized, clarified, enlarged." [25] By remaining in a continuous dialogue with the thinkers of the *living* past, Randall never appears to have lost sight of the continuity between the philosophical traditions of the past and his own work. Nor has he failed to discern what is distinctive about the critical task before him, namely to discover the uses these traditions may have when brought to bear on the problems of the living present. To his own work one may appropriately apply his own words: "The historian's understanding of the significant past, like the past itself, is progressive and cumulative." [26] Furthermore, all understanding is in terms of causes and consequences, which in turn is affected by the developments in the sciences of social behavior. What men find significant in their past is bound to the changing and developing schemes of explanation. Thus, Herodotus, Thucydides, Grote, Marx, Zimmern, Rostovtzeff, Westermann, each gives us a different "history." [27]

Randall hastens to mention another factor which renders our understanding of histories subject to change: "Our understanding of the consequences, and hence of the 'significance' of past events, changes with the further history-that-has-happened—with what has come to pass in the world of events, as a result of the possibilities inherent in what has already happened." [28] Thus the notion of "significance" is always kept tied to the ultimate context in terms of which historical knowledge must remain within experience, which is itself by nature historical. And so it is with its complement: functional relativism. We are told that "the selection of the relevant history of anything demands a future 'focus' in that thing— either in our present, or in its past 'present,' as the basis of selection." [29] And no matter what past eventuation one chooses as the focus of his investigation, the inescapable focus, the *ultimate* "for," [30] must be found in the present. Thus: "The 'proximate focus' will be relative to the historian's particular enterprise of understanding. The 'ultimate' focus will always be found in the historian's own 'present.' So long as historians live in time, such 'presentism' is inevitable." [31] Now, Randall insists on a broader understanding of "present." As a focus it includes the eventuation in the envisaged future of what a given "present" contains as tendencies. The historical "present," unless it uses the past as a deposit of resources, as material cause, and the envisaged future as posing the problems, would lack sufficient focus and remain vague with regard to "what has to be done." Against this background, and in connection with Randall's approach to Greek philosophy, there are two issues we should like to raise. The first is the problem of *genuineness* of significance; the second, the problem of the *adequacy* of an envisaged future as an ethical and cultural proposal.

If I understand Randall correctly, the "significance" of Greek philosophy *as a past event* has undergone many changes; it has had many past "presents." And his own treatment must be regarded as another "present." Thus, "significance" is plural. From the standpoint of all these "presents," Greek philosophy has the power to become significant for all of them. Now, Aristotle's own philosophy was significant also to him, not for its inherent possibilities to become "significant" for some "future" present, but *actually*: ἐνεργείᾳ, not δυνάμει. Suppose we ask: What is the total significance of Aristotle's philosophy? We could say (a) *all* it meant to Aristotle; (b) whatever significance it has had for each of the "presents" that found it relevant, and conceivably all such future presents. In the light of Randall's insistence upon *our* present as the determining context of significance, we can only talk genuinely about *our* Aristotle. We are thus forced to admit that any answer we give to the issue of the significance of Aristotle for any other "present" is but an interpretation of an interpretation. On Randall's view then it is futile to ask for significance in the sense of (a). In fact, it is as futile as the ill-reputed old quest, "What is the universe as a whole?"

Randall admits that his naturalism is continuous with that of the Greeks, and in a serious sense the "significance" Greek philosophy has for him is a working out of "the possibilities inherent" in the past event. But insofar as his naturalism is an enlarged Aristotelianism, Aristotle's philosophy is more than "possibilities inherent." Part of the "significance" of Randall's *present* is what must have actually been significant for Aristotle himself. The point I am trying to make is that his interpretation of Aristotle is far from arbitrary. In fact it is *genuine* to the extent that he can establish his claim to have recaptured the meaning and intent of the original. In view of Randall's brilliant contributions in the history of philosophy, we must also add here that he has helped us to understand the significance Aristotle's philosophy has had for the diverse post-Aristotelian "presents." I must insist that I discern a claim to partial identity here. One would surmise that it is Randall's conviction that his own critical *re-actualization* of what was actually there in Aristotle's philosophy is reasonably *more adequate* than the significant uses which Aristotelianism has had for many a past "present." It is safe then to say that Randall will accept the possibility of attaining genuine significance, and that given a number of interpretations—"presents"—some are more adequate to the subject than others. In other words, his objective relativism is free from the charge of caprice. It is *objective* in a serious sense and it allows for genuineness.

There is another point that deserves discussion. Suppose we say that the hitherto total significance of Aristotle is what "significance" it has collectively had for all past presents. Now, Randall never tires of pointing out the diverse uses in which many a medieval and modern "present" has put the Greek tradition. We would agree that the philosophies of the Greeks had for each of these diverse "presents" a significance "relative to" respective problems. Suppose now that a certain significance can be shown to be far from genuine, and hence *distorted*. Are these distortions to be included as part of the "inherent possibilities" of Greek philosophy? If so, the danger is that we may be forced to put every "significance" in a bad light—a conclusion hardly attractive to historical knowledge—and comparably question Randall's own critical "re-actualization" of Aristotle's original significance. Somehow, Randall's theory of history, though not his enlarged Aristotelianism, leaves the door open to misunderstanding. We simply cannot let the matter rest with that part of the theory which supports the position that each "significance" or "understanding of consequences" is simply a "fresh understanding" without running the risk of compromising cumulative scholarship to approximate some *original* significance. The theory may work well as a scheme to understand what has happened, but it will not tell us how genuine and *good* was the understanding. To give up the quest for ultimate and total significance is one thing; but we must insist upon criteria for evaluating each significance. The problem discussed is related to this portion of his theory of history, not the "significance" the classical tradition has with respect to his "present." The latter is a theme more intimately related to the quest for a science of values.

Randall's analyses of Greek philosophy show that he neither forgets nor neglects the autonomy and originality of philosophical traditions. But our problem has to do not with the ultimate significance of Greek philosophy, but the significance it took on in the philosophy of John

Herman Randall. He has already come to grips with the former issue:

> The ultimate significance of any history-that-happens will not be completely grasped until all its consequences have worked themselves out and can be discerned. The "meaning" of any historical fact is what it does, how it continues to behave and operate, what consequences follow from it.[32]

In order to treat the latter issue we must turn to Randall's interpretation of Greek philosophy. We may proceed by asking the following question: What are these things that have histories? Randall speaks of histories of societies, cultures, institutions, ideas, philosophy, religions, science, art; and he says: "everything in our world has *a* history. . . . Everything is *historical* in character. . . . History is at once a trait of all subject-matters, something to be discovered and understood about each of them; and a distinctive way of inquiring into any subject-matter." [33] He sees the theory of history as a branch of metaphysical analysis: "a critical examination of a certain kind of subject-matter, those traits or aspects of existent things that are said to be 'historical,' and of the intellectual instruments for dealing with that subject-matter." [34] This enterprise is taken to be analogous to what Aristotle does in his *Physica*. This is again part of his enlarged Aristotelianism. There is, however, a difference in the way Randall and Aristotle understand *ousia;* though Randall believes that he put the Aristotelian *ousia* in the language of experience—primarily Dewey's language:

> Dewey's term for Οὐσία or Substance in this sense is clearly "the situation," conceived as a "universe of action," and I have found it extremely suggestive to follow up this equating of Aristotle's term with Dewey's. For Aristotle's world of individual οὐσίαι or "substances," conceived concretely and φυσικῶς as determinate processes operating in a context, and Dewey's world of "specific situations" or "universes of action," conceived as interactions, or more precisely as "transactions," are after all the same world.[35]

The world of specific situations and the world of individual substances may well be *the same world*, but it is not clear that Aristotelian *substances* are identical with Deweyan *situations*. It is only through an enlarged Aristotelianism *within the language of experience* that this may be so. In other words, the difference we mentioned vanishes only through Randall's reconstruction of Aristotle's metaphysics. Now suppose we take Aristotle's substances in the way he presumably viewed them, can we still come up with the same results concerning the "significance" of their history as with *the things* Randall speaks of as having histories? The problem is this: If Aristotle's and Randall's substances differ, so do their histories, and so does the significance each comes to have. The difference shows up when we try to apply Randall's own view of significance to Aristotle's substances. It turns out that what in Aristotle stands for "cumulative consequences" takes on a different meaning from what it has in Randall's theory of substance—a theory which takes history and time seriously. This is so because Randall has decidedly reconstructed the formalistic ontology, the "structuralistic formalism," [36] of Aristotle's substances to arrive at situational substances where change, continuity, process, history, time possess a firm and secure place in the interpretive schemes of a philosophy of experience.

There is a close affinity between Aristotle's and Randall's frameworks of thinking about substance. Both are organic in the sense that both philosophers learned from *biology*. Not only has Randall reconstructed Aristotle's model in the light of the rich implications and suggestions evolutionary biology disclosed; he has earned the distinction of being the foremost and best interpreter of Aristotle's biological motivation. In his excellent and exciting essay "The Changing Impact of Darwin on Philosophy," he points out that the fundamental impact of Darwinism was the rediscovery of process and the reinterpretation of experience and science in terms of a biological and contextual functionalism: "Darwin's ideas not only transformed nature; they also transformed man." [37] This transformation of man has done away with the strictures of all formalistic realisms and functionalisms attending such conceptions of the *nature* of man, in favor of an ongoing socio-cultural and cumulative pluralism, an historical and objective relativism of substance. It has led to critical philosophies of experience where the world directly encountered is found to be basically *temporal* and *functional* in character, plural and transactional, capable of inquiry and experimental reconstruction. [38] Working with this "enlarged" Aristotelian biological conception of substance, Randall's organic model has come to display features decidedly socio-cultural and historical not to be found in Aristotle's own. Thus, Randall can say: "New consequences flowing from past events change the 'significance' of the past, of what has happened." [39] This conception of cumulative consequences is one of a piece with his bio-social experimentalist view of substance, a view that takes historical continuities and time seriously. Aristotle's model for τόδε τι has been left behind.

This preoccupation with time and history Randall does not have in common with Aristotle. It may well be the case that, by enlarging Aristotle, Randall has two strains of naturalism, one Aristotelian and one Darwinian-Deweyan, which cannot be brought together without sacrificing a serious aspect of Greek naturalism that Randall admires but has not fully provided for in his own present "significance," namely, the Greek ethos. When Randall replaces Aristotle's substances with transactional experience he also elevates the socio-cultural dimension of the encountered situation above the individual substance, the individual man. The objection may be raised that whereas encountered situations are *organic*, they are not *organisms*. Aristotle would say that the organism is the existential ultimate; the human *ousia* is the individual man. But in the metaphysics of experimental naturalism, the Aristotelian substance is placed *within* experience, the consequence being that the open-textured nature of human transactions is turned into a condition of our understanding of human nature. The result is, the Sophists were right and Plato and Aristotle wrong. To phrase the matter more abstractly: the organic includes the organism. Now, the real difficulty emerges when we try to specify the relationship between the ethical overtones of the Randallian notion of "significance" to the Greek view of ethics and their *single* culture. Just as Aristotle's substance is fundamental to his theory of ethics both as a philosophy of individual achievement and a theory to formulate the social good, similarly Randall's own experimental approach to ethics, his open, cumulative pluralism, is in essential agreement with his theory of substance. The philosophical statesmen of the Greek ethos took neither time nor history seriously; this is not the case with Randall, who ranks among the chief interpreters of our times and ethos. Hence, in this respect, Randall's notion of significance would have perplexed the Greeks. And though we have come to put the Greek tradition within experience, it is doubtful whether the Greeks would attach much value to the seriousness with which we take the organic and methodologically powerful model of *experience*, and its attendant emphasis on change, function, process, and experimental adaptation, and with the aid of which our critical philosophies of naturalism have worked out suitable categorial theories.

The Greeks had a single culture. We, the moderns, are faced with the complex problem of adjusting the diverse schemes of values within our plural culture and its splintered discontinuities. Except for the worshippers of radical pluralism and unmitigated individualistic ethics, the more sober men have always been strong advocates of co-operative social and political ideals. But be this as it may, it remains a fact that our times still exhibit facets of cultural disunities. The modern Western man is neither a single group, nor have our institutions promulgated the ethos of a single culture, despite the fact that all the ideologies and social manifestoes of our times were conceived in the heat of this vision. It is also a fact that our philosophers of social intelligence, especially of the American brand, had comparably declared themselves in favor of a promising unifying ethical ideal: a program which they hoped would effect the sort of harmony of social and cultural values that we call an ethos. Now, in the absence of a pattern of converging institutional practices that could lead to the emergence of a unifying naturalistic ethos, it seems only correct that our philosophies of experience should try to work out a conception of experience that would accommodate the very social realities our philosophies had set out to understand and render intelligible in the first place. Thus, it is of little surprise to see that the transactional conception of experience is genuinely pluralistic and wedded to the categories of change and process, of functions and reconstructions; that is, to conceptual tools better suited to an open-textured view of man in time and history with no fixed boundaries and constants. This being the case, we need not feel perplexed over the fact that all we can have is a limited understanding of the Greeks. We must simply take the consequences of the design and interpretive efficacy of our intellectual tools. Methodological and instrumentalistic naturalism has its virtues, but it also had its limitations. Just as the theory of experience as transaction is fundamentally pluralistic, so is the philosophy of pluralism limited in its interpretive scope and its power to effect unifications. Both are philosophies in tune with the need of our historical present. Randall's insights are indeed profound and fecund. He is the outstanding philosopher of historical self-consciousness. By working out the implications of the transactional character of historical experience he has alerted us to the *interpretive* scope and cultural efficacy of the instrumental theory of knowledge. In a word, he has forced to the foreground the *ethical* problem of naturalism and sharpened the issues for a science of values. He has put the problem of the modern quest for ethos in philosophical perspective.

But the Greeks had their ethos, a community of ideals, their crystallized set of excellences, and their own framework for social co-operation—all won through long struggles to adjust the inherited but conflicting traditions, as evidenced for instance in Aeschylus' *Oresteia*. This Randall knows, but his loyalty to naturalistic pluralism has led him to find the intellectual formulation emerging from the philosophic outlook of their unified culture a limiting element. Hence, he refused to value it and include it in the significance the Greek tradition has for us. It has become evident that our philosophizing has no use for it. This is a criticism coming from a philosopher deeply concerned with those pressing problems of man that are generated by novel experiences conflicting with a plurality of cultural traditions; it is criticism meant to draw attention to the limitations—the relative irrelevance—that a portion of a significant tradition entails for our response to the demands of pluralistic cultural change. What Randall has brought to question is the instrumental value of the Greek ethos to solve the problem of discontinuities in our present realities.

It is difficult to say whether Randall wishes to distinguish between the

need to effect appropriate solutions for problems arising in cultural conflicts and the desirability for pushing toward some unifying naturalistic
ethos. Methodologically, he is an objective relativist and hence must give
priority to the open-textured and historical character of experience. The
desirability of formulating what amounts to an ideal good, a projected
ethos for our culture, so Grecian in flavor, is acknowledged but compromised. At best, it is a myth. The Greeks could speak of "the best"; but
not we. He says:

> The ultimate objective of knowing or evaluation is thus the comparative
> of an adverb, "better." . . . It is not the superlative: which way is "best"?
> "Best" can mean only, "best under specified conditions," "best in a given
> context," " best for that situation"—and this means, "better than the other
> possibilities." "Platonism" in dealing with values, the contention that we
> cannot know what is "better than" anything else unless we have a prior
> knowledge of what is "best," has no supporting evidence, and is contra-
> dicted by our constant experience. . . . What is "best" absolutely is like all
> superlatives and ultimates, a "myth.". . . The ultimate "better than," and
> hence the "best" for any determinate situation, which is the ultimate
> objective for human inquiry and science, is How can mankind best live
> with the power of the scientific method?—a power possessed by no pre-
> vious culture, bringing with it new powers in detail, and setting new
> limits, wholly novel opportunities and responsibilities.[40]

But this is Randall the advocate of the scientific method speaking here.
We are still left with the persisting problem of our polyethic culture, even
if the particular sort of ethos the Greeks attained is not the proper thing
for us to resurrect. However, the fact that they did work out a single ethos,
their facing and solving this problem, is not historically irrelevant after
all. After the Greeks effected their ethos, theirs was the task of sustaining
it through exemplary action and the sort of high-minded talking that
demanded utmost clarity, dedication, and faithfulness to their envisaged
excellence. In comparison, modern man has defined his tasks differently.
We have found it easier to settle for power, transient adjustments, high
technology, and the speediest of adventures that go with efficient methods
and hollow souls. Of course, this is no shocking news to Randall, however
impressive he finds the organic model of experience as transaction in
enabling us to understand, define, and solve social problems. But ultimately, the instrument is not the end, and the philosophy of experience as
transaction, even if it has enabled us to put things back in it, is still primarily methodological. Its inclusive breadth does not by itself establish its
unlimited efficacy. As a philosophy of *technē* it is not free of short-
comings.

We may now rephrase the difficulty: While Randall's transactional philosophy of experience makes possible a powerful and useful theory of history, the notion of "significance," when applied to what he finds significant in the classical tradition, leads to the problem of how to interpret and assimilate the Aristotelian view of the human individual and the classical conception of a unified ethos without violating the initial meaning of either. This part of Greek naturalism, to be sure, one which does not make time and change ontologically ultimate, is hardly in unison with Dewey's naturalism of experience, which breaks the boundaries of Greek substance to make room for socio-biological situations and their continuous transformations. The alternatives seem to be shaping in terms of either more history and plurality or more constancy and individuality. The problem is real: the one-and-the-many once again.

The central issue all along has been to inquire into *genuineness of significance* in Randall's approach to Greek philosophy and culture, and to discuss the basis of his evaluation. What our analysis has yielded may be put as follows: (a) His theory contains two strains of naturalism, and (b) his thesis on historical significance is intimately related to his taking time seriously. According to the latter, the entire historical past, all history, is potentially present; it has inherent possibilities of being of some consequence insofar as anything can be selected by any one, at least one person, to whom it will be of some consequence. Though we may never get to know what the entire historical past is, nor ever realize in some given present all its inherent possibilities—for what we have here is an open historical experimentalism—we may remain sure that the historical past is more than we can talk about, and at least what has been presently realized as significant. Like nature, history is never exhausted in any given discourse or any specific universe of action. It is plural, open, dynamic, continuously realizable, but at least and always significant through the present.

Thus, according to Randall, to speak of the significance of Greek philosophy is to speak of those of its inherent possibilities that have become consequential to and realized through some present. But the issue now becomes—a central issue for Randall's historical naturalism—what is a "present"? Is his naturalistic conception of a *present* Deweyan or Aristotelian? Though methodologically it is Deweyan, I propose that ontologically Randall's "present" is basically Aristotelian. The *present* that makes Greek philosophy significant is some given present, some individual's present; *Randall's own present*, the present of an Aristotelian substance. That "present" is plural goes without saying; there are as many presents as there are individuals qualified or motivated and prepared to render significant some given past. Furthermore, each individual may come to have a whole sequence of *presents*, a chain of significances, which may be cumulative, though not necessarily progressive. How a chain of presents becomes cumulative and progressive is a special problem in one's intellectual development and need not be explored here. Now, if it can be shown that "presents" are ultimately Aristotelian, rather than Deweyan, except in the methodological sense we mentioned, then Randall's theory of history stands in need of ontological strengthening decisively in favor of his Aristotelianism.

V

I should like to close this paper with some observations on Randall's two strains of naturalism and what follows for the practice of philosophy as a result of the emphasis on the Darwinian-Deweyan strain. In a serious sense, the placing of Greek naturalism within the Darwinian-Deweyan strain, this placing the classical tradition *within* experience, tends to inhibit the practice of certain philosophical pursuits for which the Greeks have been especially admired. The problem here, more specifically, arises from the restrictions placed upon that part of the classical tradition which can be reconstructed, the uses to which it can be put from the standpoint of a criterion of significance such as Randall's objective relativism allows. We have already seen how Randall is led to take "best" as "best for" determinate situations.

We must now try to explore the implications of this position and see what it tends to inhibit as non-salvageable in classical philosophy. In all fairness it should be stated that Randall does not limit experience to "scientific" or, with Kant, "possible" experience; indeed, he takes it in the inclusive sense to mean all kinds and forms of experience. His philosophical formulations are meant to render intelligible the pluralistic aspects of experience, all "universes of discourse" and of value. In this respect he is intimately continuous with the Greeks, with Plato's pluralism of ideas when conceived as "means" to illumine the total domain of human conduct, all types of experiences, activities, and aspirations. The Greeks would say, "the whole man"; Randall and Dewey, "the pluriverse" in experience. Randall has written extensively on the long struggles of modern philosophy to arrive at a critical conception of experience free from reductionistic fallacies and one that no longer truncates the pluralistic nature of experience. As a result, "nature is once more for us, as for the Greeks, full of implicit ends and ideals, full of 'value'"; also, "the nature our philosophies describe today is a nature of which human life is once more the most complex and fullest expression." [41]

There is no doubt about Randall's firm belief in the vitality of the classical tradition. Now, when he discusses the vitality of a philosophic

tradition he sees it as a function of its power to become transformed. On
the other hand, transformations have to take place because of the presence
of pressing problems, cultural conflicts, fresh intellectual experience, and
social change. Whatever his admiration of Greek philosophy, Randall
has been quick to detect limitations in the intellectual formulations of the
Greeks with regard to serving our own needs. There is vital thinking
going on today. Such vitality is manifested in the boldness with which
our thinking transforms our philosophical traditions. But in transforming
them, in reconstructing what we find of significance in them, something
is necessarily left out. But how can we be sure that much of what is
omitted in our transformation of the classical tradition is not of real significance as well? Can we really put all our trust in our pressing problems? Is it wise to leave this matter altogether up to what might be a
somewhat chaotic interlocking network of all sorts of contemporaneous
needs? Might it not be that what we have left out proves, not an instance
of vitality in our thinking, but a certain weakness? Again, are reflective
responses to freshness, novel social experience, drummed up cultural problems, and felt conflicts necessary and sufficient prerequisites for claiming
the occurrence of vital philosophical thinking? Is it not conceivable that
vital thinking may also go on when social experience enjoys relative
smoothness and irenic actualizations?

Randall's contextualism gives the impression that vital thinking flour-
ishes mainly when life abounds in challenges and changes, when experience is stirred with problems and conflicts. Thus, we are given to believe
that the proper way to have vital thinking is to live in a kind of "sweat-
of-the-brow" world. It further seems that Randall is prepared to defend the
position that vital thinking in values, to find out "what has to be done,"
blossoms in situations of conflict. Geared thus to this type of situation,
ethical thinking in its basic features is not only experimental and flexible,
it is dominantly social and tied to a passion to champion all sorts of
reconstructions. When ethical thinking becomes so strongly attached to a
philosophy of experience advocating change, it runs the risk of turning
change itself into a value. It is then guilty of the same metaphysical addic-
tion Dewey "found" and castigated in the old-fashioned "philosophies
of being," the sin of turning *permanence* into an ideal value, into a supreme feature of knowledge and reality. If it is proper to enlarge the
expression "situation of conflict," intending no violence to it, but so as
to make it include the *current* conflict between two sorts of ethical thinking—the one attached to a philosophy of experience with its emphasis on
change, and the other to a philosophy of being with its accent on permanence—it would then seem that we have a genuine problem that calls
for reconstruction of the situation. It is highly probable that our efforts

to meet the challenge might force us to expand and invigorate our initial understanding of what it is to do vital thinking in ethics. For refusal to do so would be tantamount to a stubborn act of condemning ourselves and starving our *present* to the point of atrophy.

There is much in the Greeks that is relevant to our time. I mean here not only in their ideal ends but also in the well-designed conceptual tools through which they sought to articulate what they found lasting in experience and unchanging in nature. They sought what Heraclitus called "the hidden harmonies," the structures and the *logoi* of things and values; and indeed they found some. All along they were confident in the belief in the genuine connection between the search for the logos and the pursuit of excellence. It would be unfair to accuse the Greeks of ever having denied the reality of change or of refusing to give experience a respectable place in their philosophies of being. That they sided with Being rather than Experience goes without saying. However, we have to admit that part of their lasting significance lies in the fact that they exhibit in their thinking not only an admirable toughness but also an amazing balance and vitality. Their solutions are still achievements of *metron*, and profound visions of Being and Becoming. Without appreciation of this controlling feature of the Greek *theoria* the classical attainments in philosophy lapse helplessly into a series of interesting but dated discoveries in the development of logic and science. When we take out of their philosophy the delicate interdependence between the love of wisdom and the aspiration to excellence of ethos, we cut down mercilessly the power of this tradition to figure significantly in our *present*.

I submit that it is not Randall's intention to side with those who advocate doing away with the Greeks. As we have seen, his work has explicitly and effectively defended the classical tradition. What seems, however, to be a source of trouble is a certain ambivalence that is created through a tension between two countervailing movements in his writings. On the one hand, we have his open praise and documented defense of the Greek culture and thought, for instance, when he writes that "Plato and Aristotle, and the Stoics and Epicureans, are our intellectual contemporaries . . . they are companions and teachers in the present-day philosophical situation, as they have always been." [42] On the other, we have the implications of his theory of historical knowledge, his philosophy of experience as transactional situation, his interpretation of what constitutes vital thinking in values. It is this side of his views that tends to inhibit the power of our *present* to assimilate certain salient features of the Greek ethos. The irony of our own situation lies in the fact that it is these very features that we need most. Without them, our ethical thinking, however vital in its preoccupation with current conflicts, is prone to rationalize its restricted scope, as it has often done; just as it repeatedly tried to convert its weaknesses into points of strength.

I suppose I find it difficult to believe that we can seriously hope to effect the science of values Randall has so correctly labelled as the most urgent *desideratum* of our times, while in the same breath we promote philosophical interpretations of human experience which force our ethical quest to land, before it has even gotten off its grasshopper-like feet, in the misty jungle of our innumerable relativisms. It seems that after twenty-five centuries of reflection in ethics that Protagoras, not Socrates, was the wisest of the Greeks. What is baffling here is that we persist in admiring Socrates. What is also baffling in all this is that in seeking the optimum of freedom we have defeated every serious effort to come to grips with the principle of *eudaimonia*. If the function of what Randall envisages as the science of values is to serve as the instrument which would help us formulate and attain our own *theoria* of excellence and ethos, then this science would have to do more than indulge in debates about the definability of ideals. It would have to be what all the sciences are in their instrumental capacity: critical methods and inquiries into the relevant facts, and examinations of the efficacy of the means by which action can be successfully transformed into a *technē aristē*, the supreme art of the good life. As long as we shun from emboldening vital thinking in this direction, our *hubris*, our characteristic surrender to the alleged omnipotence of "change," will linger on half-illumined. The price we will continue to pay is already known: existence in the twilight of virtue.

Without this science of values we may never fully realize what we are, what the total significance of our history could have been. If the Greeks have limitations, they are not of this sort. As Randall has pointed out, it was precisely their science of values that was the triumph of the Greeks. Hence, it would seem odd that we should inadvertently perhaps try to exclude from our *present* this most needed aspect of Greek philosophy simply for the sake of saving the theory that has entailed the restriction. It may well be that our naturalistic philosophies of experience have succeeded in illuminating the sciences, in understanding their efficiency—even working for them—but it cannot be said that here we have surpassed the Greeks in ethical wisdom. The naturalism of the Greeks is at once a robust metaphysics and an ethics of excellence. Whenever we ignored either we did so at our own risk.

The Greeks faced and solved for themselves the problem of *aretē*. In our own culture—and there is good reason for saying so—we have yet to meet with success in this vital area of conduct. It is not a question of whether we can or should duplicate the Greeks, for ours is a novel situation, and Randall is right in insisting on this point just as he is right in telling us how fundamental the Greek tradition is. The real problem is whether our interpretations of experience allow us to "see more," as the Heraclitean saying would have it. But be that as it may, Randall has explained, better than any other English-speaking philosopher I know, why and what countless generations of Western thinkers failed to see in the Greeks. Positively, he has succeeded in drawing attention to the philosophical relevance of their "aesthetic vision of intelligibility." [43] Comparably, he has on many occasions stressed how the cumulative and funded body of our philosophical ideas includes the store of classic visions as ideal enterprises "on the same permanences of man's experience of the world." [44] By sharpening for our times the major issues in the philosophy of the history of philosophy, he has given us an original interpretation of the problem of the permanent relevance of the "living Greeks." As many have done before him, he has demonstrated for this generation the fecundity of the classical tradition. One of his major contributions toward a creative understanding of the history of philosophy will no doubt prove to be his showing how the Greeks lead us to challenge our own commitments and make us move on to needed reconstructions of our own cherished philosophies of experience. Modern man is forever indebted to Randall.

NOTES

1. What I am suggesting here is that in this respect Randall is closer to the Platonic quest for excellence, the pursuit of *aretē*, than he is to that part of Plato he calls "how to create a world." See his *Aristotle* (Columbia, 1960), p. 297. It should be noted that this is not all that he has found in Plato. To be sure, his knowledge of Plato is far more comprehensive than the following passage, for instance, would lead one to believe: " 'How to create a world' is a Platonic, not an Aristotelian question. It is explored in the great creation myth of the *Timaeus*, and became central in the religious 'metaphysics' of the Middle Ages" (*ibid.*). However, no hint is given here whether the creation myth of the *Timaeus* can be understood within the context of Plato's vision of excellence. In the Foreword to his *Aristotle*, Randall gives us a glimpse of the manner in which he reads his Plato: "Though a student and admirer of Plato, the present writer is forced to see much more than 'Platonism,' in the world and in Plato."

2. *Nature and Historical Experience* (Columbia, 1958), p. 10. Actually, Randall sees philosophy's "return" to Greek naturalism as a significant accomplishment. In a way, he is suggesting here that by doing so philosophy may now claim to have begun doing what in 1912 his teacher Woodbridge saw only as lying ahead in the future. "As a student of philosophy," Woodbridge said, "I know of no period in the history of human thinking which so well repays study, which so sustainingly quickens the mind and encourages the soul. There may be greater philosophical conceptions than those the Greeks have left us, but I know not where they are unless they are in the future. Their attainment I can believe to be possible only after we have recovered as a habitual possession, the Greek conception of nature which conceives her as adequate

for man's outlook because she has been adequate for his production." "Philosophy," in *Greek Literature;* a Series of Lectures delivered at Columbia University (New York: Columbia University Press, 1912), p. 228.

3. The following passage is illustrative of this point: "In its fundamental attitude, in its basic metaphysical position, contemporary naturalism is thus back once more with the naturalistic world view of the Greeks. But it has increased its resources to include all that men have learned since the ancients. . . . For it, man is still what he was for the Greeks, an intelligent and valuing animal living in an intelligible and valuable world. He now knows something about the nature of that world, and is beginning to learn how to make it serve his ends." "The Nature of Naturalism," in *Naturalism and the Human Spirit,* ed. Y. H. Krikorian (Columbia, 1944), p. 374.

4. *How Philosophy Uses Its Past* (Columbia, 1963), pp. 88-89.

5. *Ibid.,* p. 89.

6. *The Making of the Modern Mind* (New York: Houghton Mifflin Co., 1940), p. 99.

7. *Ibid.*

8. *Ibid.,* p. 100.

9. *Nature and Historical Experience,* p. 13. Originally in the essay "Historical Naturalism" (1935).

10. *The Making of the Modern Mind,* p. 615 (italics added).

11. *Nature and Historical Experience,* p. 14.

12. *Ibid.,* p. 151.

13. *Ibid.,* pp. 171-2.

14. *Ibid.,* pp. 86-87.

15. In insisting upon this point, I follow in addition the line of arguing employed in the discussion on "Substance" where Randall says: "Substance, then, the existing world, is what is encountered in all types of experience. . . . Substance may be *more* than what it is encountered as, even in our best knowledge, in our highest religious and ethical vision, and in our most inspired artistic imagination . . . Substance doubtless *is* more—but it is at least all of that" (*Ibid.,* p. 150). Furthermore, I assume that Randall himself still adheres to the views expressed in his "Historical Naturalism," an earlier essay, written in 1935, and reprinted as the Prologue in his *Nature and Historical Experience.*

16. *How Philosophy Uses Its Past,* p. 55. More formally, it is "a persistent body of ideas tied together by subtle associations as well as logical relations, which persist over the generations, and dominates and colors the thinking of those who for one reason or another have been brought up with it" (p. 47).

17. *Ibid.,* p. 48.

18. For Randall's treatment of "limitations" of philosophical traditions, see *ibid.,* pp. 55ff.

19. *Ibid.,* p. 48.

20. Randall has come closer to accepting the pluralistic side of Greek culture in his recent writings. A more qualified approach is expressed in his *The Role of Knowledge in Western Religion,* chap. i, esp. pp. 17-22.

21. *Nature and Historical Experience,* p. 12.

22. *Ibid.* Compare what Randall says in his *Aristotle* (Columbia, 1960): "Today, the concepts of Aristotle's physics, those notions involved in his analysis of process,

have been driving those of Newton out of theory. . . . Far from being wrong, [his analysis] seems today far truer and sounder than the basic concepts of Newton. And it is fascinating to speculate how, had it been possible in the seventeenth century to reconstruct rather than abandon Aristotle, we might have been saved several centuries of gross confusion and error" (p. 167).

23. *Nature and Historical Experience*, p. 13.

24. *Ibid.*, p. 54.

25. *Ibid.*, pp. 8, 10. Also, *How Philosophy Uses Its Past*, pp. 93, 99: "It is indeed true, that the chief contribution history can bring to philosophic understanding, is the light it can shed on the character of philosophy itself, as men have carried it on in the tradition of our Western culture since the days of the Greeks" (p. 99).

26. *Nature and Historical Experience*, p. 40. The term "cumulative" seems to be a troublesome one. It is not always clear when it is used to refer to individual and when to social experience. No doubt, it is meant to cover both. It is difficult to decide whether Randall wishes to stress the individual character of cumulative experience. Though we cannot undertake at this point an analysis of the issues the problem raises, one may only suggest that it would be best to discuss it in the light of Randall's distinction between things that have *careers* and things that have *histories*; the latter, one supposes, are possible because certain things that have careers are also such that can effect such things as may come to have histories. Thus, a society does not have a career; the histories of societies, insitutions, and ideas are not careers. Most pertinent to discussing this problem are Chapters 3 and 4 in *Nature and Historical Experience*.

Be that as it may, Randall means by the *cumulative* aspect of our funded body of philosophical ideas the following: (a) it is revealed "in the clarification through their use of methods, of intellectual procedures, of standards of validity," (b) it includes "the classic philosophical analyses," the analyses of historical and familiar arguments as well as certain definitive analyses of problems; (c) it encompasses "the refinement and reformulation of philosophical concepts," e.g., great metaphysical distinctions, polished and sharpened tools of criticism; (d) it refers to "the store of classic visions, of imaginative perspectives upon the world, in the light of different intellectual interests. Here is not the practice so much as the poetry of ideas. Those visions are perspectives, from differing standpoints in the activities of men and their ideal enterprises, on the same permanence of man's experience of the world." *How Philosophy Uses Its Past*, pp. 84-86. Since Randall is speaking here of *ideas*, we cannot but conclude that he is talking primarily about the cumulative aspects of things that have *histories*. The last item in the list presents a difficulty. A philosophical vision as "the poetry of ideas" is too complex an event to be classified as a thing that has a history. For instance, Plato's vision perhaps does not have a history, though Platonism clearly does. It is different with Aristotle's; since Santayana knew his "secret," that vision clearly has a "history."

27. *Nature and Historical Experience*, p. 40.

28. *Ibid.*, p. 41.

29. *Ibid.*, p. 55.

30. "There is hence no discoverable 'ultimate context,' no 'ultimate substance.' There is only the widest context that is relevant to any particular activity, process, or specific cooperation of processes, and is hence 'ultimate for' that cooperation. 'Ultimate,' that is, is always relative, never 'absolute'; it is always 'ultimate for'." *Ibid.*,

p. 199.

31. *Ibid.*, pp. 50-51.

32. *Ibid.*, p. 42.

33. *Ibid.*, pp. 27, 28.

34. *Ibid.*, p. 29.

35. *Ibid.*, p. 148. Compare also the following: "But Substance is more than mere 'context in general'; Substance is always specific and determinate. It is always encountered by men in a *specific* transaction, a *specific* cooperation . . . The specific encountering or cooperation selects its own 'relevant field' or 'context' of interaction, and thus delimits the boundaries of that particular 'universe of action,' of that particular Substance" (p. 154).

36. *Aristotle* (Columbia, 1960), pp. 295-6.

37. In the *Journal of the History of Ideas*, XXII (1961) p. 459.

38. *Ibid.*, p. 462.

39. *How Philosophy Uses Its Past*, p. 42.

40. *Nature and Historical Experience*, pp 181-2.

41. "The Changing Impact of Darwin on Philosophy," pp. 458, 455.

42. *How Philosophy Uses Its Past*, p. 81.

43. *The Career of Philosophy* (Columbia, 1962) p. 19. Compare what he says in his *Aristotle*: "Conceptions like *nous* which sum up and concentrate the ultimate intellectual aims of an entire culture, are almost impossible to translate into the tongue of a different culture, with different aims. *Nous* meant to the Greek 'intellectual vision,' and the verbs associated with it, like *theorein* and *eidenai*, are sight words, conveying the flavor of 'seeing' something. The function of *nous* is to lead to *theoria*, the kind of aesthetic spectacle properly beheld in a 'theatre,' the natural abode of *theoria*, Ultimately, when Greek culture became very much aware of its central aims, as in Plato, the function of *nous* was seen as leading to a beholding of human life in the world as a transparently intelligible dramatic spectacle. It is such an aesthetic *nous* that Aristotle is trying to bend to his own purposes, more scientific if in the end no less aesthetic" (p. 90, note 13).

44. *How Philosophy Uses Its Past*, p. 85. Compare *Nature and Historical Experience*, pp. 301-9.

PAUL OSKAR KRISTELLER
Columbia University

John H. Randall, Jr., and Renaissance Philosophy

To many of his professional colleagues, most of his students and readers, and to large sectors of the general public, Randall is primarily known as a contemporary thinker who has been continuing the work of his teachers John Dewey and Frederick Woodbridge at Columbia University. His philosophical position is often described by others, and even by himself, as that of a pragmatist, functionalist, and naturalist. As a teacher and lecturer, and in many of his publications, Randall has been much concerned with the problems of science and of general methodology, of society and religion, and he has laid the foundations of a comprehensive metaphysical system along naturalistic lines. Randall has thus played an active role in the philosophical discussion of many problems during the last few decades, and the importance of his contribution to contemporary American thought will be discussed by several other contributors to this volume—and no doubt on many future occasions.

Unlike many other American philosophers of his time and generation, Randall has always shown a strong and active interest in history, and especially in the history of philosophy. This interest has no doubt centered around Aristotle and the Aristotelian tradition, to which Randall has always felt a special affinity and allegiance; but in a broader and quite generous way, Randall has tried to study and to understand also those ideas and traditions which he finds less congenial, such as Platonism, and has actually been aiming at a comprehensive interpretation of the entire history of Western thought. In this endeavor, he has been guided by a strong sense of the relevance of the past to the problems and solutions of modern thought, and of the close links that connect contemporary philosophy, even where it seems least conscious of it, with the entire tradition of Western thought, and especially with the origins of this tradition in Greek philosophy. Moreover, Randall has always been keenly aware of the fact that all philosophical ideas when first formulated depend to some extent, and in the specific from in which they are expressed, on the historical context to which they belong. Without denying the inner continuity of philosophy as a technical and academic enterprise, Randall has been more willing than other historians of philosophy to admit the impact which technical philosophizing has received at various times from intellectual and historical developments outside its own area, and its reflection especially of the political, religious, and scientific developments of the time. In this way, Randall has not merely recognized the importance which the history of philosophy, and intellectual history as a whole, has for the philosopher, but has been an actual practitioner of this study, and has made important contributions to it in his long career as a teacher and scholar, through his courses at Columbia University on the general history of philosophy and on many individual philosophers of the past, and through many books and papers, from his early *Making of the Modern Mind* (1926) to his recent *Career of Philosophy* (1962).

Within the broader history of Western thought, the period of the Renaissance has been comparatively neglected. It is Randall's merit that he has always assigned to this period an important place in intellectual history, and in the history of philosophy; and although he was preceded in this respect by Fiorentino and Dilthey, Cassirer, Gentile, and other scholars, he was probably the first historian of philosophy to do so in this country. If American philosophers take any interest in the Renaissance, and if other Renaissance scholars can expect some help and co-operation from among the philosophers and historians of philosophy, this is largely due to the influence of Randall, to the effect of his work as a teacher and writer, and to the encouragement given by him to other scholars.

The reason for Randall's specific interest in the Renaissance is not so easy to indicate, and probably more than one factor must be considered. Randall's interest in Aristotle and Aristotelianism certainly opened his eye to the importance of Renaissance Aristotelianism. In his more general historical studies, Randall could not fail to note the difference that seems to separate the age of medieval scholasticism from that of modern science and philosophy, the prevalent religious orientation of the Middle Ages from the more secular and "humanistic" values of modern times, and to recognize the important role played by the intellectual ferment of the intervening centuries in the transition from the earlier to the later age. Moreover, Randall's sensitivity for the links which connect the technical philosophy of an age with its other intellectual forces obviously sharpened his understanding for a period of thought whose philosophy cannot be properly understood without a constant awareness of its cultural development as a whole.

As a result of this genuine interest in the period, Randall's contribution to Renaissance studies is not limited to his publications, important as they are. He has been influential as a teacher and lecturer, and as a director of doctoral dissertations, and has encouraged and influenced the work of numerous other scholars through private conversation and public discussion, through correspondence and editorial advice, and by criticizing and reviewing the books of others. He has generously collaborated with others on a variety of joint enterprises; and I may be permitted to cite the bibliographical article, "The Study of Renaissance Philosophies," which he published jointly with me, and the volume of translations from Renaissance philosophers, *The Renaissance Philosophy of Man*, which he edited jointly with Ernst Cassirer and me, and to which he contributed long sections of a general introduction, and an important paper on Pomponazzi. As one of the editors of the *Journal of the History of Ideas* and *Studies in the Renaissance*, Randall has for many years played an important part in fixing editorial standards and policy, and in endorsing or improving the work of younger scholars before it was published. As chairman of the Columbia University Seminar on the Renaissance, Randall has been instrumental in keeping this group alive as a local and regional center of discussion where scholars from many fields of Renaissance studies and from many parts of the world would find an opportunity to discuss their views and methods and to learn from each other. Randall's interest in Paduan Aristotelianism has led to a special link between this Seminar and the University of Padua, which has been symbolized by the joint publication of a series of studies. When the time seemed to have come to organize Renaissance studies in this country in a permanent fashion and to found the Renaissance Society of America, Randall belonged to a small group of scholars who took the initiative and decisive action, served as the first president of the Society, and has played an important part on its executive board ever since. It would be hard to estimate how many scholarly enterprises and projects of others have been helped, or even made possible, by the generous endorsement Randall gave to them, including many that he would never have undertaken himself, and even many that he would find personally uncongenial, but whose usefulness for the progress of scholarship he would recognize and understand.

Randall's most specific contribution to Renaissance scholarship, aside from the bibliographical article and the general introduction to the Chicago volume which he wrote jointly with me (and in which it would by now be difficult even for ourselves to separate our individual contributions), is primarily embodied in a group of three articles, first published in the *Journal of the History of Ideas* or in the Chicago volume, and more recently, in a revised and more fully documented version, collected in a volume published in Padua under the title *The School of Padua and the Emergence of Modern Science* (1961), and in a very large section devoted to the Renaissance in his recent *Career of Philosophy*. Aside from the general appreciation Randall shows for other strands of Renaissance thought, such as humanism or Platonism, his chief contribution consists in his detailed study and evaluation of Paduan Aristotelianism.

In order properly to understand this contribution, it is necessary to remember the previous history of the problem. Most historians of the Renaissance, and of Renaissance thought, tended to emphasize the roles of humanism and Platonism, and to stress the gradual emergence of an anti-Aristotelian metaphysics opposed to the Aristotelianism of the later Middle Ages. In this view, the Aristotelianism of the Renaissance, whose existence could hardly be denied, appeared merely as a regrettable survival from the Middle Ages, sustained by the inertia of academic institutions and of professional philosophers who failed to understand the significance of modern ideas, and whose works might as well be ignored by those who wish to understand the more vital thought of their own time. Only a small group of historians, following the work of Renan, held a more favorable opinion of Renaissance Aristotelianism, and praised especially the Paduan Aristotelians—or the Paduan Averroists, as they were often called—as the standard-bearers of free thought, and as forerunners of the Enlightenment, without crediting them otherwise with any specific contributions to modern philosophy or science.

Also, the historians of science usually presented the achievements of the seventeenth century as a final triumph of truth over the antiquated Aristotelian doctrines held during the Middle Ages and to some extent until the sixteenth century. When a new approach to the problem began with the work of Pierre Duhem, the prevailing tendency was to rehabilitate medieval science, and to claim that it prepared or even anticipated the discoveries of Galileo; but the credit for this accomplishment was usually given to the fourteenth-century physicists and logicians of Paris, and more recently, of Oxford. The fact that their work was transmitted to Leonardo, Galileo, and others through the Italian Aristotelians of the fifteenth and sixteenth centuries was known to Duhem and to some of his followers. Yet many historians of science have been able to maintain until quite recently that the auspicious progress of science in the fourteenth century was arrested during the fifteenth, and that this regrettable fact was due to the influence of Italian humanism.

It is at this point that Randall's study and interpretation of Paduan Aristotelianism has filled a gap and corrected the picture prevalent until fairly recent years. In keeping with a scholarly tradition going from Renan to Nardi, Randall has emphasized that the Aristotelian philosophers of the Italian Renaissance, including Pomponazzi and Zabarella, were the legitimate heirs of the philosophical speculation which from the thirteenth century, at the university arts faculties in both Italy and northern Europe, developed around the text of Aristotle and his commentators. But he goes further to argue that the work of the northern Aristotelians of the fourteenth century, which historians of science from Duhem to Anneliese Maier have interpreted in various ways as a preparation or anticipation of seventeenth century physics, was actively continued and further developed by the Italian Aristotelians of the fifteenth and sixteenth centuries, who thus appear as the immediate predecessors of Galileo and as the mediators between the science of the fourteenth and the seventeenth centuries. Randall has studied and documented this relationship in great detail in his paper on the development of scientific method in the school of Padua, showing that Galileo's conception of the resolutive and compositive procedure in the discovery of natural causes and effects was indebted not only to the mathematicians and to the logic of Zabarella, as Cassirer had shown, but presupposes several centuries of methodological discussion carried on by the Italian Aristotelians at least since the beginning of the fourteenth century. Finally, since Randall admires the original work of Aristotle rather than its medieval adaptations, he recognizes the beneficial effect which the revival of Greek scholarship during the Renaissance had upon the study and interpretation of Aristotle, and even upon the philosophical tradition of Paduan Aristotelianism; and hence he is inclined to assign an especially important role to Jacopo Zabarella, who was both the heir of the Paduan tradition and a consummate Greek scholar, and thus became outstanding both as an interpreter of Aristotle and as a philosopher in his own right, two things which for Randall tend to appear identical.

Some of these conclusions of Randall have become by now the common property of scholars in the field of Renaissance philosophy, and they can no longer be ignored by any historian who wants to arrive at a full understanding of the development of philosophy and of the sciences during the Renaissance. I gladly confess that my own views about Renaissance Aristotelianism, its achievements and its relationship to the other intellectual currents of the period, have been profoundly influenced by Randall's work, and by the frequent discussions and conversations which I have carried on with him over a period of many years.

Randall's interpretation of the School of Padua represents in many ways a pioneer effort, and it should be developed and followed up by further studies in a variety of ways. We need more monographic studies on the more important Italian Aristotelians of the Renaissance, whether or not they were connected with the University of Padua, and many more studies on the manner in which specific philosophical and scientific problems were discussed and resolved by these thinkers. It is not the least of

Randall's achievements that his work has opened up a number of questions that call for further investigation and that may keep other scholars busy for quite some time.

Without wishing to detract from Randall's merits, and trusting the appropriateness, even on this occasion, I venture to add a few reservations and critical remarks based on my own views of the subject. In following a historical tradition which goes back to Renan, Randall is perhaps a bit too partial to Padua, a university center whose importance for these studies is undeniable, but which shared its intellectual traditions with a number of sister universities, such as Bologna and Pavia. Moreover, in stressing the contributions of Renaissance Aristotelianism, Randall does not seem to give full credit to the intellectual, philosophical, and scientific contributions made by other currents of the period, although he does by no means ignore them. I should be inclined to assign much greater importance than Randall does to Renaissance humanism as a scholarly and literary as well as a moral movement, to the intellectual contributions of Renaissance artists prior to Leonardo, to the metaphysical doctrines of the Renaissance Platonists, to the anti-Aristotelian revolt in literature, in philosophical speculation, in cosmology, and in the sciences, and to the independent developments of such sciences as medicine, mathematics, and astronomy, which were not traditionally treated within the framework of Aristotelian philosophy. In his enthusiasm for Aristotle and the Aristotelian tradition, Randall tends to minimize the distance which separates both early and more recent modern science from Aristotle and from the medieval and Renaissance Aristotelians, and to underestimate the debt—overestimated perhaps by other scholars—which early modern science owes to the artistic theory, to the mathematics, to the Platonic speculation, and at least indirectly, to the classical scholarship of the Renaissance. Hence, I should say that Randall's work supplements the work of Cassirer, Koyré, and other historians of early modern science and philosophy, but does not replace it. If I add, especially with reference to the *Career of Philosophy*, that I should have given a different emphasis to the vast impulse given by Renaissance Platonism to the history of metaphysics, and by Renaissance humanism to the development of classical and historical scholarship, I may seem to inject my own interests and preferences into a discussion where they may not belong, since Randall, like every scholar, has a right to choose those problems and those thinkers that he wishes to study or to emphasize.

In conclusion, I should like to express, not only my appreciation and gratitude for the contribution made by Randall to the study of Renaissance philosophy but also my hope and confidence that his work will bear further fruit and be continued by himself and by other, younger scholars. Even though many of Randall's specific views and statements may be subject to criticism (and I disagree with many), he has helped in a forceful way to secure for the study of the history of philosophy an important place within the context of American thought and scholarship, and to emphasize within the history of philosophy the importance of the Renaissance period, and within this period, as well as in other periods, the significance of the Aristotelian tradition. I fervently hope that in spite of current anti-historical tendencies, the example of Randall's work will not be lost on the younger generation of American philosophers and scholars.

BIBLIOGRAPHY

The Making of the Modern Mind, Boston, 1926 (revised edition 1940).

"The Development of Scientific Method in the School of Padua," *Journal of the History of Ideas*, I (1940), 177-206. Reprinted partly in: *Roots of Scientific Thought*, ed. P. P. Wiener and A. Noland (New York: Basic Books, 1957), 139-146. Revised and more fully documented in *The School of Padua* (1961), pp. 13-68.

(with P. O. Kristeller), "The Study of the Philosophies of the Renaissance," *Journal of the History of Ideas*, II (1941), 449-496. Reprinted in: *Surveys of Recent Scholarship in the Period of Renaissance* (1945).

(ed. with Ernst Cassirer and Paul O. Kristeller), *The Renaissance Philosophy of Man* (University of Chicago Press, 1948). pp. 1-20: "General Introduction," by P. O. Kristeller and J. H. Randall. pp. 257-279: Introduction to Pomponazzi, by J. H. Randall. A revised and more fully documented version of the latter piece in *The School of Padua* (1961), pp. 71-114, under the title: "The Place of Pomponazzi in the Padua Tradition."

"The Place of Leonardo da Vinci in the Emergence of Modern Science," *Journal of the History of Ideas*, XIV (1953), 191-202. Reprinted in: *Roots of Scientific Thought*, ed. P. P. Wiener and A. Noland (New York: Basic Books, 1957), pp. 207-218. Revised and more fully documented in *The School of Padua* (1961), pp. 117-138.

The School of Padua and the Emergence of Modern Science. (Saggi e Testi, edited jointly by the Centro per la Storia della Tradizione Aristotelica nel Veneto of the University of Padua and by the University Seminar on the Renaissance of Columbia University, vol. I), Padua: Editrice Antenore, 1961.

The Career of Philosophy. New York: Columbia University Press, 1962.

How Philosophy Uses Its Past, New York: Columbia University Press, 1963.

NEAL GILBERT
University of California, Davis

Renaissance Aristotelianism and Its Fate:
Some Observations and Problems

One secret of Professor Randall's effectiveness in the field of the history of philosophy, both as a teacher and as a scholar, is his talent for seeing ideas not as thin lines of metaphysical reasoning spun out of abstract minds, but as the thoughts of living men of widely differing temperaments and backgrounds. He has a keen awareness of the various interrelationships between philosophy and human life. It is this feature that makes *The Making of the Modern Mind* such a valuable textbook. At a time when it is fashionable to dismiss as philosophically irrelevant the social, economic, and religious concerns of a philosopher, Randall has an unusual respect for the importance of the social and religious traditions within which philosophers work. The result is historical analysis that can be fruitful and revealing. Randall does not confine himself to the narrow consideration of the canonical texts, but places them in their social and historical context. The pages of philosophical inquiry come to life in his hands, and we begin to see how even the most iconoclastic and self-sufficient philosopher can be influenced unwittingly by tradition. I would go so far as to suggest that Randall's gift for putting himself in the place of men of different persuasions is an essential requirement for the profitable study of the history of philosophy. To be sure, his approach may be scorned by analysts who insist that there is only one way of "doing" philosophy—theirs. But their method—the piecemeal evaluation of detached arguments—has its own limitations, and the best way to overcome these limitations is through the sort of historical study that Randall represents. Locating a thinker in his religious, economic, and social context helps to bring to light the assumptions and presuppositions that he absorbs from his environment. Often these assumptions are what make his arguments meaningful: in any event, awareness of them is essential to our evaluation of a man's philosophy. Why discuss philosophers of the past at all, if we are not prepared to do full justice to them? And doing justice involves, initially, evaluating their arguments in terms of their assumptions, not ours. We need not, of course, accept their assumptions, but we should at least be aware of them, and watchful for their influence.

This is not to say that Randall's approach does not have its pitfalls. In seeing men as representatives of a given religious, economic, or social class we are always in danger of setting up a picture that does not apply precisely to any existing concrete individual. Methodologically, our research should proceed upward or rather outward from the analysis of chosen individuals. Social generalizations, like any others, must be derived by induction from at least a fair sample of a class. Furthermore, there is another temptation, related to this, that of working backward from ideas to presumed biographical details. To be sure, one can base hypotheses about a thinker's life on the written expression of his ideas. But the only way of establishing the correctness of these hypotheses is through careful historical inquiry. When we deal with "movements" (that is, philosophical tendencies characteristic of two or more men, none of whom is sufficiently "great" to merit individual attention), this temptation becomes overwhelming. Something of this sort has clearly happened with that movement known as the Enlightenment.

When dealing with a philosophical movement, we should be careful to begin by settling upon a concrete philosopher whom we can always have in mind when we discuss that movement. Moreover, we ought to keep in mind the lessons of our own experience; how many philosophers do we know who subscribe to identical views on every possible question? Perhaps we really mean to group as a "school" philosophers who share common assumptions, or, possibly, common methods of philosophical inquiry.

Now Randall's insights generally stand up well just because they are based on such induction. He brings to his generalizations a wealth of data concerning individual figures, and in particular he is careful to do justice to minor figures. As we have often been reminded, so-called "second-rate" thinkers may be as significant to the historian of ideas as the more major figures. Randall's work in the history of philosophy is not the usual rehash of what previous historians of philosophy have said. It is soundly based on direct acquaintance with the sources. The usual course of development is quite different. Its stages are as follows: (1) Some energetic pioneer delves into the thought of a given period of the past, develops what he regards as useful terms for describing that thought, and presents a picture that is as faithful as he can make it. All too often, however, he unwittingly absorbs assumptions from the writers with whom he is dealing, assumptions that may hide in the very terms he uses to characterize them. (2) Subsequent scholars, too lazy or confident to engage in the arduous and often boring task of familiarizing themselves with the writings in question, take over the pioneer's labels and descriptions uncritically (however critical they may be of the pioneer's conclusions). Thus begins the endless chain of repetition, from one dreary parasite to another, until labels that originally had some point lose touch with social reality altogether and end up in that graveyard of all social abstractions, the writings of sociologists (along with "Puritanism," "Medieval Other-Worldliness," "Asceticism," "Averroism," and many others).

Against such contingencies the only safeguard, to my way of thinking, is the old-fashioned, much scorned, but still indispensable drudgery of biographical research, research that focuses upon the individual human being in his entirety and takes total responsibility for doing justice to him and to his thought. Armed with the results of such inquiry, we are then prepared to venture more confidently upon the hazards of generalization, secure in the knowledge that we have a firm grip on reality at one point at least. Even the shakiest or newest generalization about thinkers of the past ought to hold with utter finality for at least one such clear-cut case. And *ex uno nosce omnes*.

To illustrate this point, let me introduce a concrete case, a problem that I happen to be working on intensively at present. Let us suppose that we are interested in seeing how Italian rationalism spread to other countries during the Renaissance. We are quite familiar, thanks in considerable measure to Professor Randall's work in this area, with the general outlines of Italian Aristotelianism .We know how remarkably free from superstition someone like Pomponazzi was, how sharp and cogent in his reasoning, and how reluctant to assert anything for which he could not find a strong warrant in reason or experience. We have the clearest possible picture of this man's thought, and we feel perfectly justified in calling it "rationalism," and, since Pomponazzi taught for a considerable number of years in Padua, his rationalism is clearly "Paduan." Pomponazzi's philosophical views are striking and rather different, we suspect, from those held in his time by men in England, France, or Germany. Let us put in the hands of a scholar the legitimate enterprise of investigating how and by what channels this thought might have reached other lands.

Now, if we have chosen an incompetent scholar, how will he proceed? His first step, undoubtedly, will be to forget completely, to dismiss from his mind altogether, whatever detailed knowledge of Pomponazzi's philosophy he happens to possess. Gone will be the subtleties, the qualifications, the nuances, of the Italian's thinking. In replacement, the mere phrase "Paduan rationalism" will suffice: all scholars who have actually read Pomponazzi (never a large number, anyway) have agreed that Pomponazzi represented it, and so it will be convenient to dispense in the future with tiresome details and work instead with the label "Paduan rationalism."

His second step will be to make the natural but fatal assumption that everyone who ever left or visited northern Italy bore the stamp of this "Paduan rationalism" for the rest of his life. If we think clearly and concretely for a moment, we can see how preposterous such an assumption is. Why should a law student at Bologna, for example, have necessarily acquired any acquaintance whatever with Pomponazzi's thought? Or, even if he did, why should he necessarily have endorsed it? Or, for that matter, why should he even have remembered it?

Nevertheless, if our incompetent scholar steps up into the thinner atmosphere of abstraction, it is easy for him to convince himself that anyone who studied in northern Italy during the Renaissance must have caught the contagion of Paduan rationalism. In order to do this successfully, he must resolutely keep from thinking about certain Paduan students such as Reginald Pole, upon whom a stay at Padua left no visible signs of scepticism or rationalism. Such disturbing "exceptions" are dealt with in a most effective way: their existence is ignored.

Having taken these two steps, our scholar then finds it an easy matter to populate northern Europe with missionaries of "Paduan rationalism"; he simply lists all Frenchmen, Englishmen, or Germans who were near Italy at any time in their lives, and then scans their writings (if they left any, that is; if they did not, so much the better) for anything that can be construed as the least bit antireligious, in any sense whatever of that term. The result: a clear-cut thesis about the spread of rationalism, one that can be peddled even to freshmen, but that may not bear much resemblance to reality.

This technique worked wonders for a French scholar, Henri Busson, to whose work on rationalism in the literature of the French Renaissance Randall gave a favorable if brief review in 1923. This bulky *thèse de doctorat* presented a picture of Renaissance thought somewhat like the one I have just caricatured. It contains, however, a wealth of bibliographical data that has swept critics off their feet. Hardly anyone, Randall included, has bothered to challenge the details of Busson's treatment. The general picture it gave was dramatic and intriguing, and hence was accepted as true.

"Rationalism," in Busson's view, was imported from northern Italy into France. With his own sympathy for the anticlerical Paduans, Randall was quite ready to accept Busson's hypothesis. Now it cannot be denied that there are some grounds for Busson's view. Before he wrote, another French scholar, Emile Picot, had pointed out in great detail the interesting fact that during the fifteenth and sixteenth centuries literally hundreds of French students had attended the Italian universities of Bologna, Pavia, Ferrara, and Padua. Later, many of these French students occupied posi-

tions of extraordinary influence in their native country during the grievous
Wars of Religion. Busson makes of the "former students of Padua" in
France a sort of sinister confraternity, dedicated to the subterranean promotion af Paduan Averroism. He is able to show that many of these men,
not surprisingly, kept in touch with one another during the course of their
later lives. But the evidence presented by Busson also shows that what
united the "Paduan alumni" was, usually, their common enthusiasm for
Italian humanism, especially their passion for Greek learning. Otherwise,
they form a disparate crew, ranging from atheists to highly respectable
dignitaries of the Church, from scientists to poets. One would think that
this diversity alone might throw some doubt on the idea of a monolithic
"Paduan rationalism" in France.

Less tendentious scholarship will not, I suspect, be able to substantiate
such claims. Busson's scholarship can be distressingly slipshod. Let us take
one example. Busson laid great emphasis upon a certain Italian philosopher
named Francesco Vimercato, whom he considered the chief champion of
Averroism in France. According to Busson, this Vimercato (called by him
"Vicomercato") achieved such a reputation for medical skill in his native
Milan that King Francis I asked him to come to Paris and made him his
personal physician. Later, Francis named him to the post of "Reader in
Greek and Latin Philosophy" in the Collège Royale, a post that enabled
Vimercato to spread Averroist doctrines with the greatest impunity.

This picture has at least one obvious flaw in it: it makes King Francis,
never known to be an advocate of free thought, into a sponsor of Averroism. Indeed, it represents him as searching throughout Italy for a Paduan
rationalist. Unfortunately for Busson's thesis, the man who was "called to
Paris" or at least made physician to the King, was not the same as the
"Francesco Vimercato" who taught at the Collège Royale. It is possible to
establish this fact by evidence that Busson himself adduces. Using evidence not known to Busson, it is possible to show that in 1540 the philosophical Vimercato was still unknown to the French King. The medical
man and court doctor died in 1546, leaving the scholar of the same name
(apparently no relation) to carry on for at least thirty years more. The
philosophical Vimercato moved to Savoy in 1561; from that time on, his
influence in Paris, such as it was, must have been exercised through dis-
ciples or through his published writings.

Let us now take the approach of a competent scholar. We would begin
by ascertaining the correct facts about Vimercato's life (the correct Vimercato, that is). Then, using these facts, we can place him in the social fabric
of his day. What picture emerges?

We see a diligent scholar who was probably not noble as Italian
biographers have suggested. To judge from his frequent pleas for money,

he was not wealthy, but was dependent for his livelihood upon his teaching and upon the largesse of bishops and cardinals, kings and dukes. We see a man who—understandably, perhaps, in view of these connections—did not parade his religious heresies, if he had any. Sifting through the biographical details of his life, we find that Vimercato moved in circles that could indeed be identified as non-orthodox from the point of view of the Roman Catholic Church. It is not, however, easy to characterize these circles in more positive form. A general knowledge of the refugee movements of the times indicates that Vimercato left Italy at a time when Protestants and other "heretics" were leaving Italy in considerable numbers, that he sought the protection of a French bishop (Du Châtel), known to have been favorable at that time of his life to the Reform, and that he left Paris almost certainly at the request of Du Châtel's pupil Marguerite de France, who late in life married the fiery Duke of Savoy. When we learn that Marguerite was considered one of his number by Calvin himself, although "fearful to declare herself openly," and that she was ready at all times to extend help and protection to French Protestants, we begin to suspect that her protégé in Savoy, Vimercato, may have been sympathetic to the new religious movement himself. This suspicion is reinforced by a letter Marguerite wrote to Vimercato at a time when he was the Duke's ambassador to Milan, asking him to help a French gentleman languishing in the hands of the Inquisition.

Equipped with these biographical facts, which enable us to place him in his social, religious, and economic context, we are certainly better prepared than Busson was to give proper weight to philosophical doctrines expressed or discussed by Vimercato. Vimercato, it seems, was chronically reticent when it came to expressing his own philosophical views. He was inclined to retreat, like the Latin Averroists four centuries before his time, to the safe and straightforward exposition of Aristotle. But it is clear that he might have had reasons other than "Averroism" for such reticence.

Research into this particular problem will be greatly expedited by a determination to see the philosopher Vimercato as a breathing, living human being, moving unobtrusively through some of the most troubled periods in European history. Such research can replace a label with a human being, and give us a picture that at least applies to one man without any qualification.

If this picture adds to our understanding of the whole movement of thought in the Renaissance, then that is again due in part to Professor Randall and his insistence on seeing philosophical developments against their economic, social, and religious background.

II

I should like to turn now from this private testimonial to the influence of Professor Randall on one of his appreciative pupils, and to present a historical problem that in my opinion desperately needs attention. It may be put briefly thus: what really did cause the decline of neo-Aristotelianism? This might seem to be a foolish or even stupid question. Who does not know that Copernicus and Galileo spelled the end of Aristotelian cosmology? Or that Descartes overthrew Aristotelian logic? Or that Newton's physics finally tied up the loose ends of the "new philosophy" and swept all memory of Aristotle from the minds of scientific men?

These facts must be acknowledged; and yet when we have done this, does not a problem still remain? For the men of the seventeenth century scrapped Aristotle's philosophy of nature, but his metaphysics remained to haunt them, and his logic of science, as presented in the *Posterior Analytics*, lingered to channel the thinking even of such scientists as Newton, as Professor Randall has remarked. The "substantial forms" of the Schoolmen may have been banished by Descartes and Spinoza, but their central role was taken over by "matter" (surely itself an Aristotelian concept) governed by "gravity." If "substantial forms" are a non-explanatory, metaphysician's trifling with words, what of "matter"? And if "substantial forms" are not to be tolerated as basic explanations, what of "gravity"? an "accidental form" if ever there was one, and not unfamiliar to the student of Aristotle, either.

Randall has done as much as anyone to restore Renaissance Aristotelianism to philosophical respectability: in his lectures at Columbia University, in his numerous articles, and in influential books such as *The Making of the Modern Mind* and *The Career of Philosophy*. He has focused on Italian Aristotelianism, particularly as it developed at Padua, and he has stressed the relationship of this university tradition to contemporary developments in medicine and physical science. He has not given such a conspicuous place in his analysis to the development of Aristotelianism in the Iberian Peninsula or in Germany. Yet Iberian Aristotelianism was a rich stream. To be sure, such names as Vittoria, Fonseca, Soto, Toledus, and Suarez are, unfortunately, just names to most of us—but then, so were the names of Pomponazzi and Zabarella before Randall called our attention to them.

We perhaps ought to remind ourselves that neo-Aristotelianism once did enjoy respectability with historians of philosophy and scholars in general. Glance, for example, at the *Critical History of Philosophy* of Johann Jakob Brucker (1696-1770): you will find extensive and respectful treatment of the "genuine" Aristotelians, as Brucker calls them—men who attempted to present the authentic philosophical view of the Stagirite.

Brucker puts the Aristotelians of the Renaissance where I think they belong: as revivers of an ancient school of philosophy. The other Aristotelians might be called (in a sinister modern term) "revisionists" rather than "pure and sincere" Aristotelians or advocates of the straight Aristotle. This is the category into which Brucker puts such men as Zabarella, Pomponazzi, Leonicus Thomaeus, Mazzoni, Caesalpinus, and Cremonini, blithely disregarding in the process those national boundaries that subsequent scholars have been unable to cross.

Aristotle, then, had his own Renaissance; and his followers in the sixteenth and seventeenth centuries could be thought of by an eighteenth-century historian as attempting to do for Aristotle what Ficino had done for Plato, or Lipsius for the Stoics. I suspect that this is in fact the most suitable category in which to place the Renaissance Aristotelians.

If Aristotelianism still enjoyed such a favorable press in the seventeenth century, what accounts for its subsequent decline in popular esteem? Several factors, I believe. (1) A major factor was the attack of the Humanists, who leveled such ridicule at "School Philosophy" that all phases of Aristotelianism—Nominalism, lingering theological realism, Iberian or Italian "genuine" Aristotelianism, and even, perhaps, eclectic school traditions such as semi-Ramism, suffered from association with Aristotle. Secondary-text writers have tended to accept Humanist criticisms at face value, and have written off university Aristotelianism without a hearing. To a certain extent, this is testimony to the effectiveness of Humanist rhetoric and ridicule. People continue to read Erasmus' *Praise of Folly*, which contains some sharp slashes at Terminist logic (an offshoot of Aristotelian logic); but no one, other than specialists in the history of logic, would think of looking into Peter of Spain's textbook in Terminist logic.

(2) Another factor in the decline of Aristotelianism would, of course, be the "new philosophy," that is, the rise of Cartesianism, of the materialism of Gassendi and Hobbes, or the corpuscularism of Robert Boyle. The assumption commonly made about these movements is that they had only to put in their appearance in order to conquer, with the Aristotelians creeping ignominiously away in defeat from the universities. The universities, let us recall, were the locale of the battle for the minds of European men. Occasionally a man such as Jungius in Germany took the battle down into the lower schools, but most of the enemies of the new philosophy occupied chairs of philosophy in the universities, and it was from these that they had to be dislodged.

(3) A third factor played a role in the demise of Aristotelianism: the new religious movements, including the Reformation, the separation of the Anglican communion, and (later) the rise of Pietism—no doubt these

religious developments contributed to make the environment increasingly hostile to an Aristotelianism that had become associated, in many minds, with Roman Catholic theology.

Finally, (4) there was the general rejection of bookish learning so characteristic of the seventeenth century, with its emphasis upon Reason and Sense-Experience.

All of these explanations have their champions; and all, it must be admitted, have a certain validity. Yet put them all together and they still come short, to my mind, of explaining the decline of Aristotelianism. For one thing, these factors were all operative in seventeenth- and eighteenth-century Germany, where nevertheless Aristotelianism persisted with remarkable vigor.

If the proper category in which to put Renaissance Aristotelianism is that of historical scholarship, and if this tradition is no more incompatible with original and sound philosophizing than is the study of mathematics, or of jurisprudence, then why should it ever have been superseded in the universities of Europe? No one would say that philosophy at Oxford has suffered incurable damage from the constant study of Aristotle's *Ethics*, or from the presence of Sir David Ross. Then who would begrudge the Aristotelian scholar his chair of philosophy? The answer must be, I suspect, someone who wished to occupy that chair himself. We all know from our own experience that academic opponents are capable of misrepresenting the views of those whom they wish to displace. The process by which Aristotelians were gradually ousted from university positions in the seventeenth and eighteenth centuries has been very little studied. We know far too little about the academic in-fighting of the period to speak with much assurance about the replacement of teachers committed to Aristotle by new men. The transition is perhaps most fully documented for Holland, where Cartesianism (a historically striking phenomenon) had considerable and early success in driving Aristotle from the schools. We also have some adequate works on the late stages of Aristotelianism in Germany. But the death throes of Aristotelianism are far less well documented for the universities of France, of England, and of Spain and Portugal. We may have scattered information on the decline of Aristotelianism in these schools, but this information has not been hammered into any acceptable scholarly synthesis. There have been only a few monographs on trends at particular schools.

Unfortunately, historians are still, for the most part, interested chiefly in the origins of universities, which means the thirteenth century for a few universities, or the fourteenth, fifteenth, or sixteenth centuries for a great many others. Not until we reach the founding of the great German universities in the nineteenth century do historians provide us with useful materials for analyzing the sort of shift in emphasis we would like to study: changes in departments, in chairs, in curricula, in student patronage, in financial support, and so on.

What I have just been exploring is (5) a possible fifth factor in the decline of Aristotelianism, which might be called institutional lag, or the persistence of institutionalized habits of thought past their usefulness. The main point to be made here, I suppose, is that no one has yet investigated this issue thoroughly from a historical standpoint. By way of contrast, we might ask ourselves whether the historian of medieval philosophy could dispense so flippantly with the institutional background of his thinkers? Can Abelard's philosophical development be studied without reference to his flight from Paris, or Ockham's political and social thought be understood without knowing where he taught and with whom? Even individual Renaissance Aristotelians are identified with the universities at which they taught (the "School of Padua"), to say nothing of such influential groups as those anonymous Jesuit commentators forever associated with the University of Coimbra. Why, then, do we lose sight of institutional settings when it is the institutional affiliation, presumably, that accounts for the persistence of Aristotelianism at a time when the "New Science," the "world of nature," the "New Religion," and all the rest of the putative factors would make it obsolete?

I want finally to advance a most impertinent and naive suggestion: (6) could it possibly be that Aristotelians themselves were becoming aware of serious deficiencies or contradictions in the system of their master? I know that it is not at all fashionable to attribute intelligence to our professional predecessors (or even peers). Yet I am convinced, from what reading I have done in the works of Renaissance and seventeenth-century Aristotelians, that they were men of considerable acumen. If anything, they were too sharp for their own philosophical good. I believe that Aristotelian scholarship reached an absolute impasse in the sixteenth century, when men were able to read the Greek text of Aristotle, or at least, to profit from the scholarship of men who could read Greek. Problems within Aristotle's system of thought could no longer be glossed over by clever constructive interpretations, or by the invention of verbal distinctions designed to meet charges of internal inconsistency. Aristotelians could no longer fall back upon a long series of elaborate glosses fabricated in order to preserve the Master from the charge of obscurity or to meet philosophical difficulties. The problems, in short, stared up at them from the text of Aristotle himself, and no amount of Talmudic ingenuity could rescue the Philosopher from his difficulties.

The most important such difficulty concerned the distinction of matter and form, which surely lies at the heart of Aristotelian metaphysics, and runs through all of his thought, being related in complex ways to the distinction between potential and actual, as well as to the Platonic problem of the Many and the One. Already difficulties had been found in late antiquity in applying this distinction to the nature of the human soul, which, as actuality and as form, would seem to be at the opposite pole, metaphysically speaking, from the body, which is matter. The status of the soul in Aristotle's metaphysics troubled many students of Aristotle, such as the Greek commentators, who certainly cannot be accused of having been encumbered by theological commitments. It is customary to regard the Renaissance concern with the soul as a reflection of the religious issues of the day. A deep concern for immortality, so this theory runs, underlay the ardent desire of students at Italian universities to hear about the soul. "*Anima! Anima!*," they cried, when their instructors tried to switch the topic of lectures to something other than the *De Anima*. Yet is it not possible that the interest of these students was strictly philosophical? Might they not have been deeply concerned with the consistency of the metaphysical system presented to them for their acceptance, as a rational structure built upon sense experience? If so, they would have been understandably disturbed when it was argued, as by Pomponazzi, that the Averroistic thesis of the unity of the intellect, contrary to experience as it seemed, represented the most satisfactory interpretation of Aristotle and, indeed, alone rendered his metaphysics consistent.

These commentators were studied avidly in the Renaissance—more avidly than they have ever been studied since. One might attribute this to the fact that the Greek commentators had just been printed in the sixteenth century. But why were they published, if not that they promised to shed some light on significant features of Aristotle's philosophy? Their vogue accounts for the prominence of the debate over the nature of the soul; was it a *forma dans esse*, or a *forma informans*? Was Alexander closer to the spirit of Aristotle's metaphysics than Simplicius? These questions, I believe, bothered Renaissance Aristotelians because of their *philosophical* implications, just as they have bothered many a later student of Aristotle. I suspect that these internal problems of philosophical exegesis had as much to do with the disappearance of Aristotelianism as did the external factors usually cited. But what we obviously need is another Gibbon to trace the movement's decline and fall.

WILLIAM F. EDWARDS

State University of New York at Buffalo

Randall on the Development of Scientific Method in the School of Padua—a Continuing Reappraisal

I

No piece of Prof. Randall's writings has been more influential than his "Development of Scientific Method in the School of Padua," first published in the *Journal of the History of Ideas* in 1940.[1] Historians of philosophy have been less ready to accept the thesis he presents there than historians of science, perhaps because their views on the origin of modern thought have been longer established and cannot be so easily changed. Expressed most simply, the view has been that both modern philosophy and modern science arose out of a revolt against Aristotle and the intellectual system founded on his thought. Modern science is supposed to have arisen when scientists closed the books of Aristotle, and opened the book of nature. Modern philosophy, similarly, is supposed to have come into being partly as a result of the Humanist rejection of Scholasticism, partly as a result of philosophers' following the lead of the new scientists of the sixteenth and seventeenth century.

Admittedly, this is an overly simple statement of the view of the origin of modern thought traditionally presented. Historians of science, in particular, and historians of philosophy oriented towards the history of science have been willing to recognize a continuity between the old and the new. But there is still a widespread reluctance to admit that the break customarily posited between the medieval and the modern was not really so clean or absolute as we were once inclined to imagine. Above all, there seems to be a reluctance to admit that the Aristotelian tradition of philosophical and scientific thought did not come to an abrupt end, at least among those who mattered, in about the year 1600. If a continuity is admitted, then it is insisted that it must have been through the Platonic, not the Aristotelian, tradition. The uniqueness of modern science, compared to medieval, has been its mathematizing mode of thought; and as the Aristotelians were little given to this kind of thinking, it is concluded that early modern scientists, like Galileo, must necessarily have found the Aristotelian tradition sterile.

It was this assumption Prof. Randall challenged in his "Development of Scientific Method in the School of Padua." Following the lead of E. Cassirer, who had pointed out in his *Erkenntnisproblem* that the concept of scientific method presented by Jacopo Zabarella (1533-1589) was—except for the fact that mathematics plays no part in it—the same as that of Galileo,[2] Prof. Randall went on to show that the concept of scientific method presented by Zabarella in his *Logic* of 1578[3] had actually been about three hundred years in developing. Starting with Peter of Abano (d. 1315), Prof. Randall traced the evolution of the concepts of "resolutive" and "compositive" method down through the fourteenth and fifteenth century commentators on Galen's *Ars Medica* and other writers closely allied to this tradition of commentary, to Agostino Nifo (d. 1546), Zabarella, and Cesare Cremonini (d. 1631), showing how the two concepts were gradually combined into a single theory of method of the kind described (and in the same language) by Galileo and other early modern scientists. Like Cassirer, Randall stressed the fact that there was a missing element in the theory of method developed in the "School of Padua," viz., mathematization of the *principia* discovered by resolutive (or inductive) method, and concludes only that the Paduan Aristotelians worked out the fundamental logical concepts that do in fact constitute modern scientific method. The crucial step of introducing mathematics and in effect of converting the Paduans' "compositive" method to mathematical deduction was taken by Galileo.

More will be said in what follows about the concept of method developed by the Paduan Aristotelians, but as its explication is not the main purpose of this paper, additional remarks about it will be incidental. Here my principal motive is to defend Prof. Randall's thesis against some of the criticisms that have been made of it since its publication in 1940. I do not wish to argue that the thesis is perfect as he states it—only that it is substantially correct—nor that the evidence he adduces to support it is complete.[4] Again, I do not wish to maintain that the objections brought against it are of no force, or value. On the contrary, they are themselves contributions to our understanding of the origins of the method of modern science. But it seems to me that their value is lessened by an overly narrow or what might almost be called a partisan view of the development of the modern concept of scientific method—a narrowness or partisanship not justified by a careful examination of the relevant traditions.

The nature of the partisanship is indicated clearly enough by the title of the essay—"Galileo's Platonism"[5]—in which Cassirer, seeming to retreat from his earlier view, attacks the thesis propounded by Prof. Randall in his "Development of Scientific Method in the School of Padua." Accepting the "results" of Prof. Randall's research, but not his "conclusions," Cassirer argues that Galileo "found the first clear and sharp distinction between 'analysis' and 'synthesis' " in Euclid; that he gave to "the Greek classical method of 'problematical analysis' a new breadth and a new depth" by applying it to a subject to which it had never before been applied, viz., physical thought; and that he borrowed only his terminology—"resolutive" for "analytic," and "compositive" for "synthetic" method—from the Aristotelians.

Prof. Neal W. Gilbert, in a recent note in the *Journal of the History of Philosophy*,[6] carries Cassirer's argument even further, and suggests not only that Galileo's concept of method can be derived completely from the Greek mathematicians but also that there does not seem to be any reason to suppose that he borrowed even his terminology from the Aristotelians. This, Gilbert surmises, could just as well have come from "the Greek mathematical works so recently made available to him by Federigo Commandino." Gilbert is further impressed by the fact that "the methodology of the Aristotelians relied exclusively on the syllogism," condemned by Galileo as useless for the purposes of scientific discovery, but for Zabarella, "a loyal Aristotelian," the single instrument of science; moreover, there is "no mention of Zabarella in the whole mass of Galileo's writings," and "no evidence that Galileo ever owned a copy of Zabarella's logic," and so on.

While it is not true that there is no mention of Zabarella in the whole mass of Galileo's writings,[7] Gilbert's arguments are telling because there is no one who has a more extensive and closer knowledge of Renaissance speculation on method than he does;[8] and I do not wish to leave the implication that the statement I have just given of them is by any means complete. It is not. But neither do I wish here to reply to Gilbert's arguments in detail. Instead, I should like to argue more generally that both he and Cassirer fall into the same error: that of *separating* the medico-philosophical (or Aristotelian) and the mathematical traditions too completely, and of supposing that what is found in the one must necessarily be absent from the other, or—if not that—at least that the inspiration for Galileo's thought must be found exclusively in one or the other.

Such assumptions find little support in the medico-philosophical tradition of speculation on method, of which Prof. Randall's "Development of Scientific Method in the School of Padua" is a highly useful preliminary exploration—and for two reasons: (1) the earliest of the commentators on the *Ars Medica* were already debating the question whether the "analysis" of which Galen speaks in the prologue is the same as the "analysis of the geometers"; and (2) the concept of "regressive" demonstration[9] developed by the Averroist-Aristotelian commentators on the *Ars Medica* and the *Posterior Analytics* was itself at bottom nothing but an attempt to provide the natural sciences with a method that would be equivalent in degree of certitude (or as nearly so as possible) to the kind of "absolute" demonstration Averroes saw in mathematics. Whether the early commentators on the *Ars Medica* really succeeded in understanding and imitating "the analysis of the geometers" in their medical methodologies, or whether Averroes and his followers really understood and reproduced in the theory of method they proposed for the natural sciences the "absolute" demonstration of the mathematicians they took as a shining model of scientific method, is beside the point if the question is whether the Aristotelian concept of method was developed independently of mathematical thought. It was not. Twice, at least, before the advent of Galileo the mathematical and philosophical traditions met and merged. Indeed, rather than to maintain that they met for the first time in Galileo (as Cassirer does), it would be more plausible to suggest that in Galileo we have the third and final stage of a merging process that began over five centuries earlier, with 'Ali ibn Ridwan (d. 1061), and his influential commentary on the *Ars Medica* of Galen.

II

This is the position I should like to defend in this paper, and while it will not be possible to substantiate it fully here, the evidence on which it is based may at least be presented in a summary form. Whether 'Ali ibn Ridwan—or "Haly," as the Latin commentators called him—was the first to interpret that *analysis* Galen defines in the prologue[10] of the *Ars Medica* as the same as that of the "geometers,"[11] and to propose, in effect, the application of that method in medicine, I am not certain; but he is the first commentator on the *Ars* cited by Peter of Abano and later Latin expositors of that work. Nor is it quite certain from what he says and the examples he gives that he is proposing what we would consider to be a method in a significant sense, that is, a scientific method, or a method by which authentic new knowledge may be obtained. The reason for the uncertainty is that what Galen defines in the prologue of the *Ars Medica* is not scientific method in the modern sense, but three "ordered modes of instruction" (*didaskaliai taxeos echomenai*, or, in Latin, typically, *doctrinae ordinatae*). He is thus thinking primarily of the "method" that would be used in the organization of an already existing body of knowledge, like medicine, for presentation to students in a classroom or in a written work. Of this kind of method, he says there are three: the first is produced by resolution (*kat analysin, per resolutionem*) of the idea of an end (*ek tes tou telous, ex finis notione*); the second by composition (*ek syntheoseos, ex compositione*) of the things that were discovered by resolution; and the third by dissolution of a definition (*ex horou dialyseos, ex definitionis dissolutione*).[12] Either the early commentators did not understand what kind of method Galen defines here in the prologue (which is unlikely), or they did not think it important to distinguish sharply between this kind of method, by which an entire discipline is coherently or logically organized, and the kind of method by which particular problems within a discipline are solved. Their task as they saw it was simply to relate what Galen says in the prologue of the *Ars* to the other theories of method known to them, viz., the *analysis* and *synthesis* of the Greek mathematicians, and the two kinds of demonstration—*hoti, quia,* or of the fact, and *dioti, propter quid,* or *of the reasoned fact*—defined by Aristotle in the *Posterior Analytics.*

Haly makes a simple and straightforward identification of Galen's *analysis* with geometrical analysis—"the geometers and the founders of the sciences know this mode of instruction," he says[13]—and also with Aristotle's demonstration *hoti* or *quia.* So whether he intended to or not, he is suggesting that Galen's analytic or resolutive mode of instruction is really a method for the solution of particular problems—that is, a scientific method in the modern sense—and that is the way he was understood by Peter of Abano and other commentators on the *Ars*[14] up to Nicolo Leoniceno (1428-1524) in the sixteenth century. Having taken this step, it is natural that Haly should go on to identify Galen's synthetic, or compositive mode of instruction with Aristotle's demonstration *dioti,* or *propter quid.*[15] If he means also to equate it with geometrical synthesis, he does not say so, but it seems a safe assumption that he did. This leaves the definitional mode of instruction defined by Galen standing by itself, since neither the Greek mathematicians nor Aristotle posited a third kind of method to which it might correspond. What to say about definition remained a problem in the tradition of commentary on the *Ars* till, again, Leoniceno, who could present it, along with resolution and composition, merely as a third way of ordering a body of knowledge for teaching purposes. It was evident to the earlier Latin commentators too that definition, unlike resolution and composition, could not be a method for acquiring new knowledge. There was nothing in Aristotle to justify such a view, and most of them concluded rather weakly that while definiton is of no use in obtaining new knowledge, it is at least a compendious way of teaching and writing an art, and more conducive to memory than either of the other two.

Returning to Haly's interpretation of the Galenian analysis, it does not seem to occur to him that the analysis employed by the geometer in the solution of his problems, or the construction of his proofs, may require some modification before it can be transferred to the subject-matter of the *medicus*. A physician asks, e.g., what is the cause of this fever, in this patient? The geometer asks, can this triangle be inscribed in this circle?[16] And these may not be questions answerable by exactly the same logical procedures. The essence of geometrical analysis, as it is defined by Plato in the *Meno*, Euclid (or Eudoxus) in the *Elements*, and Pappus, is to assume what we wish to demonstrate, and then work back through the consequences of that assumption till we come to something we know to be true (or false). Here is Pappus' definition of it: "... in analysis we assume that which is sought as if it were (already) done (*gegonos*), and we inquire what it is from which this results, and again what is the antecedent cause of the latter, and so on, until by so retracing our steps we come upon something already known or belonging to the class of first principles. . . ."[17] Thus, the moment we come on something we know to be true, we also know that our original assumption is true, and we may turn around and work back to it through the same chain of consequences by which we reached it (this, of course, will be *synthesis*, and may take the form of an actual construction—we have all worked enough geometrical problems to know how this is done). But if the physician employs this kind of analysis in diagnosing the causes of a disease, he does not arrive at "something already known." The geometer does—he comes to a proposition he has already proved, or to the self-evident definitions, axioms, etc., he has laid down in the beginning. But the physician comes to something he only *thinks* may be the cause of the disease in question, and his analysis stops when he comes to some factor he can *control*, or *manipulate*. If he concludes, as medieval physicians were in the habit of doing, that the cause of a fever is a "cold stomach," caused by a generally cold "complexion" in the patient, which in turn is caused by exposure to cold air, then it is up to him to warm the patient up, and *wait to see* what happens. Only if the chain of causal actions his own action sets up results in an abatement of the fever will he *know* that his analysis was correct.

The situation of the physician vis-à-vis the use of geometrical analysis is exactly analogous to that of the natural philosopher, whose task is to analyze natural effects into their causes; and it was a consideration of the differing *knowledge-situations*, so to speak, of the geometer on the one hand and the *medicus* and *physicus* on the other that led Averroes and the Averroists to develop different theories of scientific proof for the mathematician and the natural scientist. It is strange that Haly does not see the need for this. Peter of Abano did, as we shall see in a moment. But in modeling his concept of medical analysis on that of the geometer, Haly does not seem to have in mind the diagnosing of the causes of a disease.

Rather, he seems to be thinking of the original construction or constitution of the art of medicine itself. By way of example of analysis in medicine, he says:

> We wish to learn the art of medicine; we find accordingly that the art of medicine has two parts, of which one is the acquisition of health, and the other the preservation of health; we consider, therefore, the acquisition of health, and we find that it is effected through cures, diet, and medicines; and (then) we consider the preservation of health, and we find that is effected through diet, and regimen. Then we consider each one of these things (that is, cures, diet, regimen, etc.) and we do not cease to descend (thus) until we come to known sciences, and to the things that must be posited as the principles of medicine.[18]

If this is what analysis is for Haly, it must be admitted that it bears a striking resemblance to geometrical analysis, but it is hard to see how he could have thought it identical with the Aristotelian demonstration *hoti* or *quia*. Given the view, that is, that the principles of medicine are borrowed from the more basic science of physics—and this was the view that prevailed—then the *medicus*, in the type of analysis Haly describes, will eventually come to "known sciences," as he puts it, or to "something already known," as Pappus expresses it. He will come to principles that have already been demonstrated by the *physicus*, and he will be in the same happy knowledge-situation the geometer is. But the analysis he has carried out will not be the kind we should be inclined to demand of a practicing physician or natural scientist—it will not be an analysis of effects into their causes, whether the effects in question are fevers or eclipses of the moon—and the concept of analytic method deriving from this use of analysis will not be method in what we take to be a scientific sense.

Analysis as a method for discovering the *causes* of an *effect*, rather than the principles of an art or science, first begins to emerge clearly in the thought of Peter of Abano (d. 1315) and, as might be expected, takes the form of a reinterpretation of the prologue of the *Ars Medica*. Peter was acquainted not only with the commentary of Haly on the *Ars* but— much more important—with the extensive writings on logic and method of Averroes (1126-1198), and since the new interpretation he gave to the prologue of the *Ars* is largely traceable to the latter, something must be said here about the Commentator's views on the method of mathematics. There is no evidence that Averroes knew Haly's commentary, and there is no *clear* evidence that he knew, directly at least, the work of the Greek geometers, or the geometrical concept of analysis. He did not himself comment on the *Ars Medica*, and only a commentary on that work would provide us with a certain answer to the question whether the "absolute" demonstration he defines for mathematics—*demonstratio simpliciter*, as it is usually called in the Latin translations—was *his* interpretation of what the analysis of the geometers is. It has all the earmarks of being that, and in any case there can be no doubt about Averroes' profound interest in the method of mathematics. His writings abound in discussions of it, and in comparisons of the method of the mathematician to the method of the natural scientist. He was struck—one might almost say obsessed—by the fact that mathematical demonstrations furnish both of the kinds of knowledge defined by Aristotle in the *Posterior Analytics*: both knowledge of the fact, and of the reasoned fact, while in natural science the *quia* and the *propter quid* of things can almost always be discovered only by the use of two kinds of demonstration separately. When the mathematicians gets down to his known principles, he knows both *that* the thing he originally assumed is true, and *why* it is true. But it is seldom that a natural scientist can construct that kind of demonstration.[19] If asked why he cannot, Averroes' answer would be, as it was time after time, that the *causes* of *res naturales* are not naturally known to us, while those of *res mathematicae* are. [20] By naturally known, Averroes means "sensible," and only the effects of natural causes, not the causes themselves, are sensible. Does Averroes then mean that the causes of *res mathematicae* are sensible, and for that reason better known to us? It hardly seems possible that he could, though some of the Averroists tried to interpret him that way, and explain his "absolute" demonstration by saying, in effect, that it starts from sensible causes, which do not first have to be discovered through effects. But a "sensible" cause would be a contradiction in terms. Psychologically, we are unable to look on anything sensible as a "cause"—it is always, by the very fact that it is sensible, an "effect"—an effect needing to be explained through a "cause." The only clue Averroes gives us to what he means when he distinguishes between "things better known to nature"—these would be the kind of causes from which mathematical proofs start—and the "things better known to us"—these are always to be understood as sensible things—is to say that if we made *res naturales*, then their causes would be as well known to us as they are "to nature." We know the causes of *res artificiales* because we make them,[21] and though Averroes does not to my knowledge ever say that we know the causes of *res mathematicae* because we make them too, I do not know of any other way to interpret him.

The point to be stressed in all this is that for Averroes the types of scientific demonstration are determined by the knowledge-situation of the user of them, or by his relation to the causes of the things he seeks to explain or prove. The mathematician is in the peculiar situation of not knowing whether the things he seeks to demonstrate are true till he has found their causes. These causes are naturally known to him, and when he reaches them he knows both that the things he assumed *are*, and *why* they are. As Averroes expresses it, his demonstrations are at once *demonstrationes causae et existentiae*. But the physicist is in a peculiar situation too. He always, or almost always, knows that the things he seeks to explain—natural effects—*are*. They are given by sense, and what we already know we cannot seek a demonstration of. He therefore seeks a demonstration of their causes, *demonstratio causae*, and the demonstrations given in his science, unlike mathematics, are almost all of this type. Some of them will be *demonstrationes existentiae*, if the necessary knowledge of causes has already been obtained by *demonstrationes causae*. Rarely will they be *demonstrationes causae et existentiae*, or "absolute."[22]

There are obscurities in the Averroistic theory of scientific demonstration, but there are also important insights, not always fully articulated, into the nature of the problem of method in the natural sciences. If Averroes is right, then the analysis of the geometers, or the method of mathematics, is *not* transferrable to medicine and physics, which must be content with the kind of demonstrations proper to their subject-matter, *hoti* and *dioti*, *existentiae* and *causae*, *quia* and *propter quid* (these are all interchangeable terms). On the other hand, if the physicist can by demonstration *causae* discover the causes of things, and by demonstration *existentiae* establish the existence of effects through discovered causes, why is it not possible for him, in this roundabout way, to prove things with all the certainty or as "absolutely" as the mathematician does? This idea— that of a "regress" in demonstration, in which first demonstration *quia* (effect to cause) would be employed, and then demonstration *propter quid* (cause to effect)—is present in Averroes only in a germinal form. Or rather, its component elements are scattered through his diffuse logical writings, and had first to be collected and integrated before the full-fledged theory of regressive demonstration could emerge. There are more of these elements than have been mentioned here, but they are all in Averroes in one place or another; and gather them together and build them into an impressive theory of method for the empirical sciences is what the Latin commentators on the *Ars Medica* and the *Posterior Analytics* gradually did.

It is not possible here to examine the thought of all these commentators, or to determine what their individual contributions were, but one or two of them may be looked at. Returning to Peter of Abano and the now familiar question whether Galen's analysis is identical with that of the geometers, Peter answers that (1) Haly was right in identifying the Galenian analysis with Aristotle's demonstration *quia*, but that (2) mathematicians do not use demonstration *quia*, but demonstration *propter quid*. The analysis of the geometers and the kind Galen talks about are therefore *not* identical, according to Peter. Attempting to explain how Haly could have said that they are, Peter stresses the fact that all Haly said was that the Galenian analysis (or demonstration *quia*) is *known* to the geometers, not that they *use* it. It is known to them, Peter maintains, because they employ demonstration *propter quid*, and these two kinds of demonstration—*propter quid* and *quia*—are "connected."[23]

This is a rather weak explanation, and Peter probably thought that Haly was wrong in saying that Galen's analysis is equivalent to Aristotle's demonstration *quia*. Having himself taken the position that mathematicians used demonstration *propter quid*, Peter also has the task of explaining how Averroes could have held that they use a third and special kind, viz., *demonstratio simpliciter*, or absolute demonstration. Here again he is perhaps overly ingenious, but since he is working in an interesting direction one does not find it hard to forgive him. The Commentator, he says, did not mean that the mathematician constructs a kind of demonstration that is different from the other two. What he meant was that the mathematician constructs a demonstration *propter quid*, and that through this single demonstration the effect becomes both absolutely known (i.e., through its cause) and known to us, just as if a (separate) demonstration had been given of it.[24] In other words, the only difference between demonstration *propter quid* in mathematics and in the natural sciences is that in the former no prior demonstration *quia* (to discover the cause) is necessary, whereas in the latter it is.

It is surprising that Peter does not go on to posit a regress in the method of the natural sciences. Unlike Haly, he does not understand the "end" from which Galen says resolution, or analysis, begins as the aim or purpose of a science, and resolution itself as a process by which the means to that end are discovered. Rather, he says, the "end" from which resolution begins is to be understood as an "effect,"[25] and with this reinterpretation, in which the influence of Averroes is evident, he has succeeded in giving the Galenian concepts of analysis and synthesis the meaning they needed to become genuine methods for the discovery and verification of the causes of natural effects. In addition, as already noted, he says that analysis (demonstration *quia*) and synthesis (demonstratio *propter quid*) are "connected." *How* they are connected, Peter unfortunately does not specify. The conclusion that they are connected in the sense that demonstration *quia* supplies us, in the natural sciences, with the knowledge of causes that makes demonstration *propter quid* possible (hence, demonstrations of the type Peter says the mathematicians use) seems to have been staring him in the face. But if it was, Peter did not see it, and the most we can say for him is that he takes some of the necessary preliminary steps towards the working out of the concept of regressive demonstration needed in the empirical sciences.

Peter's reluctance, or inability, to go the whole way towards developing a substitute for mathematical demonstration in the natural sciences is all the more surprising in view of the fact that another of the great contemporary *medici*, Taddeo degli Alderotti (Thaddeus Florentinus, d. 1303), had already reached the concept of a regress in demonstration. In fact, he explicitly uses the term *regressus*, and so far as I am aware is the first of the medical commentators to do so. It appears, too, that Peter knew Taddeo's commentary on the *Ars* when he wrote his own *Conciliator*, since he specifically attacks the position Taddeo takes on the question of what Haly meant when he said that the Galenian *doctrina resolutiva* (or analysis) is known to the geometers. Like Peter, Taddeo holds that the mathematicians use demonstration *propter quid*, not *quia*; and since Haly identifies demonstration *propter quid* with the Galenian *doctrina compositiva*, not *resolutiva*, how is it possible for him to maintain that *doctrina resolutiva* is known to the geometers?

Peter's answer to this question, as will be recalled, was that geometers only *know doctrina resolutiva* (demonstration *quia*), they don't *use* it; and Taddeo's answer is at least as ingenious, and far richer in consequences. *Doctrina resolutiva*, Taddeo says, is twofold: there is first a resolution of what is sought into its causes, and then there is a regress from the causes back to what is sought. In the first part of this process, we have demonstration *quia*, because there is a passage from effect to cause; but in the second part, we have demonstration *propter quid*, because in the regress occurring here there is a passage from the cause back to the effect. Thus it can be said that *doctrina resolutiva*, or demonstration *quia*, is known to the geometers, because it includes demonstration *propter quid* (*doctrina compositiva*) as an integral part of itself.[26] Peter emphatically rejects this position, and apparently the idea of a regress in demonstration along with it. Assuming that he understood Taddeo's position, it is hard to see why he rejected it, since it is a natural and almost inevitable development from his own. But even though the double resolutive-compositive method Taddeo describes—which is, precisely, the analysis of the geometers modified and adapted to the requirements of the empirical sciences—did not receive the approbation of the influential Conciliator, it was the concept that triumphed in the medico-philosophical tradition. Later commentators did not agree with Taddeo that composition is a *part* of resolution, but they did agree that in the natural sciences we do not have genuine knowledge till we have completed the double process of resolution and composition he describes.

III

The commentators on the *Ars* continued to debate the question of the relation of geometrical analysis, the Galenian *doctrina resolutiva*, and the Aristotelian demonstration *quia* long after Peter and Taddeo. Torrigiano dei Torrigiani (d. 1350), a younger contemporary of theirs, plunged into the debate with a position so radical he came to be called *Plusquam Commentator*—that is, a commentator who went farther than a mere commentator should. He held that geometrical analysis, *doctrina resolutiva*, and demonstration *propter quid* (rather than *quia*) are all equivalent, and argued, in my opinion, both eloquently and soundly for this position.[27] After all, both Peter and Taddeo—certainly Taddeo—had all but said the same thing, and only avoided saying it by what looks very much like a bit of legerdemain. The trouble with Torrigiano's position, in comparison with Peter's and Taddeo's, is that it does not allow for a regress, and so—if accepted—would have blocked any futher progress in that important direction. I would like to examine Torrigiano's position in detail here, as well as those of Gentile da Foligno (d. 1348), Jacopo da Forli (d. 1413), Hugo of Siena (d. 1439), and others who joined the controversy started by Haly's cryptic remark that *doctrina resolutiva* is known to the geometers, but space does not permit. Suffice it to say that the problem of the nature of analysis remained a central one in the medical tradition of commentary, so that contact with the mathematical sources was never lost.

New problems were added by both the commentators on the *Ars*, the *Posterior Analytics*, and the *Physics* as the tradition matured. It is important to point out that the tradition had this triple base from almost the beginning—the prologue of the *Ars*, the prologue of the *Physics*,[28] and certain passages in the *Posterior Analytics*—and that the commentators on these different works tended to develop and stress somewhat different problems. If commentators on the *Ars* tended to stress the problem of analysis, commentators on the *Posterior Analytics* and the *Physics* were prone to devote their attention mainly to regressive demonstration, and problems associated with it. One of these was whether regressive demonstration is circular, and if it is not—a conclusion all the Averroists were ready to defend—precisely how and why it is not. This, too, should be said, that concentration on the concept of regressive demonstration by commentators on Aristotle resulted in a tendency to lose sight of the origin of that concept in the early controversy about how the geometrical, Galenian, and Aristotelian theories of scientific proof are related. The Aristotelians never lost sight of Averroes' *demonstratio simpliciter*, with its mathematical origins, but following the bent of the Commentator's own mind they came gradually to pay ever closer attention to the psychological foundations on which a complete theory of method in the natural sciences must rest, and to neglect the question of the relationship between their own theory of method and the analysis of the geometers. But their attention to the psychological foundations of method is precisely the strength and special contribution of the Averroists in the development of the modern concept of scientific method. An illustration of this special orientation was their working out of the idea of a *negotiatio intellectus*, a third stage in their originally two-stage method intervening between the other two, in which the causes discovered or isolated by resolution are psychologically *recognized* as causes, and thus become capable of functioning—for *us*—as premises in demonstration *propter quid*, or composition. They are, of course, causes, and known as causes, "to nature" all along, but the problem is to explain how they become known *as* causes to us.

But all in all, there was a continuous and ever more sophisticated and penetrating analysis of the problems first posed by Haly, Averroes and the early Latin commentators throughout the fourteenth, fifteenth, and sixteenth centuries—problems which, as we have seen, had their origin in an attempt to conciliate mathematical, medical (Galenian), and philosophical (Aristotelian) theories of method. It is not here maintained that this attempt, however fruitful, was completely successful. The glory of successfully completing it belongs to Galileo, and I should be the last to wish to try to take it away from him. That he did successfully complete it is evident more from his actual procedures in the solution of scientific problems than from anything he had, explicitly, to say about method. Indeed, he said extremely little on this subject, though from the few and fragmentary statements we have it seems clear that he posited the double, resolutive-compositive method—hence, a regress in the method of the natural sciences—about which discussion in this paper has centered. He may not have known Zabarella, the clearest and best of the Aristotelian writers on method in the sixteenth century, but he knew and cited Averroes, as well as many of the Averroist Aristotelians—Paolo Veneto, Alessandro Achillini, Agostino Nifo, Marcantonio Zimara, etc., all of whom, with the exception of Achillini, were important representatives of the tradition of methodological speculation explored by Prof. Randall in his "Development of Scientific Method in the School of Padua," and elaborated in one of its special aspects here. How, then—or why—shall we maintain that this whole tradition was unknown to (or despised by) Galileo? Why must we suppose that he bypassed this rich heritage, and went directly to the Greek mathematicians for his concepts of *metodo risolutivo* and *compositivo*? That a fresh study of these ancient sources enabled him to take the final and most rewarding step in the adaptation of the analysis of the geometers to the subject-matter of the natural sciences need not be denied, but that he did not profit from five centuries of labor by others in the same vineyard seems—in the light both of the record and of what we know of Galileo's wide-ranging and acquistive mind— too much to be asked to believe.

N O T E S

1. *Journal of the History of Ideas*, I (1940), 177-206; reprinted in *The School of Padua and the Emergence of Modern Science* (Padua: Antenore, 1961), pp. 13-68.

2. *Das Erkenntisproblem in der Philosophie und Wissenschaft der Neuren Zeit*, Vol. I (Berlin: 1922), p. 139. After outlining Zabarella's concept of method, Cassirer says: "Alle diese Ausführungen sind von Galileis Methodenlehre, in der wir sie völlig gleichlautend wiederfinden werden, nur durch einen einzigen Zug getrennt, der allerdings entschiedend ist. Die Rolle, die der Mathematik in der 'beweisenden Induktion' zukommt, wird von Zabarella nirgends begriffen: . . ."; and this is true.

3. *Opera Logica* (Venice: Paulus Meietus, 1578).

4. I hope in forthcoming papers to add considerably to the evidence on which Prof. Randall bases his thesis.

5. In *Studies and Essays in the History of Science and Learning Offered in Homage to George Sarton on the Occasion of his Sixtieth Birthday . . .*, ed. M. F. Ashley Montagu (New York: Henry Schuman, 1944), pp. 277-297.

6. "Galileo and the School of Padua," *Journal of the History of Philosophy*, I, No. 2 (Oct. 1963), 223-231.

7. Galileo does not cite Zabarella in any of his works included in the *Edizione Nazionale*, but mentions him in a little-known poem entitled "Contro gli aristotelici," edited and published by A. Favaro in the *Atti del Reale Istituto Veneto di Scienze, Lettere ed Arti*, Series VII, Vol. III (1891-2), pp. 1-12. There are apparently two speakers in this poem: Galileo, and an Aristotelian whom he calls "Bozzio." Since the mention of Zabarella occurs in a passage in which Bozzio is speaking, it cannot be considered of any particular significance. Though the mention is favorable, it obviously proves neither that Galileo thought highly of Zabarella, nor that he was acquainted with the latter's logical thought.

8. No book has been more helpful to me in my study of Zabarella and the history of method in the Renaissance than Prof. Gilbert's *Renaissance Concepts of Method* (New York: Columbia University Press, 1960).

9. "Regressive," in the sense that one first employs demonstration *hoti* or *quia* to reach the cause of an effect, and then—turning about—demonstration *dioti* or *propter quid* to exhibit the effect through its cause.

10. The so-called "prologue" of the *Ars Medica* is the first chapter of the first book of that work.

11. The geometers to whose concept of analysis Haly refers must be Euclid, in the 13th book of the *Elements*, of which Eudoxus is the author); Pappus (quoted by Heath in his edition of Euclid's *Elements*, Vol. I, p. 138); and Plato, in the *Meno*, 86e.

12. *Claudii Galeni Opera Omnia*, ed. C. G. Kuhn, Vol. I, p. 305.

13. "Et geometrae quidem et authores scientiarum sciunt hunc modum doctrinae; et Aristoteles quidem iam posuit ipsum in Analyticis, id est, in libro Posteriorum."

Haly's commentary can be found in *Plusquam commentum in parvam Galeni artem* . . . (Venetiis: Iuntae, 1557). The statement quoted is on folio 175v.

14. With the possible exception of Hugo of Siena, who seems to have suspected that Galen meant "method" in the other sense defined above.

15. "Et demonstrationes quidem omnes fiunt in his duabus doctrinis; demonstratio autem quare fit per compositionem; et demonstratio quia fit per dissolutionem" (*op. cit., ibid*).

16. I use this example because it is the one used by Plato in the *Meno*, 86e.

17. Quoted by Heath in his edition of Euclid's *Elements* (New York: Dover Publications, Inc., 1956), Vol. I, p. 138.

18. *Op. cit., Ibid.*

19. It is unclear to me under what conditions a physicist can *ever* construct this kind of demonstration, though Averroes gives an example of it in his *Epitome in Libros Logicae*, in the section entitled *De Demonstratione*. The gist of it is that both the fact that the equatorial region is uninhabited and the reason it is unhabited can be deduced from the knowledge that it is always extremely hot there. This latter knowledge an astronomer could have from his knowledge of the position of the sun in relation to the equatorial regions throughout the year, and would presumably never have to go to the equator to verify the conclusions mentioned. The unhappy result of this demonstration suggests that the use of *demonstratio simpliciter* should be even *rarer* in the natural sciences than Averroes supposes.

20. ". . . illa, quae sunt cognita apud nos in rebus naturalibus, non sunt illa, quae sunt cognita simpliciter, id est, naturaliter; quod est contrarium in mathematicis; illa enim quae sunt cognita in illis simpliciter, et sunt causae priores in esse, sunt cognita apud nos" (Commentary on the *Physics*, Bk. I., text. 2).

21. "Si igitur nos ageremus res naturales, tunc causae essent notiores apud nos; sed quia nos non habemus agere eas, ideo dispositio in eis apud nos est contraria dispositioni in rebus artificialibus" (Commentary on the *Physics*, Bk. I, text. 3).

22. "Via doctrinae huius libri sunt species doctrinae usitatae in hac scientia; et sunt modi omnium disciplinarum, scilicet, tres modi demonstrationum, scilicet, signi, et demonstratio causae, et demonstratio simpliciter; quamvis signum et causa sunt plus usitata in hac scientia; et aliquando est usitata demonstratio simpliciter" (Commentary on the *Physics,* Preface). *Demonstratio signi,* or a *signo,* is the same as *demonstratio quia.*

23. "Amplius Haly dicit quod ipsam (i.e., doctrinam resolutivam) sciunt Geometrae; et isti demonstratione utuntur propter quid; et subdit demum, et scientiarum auctores sciunt hunc modum doctrinae . . . dicendum quod Haly minus bene dixit, unde plures sequaces ipsius in baratrum ignorantiae detrusit; vel quod inquit geometrae bene sciunt eam, sed non quod utantur ipsa, quia si sciunt demonstrationem propter quid, sciunt et quia, cum sint connexae" (*Conciliator*, Difference 8).

24. "Non tamen intendit Commentator quod mathematicus construat demonstrationem simpliciter tanquam aliam ab illis duabus; sed quod facta demonstratione propter quid, qua utitur mathematicus, effectus simpliciter notificatus ab ea per causam est etiam notus quo ad nos, ac si ad ipsum foret facta demonstratio" (*ibid.*).

25. ". . . resolutiva (doctrina) dicitur fieri ex finis notione, id est, effectus; finis enim et effectus idem est, secundum Boetium in Topicis" (*ibid.*).

26. "Ad hoc dico quod Haly dicit verum. Sed dico quod doctrinae resolutivae est

duplex actio, scilicet, resolutio quaesiti in suas casusas, et alterius est regressus ex causis super quaesitum. Unde quo ad primum quaesitum vel progressum potest dici quod in doctrina resolutiva fiat demonstratio quia; proceditur enim ab effectu ad causam. Sed quo ad secundum fit demonstratio propter quid, quia fit processus in regressu illo a causa super effectum" (Thaddei Florentini . . . in C. Galeni Micratechen Commentaria . . .' Naples: 1522, 3r-v).

27. See *Plusquam Commentum in Parvam Galeni Artem* . . . (Venetiis: Iuntae, 1557, ff. 3r-4r).

28. The "prologue" of the *Physics*, as in the case of the *Ars Medica*, is the first chapter of the first book.

H. S. THAYER

The City University of New York

Historical Patterns, Empiricism, and Some Reflections on Ockham and Berkeley[1]

In the second chapter of his recent book, *How Philosophy Uses Its Past*, Randall writes:

> I have been led to mark the occurrence of many historical patterns of various types, patterns in the careers of philosophical ideas. These different types of historical pattern, which I have been forced to recognize as illustrated over and over again, are characteristic of different strands in the philosophic enterprise.[2]

No one who has heard him speak or read his writings can fail to appreciate the clarity and perceptivity with which he has delineated and articulated these patterns. With wonderful skill, in his *Career of Philosophy* he traces and explores the patterns of ideas of modern philosophy, combining a richness of relevant detail with historical breadth and perspective.

The Career of Philosophy is about the past, revealing the course of philosophy in the West; it is designed to be absorbed by any intelligent reader. *How Philosophy Uses Its Past* seems to be addressed primarily to philosophically minded readers; it is a kind of philosophic reflection upon how we might think about the past, about the materials so ably described in *The Career of Philosophy*. While *The Career of Philosophy* is about the history of philosophic thought, *How Philosophy Uses Its Past* is about philosophic and historical wisdom. It is a sign of our age and inheritance that the latter should be a far slimmer volume than the former.

A significant feature of John Herman Randall's philosophy of intellectual history is that discernible patterns of ideas are not products of "dialectical necessity." The historical patterns of ideas—their recurrence, repeated exemplification, and continuities—are, for him, matters of empirical generalizations and sagacious observation. The past, the movement of ideas, and the arrangements they appear to take are not derivable from a "unifying law or formula of intellectual history."[3]

This thoroughly sane attitude toward the history of ideas has its advantages and disadvantages. The advantages accrue to the readers of such a historian; they shall probably be taken as close to the Truth of history, to as insightful and sympathetic a grasp of the problems, conflicts, and assumptions generating the meaning of historical ideas as is possible. The disadvantages lie with the historian. He must become an acute and patient student of the materials, of the ideas and the historical background. In time and labor he suffers in comparison with the historian who comes to history with a ready-made scheme of historical interpretation, of how things "*had* to happen," of what the philosophers "really meant to say."

In his empirical attitude toward the history of ideas, Randall stands apart, even from that suggestive and critical commentator on historical thought John Dewey. For where Dewey wields a scheme of sorts, viz., that philosophy has always tended to be a defender of "vested interests," and in a conspiracy against change and new experience,[4] Randall sees philosophers engaged in an extremely complex intellectual task of adjusting conflicting social forms, values, and new advances in knowledge.[5]

While Randall's empirical view of patterns seems to make eminently good sense, I find that questions arise resulting partly from what he says and partly from what he does not say concerning his approach to philosophic history. For, in addition to the view that the developments of patterns of ideas are contingent and result from cultural transitions and conflicts, not dialectical laws and necessities, Randall accepts another significant fact of inquiry and intellectual method. Namely, that we bring to experience, to "facts," certain leading principles and procedures of organization and interpretation. "All instruction given or received by way of argument proceeds from pre-existent knowledge,'" says Aristotle in the famous first sentence of *Posterior Analytics*. The "pre-existent knowledge" is, of course, not the recollected episodes of a previous existence, not platonic memories. The pre-existent knowledge is the cumulative experience—the facts, habits, and procedures of inquiry, however crude—already acquired in the past. This empirical insight into the act of empirical inquiry, restated by Kant, a number of romantic idealists, and by the pragmatists, is also set forth by Randall:

> Historically considered, the appeal to "experience" is never the first step in philosophizing. In any concrete enterprise of criticism, the concept of "experience" is not the starting-point, not a "datum," but an instrument of criticism . . . experience is never approached "immediately"; it has already been conceived in terms of some antecedent scheme of analysis . . . "experimental" method . . . always starts frankly from a whole antecedent body of ideas. It approaches experience not only with some hypothesis to be confirmed or criticized . . . experimental method assumes to begin with the funded body of knowledge already acquired in the past. . . . So the

start of the appeal to experience is always with some codified experience of nature already won, some understanding already achieved of nature, some knowledge previously acquired.[6]

Now the historical patterns of ideas, the products of detection and empirical generalization on Randall's part, are clearly the "facts" and "experience" of central interest to the philosophical historian. These "facts" may be hard won, earnestly discerned, though only after patient study and thought. The patterns are clearly not immediate data of historical experience. Since, as Randall says, experimental method starts from a whole antecedent body of ideas, the experimental-empirical historian will employ antecedent hypotheses and interpretive principles to launch and guide the effort of analysis and exploration into patterns of ideas.

My main query, then, is: What are the antecedent regulative assumptions and controlling hypotheses that Randall makes use of in sighting and coming to just those historical patterns he carefully portrays in *The Career of Philosophy?* Some of these antecedent codifying instruments of historical inquiry are clearly seen in the first two chapters. They are the implications of cultural change and, salient among these, the coming and recurrent challenge of new knowledge—of science—into the inherited intellectual and moral schemes of European classical thought.[7] In general, the changes in social, moral, and intellectual experience in the rapidly expanding culture of Europe since the thirteenth century have generated our fundamental philosophic problems and called forth a series of distinctive responses to them. Such is the historical matrix of the career of philosophic ideas for Randall; one that he brilliantly unfolds and illustrates in *The Career*. But concerning the details of this matrix, as conditions for selection, as vantage points for discerning and focussing upon patterns and clusters of ideas, I would like to learn more from Randall. One might ask also: Does philosophic thought always begin as a response to a *problem?* Is Western philosophy since the early Middle Ages always and only a record of "adjusters"?[8] That all thought begins with a *problem*, that living is a matter of adjusting with the world, are characteristically Deweyan convictions. But does Randall recognize other genetic and motivating conditions of philosophic thought—artistic promptings, say, or from a love of myths, or even the occasional call of Truth?

In the pages to follow I shall try to illustrate my question by directing and narrowing it down to a concrete example.

II

One historical pattern, elaborated in *The Career of Philosophy* and serving in an illustrative capacity in *How Philosophy Uses Its Past*, is the tradition of British Empiricism. Despite a war with England, which the British still assure us was not a war but a separation (an adjustment), and the dominance of German thought in America during the last century, British Empiricism is conspicuously alive in much contemporary American philosophy. The vicissitudes and career of this pattern of ideas are traceable in America; why and in what way this is so, we will see more clearly in Volume Three of *The Career*.

Randall depicts the assumptions and the pattern of modern empiricism as deriving from Ockham, in the fourteenth century, and continuing on through Hobbes, Locke, and Newton to Berkeley and Hume, and then on through Mill to Russell.[9] The cardinal assumptions and features of the pattern are: (1) science is not demonstrative of reality but descriptive of events; (2) the immediate data of scientific knowledge are not *objects* but *ideas*, sense-data, or contents of the mind; (3) a spectator theory of mind (i.e., a wholly passive mind acted upon by external objects and powers); (4) a genetic criterion of criticism and validation of beliefs and knowledge-claims.[10]

How definitive or rigid is this "pattern" to be maintained? In *The Career* Randall comments that

> Ockham's theory is a form of presentational realism: In knowing a passive mind directly perceives particular real objects, their properties and relations. . . . This complete passivity of the mind, this spectator theory of knowledge, has persisted as the fundamental assumption of the empiricist tradition; together with those of a structureless world of pure particulars, and of the contents of the mind itself as the immediate object of knowledge, it has formed the major British tradition.[11]

Now the extent to which we find that Ockham's view of mind, knowing, and science *is* British Empiricism (or "the position to which the English thinkers, Hobbes, Locke, and Newton, turned to interpret seventeenth-century science"[12]) depends upon what we take to be the stuff of this empiricism. The four assumptions and the pattern stated above are not without need of clarification and qualification unless we are to read Russell and Hume into Ockham. A few comments may bear this out.

(1) While mental terms or concepts, *passiones animae*, are "things," are contents of mind or inhere in soul, they are treated by Ockham as *acts*. The mental "thing" here is an intellection by which something is thought or conceived. This is *actus* in the sense of *actio*: operation. In the *Reportatio* (e.g., Bk. 2-4 of the Commentary on the Sentences) Ockham argues for a *fictum* version of universals. Here a concept or universal does not possess real existence, it is only a "thought object," *esse objectivum* (which we would now call a "subjective entity," reversing medieval us-

age). But later Ockham rejected this analysis[13] and argued for an *intellectio* explanation.[14] Details must be waived here; but the important point is that, in rejecting the *fictum* version,[15] Ockham was critically abandoning a doctrine that is very close to (if not identical with) the later epistomological theory of ideas as mental pictures or images and the doctrine of abstract ideas. These were the very doctrines, subsequently developed by Descartes and Locke that were so roundly and effectively criticized by Berkeley.

The view, so characteristic of *some* later Empiricists (e.g., Locke, Hume, Mill, Russell), that an idea is similar to the object it represents (or that some ideas "resemble" their causes) is accordingly rejected by Ockham. For him, the supposition of any intermediary mental "thing" between thought (active cognition) and its object (things) is unwarranted and (via his razor) unnecessary. Asking, "What in the soul, is this thing which is a sign?" he answers:

> Some say it is nothing but a certain fiction produced by the soul. Others say that it is the act of understanding. And in favor of these there is this to be said: what can be explained on fewer principles is explained needlessly by more. Everything, however, which is explained through positing something distinct from the act of understanding can be explained without positing such a distinct thing. For to stand for something and to signify something can belong just as well to the act of understanding as to this fictive entity; therefore one ought not to posit anything else beyond the act of understanding.[16]

But, then, this version of mind and knowing, emphasizing activity (though not, of course, an "active intellect") and stressing the operation of signifying, would seem to enjoy the functionalism that Randall finds missing, and fatally so, from empiricism. I should think that this "functional" version of knowing would not be unlike what Randall finds in Aristotle—not the Aristotle talking as *physikos*, but as *logikos* or *dialektikos*.

(2) For Ockham, while the *origin* of knowledge is experiential of individual things, the content of knowledge is not. It consists of ideas, concepts, acts of cognition of a universal kind. These latter, of course, are signs; they relate to the "things" they are "about" as signs to things signified. Now this relation is one of cause and effect; things, objects, *cause* the cognition, but only partially, for the intellect is also a cause. Thus the object *and* the intellect are co-operative causes in making the object known. Once again, mind is an activity through which knowledge becomes possible.

Moreover, Ockham holds that, roughly, mental events are similar—

exhibiting *similitude*—to *both* the object represented *and* the intellect as a cause. That is, thought stands in the relation of *similitude* with reality. But this is not a simple or crude copy theory of thought imaging reality. *Cognitio est repraesentans*, but this often means cognitions are caused by the object *and* intellect.[17]

I raise these two points, not as a quarrel over interpreting Ockham, but to suggest that the founder of British Empiricism did not himself hold the position or quite the assumptions that make their way into the later pattern. Ockham's assumptions and method of analysis seem to me to be very far from those of Locke, the great spokesman for empiricism in the seventeenth and eighteenth centuries. Indeed, Locke is partly Cartesian, partly experimental empiricist—a theoretical-on-the-fencer (like all good liberals). This same dual or divided position Randall pentratingly shows to have been implicit in Newton's conception of science and method.

The pattern of early modern empiricism is complicated. The greatest critic of Locke in behalf of common sense was Berkeley. His criticisms remind one of those that Ockham had directed against Augustinian and Averroistic theories of knowledge and science. Three of the four assumptions of empiricism listed above hardly hold for Berkeley. Excepting the first (i.e., science as descriptive), Berkeley does not fit into the pattern. To be sure, the *datum* of knowing, for Berkeley, consists of *ideas*. But this merely means that science has as its subject matter "things," sensible, perceivable qualities. Mind is an active power, a *spirit*—an activity of perceiving, not a Cartesian container of ideas nor a Newtonian mechanism.

What is the essential feature of this mind which, since it is not a thing or object, cannot be immediately perceived? Berkeley answers: perceiving and inferring (i.e., thinking); generally, with the aid of language created for the purpose,[18] to infer from given experience other "attended" experiences. Experience, thus interpreted and codified serves as marks or signs, forewarning of other future experiences. Here, too, Berkeley is an heir of the Ockhamite tradition. Experience intelligently interpreted is significant of further experience:

> . . . the connexion of ideas [i.e., things] does not imply the relation of *cause* and *effect*, but only of a mark or *sign* with the thing *signified*. The fire which I see is not the cause of the pain I suffer upon my approaching it, but the mark that forewarns me of it.[19]

The "mark that forewarns" is a sign that has become interpreted and the material for predictions based upon past experience and observed "connexions of ideas." The fire I see is a sign that, under certain other conditions, I will suffer pain. To be thus forewarned of how the fire seen *might* (under specified conditions) be felt, is an aid in avoiding that possible experience.

While this last point does not receive great emphasis in Berkeley's writings, it is frequently encountered. And it is a point of some interest. For clearly Berkeley was setting forth a theory of empirical knowledge in which the act of knowing takes a conditional form (often, as in the above case of the fire, as counter-factual conditionals[20]) and in which the significance of an idea (e.g., fire) *is* the class of empirical consequences ("connexions") that *would* follow from the fulfillment of certain antecedent conditions.

A simple schematic way of stating this last idea may help to make it clearer and will prove useful for elucidating some matters to come.

Let us adopt the following conventions: Let $I_1, I_2, I_3 \ldots$ etc., represent single *ideas* (or sensations); let $C_a, C_b \ldots$ etc., represent the "regular" *conditions* under which, as Berkeley says, "such and such ideas are attended with such and such other ideas, in the ordinary course of things."[21] These "trains" or attendances of ideas make up the "Laws of Nature" according to Berkeley.[22] Let us finally, then, use the symbol of the arrow '$\rightarrow$' to represent the *sign* function, the *signification* of ideas. The arrow symbol represents that capacity of an idea I_1 to serve as a "mark" or "to signify" (using Berkeley's terms). So I_1 becomes: $I_1 \rightarrow . \ldots$ The arrow represents the all important field of *relations*, of "connexions" among ideas. And of connections, Berkeley insisted, they are not necessary relations nor forces or powers. Ideas are related to other ideas as *signs* to things *signified*, "by an habitual connexion that experience has made us to observe between them."[23]

Now, reverting to the passage quoted above, to see the *fire* (i.e., the visible idea I_1) as a sign of *pain* (i.e., the feeling I_2) under certain conditions (i.e., my approaching the fire, conditions C_a) is to reason:

(i) I_1 and $C_a \rightarrow I_2$.

To avoid the unpleasant consequent in (i), the sensation of pain I_2, I act to change or avoid conditions C_a, thus seeing to it that the conditional (i) is unfulfilled.

If knowledge consists of conditionals like (i) it follows logically that, for Berkeley the mind (or Spirit) does more than perceive things. Perceiving may guarantee the existence of the thing perceived, but the mind also *reasons*, that is, discovers and infers the relation of the momentarily perceived thing to other possible perceived or experienced things under given conditions. The conditionals of knowledge require reasoning, not merely perceiving. Sometimes Berkeley calls this other activity "reasoning"; sometimes, as in one of the excellent summary statements of the position we have been studying, he calls it "experience" and "foresight":

> ... we learn by experience, which teaches us that such and such ideas are attended with such and such other ideas, in the ordinary course of things.
>
> This gives us a sort of foresight which enables us to regulate our actions for the benefit of life. . . . That food nourishes, sleep refreshes . . . all this we know, not by discovering any *necessary connexion* between our ideas, but only by the *observation* of the settled Laws of Nature. . . .[24]

Since man acts to fulfill, or to avoid fulfilling various possible experiential conditionals, this theory of knowing suggests a thoroughly active conception of knowledge as an ordering of experience and a deliberate modifying and arrangement of future experience:

> We may, from the experience we have had of the train and succession of ideas in our minds, often make, I will not say uncertain conjectures, but sure and well-grounded predictions concerning the ideas we shall be affected with pursuant to a great train of actions, and be enabled to pass a right judgment of what would have appeared to us, in case we were placed in circumstances very different from those we are in at present. Herein consists the knowledge of nature. . . .[25]

Berkeley was fond of a venerable analogy according to which the system of nature is likened to a language.[26] The "connexions" of things, $I_1 \rightarrow I_2 \rightarrow I_3 \rightarrow \ldots$ (of our earlier scheme and (i)), is compared to the order of words, or signs, in a system. Knowledge is then described as a discerning of the grammar of nature. Although the theme, and the analogy, are found in earlier writings,[27] this is brought out most clearly in *Siris*:

> There is a certain *analogy, constancy,* and *uniformity* in the phenomena or appearances of nature, which are a foundation for general rules: and these are a Grammar for the understanding of Nature, or that series of effects in the Visible World whereby we are enabled to *foresee* what will come to pass in the natural course of things.[28]

Again:

> As the natural connexion of *signs* with the *things signified* is regular and constant, it forms a sort of Rational Discourse. . . .[29]

Three conclusions can be drawn from the sketchy observations we have been making.

(1) For something to be a *sign*, as distinct from sheer sensation (or idea), the mind must make its contribution. Mind invests the raw data of sense with "significance." The once-naked datum, for all of its engaging simplicity and aboriginal vivacity, gets reformed by that bustling missionary thought. The datum's unique presence is turned into something

transitional and referential: the palpable *thing* becomes a *sign* of other things. Such is the conversion of native sentience to the civilized mores of knowledge.

One grants, of course, that for Berkeley, Divine Mind also infuses the empirical world with significance. But in the absence of knowers, of minds (and God), if fire could be supposed to exist at all, it would *be* as a flame, perhaps, but void of all significance. As a *sign* of other experiential conditions (as endowed with the arrow function lately discussed) *that* fire would not *be* at all. This is to say that the intelligible character of fire, or any thing, consists in its interpretative content. But it is minds that do the interpreting. So he says:

> We know a thing when we understand it; and we understand it when we can interpret or tell what it signifies. Strictly, the Sense knows nothing. We perceive indeed sounds by hearing, and characters by sight. But we are not therefore said to understand them.[30]

Understanding, Berkeley adds, is of "the connexion of natural things."

In other words, a single entertainment of sensation, unrelated to past experience, custom, and habit, would not constitute knowledge, for Berkeley. For the sensation would not be "understood" as a sign.[31]

(2) In saying, as he does above, that "the sense knows nothing," Berkeley is not repudiating his earlier radical empiricism. He is simply making explicit what is a logical condition of the position he has maintained from the start. The single sensation, the idea as such, is not knowledge, as we have been noticing above. This feature of his epistemology is interesting, among other reasons, for its anticipation of the analyses of the role of sensation in knowledge of Peirce, Dewey, Mead, and Lewis.

(3) Berkeley's theory of mind thus turns out to be almost a complete reversal of Locke's position. Instead of Locke's realm of bodies acting upon passive minds, for Berkeley operative minds act upon passive things or ideas. Yet the "things" are also signs. An idea is both a brute particular item of sense *and* a mark; a thing, an *I*, but also a referring thing, an *I→*. So in ideas, in data or things, there are also operative conditions or possibilities, the *dynameis* of classical tradition, or Locke's *powers, to be significant*. Thus construed, knowing becomes a co-operative activity, an active interpreting of things capable of signifying other things. This is, I think, implied throughout Berkeley's analysis of ideas or things. In his later philosophizing Berkeley invokes Platonism, ancient and Cambridgian, in expressing the view, not of a passive order of natural objects, but of nature as "*ratio mersa et confusa*—reason immersed and plunged into matter, and as it were fuddled in it and confounded with it."[32]

The upshot of these last pages is that, for Berkeley, knowing is not a purely passive reception of ideas. Knowing—if I may so put it—is of the arrows of ideas, and not even the brilliance of a Zeno can keep the arrow from moving. Knowing is a purposive transforming of the materials of future experience. Surely here is a conception of knowledge that renders experience experimental.

These themes in Berkeley seem to me to point to a new historical pattern in the empirical tradition; it is not a sounding of the same notes of his predecessors. Berkeley rightly saw himself as a critic and rebel among the philosophers. Here, as he said, "I side in all things with the mob." He was trying to teach empiricism some common sense.

Berkeley's pattern suggested to Mach and William James a reductive radical empiricism and a thoroughly instrumentalistic conception of science. To Peirce, it suggested (despite its nominalism) the leading principles of pragmatism.[33] In spite of his propensity to indulge in a variety of rather different explanations of the source and content of pragmatism, I take seriously Peirce's comment in a letter of 1903 to James: "Berkeley on the whole has more right to be considered the introducer of pragmatism into philosophy than any other one man, though I was more explicit in enunciating it."[34] Peirce also turned to Kant, but the aspect of pragmatism that Kant suggested to Peirce is very close to what, as we have been seeing, is found in Berkeley. It is the pattern that had made its way on the continent, partly under the aegis of Hume, as a sceptical empiricism capable of interpreting the procedures and results of science while cutting away the foundations of Reason upon which science rested—thus saving Faith and Values from science and, indeed, rendering science as an act of faith.

Berkeley's insistence that meaningful language be explicitly correlated with sense experience; that the meaning of an expression is its specifiable empirical consequences (for Berkeley is the ancestor of the "verifiability theory of meaning" and "Operationalism"); that all predication, all description and claims about the objects of experience or what things *are*, is predictive; that given data are inferentially significant of other data (in the manner indicated in (i) above)—all of these insights are also central to the pragmatism of John Dewey and C. I. Lewis. For both agree with Berkeley that meanings have a futurative reference in experience (as Peirce puts it) and that immediate experience is not knowledge, but a condition of (or material for) knowing by providing conditions for a probability-judgment concerning future experience. And, as alluded earlier, to anticipate the future is to evaluate, modify, partially control, and reconstruct what is passing and is to come.

In Randall's account of the pattern of empiricism—pointing to the repeated dilemmas occasioned internally by the attempt of empiricists to weave the strands of Platonism, Augustinian and Cartesian, into the pattern—I miss the recognition of the position advanced by Ockham and Berkeley, the two most skillful exponents of empiricism; namely, that of the instrumental and pragmatic spirit which Dewey later called "neo-empiricism." Randall finds this latter spirit emerging from Hume,[35] from how Hume practiced, if not quite from what Hume preached.[36] But the most concise and careful *statement* of this position is in Berkeley, recent attempts to minimize the influence of Berkeley on Hume notwithstanding.

III

In these pages I have been raising questions about Randall's philosophic approach to historical patterns of ideas. The questions have not been prompted in that spirit of perplexed despair with which Amy Lowell ended one of her poems: "Christ! What are patterns for?" My questions, rather, are prompted by an interest in learning more about the "cluster of assumptions" that Randall argues is always inherent in every tradition of philosophizing—specifically, the cluster that Randall has relied upon in developing his own penetrating study of the career of philosophy. My suggestion, in the example of British Empiricism thus pondered above, is that several patterns and several conflicting clusters complicate the history of this tradition and complicate as well all attempts at a general characterization.

But I have not been exclusively concerned to raise questions. In a very suggestive essay, Dewey has shown how "from a study of Locke himself" the "ordinary interpretation" is framed in a way that forces attention to epistemological dilemmas and misses the genuine if incomplete development of a relational and functional theory of knowledge latent in the *Essay*.[37] Randall has explored a not dissimilar theme in Hume.[38] I have here tried to indicate the merits of much the same approach in the study of Ockham and Berkeley.[39]

In *How Philosophy Uses Its Past*, Randall very convincingly argues that a philosopher with a future will know something about the past. He exemplifies his argument.

Felix qui potuit rerum cognoscere causas.

NOTES AND REFERENCES

1. I am indebted to Professor John P. Anton for some valuable critical comments on an earlier version of this paper.

2. *How Philosophy Uses Its Past* (New York: Columbia University Press, 1963), p. 37.

3. *Ibid.*

4. See, e.g., *Reconstruction in Philosophy*, chap. i, "Changing Conceptions of Philosophy," for a general statement of Dewey's view of the traditional function of philosophy. For a more extended statement, *The Quest for Certainty*, first three chapters.

5. See *The Career of Philosophy*, vol. I (New York: Columbia University Press, 1962), pp. 19-20.

6. *How Philosophy Uses Its Past*, pp. 42-43.

7. Lest I be thought insular to Randall's other writings in connection with the question I have raised, I add that I do recognize any number of illuminating insights and accounts of genetic-functional "causes" of ideas in the books cited above, in *The Making of the Modern Mind*, and, especially in *Nature and Historical Experience*. Still, these studies, concerning the specific issue in question, seem to me to provide us with valuable preliminary hypotheses, suggestions. What I am asking for is a fully stated theory, the integral framework of these assumptions and hypotheses—in short, the full *pattern* of ideas that Randall brings so effectively to his historical work and to his depictions of, and critical philosophizing about, the history of ideas.

8. Cf. *The Career of Philosophy*, vol. I, p. 20.

9. See *Ibid.*, chap. ii, and especially p. 43.

10. For Randall's statement of the four assumptions, see *How Philosophy Uses Its Past*, pp. 64-65.

11. *The Career of Philosophy*, p. 43.

12. *Ibid.*, p. 43.

13. In *Quodlibeta*, for example.

14. *Summa logicae*; *Quaestiones super libros Physicorum*, for example. For a discussion of this, see Philotheus Boehner, *Collected Articles on Ockham* (New York: The Franciscan Institute, St. Bonaventure, 1958), pp. 169-72.

15. Randall, it seems, attributes this first theory to Ockham without mentioning Ockham's later rejection of it and development of the *intellectio* version of universals.

16. *Summa totius logicae* (1508 edition) I. 12.6r. Quoted from Ernest Moody, *The Logic of William of Ockham* (New York: Sheed and Ward, 1935), pp. 49-50. See, also, *Quodlibeta* IV. Qu. 19, in R. McKeon, ed., *Selections from Medieval Philosophers*, vol. II (New York: Charles Scribner's Sons, 1929), pp. 390-91:

> "I say that as well the first intention as the second intention is truly an act of understanding, for by the act can be saved whatever is saved by the fiction. For in that act is the likeness of the subject, it can signify and stand for external things. . . . Wherefore it is clear that the first and second intention are really distinct, for the first intention is the act of understanding signifying things which are not signs. The second intention is the act signifying first intentions."

17. For an account of meanings of *repraesentare*, and the several senses thereof, see Boehner, *op. cit.*, pp. 166-67.

18. Although he recognizes other uses, emotive and persuasive of language as well.

19. *A Treatise Concerning the Principles of Human Knowledge*, sec. 65.

20. That is, the fire I see warns me of pain I *would* suffer *if* I move in such and such a direction. I thus decide *not* to fulfill this conditional. For Berkeley's recognition of

the role of counter-factual conditions see the next to the last sentence of the passage quoted below and identified in note 25 below.

21. *Principles*, sec. 30.

22. *Ibid.*

23. *An Essay Towards a New Theory of Vision*, sec. 147.

The scheme we have adopted here also applies to Berkeley's analysis of objects. Objects are collections or "a congeries" of ideas or "sensible impressions," cf. the Third Dialogue. Thus when we see the circular orange patch I_1, we expect—by custom, habit, and past experience, argues Berkeley in clear anticipation of Hume—the rest of the sensible properties of the orange to be present. The common name "orange," says Berkeley, is not the name of an idea, but names a collection. Here, I_1 (color) $\rightarrow I_2$ (taste), $I_1 \rightarrow I_3$ (odor) . . . etc. Moreover, *any* one idea, or member of a congeries may signify the rest, thus: $I_3 \rightarrow I_1$, $I_2 \rightarrow I_1$, etc. As Berkeley argues in the *Theory of Vision*, visible ideas become associated with ideas of touch: what we see is a sign of what, under C_a, we would touch. But in the dark, ideas of touch serve as signs of what we would see if it were light. For more, see Berkeley's discussion of the die in the *Principles*, sec. 49:

> "to me a die seems to be nothing distinct from those things which are termed its modes or accidents. And to say 'a die is hard, extended, and square' is not to attribute those qualities to a subject distinct from and supporting them, but only an explication of the meaning of the word *die*."

24. *Principles*, secs. 30-31. That the mind has other powers in addition to that of *perceiving* is often neglected in the study of Berkeley. He appeals to our having a *notion* of our own minds (for which see note 30 below). In *De Motu*, sec. 21, he says that "things that are sentient, percipient and understanding" we know by a kind of internal awareness: *rem vero sentientem, percipientem, intelligentem, conscientia quadam interna cognovimus.* But of other powers, see secs 2-3 in *Principles*; his citing sense and reflexion, in *ibid.*, sec. 35; the definition of *spirit*, sec. 138: "by the word *spirit* we mean only that which thinks, wills, and perceives. . . ."

25. *Ibid.*, sec. 59.

26. The comparison goes back at least to Plato's *Cratylus* and *Theaetetus*. It often appears in Renaissance and seventeenth-century writers.

27. Thus see the *New Theory of Vision*, sec. 147; *Principles*, sec. 44.

28. *Siris*, sec. 252.

29. *Ibid.*, sec. 254.

30. *Ibid.*, sec. 253. Here, and in preceding paragraphs I do not make or find a fundamental distinction between an "early" and "later" philosophy in Berkeley. The points under discussion here, the theory of signs and things signified, are found in the *New Theory of Vision* (1709) and *Principles* (1710), as well as in the later Platonizing of Siris (1744). See above, note 27, for a case in point. In some passages of the *New Theory of Vision* and *De Motu* (1721) Berkeley does talk the traditional epistemology of Locke and Descartes. But this I take to be a concession to tradition in order, in each work, to make more acceptable the radical central thesis being argued. So, too, the lame, really ironic, compliment in *De Motu*, sec. 30, to Descartes for doing the "most justice" among moderns to the distinction between thinking beings and extended beings. For the distinction was hardly new and had become a special problem for the Cartesians.

I do not deny the existence of problems and conflicting interests in Berkeley's philosophy, such as the famous appeal to a *notion* of soul or spirit—in the absence of an *idea* of the same—in the second edition of the *Principles*, secs. 2, 140, and 142; and in *De Motu* the disparaging use of *notion* in sec. 23.

31. As early as the *New Theory of Vision* he points this out. See the argument about a first experience of sight (or a blind man suddenly made to see), sec. 41. See also secs. 147, 153. In either case the visible idea is simply *l* and not *l* → (to recall the earlier symbolism). The idea does not function as a *sign*.

For the moment, and in the next paragraphs, I am arguing that Berkeley is committed to a theory of sense qualities that maintains not only that these *exist* under certain conditions, but also under certain conditions *do* something. For further important philosophizing on this theme I refer the reader to Dewey's essay "Qualitative Thought" in *Philosophy and Civilization*, and also to Randall's "Qualities, Qualification, and the Aesthetic Transaction," ch. 10 of *Nature and Historical Experience*. In the latter, see especially the critical analysis of "immediate experience" and the manner in which sensed qualities are said to be "powers to operate" in certain situations, and to "*do* something," *ibid.*, pp. 276-85.

32. *Siris*, sec. 255. He is citing the doctrine of Cudworth.

33. That is in his 1871 review of Fraser's edition of *The Works of George Berkeley, North American Review*, No. 113 (Oct., 1871), pp. 449-472. Berkeley's influence on Peirce and James and his role in the development of pragmatism are dealt with in my forthcoming book *Meaning and Action: A Critical History of Pragmatism* (New York: The Bobbs-Merrill Company, 1967), esp. sec. 27 and Appendix 5.

34. Quoted in R. B. Perry, *The Thought and Character of William James*, vol. II (Boston: Little, Brown and Co., 1935), p. 425.

When James came to restate in his own way what he took to be Peirce's doctrine, he gave it a very Berkeleyan formulation: "To attain perfect clearness in our thoughts of an object, then, we need only consider what conceivable effects of a practical kind the object may involve—what sensations we are to expect from it, and what reactions we must prepare" (*Pragmatism* [New York: Longmans, Green, and Co., 1907], pp. 46-47).

35. Thus in *The Career of Philosophy*, vol. I, the chapter on Hume's theory of knowledge is significantly called: "Hume: Empiricist and Pragmatist."

36. *Ibid.*, see especially p. 643.

37. "Substance, Power, and Quality in Locke," *Philosophical Review*, XXXV (Jan. 1926), 22-38. Reprinted in *Freedom and Experience*, Essays Presented to Horace M. Kallen (Cornell University Press, 1947), pp. 205-20.

38. See above, note 35.

39. My comments are also directed to the very illuminating discussion of the critical reconstruction in the empirical tradition in *How Philosophy Uses Its Past*, esp. pp. 67-69. Randall finds the critical transformation of "the spectator theory of knowledge, or the complete passivity of the mind in knowing" to begin with Hume and made central in Kant's "'Copernican' view of knowledge." For reasons stated earlier, I would find this reconstruction of one of the assumptions of traditional empiricism to have commenced as early as Ockham but to have its most significant historical development with Berkeley.

GEORGE L. KLINE
Bryn Mawr College

Randall's Reinterpretation of the Philosophies of Descartes, Spinoza, and Leibniz

The first volume of Professor Randall's *The Career of Philosophy*, subtitled *From the Middle Ages to the Enlightenment*,[1] discusses the major thinkers of the seventeenth century in Book Three, "The Assimilation of Science" (pp. 363-531). Among the philosophers considered at some length are Descartes, Geulincx, Malebranche, Pascal, Spinoza, and Hobbes.[2] The second volume, subtitled *From the German Enlightenment to the Age of Darwin*,[3] discusses Leibniz in the first two chapters of Book Five, "Building the German Tradition."

In this paper I shall be concerned almost exclusively with Randall's interpretation of Descartes, Spinoza, and Leibniz. In addition to the two volumes of *The Career of Philosophy*, three other recent books by Randall which contain material on all three thinkers will be freely drawn upon. These books are: *Nature and Historical Experience* (1958), *The Role of Knowledge in Western Religion* (1958), and *How Philosophy Uses Its Past* (1963).

I

Professor Randall's characterization of Descartes seems to me both original and illuminating. In his view, the traditional "father of modern *philosophy*" was at heart a mathematical *physicist*—though a pious one[4]—and not primarily a philosopher at all. Descartes, he writes, "cared for little outside physics, and knew less" (I 373). Randall sees Descartes as much closer in interest and talent to—among twentieth-century thinkers—a James Jeans than a Dewey or a Whitehead.[5]

Randall makes a strong and plausible case for the contention that Descartes' major intellectual contribution was the invention of analytic (or "coordinate") geometry, the brilliant synthesis of algebra and Euclidean geometry which made it possible to plot any "curve" (straight line, ellipse, circle, parabola, hyperbola) on "Cartesian coordinates" and express it by means of a definite alegbraic equation.[6] By use of this new, elegant, and powerful mathematical instrument Descartes was able to express adequately, in algebraic form, any given configuration of *res extensa*. The requisite mathematical instrument for the adequate expression of the movements of *rēs extensae*—namely, the differential calculus—was invented a generation later, independently, by Leibniz and Newton.

Perhaps Randall puts the case too strongly when he says that Descartes always regarded philosophy as a "handmaiden of science." But he is certainly right in asserting that Descartes felt called upon to "defend the divine right of mathematics against Aristotle" (I 385).

Randall exhibits the major Cartesian *aporiai* in metaphysics patiently but devastatingly: first, the unbridgeable dualism of unextended *res cogitans* and unthinking *res extensa*. As Randall had written earlier, "When a Descartes—or a Kant—divides the world between the two realms of what his intellectual method can deal with [i.e., *res extensa* in Descartes, the "phenomenal" in Kant] and what it cannot [i.e., *res cogitans* in Descartes, the "noumenal" in Kant] that soon appears as a methodological inadequacy, and men like Spinoza and Leibniz—or the whole generation of post-Kantians—set to work to develop a more adequate method that will not clash with the required unity of knowledge."[7]

A philosopher who would stoop to the pineal gland[8] to attempt to explain the interaction of entities (the human "mind" or "soul" and the human body) which by definition have nothing in common, must indeed have been primarily interested in a discipline other than philosophy!

The second *aporia* of Descartes' thought is generated by his "epistemological subjectivism."[9] It is the problem of whether, and, if so, how we can know anything external to our own consciousness, and, in particular, whether, and how we can know that "other minds" exist, or infer what other people's experience is like. Contemporary metaphysics, Randall has written, "is still focused upon the 'mind-body problem' inherited from Descartes."[10]

Descartes, reversing the tradition of the Renaissance, made man a stranger in the natural world, the human psyche *(anima, âme)* a stranger in the billiard-ball universe of extended things, much as Plato had made the human body a stranger in the ideal world of pure and intelligible forms (cf. I 394).

Generalizing slightly beyond Randall's account, we might say that Descartes' three principal metaphysical tenets (like his major theological tenets) were all tradition-bound: his rationalism, anti-empiricism, and "substantialism" all came from the Greeks—the first two most clearly from Plato, the third from Aristotle.

Descartes' three most original contributions were not to be found in metaphysics at all. One was a mathematical invention (the coordinate or analytic geometry already discussed), two were (related) methodological inventions: the famous methodological doubt and the subjective criterion of truth—truth is what is clearly and distinctly conceivable—both of which may be expressed succinctly in the expanded *cogito* argument, *"dubito, ergo cogito, ergo sum—res cogitans."*

The roots of the last of these methodological doctrines may be traced to the Scholastics and to Augustine,[11] and those of the second to such ancient skeptics as Carneades. However, as Randall makes clear, Descartes himself did not really doubt anything very seriously; he was neither a suffering "existential" doubter nor a hardened destructive skeptic. Descartes wanted to "doubt" his way to the epistemological bedrock of "clear and distinct" ideas: *dubito quod intelligam.* But he knew all along that the indubitable bedrock was there, concealed beneath the yielding swamps of dubitability. In psychological terms, as Randall perceptively remarks, "probably there never lived a more self-confident mind than Descartes" (I 386).

Randall reminds us that Descartes had done a good deal of serious work in mathematics and mathematical physics before he turned to philosophy. Although the details of the Cartesian vortex-theory are now of no more than historical interest, the central assumption of his physics— namely, that there is no absolutely *empty* space, but that something is happening everywhere at all times—has, with field theory and relativity physics, come into its own, displacing the opposed Newtonian assumption of an absolutely empty and eventless "spatial container" (cf. I 379).

Descartes was more mathematician than physicist; the Cartesian "mechanistic theory resembles the mathematical atomism of the *Timaeus* and the Platonic tradition, rather than the atomism of Democritus and the Epicureans" (I 378). Descartes presented modern thinkers with a dilemma: "either science but no world, or a world but no science" (I 367). I take this to mean: either pure mathematical formalism purged of (sense) experience and aloof from the empirical world, or an empirical world innocent of, or immune to, mathematical formalism—and hence unintelligible. Francis Bacon had opted, blunderingly and dogmatically, for the second alternative; Descartes himself opted, clearly and distinctly, for the first.

Randall sees an intimate connection between Descartes' metaphysics and his philosophical theology: "Descartes, who drew upon a variety of traditional theological ideas as the support and bulwark of his new mechanistic philosophy of nature, . . . built God into the very foundation of that philosophy, as the continual Sustainer of the universe."[12] This last point refers, I assume, to Descartes' insistence that it takes as much power or energy to maintain something in existence as to create it in the first place, a corollary to his admission that finite, plural *rēs extensae* are not "substances" in the strict sense of "self-sufficient entities, needing nothing but themselves in order to exist (and to continue existing)," and that only God is a substance *stricto sensu*—a point taken up and generalized by Spinoza.

II

Parallel to Randall's interpretation of Descartes as a mathematical physicist is his interpretation of Spinozism as a generalization of Cartesian analytic or coordinate geometry. Again the interpretation is both original and illuminating; but I think that in Spinoza's case it encounters difficulties not present in the case of Descartes. Randall points out that for Spinoza the same reality—say, a circle—can be conceived under the aspect or attribute of extension (in geometry) and also under the aspect or attribute of thought (in algebra: $x^2 + y^2 = r^2$, or, in Randall's own notation, $a^2 + b^2 = r^2$).

The difficulty which I see with this highly suggestive reformulation of Spinoza's doctrine of attributes is related to a difficulty in Randall's interpretation of Spinoza's doctrine of ideas. To introduce this topic, let me make a brief historical excursus.

The ancient doctrine of "ideas" (or "forms") was an *objectivist* doctrine; for both Plato and Aristotle "ideas" were "out there" in the real world. (They were, in some sense, separate and separable from the sensible world for Plato, not thus separable for Aristotle; but this disagreement about the mode of "embodiment" or "enaction" of ideas or forms does not affect the essential agreement of the two Greek thinkers as to their "ontological status.") In contrast, for Locke and the tradition of British empiricism, to which contemporary English-speaking philosophers—*volens nolens*—are terminologically heir, ideas are *subjective*, purely "mental," realities. Lockean ideas are not "out there" but "in here," in the mind.

It seems to me that Spinoza, who stands chronologically between the two opposed traditions, also stands theoretically between, or outside, them. Spinoza's "ideas," as he himself explicitly tells us, are not passive images or "pictures"[13]—like the subjective mental entities of Locke—but neither are they unchanging, eternal forms—like the objective, non-mental entities of Plato and Aristotle. They are active and, in a sense, "constructive."[14] Spinoza likes to refer to the "constructive definition" of geometrical entities, e.g. the circle, as an example of "idea" in this active sense.[15] But what is more directly to our point, they must be described as "neither-nor" or else "both-and": they are neither purely objective nor purely subjective; rather, they are, in some sense, both objective and subjective. They exist "in the mind"[16]—which, to be sure, is an integral part of nature—as much as they exist "out there in the world." Indeed, it is only through them, through "adequate ideas," that Spinoza's longed-for "union of the mind with the whole of nature" can be consummated. This is the point of his famous statement (in *Ethics*, II, vii) that "the order and connection of ideas is the same as the order and connection of things."

It seems to me that Randall's interpretation of Spinoza's doctrine of ideas and attributes, for all its suggestiveness, misses the "subjective" or "Lockean" dimension of the ideas. Thus, when Randall writes that for Spinoza ideas are the "intelligible aspects of bodies" (I 438) or, again, that the Spinozistic idea is "an Aristotelian form made mathematical" (I 444), I sense an undue Aristotelianizing, or objectifying, of Spinoza's position. To be sure, Spinoza's doctrine of ideas (and of their "objective correlates," the *ideata*) is dense and difficult. We must be grateful for the light which Randall's interpretation casts into these dark places. My only reservation has to do with what I take to be the one-sidedly Peripatetic source of the illumination.[17]

To return now to the problem of the attributes: Spinoza says that a circle, for example, can be, and be conceived, under the attribute of extension as well as the attribute of thought. I am not convinced that this claim can be interpreted, as Randall suggests, in terms of the distinction between geometrical and algebraic formulation. Perhaps I have loaded the dice by using the word 'formulation'; but my point is that both algebra and geometry are, as Descartes would have said, "modes of thought" (*modi cogitandi*).[18] For Spinoza, both algebraic and geometrical ideas are *ideas*. Their respective *ideata* may well coincide, as in the case of (a) the quadratic equation, $x^2 + y^2 = r^2$, and (b) the "plane closed curve" of equal radii traced out by a compass, whether "mental" or "physical"—both of which refer to the *ideatum* circle. But, unless I have missed Spinoza's meaning, such an *ideatum* is a mode (i.e., modification) of the one Substance under the attribute of *extension*, whereas its idea, whether algebraic or geometrical, is a mode of the one Substance under the attribute of *thought*.[19] It is *this* distinction which Professor Randall's ingenious suggestion seems to me to blur.

On other points, I can only concur in Randall's judicious and sensitive treatment of Spinoza's system. On the controverted question of Spinoza's intellectual ancestry, Randall strikes a sound balance between the opposed claims of total originality and total derivation from the ancient and medieval tradition. What is "Hebraic" in Spinoza's conception, he rightly argues, is the notion of Law as a stable and pervasive moral order, which Spinoza—in this respect a good Cartesian—identifies with the mathe-

matical order and intelligible structure of the world. "The fact of order
or intelligible structure," Randall writes, "was for Spinoza something
overwhelming, overpowering" (I 437).[20]

However, it seems somewhat less than fair to say that Spinoza "sought
to bend the new physics to the support of old values" (I 367), or to describe him as "the last major representative of the medieval way of life,
of the medieval religious values, in the setting of the new science" (I 436).
For, after all, as Randall would be the first to admit, this "profoundly
religious man" (I 443) was strikingly independent in his religious thought
and feeling. What medieval thinker would have been capable of Spinoza's
austere saying, "He who loves God cannot strive that God should love
him in return"? (*Ethics*, V, xix.)

Spinoza's critique of personal repentance, like his rejection of cosmic
teleology, seem quite remote from "the very substance of medieval religion, its piety and its scheme of otherworldly values" which, according
to Randall,[21] Spinoza was concerned to preserve.

Randall does greater justice to Spinoza as religious thinker when he
groups him with those "to whom salvation comes . . . from elevating the
spirit to cosmic impartiality, to the majesty and order of the universe. For
such, religion is a cosmic sense, a recognition of man's utter dependence
on a power which yet satisfies the demand of his intellect for understanding. And for the Spinozas and the Einsteins such a religion does afford a
peace intense if austere."[22]

I would agree with Randall that Spinoza's denial of potentiality
("everything in his mathematical universe is 'pure actuality'") constitutes
"the greatest inadequacy in [his] metaphysics" (I 442)[23]—or, at least, *one*
of its greatest inadequacies, his strict determinism being another. I would
also concur in the judgment that the last three books of the *Ethics* are its
core, and that "however inspiring or true" they may be, "they are not
adequately grounded in the first two" (I 446).

One might wish to split a few hairs over Randall's denial that Spinoza
was in any sense a "panpsychist"; or his reduction of all Spinozistic
causality to "formal causality"—at least if the concept of formal cause be
taken in a strictly Aristotelian sense (cf. I 439). One might even permit
oneself the terminological (and marginal) objection that "pleasure" seems
a trivializing and somehow "utilitarianizing" translation of Spinoza's
laetitia. (Cf. I 453.)

III

Professor Randall contrasts Leibniz to Spinoza in terms reminiscent
of his contrast between Descartes and Pascal ("great thinker" vs. "great
man"). He says that, unlike Spinoza, Leibniz had no "vision" of the

world, only a "system." Furthermore, Leibniz's most systematic works (the *Theodicy*, *Monadology*, etc.) are his "weakest and least valuable" (II 4). In fact, the *Theodicy* is "the worst perpetration of any major philosophical figure," and "Leibniz was probably guilty of more silly and inane ideas than any other great thinker . . ." (II 8).

Still, Leibniz *was* a major philosopher; but where he is impressive is "in his acute and penetrating analyses of individual problems, in the extraordinary imagination with which he could generalize particular ideas . . ." (II 4f). Randall finds in Leibniz's specific analyses "profound insights and brilliant suggestions." He lists among the Leibnizian contributions that have retained their currency and vitality: mathematical logic, the idea of a universal language, the notion of intelligible perspectives, the relativistic conception of space and time, and the doctrine of "objective relativism." (Cf. II 9.)

Like Descartes, Leibniz exhibits "the intellectual attitude of the mathematician." Randall sees this as "the source both of his extraordinary fertility in those realms where mathematical analysis is fundamental, and of his failures and ludicrous missing of the point in those where it is irrelevant" (II 9). In Pascalian terms, Leibniz had *l'esprit géometrique* to an unusual degree, but he lacked *l'esprit de finesse*; and he couldn't tell when the one and not the other was appropriate. In consequence, he had difficulty distinguishing his own nonsense from his profundity. (Cf. II 10.)

Unlike Descartes, Leibniz combined his mathematical skills and insights with themes drawn from Aristotelian metaphysics. The resulting position Randall calls, in a happy phrase, "mathematical Aristotelianism." Of course Aristotle himself was no mathematician; but he was a logician with an acute sense of form and structure. As Randall puts it, Leibniz's "Aristotelian emphasis on the unity of a general type of structure or formula" was balanced by his "equally Aristotelian emphasis on the individuality or particular value of each member embraced" (II 23). Leibniz lacked Aristotle's respect for facts and sense experience; but he accepted Aristotle's concept of "individual substances" *(ousiai)* and particular processes, as well as Aristotle's stress on the unity of matter and form.

Randall spells out four respects in which the mechanical conception of nature that Leibniz inherited from Descartes was—and was felt by Leibniz to be—defective: (1) "the static and geometrical structure of Cartesian extension left all events and real changes unintelligible"; (2) "the Cartesian physics makes individuality, the existence of real concrete things, unintelligible, and they vanish into the universal order, like the modes of Spinoza"; (3) this conception "makes the fact of function, of the organic relations of living and knowing, of ends and purposes, unintelligible"; (4) it leaves the laws of mechanics as "brute data," ultimately dependent on the "arbitrary will of God" (II 20f). It was to remedy these defects that Leibniz, as mathematician, moved beyond Descartes, inventing the infinitesimal calculus in order to give a rational account of change and process, as Descartes had invented coordinate geometry in order to give a rational account of static extension. "Leibniz," Randall observes, "really thought in terms of the calculus, not of geometry and matter in motion, like Newton."[24]

This was Leibniz's strength, but also his limitation: "Just as Descartes, having found a method of rendering extension intelligible, ever after conceived the whole of nature as pure extension: so Leibniz, having rendered an infinite and continuous series intelligible, conceived all things as such series" (II 22). The idea of a constant mathematical law or function of a series found special application in Leibniz's metaphysics, being invoked to explain the series of internal changes in a given monad, as well as the series of changing relations among monads. Of course these relations are indirect, mediated by "pre-established harmony," since the monads themselves do not interact, being "without windows." (Cf. II 22, 32.)

In matters of religion, Leibniz was an indefatigable theoretical and practical conciliator, but in matters of philosophical theology he remained a "pure mathematician," treating theology as "a postulate system, whose assumptions he could freely manipulate." According to Randall, Leibniz's "new speculative mathematical theology" had a powerful historical impact, furnishing the "main outlines, minus Leibniz's own original and suggestive mathematical ideas, of the rational theology of many of the great Romantic thinkers."[25]

On the one hand, Leibniz represented "a far more radical break with the essence of medieval or Reformation piety than Spinoza," since "for him there was no mystic resignation to the great nature of things, no selfless and detached intellectual love of God" (II 15). In various works, especially the *Theodicy*, Leibniz treated God like any other mathematical function, a procedure, as Randall drily remarks, that is "blasphemous only to those who believe in God." In the *Theodicy* Leibniz used traditional theological language to express the essentially secular confidence ("best of all possible world") nourished by the "vision of a scientific determinism" (II 16).

On the other hand, Leibniz was not a religious genius; he wholly lacked Platonic *Eros* as well as Spinozistic *amor Dei intellectualis*. Leibniz was a typical speculative thinker in the German tradition. He had "the sense of the multiplicity of human values, the intense need for some all-embracing scheme that would afford an intelligible reconciliation of them all, moral, aesthetic, and religious, as well as purely scientific" (II 3f). Yet the "synthesis" which he offered was weak and one-sided. It included mathematics and science (at least physics), but was singularly unconvincing in its attempts to include morality, art, and religion.

Perhaps this is just another way of saying what has been implied by the foregoing discussion of Descartes and Spinoza—that both Descartes and Leibniz were primarily mathematicians and only secondarily or partially philosophers,[26] in contrast to Spinoza, who was totally and powerfully a philosopher.[27]

To have shown this, as Professor Randall has done, in a synoptic and synthetic reinterpretation—almost Hegelian in its sweep—of the relation of emerging science and traditional philosophy in *le grand siècle*, is indeed an impressive achievement.

NOTES

1. New York: Columbia University Press, 1962. 993 pp. This volume will be referred to in the sequel by roman numeral I and page number enclosed in parentheses, e.g., (I 214).

2. At one point, Randall refers to Spinoza and Leibniz as "the only living philosophers of the seventeenth century" (I 20). His own careful and generally sympathetic treatment of Pascal (I 413-425) would seem to be an implicit denial, or at least a significant qualification, of that judgment. For example, he remarks—both wittily and judiciously—that "Pascal was a great man, where Descartes was only a great thinker" (I 414).

3. New York: Columbia University Press, 1965. 675 pp. Ch. i is entitled, "Leibniz and the Presuppositions of German Thought"; ch. ii, "Leibniz and the Mathematical Ordering of the Universe." This volume will be referred to by roman numeral II and page number enclosed in parentheses, e.g., (II 34).

Randall has chosen to group Leibniz with other German thinkers in Volume II rather than with the other seventeenth-century thinkers in Volume I. Leibniz is thus placed at the head of a tradition which continues through Wolff, Kant, Fichte, Schelling, and Hegel, to Marx and Engels. (In the forthcoming Volume III this German tradition will be continued down to Wittgenstein and Heidegger.) Such a scheme of organization has obvious advantages: the linguistic, cultural, and intellectual continuities of a given tradition can be more readily exhibited. Still, one misses a sustained treatment of Leibniz (there are numerous passing references to him in Volume I) in that section of a history of philosophy devoted to Descartes, Malebranche, Spinoza, et al. There is, after all, something to be said for sheer chronological continuity!

4. In the *Discourse on Method*, Randall writes, Descartes "made God the ultimate epistemological guarantee, and initiated that pernicious strain in modern philosophical theology which finds epistemology the royal road to the Divine. Descartes was, in fact, a pious physicist—than which, as we have learned again of late, there can be no greater subverter of all sound theology" (*The Role of Knowledge in Western Religion* [Boston: Starr King Press, 1958], pp. 63f).

5. This may be a bit unfair to Descartes, since Jeans, whatever his merits as a physicist, astrophysicist, and popularizer of science was not—like Descartes—a creative mathematician.

6. The straight line, of course, is expressed by a "linear" equation (e.g., $x=y$); the ellipse, circle—which, strictly speaking, is only a special case of the ellipse—parabola, and hyperbola by "quadratic" equations (e.g., $x^2+y^2=r^2$ for the circle).

7. *Nature and Historical Experience* (New York: Columbia University Press, 1958), p. 203. "Descartes," Randall adds, "can justly claim the dubious honor of having initiated 'modern philosophy' and its 'problem of knowledge'" (I 393).

8. Spinoza calls Descartes' theory of the pineal gland a "hypothesis more occult than any occult quality" (. . . Hypothesin . . . omni occulta qualitate occultiorem [*Ethics*, Pt. V, Preface]).

9. Descartes himself did not use the term 'subjective,' but he did use the term 'objective' in a sense very close to the modern—i.e., post-Kantian—sense of 'subjective' (although perhaps even closer to the modern sense of 'mental' or 'conceptual'). Randall is at pains to clarify this important terminological point, which many translators of, and commentators upon, Descartes' philosophical writings have left in total confusion. For Descartes and Spinoza, Randall explains:

> to exist "objectively" [*objective*] in the understanding is contrasted with existing "formally" [*formaliter*] in itself. It is primarily due to Kant that present usage has come to reverse the terms of the distinction, so that today the contrast between "subjective" and "objective" existence corresponds to what Descartes [and Spinoza] understood as the contrast between "objective" and "formal" existence (I 387n8).

It would also have been helpful, I think, to point out that the term 'evidence' (*evidentia, évidence*) was used in the seventeenth century in a sense quite different from ours—e.g., when we speak of "empirical evidence" or "examining all the evidence." 'Evidence' in the seventeenth century meant "obviousness" or "self-evidence." Randall's references to the term, without a *caveat lector*, in his discussion of s'Gravesande (I 402) and Geulincx (I 408), are likely to mislead.

10. *Nature and Historical Experience*, p. 122.

11. As Randall has remarked elsewhere, in contrast to both Spinoza and Leibniz, who adopted the "realistic Aristotelianism of Thomas and the anticlerical Italian schools," Descartes went back to the "Augustinian philosophy of knowledge and science" (*How Philosophy Uses Its Past* [New York: Columbia University Press, 1963], p. 49).

12. *The Role of Knowledge in Western Religion*, p. 63.

13. *Ethics*, II, xliii note, xlviii note.

14. *Ibid.*, II, Definition 3 and explanation.

15. *The Improvement of the Understanding*, in James Gutmann, ed., Spinoza, *Ethics* (New York: Hafner Publishing Co., 1949), p. 32. For Spinoza's "constructive" or "genetic" definition of a sphere, see *ibid.*, p. 24.

16. Spinoza often speaks of ideas as being "in the mind" (*in anima*) in *The Improvement of the Understanding*, where he also classifies ideas as "true," "false," and "fictitious" (*idea vera, falsa, ficta*) (Gutmann ed., pp. 11, 23, 27). He even says that an idea "is in itself nothing else than a certain *sensation*" (*ibid.*, p. 24; italics added). (". . . est . . . in se nihil nisi talis *sensatio*" [*Opera*, ed. van Vloten and Land, The Hague, 1914, I, 24; italics added].)

17. Randall himself credits his teacher, F. J. E. Woodbridge, with the interpretation of Spinoza's ideas as "wholly objective": "ideas are not 'in the mind.' Rather, the mind is *in ideas* . . ." In consequence, "there is no panpsychisr" in Spinoza's philosophy. (Private communication, April 29, 1964). Randall also attributes to

Spinoza the Averroist position that "the universe itself thinks in men, and by means of men" (*Nature and Historical Experience*, p. 223; italics removed).

18. An idea, Spinoza insists, "is something different from its correlate; thus a circle is different from the idea of a circle. The idea of a circle is not something having a circumference and a center, as a circle has . . ." (Gutmann ed., p. 11). (". . . idea . . . est diversum quid a suo ideato: Nam aliud est circulus, aliud idea circuli. Idea enim circuli non est aliquid, habens peripheriam et centrum, uti circulus . . ." [*Opera*, I, 11].) Spinoza sometimes contrasts the idea as subjective with the idea (form) as objective in terms of *essentia objectiva* ("subjective essence") and *essentia formalis* ("objective essence"), using the terms *objectiva* and *formalis* in the special Cartesian sense noted above (see footnote 9). Cf. *Improvement* . . ., Gutmann ed., p. 12; *Opera*, I, 13. This formulation cuts two ways: the term *essentia* tends to support Randall's interpretation, but the opposition of *objectiva* and *formalis* tends, I think, to support the interpretation which I have been defending.

19. That Randall would reject this interpretation may be inferred from his account of Spinoza's thought in *The Career of Philosophy*, Volume I. He has recently made this rejection explicit, expressing doubt that Spinoza would consider both algebra and geometry "modes of thought," and adding: "I suspect that like Descartes he failed to distinguish extension and geometry, and identified the domain of physics with that of geometry. . . . Algebra is the structure of thought, geometry the structure of extension; and both are the same structure conceived under different attributes" (private communication, April 29, 1964).

20. Perhaps the distinction between law as *pre*scriptive or prescribed regularity (normative law) and law as *de*scriptive or described regularity (law of nature), might have been made explicit in this connection, if only to throw light on the way in which Spinoza tries systematically to fuse the two conceptions.

21. *The Role of Knowledge in Western Religion*, p. 65.

22. *Ibid.*, pp. 119f. More recently Randall has called Spinoza the "most eternal of philosophers," adding that, despite his "passionate devotion to all the medieval values," Spinoza "seems a startling foreshadowing of that liberal 'pantheism' that was to dominate so much of nineteenth-century thinking. (*How Philosophy Uses Its Past*, p. 26).

23. Earlier Randall had written that "Spinoza was able to carry to the limit the denial of all potentiality . . . ," making no distinction between "what things *do* and what they *can* do; all 'powers' have vanished, and everything is actuality" (*Nature and Historical Experience*, pp. 103, 233).

24. *How Philosophy Uses Its Past*, p. 53.

25. *The Role of Knowledge in Western Religion*, p. 64.

26. However, one does not have to go quite as far as Randall does when he calls Leibniz "a journalist among philosophers" (II 5), or as Victor Lowe does when he says that in the twentieth century Leibniz might well be the chief accountant for a large corporation, occupied with the design and construction of elegant and elaborate bookkeeping machines. (Cf. Victor Lowe, *Understanding Whitehead*, Baltimore, 1962, p. 127.)

27. One recalls Bergson's striking statement that whenever he looked into Spinoza's *Ethics*, he felt that "telle est exactement l'altitude où le philosophe doit se placer, telle est l'atmosphère où réellement le philosophe respire" (*Chronique des lettres françaises*, No. 26 [1927], p. 203; quoted in H. F. Hallett, *Aeternitas*, Oxford, 1930, p. xi).

RICHARD H. POPKIN
University of California, San Diego

Randall and British Empiricism

In the present period of adulation of the achievements of the British empirical philosophers, John Herman Randall has been one of the very few to speak out in opposition. His many attacks on this tradition are joined together in *The Career of Philosophy*, especially in Book Four, chapters 2-6, in which he endeavors to trace the career of certain fundamental problems involved in Newton's formulation of the nature and interpretation of science through Newton, Locke, and Berkeley, to "the most consistent of the empiricists," David Hume. Newton's fundamental assumption that "the ultimate validity of science lies in its foundations in sense," that "the ultimate subject-matter of science . . . can consist only of what is directly given in sensation, that the origin and justification of science . . . must be sought in ideas received through the senses" is "an assumption which makes inevitable the 'problem of knowledge' that has created so many technical difficulties for subsequent philosophical thought, and is the tragic guilt initiating the long drama of epistemology."[1] Randall vigorously describes and analyzes the drama, contending that various confusions and tensions in the empirical tradition, between what is a real property of an object and what is a property known in experience, between *what* we know in experience and *how* we know, and so on, finally led to Hume's transformation of the empirical interpretation of science into a kind of pragmatism. And through Hume's efforts, the British empiricists have been left with a strange view, namely, "we know the world only by experience, not by reasoning; yet what we know is not the world, but only experience. We must defer to facts, but there are no facts, only ideas."[2] They have been left with an interpretation of science that appears to make science meaningless and unintelligible. Hume's legacy, his contention that science is "descriptive," not demonstrative, has been accepted by the British empiricists, and has left them in "the difficult position of trying to convince scientists that science ought to be different from what it actually is."[3]

In developing his story, Randall raises many crucial points that have

too long been ignored, suppressed, or overlooked by those imbued with
the ideas and ideology of the British empirical tradition. In this essay I
do not want to deal specifically with the philosophical issues Randall discusses, but rather with some historico-philosophical ones. If I may speak
autobiographically for a moment, my own vital concern with the history
of philosophy was first activated and encouraged by John Herman Randall
almost twenty-five years ago when I was an undergraduate at Columbia.
He stimulated both my interest in the development of ideas, and in the
nature of investigations and interpretations of the careers of these ideas.
As a result of studying with him and others, I have been concerned, in
part, about why certain patterns of development of ideas have been accepted as adequate and sufficient accounts of what has happened in the
past, and what is relevant for us today. And this concern has led me to
be suspicious both of the role Hume has been given, the tradition he has
been placed in, and the achievements he has supposedly bequeathed to us.
It seems to me that we have all, to some degree, accepted a kind of historical mythology about the activities of the triumvirate Locke, Berkeley,
and Hume, which makes certain problems and solutions they presented,
in whole or in part, crucial stages of *our* intellectual drama, which we
either live in, or fight against. The importance of what we are doing and
thinking somehow gets measured in terms of how it fits in this drama of
the development of British empiricism two centuries ago.

A long time ago Randall made me realize that people write histories,
including histories of philosophy, as a way of dealing with present-day
problems and concerns, and of proposing means for their future solutions.
In terms of these problems and concerns, a focus of selection of past data
emerges, by which a career or development is singled out, showing usually
how some good cause is progressing towards its future triumph, or some
bad cause is moving towards its ultimate future failure.

Histories of philosophy seem, much more than political or social histories, to be filled with anomalies and anachronisms. A thorough study of
the development of histories of philosophy from the end of the Renaissance onward would probably show this quite clearly. Who is considered
a serious and important philosopher of the past by historians of philosophy
of a later time too often seems to be the result of odd and curious factors.
The philosophical texts that are used in schools, the material that exists
in translation into the language of the historian, the selections of what
was considered important by earlier historian-polemicists in terms of
which theories they were opposing, and which they were favoring—these
and similar factors appear to play a great role in the selections of materials
by later historians of philosophy. A case in point is the debatable status of
Nicolas Malebranche, who has become a quite minor figure, a footnote to

Descartes, or a name to be identified because he is mentioned by a serious and important philosopher like Leibniz, or Locke, or Berkeley, or Hume. Malebranche's major work, *De la recherche de la vérité*, has not appeared in English since the beginning of the eighteenth century. His views are given short shrift in most textbooks, if mentioned at all. For about a century and a half he has been omitted as a major figure among the Continental Rationalists. Hence, contemporary historians of thought can continue to leave him and his ideas in oblivion, since he was long ago selected out of our intellectual development. But misgivings arise now that Malebranche's great influence on the views of Berkeley and Hume is being recognized, and it is hard to find the proper place for him in the canon of our philosophical ancestors.[4]

Bayle, who was probably the most influential thinker of his age, with an enormous impact on both Continental and British thinkers, has also, through a series of odd factors, lost his place in histories of philosophers. His major work, the *Historical and Critical Dictionary*, ceased being a useful reference source by the late eighteenth century. His critical views were milder than those of the *philosophes*, so their writings replaced his in the schools. History was written in terms of one set of his heirs, and he then deserved mention only as a forerunner of the Enlightenment. And now that there seems to be a revival of interest in many sides of Bayle's scepticism and fideism, it will be quite difficult to find him a suitable niche in histories of philosophy that can portray him both as a major figure of his own day, and as an extremely influential one in the Age of Reason, both in Great Britain and on the Continent.[5]

The history of the role of the British empirical tradition exhibits many similar elements, and suggests, at least to me, that we are all victims of an anachronistic selection, and that in terms of our present-day concerns and problems a more fruitful and meaningful rendition and interpretation of Locke and Berkeley and Hume can be made, so that they are seen not as the heroes who set the stage for twentieth-century analytic philosophy, nor as the villains who left us a hopeless legacy, but rather as three only partially related thinkers, dealing with certain major problems in various seventeenth- and eighteenth-century metaphysical and sceptical traditions. Since some of these problems are vitally ours today, these thinkers, each separately, and only slightly as a triumvirate, can be seen as progenitors of new avenues of enquiry.

The usual formulation of their roles, it seems to me, leads to a sterile and futile present-day evaluation of their texts and their message for us. If they have to be seen as forebears of today's empiricists, it really becomes more and more difficult to find great meat in their writings, and harder and harder to comprehend why their muddles, confusions, and archaic views actually have had any great impact and continue to have any importance.

Briefly, I should like first to sketch out how I think the concept of a British empirical tradition developed, what function this concept seems to play, and then propose an alternative that might make at least Locke, Berkeley, and Hume more interesting and exciting intellectual figures for us today.

The record, for what it is worth, indicates that Berkeley did not see himself as Locke's successor, nor was he so seen by his contemporaries. Similarly, Hume did not see himself as Berkeley's successor, nor was he so seen by his contemporaries. Berkeley was usually read as either the Irish Malebranche or as a member of the lunatic fringe of the seventeenth-century Pyrrhonists.[6] Hume, in the *Treatise*, claimed he was in the line of Locke, Mandeville, Shaftesbury, Hutcheson, and Butler; and when he discussed his own philosophy, it was, as his contemporaries saw, an extension of Pierre Bayle's scepticism.[7] Some of the first critics saw him as following in the irreligious line of Bolingbroke and Kames.[8] It is only towards the end of Hume's life that he and Berkeley start to be connected and linked to something that started with Locke. Thomas Reid, one of the very, very few of the time who could find much to mull over in Hume, spent twenty-five years figuring out the intellectual genesis of the monster Hume spawned in 1739, the *Treatise of Human Nature,* and finally found it in the problem of knowledge set up by the Cartesian way of ideas, and in Locke's transformation of this into empirical terms.[9] Hume, in his brief comments on Reid's interpretation, based on reading the latter's *Inquiry,* showed no sign of interest in this construction of an Anglo-Hibernian-Scottish triumvirate, with Hume as the destructive end man. Hume noticed that Reid used a "Scotticism," and differed with him on a technical point about the psychology of perception, but he did not seem to take note of what was to become the major, and practically exclusive, way of interpreting the philosophy of David Hume.[10]

The French Enlightenment figures, including many who knew Hume personally and many who jibed at Berkeley as a fool and a crank, could hardly see either of them as the philosophical heirs of John Locke, since, as far as these *philosophes* knew, it was in France—with Voltaire, Diderot, D'Alembert, Condillac, and others—that empiricism was triumphantly moving from the initial revolutionary efforts of Locke and Sir Isaac Newton to the geniune establishment of an Age of Reason which would lead to the salvation of mankind. Hume as a scientist they considered to be one of their own brothers in furthering the application of the "experimental method of reasoning to moral subjects," and thereby in furthering the reasonable reform of the social order. Hume as a philosopher they considered to be a latter-day Pierre Bayle, who just did not seem to be aware that the era of doubting was now over, to be replaced by the positive results of Newtonian science."[11] And the Enlightenment thinkers saw Berkeley, except for his scientific work on perception, as a strange curiosity, someone who had somehow managed to prove something totally incredible, that "admits of no answer and produces no conviction."[12] The French and Swiss refugees in the Prussian Academy who translated and commented on Hume's writings began to perceive a "phenomenalistic" tradition and a sceptical debacle in which Hume figured mightily, and in which Berkeley dimly emerged as the one who had set him astray and adrift. One of them, by the end of the century, even wrote a dialogue in which Berkeley apologized to Hume for leading him down the path to pure empiricism and total scepticism.[13]

Once the Sage of Königsberg was aroused from his dogmatic slumbers, then a script could be written in which Locke, Berkeley, and Hume became the steam-shovel school of philosophy. Pitted against the Continental rationalists, from Descartes to Wolff (with Malebranche pretty much left aside), who were constructing dogmatic metaphysical castles in the air, the British empiricists were demolishing all metaphysical concepts and methods. Locke supposedly destroyed the doctrine of innate ideas, but unfortunately he forgot to do the same to the theory of substance. Berkeley destroyed the conception of a material substance, but he forgot to do the same to the conception of mental substance. Finally Hume came along and destroyed the conceptions of substance, cause, demonstrative reasoning about experience, proofs of the existence of God, and so on. And according to this story, as we all know, the failure of Continental rationalism and the culmination of British empiricism into a complete and total scepticism, in spite of itself, led first to the views of Immanual Kant and critical philosophy, and then to the Hegelian synthesis. The German historian-polemicists, from Wilhelm Gottlieb Tennemann to Kuno Fischer and onward throughout the nineteenth century, constructed and developed this historical entity, "British empiricism," as a way of understanding the brilliant triumphs of Kant, Fichte, Hegel, and Schelling.[14] And in terms of the Hegelian notion of what intellectual history represents, British empiricism was not just a sequential development, but part of the March of Reason through the world, a phase in the development of the self-realization of the Absolute, whose dialetic required the thesis of Rationalism and the antithesis of Empiricism before it could synthesize itself and culminate all intellectual history in the achievements of nineteenth-century Hegelianism.

The British empiricists seem to have accepted all of this as their own history, except the Hegelian-synthesis part of the story. Perhaps because the later members of this alleged group of British empiricists were so unhistorical and so anti-historical (unlike Locke, who used "the plain, historical method," and Hume, who was one of the very few great historians the British Isles have produced), they accepted the Teutonic version uncritically, only adding a different ending. From the vantage point of the nineteenth century, and in the light of Auguste Comte's insights into the stages of human intellectual developments and Darwin's triumphs, it seemed obvious that not only had British empiricism destroyed the theological and metaphysical Dark Ages (extending, on various readings, from the date of Creation up to somewhere around 1600-1850 A.D.) but also that the continued application of its method and *Weltanschauung* would ferret out the last vestiges of obscurantism, religion, superstition, malice, evil, etc. The culmination of intellectual history for the empiricists would not be a new gaseous metaphysical theory alleging to synthesize Empiricism and Rationalism and to overcome the difficulties raised by these views, but rather it would be a scientifically oriented quasi-socialist paradise emanating from the total application of Hume's empirical descriptive and sceptical analysis of human beliefs. Bertrand Russell and many other empiricists have been revelling in the Germanic rendition of their past, and have seen it as their personal mission to continue the destructive work of their intellectual ancestors until all traditional philosophy vanishes from the scene, and only science and mathematics are left. All else being naught but sophistry and illusion, therefore commit it to the flames. And, in terms of such a past, Locke, Berkeley, and Hume have become not just three philosophers, but the only three serious and significant ones, whose places on the pedestal are in reverse order to their chronology.

Twentieth-century empiricists may still be impressed with their own achievements and potentialities for the future. If so, then we can understand why they might cling to the old German version of their past and their own reading of it in glorious and heroic terms. But should the rest of us accept the past and present in their terms? If we have doubts that present-day empiricism is an adequate philosophy for explaining science or man, why should we select an intellectual history for ourselves purporting to show how and why it does fulfill such a role? Why should we select an intellectual history in which empiricism's giants are pygmies in terms of our own concerns? As an indication of some of the problems involved in terms of the questions raised above, just consider the present difficulty that exists for European philosophers in trying to make the classic British empirical tradition meaningful in terms of present-day Continental thought. The purported contributions, according to the traditional account of the development of British empiricism, just do not seem relevant. The degree to which Anglo-American philosophers take Locke, Berkeley, and Hume seriously seems to require some incorporation of them as intellectual ancestors of present-day thinkers. Only by the most valiant efforts of reinterpretation of Locke and Berkeley and Hume, and only by connecting them with other vital traditions, are they portrayed as significant philosophers who deserve an important historical place.[15]

If we do accept the empiricists' version of their history, then one possible approach is that which Randall has been working on for many years, namely, that of arguing that this history is a history of bungling and confusion, culminating in a view so strange, namely Hume's, that no one really accepts it. Such an approach also attempts to explain why this type of view ever developed, and accounts for it in terms of Marxian factors (that is, in terms of economic factors in England) and psychological ones (that is, in terms of the strange personalities of John Locke, George Berkeley, and David Hume).

As an antidote to the hero-worship and the self-congratulation of the empiricists, Randall's approach is appealing, intriguing, and often shocking. It is developed in terms of what the Kantians and the nineteenth-century British empiricists saw as the issues out of which their views grew. The force of Randall's reading of the contributions of Locke, Berkeley, and Hume depends to a great extent both on accepting the later empiricists' view of their past and on accepting Randall's judgment of their present. If the modern empiricists are unable to tell that there is anything odd about their twentieth-century rendition of what scientific knowledge is, and what it is about, they probably will not be very much impressed at seeing how Newton and Locke created certain problems, how Berkeley straightened some of them out, and how Hume transformed the empirical view into its present form. If the empiricists are genuinely satisfied with the present form of their doctrine, then Hume's contribution is seen as a wonderful conclusion, and not as a *reductio ad absurdum* of empiricism. Those items that Randall presents as problems left unsolved by Hume or shown to be insoluble by him, his present-day admirers might well regard as more signs of his genius, in that he eliminated the further consideration of certain matters, that he put forth a view of science that made certain philosophical considerations useless, and so on. The attack Randall launches on the personalities involved, especially Hume, might well be countered by the empiricists by either constructing alternative biographical portraits based on a different selection of the data, or by a different evaluation of the biographical facts. Mossner's answer to Randall on Hume indicates how a quite different and laudatory portrait of Hume can be drawn by a different interpretation of the data, and an emphasis on other aspects of Hume's career.[16] The empiricists might also counter

Randall's evaluation of Hume's personality by replying, "So what?" Hume, they might say, could have been a dilettante, a money-mad Scotchman, a fame-seeker, an Anglophobe, or lots of other things, but nonetheless he might also have been right in his philosophical views, no matter why he happened to set them forth.

In his important work *How Philosophy Uses Its Past*, Randall states, "The understanding of every significant philosopher is ultimately the understanding of the materials he offers for our own disposal, of the concepts and distinctions and methods he has made available for use on our own problems."[17] In the light of this, I should like to suggest another alternative interpretation of the achievements of Locke, Berkeley, and Hume. In terms of certain contemporary philosophical issues, rather than late eighteenth- and early nineteenth-century developments, I feel that such an interpretation may be more rewarding. Since the concerns that shape my readings of these philosophers are different from those that Randall emphasizes in *The Career of Philosophy*, the resulting evaluations are also quite different. It is hoped that these evaluations may be of some value in applying the philosophical insights of Locke, Berkeley, and Hume to some of the basic problems of twentieth-century man, and will rescue these thinkers from their sterile roles as founders of one of the now less-exciting movements of modern philosophy.

The British empiricists' version of the British empirical tradition appears to concentrate on some of the less interesting aspects of the views of their heroes, and to leave a fairly sterile battleground, either for the erection of monuments or for the carrying on of philosophical warfare. It requires truncating the actual texts of Locke, Berkeley, and Hume to just those parts that happen to fit together, so that Berkeley's writings on notions and spirits are regarded as afterthoughts that can be ignored, since Berkeley was, after all, a Bishop; and so that Hume's writings on mathematics and on scepticism, and on scepticism about Humeanism can be ignored as being due to unfortunate lapses or moments of self-dramatization. The empiricist's version requires ignoring all sorts of major "minor" figures, like Pierre Bayle, whose known historical influence on the Empirical Triumvirate is monumental (and certainly more extensive than their individual influence on each other). It requires putting together a corpus of texts that seem less and less exciting as time goes on (maybe just because we have heard the story so many times), and that seem less and less capable of accounting for the "making of the modern mind." It requires making Locke appear a muddled and confused thinker, since he should have reached Berkeley's views about material substance, primary and secondary qualities, and abstract general ideas. It requires making Berkeley appear as the serious author of only a small part of his actual writings, since he should have seen that his "brilliant" empirical critique of Locke on the above points should also have been applied to Berkeley's own views on mental substance, spirits, notions, cause, etc.; in other words, that he should have written Hume's *Enquiry* instead of the second and third dialogues, and the strange nonsense in *Siris*. And, it requires that Hume be published in selection form lest he become a philosophical embarrassment, as well as a devastating critic of Hume—the hero of heroes of British empiricism.

Each of these philosophers when read out of context (that is, out of their roles as members of the Triumvirate) is much more exciting, interesting, and rewarding. Each of them had important, conscious reasons for not just holding the views that would have made them paradigm cases of something called "British empirical philosophy." These reasons I find the most illuminating aspects of their work, and the aspects that may throw the most light on present-day interests and concerns of all thoughtful men. For several years I have been proposing quite different interpretations of the roles of Locke and Berkeley and Hume in intellectual history, roles which make it possible to take more of their writings seriously, and to see each of them in a broader historical context.

Locke appears to me to be most interesting when considered as a latter-day Gassendist, developing an interpretation of science in the style of Gassendi in the context of the experimentalism of the Royal Society.[18] Gassendi, from whom Locke borrowed greatly, is perhaps the most interesting early "empiricist" for the twentieth century. Unfortunately, due to the aberrations of literary training, and publishers' desires to print classics that can be used in courses, practically nobody reads him anymore except for his fight with Descartes.[19] Gassendi really tried to state a philosophy of science shorn of all metaphysics, and based on empirical concepts, allowable relations, and so on, and tried to do this in terms of a most thorough acquaintance with the achievements of midseventeenth-century science. He saw the problems of accounting for concepts, hypotheses, models, inferences, etc., as acutely as anyone has since, and he tried to state an interpretation of science in which these problems had either been dealt with or had been evaded or avoided. The view he developed he considered a *via media* between scepticism and dogmatism.[20] Locke, it seems to me, was engaged in a similar enterprise fifty years later. He was less of a scientist, and less of a precise thinker, and was imbued with certain commonsensical counters to the complete scepticism that Bishop Wilkins and Joseph Glanvill had developed as a rationale for the experimental philosophy of the Royal Society.[21] He also was involved with the struggles of his friend Jean Le Clerc to find a compromise between Cartesianism and empiricism that would prevent the scepticism of Bayle and others from carrying the day.[22] In this sort of context Locke then appears as a fascinating figure who was groping with one of our major contemporary problems—what can science actually be about, and how can we relate it to us and our ways of knowing about it? Locke saw that strict empiricism was unacceptable, since it would make science nothing but a sequence of mental events whose subject-matter might be nothing, or just the product of imagination or dreams. He was willing enough to abandon the notion that science was the study of the real nature of things, but he could not accept Bayle's formulation that science was just a description of the sequence of ideas in our minds, and did not deal with things-in-themselves.[23] The basic problem involved was not really novel with Newton's work but was the old Greek sceptical one of appearance and reality, which, for Locke, was really sticky wicket. In the chapters on power, primary and secondary qualities, substance, real and nominal essences, and sensitive knowledge, I find that Locke was struggling to avoid the barren wasteland of modern empiricism, as well as the catastrophe of total Pyrrhonism, and also what he saw as untenable metaphysical views. His struggle is in many ways our struggle, only ours has become so much more complicated by the developments of the sciences.

As regards Berkeley, I would argue that another contemporary issue dominates his work—that of relating the scientific and the spiritual dimensions of the world. In this, a theme that runs through his works from the early *Philosophical Commentaries* to the late *Siris*, he was following in Malebranche's footsteps. Both Berkeley and Malebranche were thoroughly versed in the "new science" and were thoroughly committed to a religious and spiritual interpretation of what is going on. Malebranche saw that a meaningful scientific world depended upon an Intelligible World, and Berkeley saw that a perceptual scientific world depended upon a spiritual one. In the face of Spinozism, Hobbesism, Deism, and other irreligious views, both insisted that modern science only made sense as part of a theodicy. Berkeley's empiricism was always, for its author, just part of the story, and a part that showed that the empirical realm was mind-dependent. In the *Philosophical Commentaries* there was a moment when Berkeley became both the consistent Locke and the proto-Hume, and applied his analysis to "mind," which empirically he found could only be a "congeries of perceptions." Young Berkeley was not even tempted then to become a complete British empiricist. He knew better, and knew that there must be other modes of knowing than just sense perception, since there are other modes of being than just sense data. The "minute philosopher" could stay in his two-dimensional world, but, for Berkeley, the serious philosopher was already out of it, in that he knew that he lived in a world in which spirit was the basic and meaningful feature.[24] In our present-day headlong rush to bury ourselves in scientific data, which has become more and more meaningless, both Berkeley and Malebranche may yet provide us with important clues, by forcing us to see what we have lost by cutting off one crucial dimension of what we are doing, and by forcing us to ask whether we should have amputated our world so that sense and meaning were lopped off.

Lastly, Hume, on my reading, is a really giant intellectual figure, not for his analytical philosophical brilliance or originality, since I have strong doubts as to whether he ever really possessed those qualities, but rather for his role as a forlorn figure facing up to a world of complete Baylean scepticism, in which all anchors were gone, religious or scientific. From even the pre-*Treatise* days down to the end of his life, Hume was deeply immersed both in the destructive legacy of Bayle and in the hopeful optimism of the Scottish moralists. He saw himself both as the Newton of the moral sciences and as the reincarnation of the master of them that doubt, *le Philosophe de Rotterdam*.[25] Whenever Hume constructed anything in empirical theory, he very soon dissolved it in a barrage of sceptical criticism. The tension between the scientific and empirical Hume and the Pyrrhonian Hume goes on through all of his work and through all of his views. As the concluding chapter of Book I of the *Treatise* indicates, he was not able to find any mental peace in Humeanism, and could not even accept his own philosophical results.[26] On the other hand, he was not able to accept a total scepticism either.[27] Bayle was always able to face serenely the abysses of doubt, and to suggest calmly that blind religious faith was a resolution.[28] Hume, a few decades later, was already too "enlightened" to find any solace or peace in any religious tradition, and could only marvel at the fact that Nature always saved the day by irrationally sustaining our feeble reason, and making it psychologically impossible to take the doubts seriously, thereby leaving man able to do empirical science now and then until his mind once again became overheated with doubts.[29] Living in an age when science had supposedly conquered both religion and scepticism, Hume was almost alone in seeing the meaningless world that was left. In an almost prophetic manner, Hume visualized what we were all to see two centuries later, that all the bulwarks of our intellectual world had been destroyed, and no amount of empirical scientific research would make it meaningful or intelligible again. Like him, we were doomed to be haunted by an unconquerable scepticism once we asked, in a post-Enlightenment world, what do we know, how do we know it, why do we know it?

Locke, Berkeley, and Hume each posed a form of our present dilemma: that our world, for all of its scientific achievements, makes no sense. We want more certainty and more reality than Locke could find;

we are too enlightened to accept Berkeley's spiritual dimension, and to live and move in it, and to have our being there; and we are too tormented to try to live with Hume's torments. Our problem is not to try to justify experimental science, either by patching up a truncated version of the Locke-Berkeley-Hume tradition or by inveighing against it and its historical personages; rather, our problem is to find a framework in which experimental science deserves the role it has. We are becoming disillusioned with its achievements, and we despair of its future ones. It has enlightened us to the extent that it has left us bereft of our religious traditions, and it has shown us that we now are able to destroy ourselves, each other, and everything, in the most painful and terrible way, without knowing why or wherefore. The scientific rather than the epistemological drama has reached its tragic climax; and now we need all the insight we can garner from the past, so that we may yet have a future. Locke, Berkeley, and Hume, each in his *own* way, saw through the "science-will-save-us" view. And like Pascal, Leibniz, Bayle, and Voltaire, among others, they can help us see the problem more clearly—if we see them in larger focus. When, as hoped for, we do manage to find a way out, then we may be able to rewrite our intellectual history, not in terms of empiricism or rationalism, but in terms of a more promising vision of where we are going and where we have been.

NOTES

1. *The Career of Philosophy*, Vol. I, p. 584.

2. *Ibid.*, p. 617.

3. *Ibid.*, p. 650.

4. Randall's discussion in *Career*, pp. 425-33, makes a serious effort to put Malebranche back in the mainstream of 17th century thought.

5. In this respect I feel that Randall's brief treatment of Bayle, *Career*, pp. 855-57, fails to do justice to him. He appears long after the British figures he influenced, and far removed from those with whom he was in combat.

6. Cf. Harry M. Bracken, *The Early Reception of Berkeley's Immaterialism, 1710-1733* (rev. ed.; The Hague, 1965).

7. In the Introduction to *A Treatise of Human Nature* (Selby-Bigge ed.; Oxford, 1951), p. xxi, note 1, Hume gives the list of whom he saw as his predecessors. On the question of what tradition Hume falls in, see R. H. Popkin, "Did Hume Ever Read Berkeley?" *Journal of Philosophy*, LVI (1959), 535-45; and "So Hume Did Read Berkeley," *Journal of Philosophy*, LXI (1964), 773-78. The review of Hume's *Treatise* in the *Bibliothèque raisonée des ouvrages des savans de l'Europe*, Vols. XXIV and XXVI (1740-41), clearly places Hume in the Pyrrhonian tradition. Maty's review of Hume's *Political Discourses*, *Journal britannique*, VII (1752), 243-44, states that Hume's metaphysical and moral views are worthy of the pen of Pierre Bayle.

8. See, for instance, the criticisms of Hume in John Bonar, *An Analysis of the Moral and Religious Sentiments Contained in the Writings of Sopho* [Lord Kames] *and David Hume, Esq.* (Edinburgh, 1755); and John Leland, *A View of the Principal Deistical Writers That Have Appeared in England in the Last and Present Century* (3rd ed., London, 1757).

9. Cf. Thomas Reid, "Essays on the Intellectual Powers," in *The Works of Thomas Reid*, ed. Sir Wm. Hamilton, 2 vols. (8th ed.; Edinburgh, 1905).

10. See Hume's letter to Reid, Feb. 25, 1763, in *The Letters of David Hume*, ed. J. Y. T. Greig (Oxford, 1932), I, 375-76. Reid's answer of March 18, 1763, is given in a note on p. 376.

11. Cf. Laurence Bongie, "Hume, 'Philosophe' and Philosopher in Eighteenth Century France," *French Studies*, XV (1961), 213-227; and R. H. Popkin, "Scepticism in the Enlightenment," *Studies on Voltaire and the Eighteenth Century*, XXVI (1963), 1335ff.

12. This was Hume's line from the *Enquiry Concerning the Human Understanding* (Selby-Bigge ed.; Oxford, 1951), p. 155; compare with, for example, Diderot's view on Berkeley in *Lettres sur les aveugles*, ed. R. Niklaus (Geneva, 1951), pp. 35-36.

13. The editions by Formey, Mérian, and Sulzer give this interpretation. It was Ancillon who wrote, "Dialogue entre Hume et Berkeley," which appears in the 1796 volume of the memoirs of the Prussian Academy.

14. Cf. W. G. Tennemann, *Grundriss der Geschichte der Philosophie* (Leipzig, 1820); and Kuno Fischer, *Geschichte der neuern Philosophie*, 10 vols. (Heidelberg, 1897-1904).

15. See, for instance, André-Louis Leroy's *George Berkeley* (Paris, 1959), and *David Hume* (Paris, 1953).

16. Cf. Ernest C. Mossner, "Philosophy and Biography: The Case of David Hume," *Philosophical Review*, LIX (1950), 184-201.

17. Randall, *How Philosophy Uses Its Past* (New York, 1963), p. 93.

18. A comparison of Locke's and Gassendi's texts on similar issues is quite striking, especially when Locke's *Essay* is considered in terms of Gassendi's *Syntagma*.

19. Even though the Fifth Objections and Descartes' reply are part of our philosophical classics, it was not until 1962 that the full text of Gassendi's attack on Descartes was made available both in the original and in a modern language. As far as I know there is as yet no interest in publishing it in English. The only other work to appear in a modern langue in the last couple of hundred years is the *Exercitationes paradoxicae adversus Aristoteleos* (Paris, 1959), in French, translated by Bernard Rochet. A brief selection of this appears in my anthology, *The Philosophy of the 16th and 17th Centuries* (New York 1966). The 1658 *Opera omnia* has recently been photoreproduced.

20. Pierre Gassendi, *Syntagma philosophicum, Logica*, II, v, in *Opera omnia*, (Stuttgart, 1964, photoreproduction), p. 79. On Gassendi, see R. H. Popkin's article on him in the *Encyclopedia of Philosophy*; and Popkin, *History of Scepticism from Erasmus to Descartes* (Assen, 1964), chaps. v and vii; and Bernard Rochet, *Les Travaux de Gassendi sur Épicure et sur l'atomisme* (Paris, 1944).

21. On Wilkins and Glanvill, see Henry G. Van Leeuwen, *The Problem of Certainty in English Thought, 1630-1690* (The Hague, 1963), chap. iii.

22. LeClerc was constantly fighting scepticism and advancing his compromise in articles in the *Bibliothèque universelle et historique,* the *Bibliothèque choisie,* and the *Bibliothèque ancienne et moderne.* Locke and LeClerc became very close friends during the former's refugee period in Holland, and remained in close intellectual contract from then on. LeClerc saw Locke's *Essay* as precisely the kind of solution he was looking for to the conflicts of the time. On LeClerc and Locke, see, beside their large correspondence, Annie Barnes, *Jean LeClerc (1657-1736) et la République des Lettres* (Paris, 1938); and Maurice Cranston, *John Locke* (London, 1959).

23. See Pierre Bayle's *Historical and Critical Dictionary,* article "Pyrrho," Rem. B, pp. 194ff. in my translation (Indianapolis: Library of Liberal Arts, 1965).

24. The interpretations of A. A. Luce, T. E. Jessop, and L. L. Leroy have helped greatly in bringing out these dimensions of Berkeley's philosophy.

25. Hume's Newtonianism is evident from the title page of the *Treatise,* "being an Attempt to introduce the experimental Method of Reasoning into Moral Subjects," through the introduction and early sections. In Part III and especially Part IV, Hume reveals himself more and more as a sceptic in the Baylean tradition. On this, see my paper "Hume and Bayle," *Proceedings of the XIII International Philosophical Congress, Mexico City, 1963,* forthcoming.

26. Hume, *Treatise,* Book I, Part IV, sec. 7, pp. 263-69.

27. *Ibid.,* pp. 268-74, and sec. 1 and 2 of Part IV, esp. pp. 183, 187-88, and 218.

28. See, for example, Bayle's *Dictionary,* art. "Pyrrho," Rem. C, pp. 204-08, in my edition.

29. Hume, *Treatise,* pp. 268-74.

PATRICK SUPPES

Stanford University

Some Extensions of Randall's Interpretation of Kant's Philosophy of Science

It has been just twenty years since I heard Randall's lectures on the history of philosophy at Columbia. I was a beginning graduate student without very much prior exposure to philosophy. Randall's lectures were a memorable experience, and as I have read the two volumes of *The Career of Philosophy*, I have enjoyed recognizing viewpoints, analyses, and even phrases that I first heard many years ago in the lectures. The wit, the literary quality, and the range of learning exhibited in these lectures were famous around Columbia long before the time of my own arrival. As a young scientist turned philosopher, the most important general thing I learned from Randall was not simply to read the great modern philosophers in terms of a close explication of text, but also to realize that they must be interpreted and considered against the background of the development of modern science. What he had to say in this connection about the British empiricists and about Kant was particularly important and significant.

In a work of the historical scope of *The Career of Philosophy*, it has been impossible to treat in detail many interesting aspects of the relation between the development of modern philosophy and science. What I would like to do in this article is to offer some extensions of Chapter 6 of Volume II, which deals with Kant's critical philosophy of science. The ideas that I want to discuss do not represent general differences with Randall, or with his interpretation of Kant, but constitute a detailed documentation of some of the main theses about Kant set forth by Randall in this chapter.

I have selected four topics that are central to many classical discussions in the philosophy of science. I shall focus especially on the philosophy of physics, which also provides an insight into how Kant attempted to work out the details of his philosophy of physics. For Kant's view of these details I shall depend particularly upon the *Metaphysische Anfangsgruende der Naturwissenschaft*.[1] This important work, in which Kant attempts to work out a critical philosophy of physics, was published between the two editions of the *Critique of Pure Reason*. The relative neglect of this work in the large secondary literature on Kant in the nineteenth century can be explained only by the relative neglect of Kant as a philosopher of science. Randall's own emphasis on the intimate connection between Kant's philosophy and Newtonian physics is quite uncharacteristic of the nineteenth-century commentators.

The four topics I have selected are the relations between metaphysics and science, the application of the categories to mathematical physics, Kant's concepts of force and matter, and Kant's position on dynamical-versus-mechanical explanations of natural phenomena.

1. It is a familiar part of Kantian doctrine that the relatively great intellectual power of the mathematician comes from his monopoly of the objects given a priori in intuition. For the only pure forms of intuition are space and time, and only these forms can provide the a priori objects for the mathematical concepts of quantity and spatial figure. Corresponding to the many concepts with which the philosopher wants to deal, there are no a priori intuitions providing objects *in concreto*; constructions are thereby forbidden him and he is reduced to the mere analysis of concepts.

Actually, however, the philosopher is not quite reduced to mere empty analysis of a priori concepts. There are two other possibilities open to him, which constitute a division of the metaphysical portion of the pure, a priori part of a natural science.[2] The first possibility consists of transcendental and universal metaphysics. For this transcendental portion there are no determinate objects given a priori in intuition; transcendental metaphysics considers objects in general and thereby determines the conditions of all possible experience. The transcendental propositions of this metaphysic are not analytic, but a priori synthetic, for they provide the rules according to which we look empirically for the synthetical unity of (empirical) perceptions. This unity is required for experience itself to be possible. Although a priori synthetic, these propositions are philosophical rather than mathematical, for the mere laying down of rules governing the conditions of possible experience does not constitute construction of concepts: the conditions for the application of concepts to phenomena are determined, but not the actual construction of concepts.[3] The basic part of this transcendental metaphysic of nature is just what is developed in the Transcendental Aesthetic and the Transcendental Analytic of the *Critique*. The table of the categories provides a complete list of all the fundamental concepts which constitute pure knowledge, and the table of principles provides the rules for the objective application of the categories to phenomena, that is, empirical perceptions.[4] The *Critique*, however, does not provide a complete system of transcendental philosophy, for a detailed analysis of the fundamental concepts and a complete list of the pure derivative concepts is omitted.[5] This lacuna was never filled by Kant.

What concerns us more here is the second possibility open to the philosopher. By taking an empirical concept from experience he may develop a particular metaphysic of nature, with the restriction that nothing may be borrowed from experience except what lies in this empirical concept.[6] In this case, since the object which generated the empirical concept is given in intuition, although only empirically, the philosopher can go beyond mere analysis of the concept and make synthetic assertions about it. Furthermore, these assertions may be a priori, although not pure in the strictest sense. The core of any particular metaphysic consists in the application of the concepts and principles of transcendental metaphysic, which were developed for objects in general, to the object, such as matter, given in empirical intuition. Corresponding to the two forms of sense, the external and the inner, are the concepts of two objects, which give us the two most important particular metaphysics. One takes as its basis the empirical concept of matter, and the other the empirical concept of a thinking entity (*denkend Wesen*).[7] Here it is the particular metaphysic of matter—corporeal nature—which concerns us.

This particular metaphysic, and the transcendental metaphysic as well, can aspire to a completeness which is impossible for either pure mathematics or general physics. The reason is that in a metaphysic, the object is considered only according to the universal laws of thought, whereas in mathematics and the sciences it is considered according to the data of intuition (pure or empirical), which are infinite in their multiplicity.[8] The metaphysical enterprise is to connect the object with all the necessary laws of thought, which are definite in number. As is to be expected, the table of the categories deduced in the *Critique* provides a fixed scheme for the completeness of such a metaphysical system; for as Kant maintains in the *Critique*, this table contains all the fundamental concepts which can be concerned with the nature of things.[9] This entails that all the a priori determinations of the concept of matter in general can be brought under the four classes of quantity, quality, relation, and modality. To carry the concept of matter through these four main divisions is then precisely the task of a metaphysic of corporeal nature.

A general comment on the respective roles of mathematics and philosophy in the foundations of natural science is in order. What exactly does each discipline contribute to natural science, and why is each necessary? I am not sure that I fully understand Kant's answer to these questions, but it seems to be the following. Metaphysics is essential to natural science because it provides laws or necessary principles dealing with the existence of a thing or object, such as matter. Mathematics cannot provide this portion; for the existence of something, in contrast to its possibility, can never be given in an a priori intuition.[10] I assume that an example of this is the law of conservation of matter, which in the particular metaphysic of matter follows immediately from the proposition of universal (transcendental) metaphysics that in the processes of nature no substance can either be created or destroyed.[11] Secondly, it generally seems to be the task of metaphysics to provide the a priori principles of construction used by mathematics.[12] For lack of a well-grounded metaphysic, mathematicians have introduced and used concepts in physical science which transcend all possible experience.[13] It is the primary function of a particular metaphysic in relation to a positive natural science to provide a set of basic concepts and connected theorems which mathematics may safely build upon to develop a science, while remaining within the range of possible experience. The concept of empty space is, for Kant, a good example of an empty concept, that is, one which transcends experience; for empty space can never be an object of sensuous intuition, nor be properly derived from objects which are.[14] This is exactly the kind of logically neat concept which the mathematician, untutored in critical metaphysics, will introduce into natural science.

The positive role of mathematics in natural science is, of course, large. Kant emphasizes the necessity of mathematics by asserting that in every special doctrine, such as that of matter, there is only so much proper natural science as there is applied mathematics.[15] The reason is that in order to know a priori a determinate thing or object, such as matter, we must be able to know it from its mere (physical) possibility.[16] And the a priori knowledge of the physical possibility of a thing, in contradistinction to its merely logical possibility, can be obtained only by constructing the concept of the thing, that is, by an a priori intuition corresponding to the concept, which is nothing else than mathematics.[17] Mathematics is needed to provide the means for constructing the positive body of knowledge of proper natural science; philosophy is needed to provide a systematic set of concepts and principles which the mathematician may use and which do not transcend experience. The primary task of the *Anfangsgruende* is to carry the concept of matter through the table of the categories and thereby to provide the elements of a mathematical physics that is wholly in conformity with experience.

2. I turn now to Kant's use of the categories to find the specific determinations of matter. Within the Kantian framework a serious problem confronts us at once. How are we to begin? If the concept of matter is only clear and definite after it has been subsumed under the four functions of judgment, how can we represent any properties of matter as universal, essential, and necessary prior to this subsumption? That is, how do we

know where to begin? As August Stadler has remarked, Kant disposes of this particular problem with a casual, offhand remark that is not very satisfactory. Kant asserts: "Die Grundbestimmung eines Etwas, das ein Gegenstand aeusserer Sinne sein soll, musste Bewegung sein; denn dadurch allein koennen diese Sinne afficirt werden. Auf diese fuehrt auch der Verstand alle uebrige Praedikate der Materie, die zu ihrer Natur gehoeren, zurueck. . . ."[18] Since Kant remarks several times in the *Critique* that the concept of motion is derived empirically and is not pure and a priori,[19] from the standpoint of the Preface of the *Anfangsgruende* the relation between the concepts of matter and motion is baffling. The fundamental determination of an object of the external sense must be motion, he says, for only in this way can the external sense be affected. Now is this assertion analytic, a priori synthetic, or a posteriori synthetic? It can hardly be a priori synthetic, for it is not a proposition of mathematics, and its possibility as a valid synthetic metaphysical proposition seems to be ruled out by its assertion antecedent to the use of the categories. If it is a posteriori synthetic, Kant has violated his requirement that the *Anfangsgruende* takes from experience only the concept of matter and develops all else according to a priori principles. The only consistent alternative is that it is analytic, and this may be what Kant intends. He may hold that the concept of matter includes the concept of an object of the external sense, and that this latter includes the concept of motion. However, all of this is unstated, and the reader can only be uneasy over the nature of this fundamental assumption of the *Anfangsgruende*. In any case, Kant asserts that its introduction effectively reduces all proper natural science to a pure or applied theory of motion.[20] It is then as the doctrine or theory of motion (*Bewegungslehre*) that the *Anfangsgruende der Naturwissenschaft* is brought under the four divisions of the table of the categories. In the first division, matter is considered purely according to its *quantity* of motion, abstracted from all its qualities. This gives us the theory of phoronomy. In the second division, motion is considered as belonging to the *quality* of matter, "*unter dem Namen einer urspruenglich bewegenden Kraft.*"[21] This yields dynamics. The third division is mechanics; here, motion as quality is considered in *relation* to other reciprocal motions, or, more exactly, matter with this dynamical quality of possessing an original moving force is considered in reciprocal motion. In the fourth division, entitled phenomenology, matter in motion or at rest is considered according to its *modality*; that is, whether in its determination as phenomenon of the external sense it is determined as possible, real, or necessary.

It is the main function of the *Anfangsgruende* to elaborate this subsumption under the categories of the main divisions of mechanics, which is for Kant identical with mathematical physics. What this analysis particularly substantiates is Randall's claim that in setting forth the categories in the *Critique of Pure Reason*, Kant was "really analyzing the necessary relations in the system of Newtonian mechanics."[22]

3. Kant's analysis of the foundations of physics in the *Anfangsgruende* assigns a central role to fundamental forces of repulsion and attraction. He does not make the mistake of attempting to derive a priori specific mathematical laws that will characterize the nature of these forces, but he does derive, or at least argue for, a number of fundamental theorems, including Newton's third law of action and reaction. Without a detailed discussion of the derivation of these forces, we can still consider the central question of what is the epistemological or metaphysical relation of the fundamental forces of repulsion and attraction to the concept of matter itself. Kant emphasizes that the fundamental forces of repulsion and attraction cannot themselves be constructed; their possibility cannot be demonstrated. These fundamental forces are not derived from experience, nor can they be mathematically constructed from other concepts, which would be necessary to demonstrate their possibility. They are jointly the ultimate ground for the possibility of matter. If one asks why matter fills its space by these original forces, the only answer is that they are necessary conditions for the construction of the concept of matter. Reason can do no more than reduce the diverse forces appearing in nature to these two fundamental ones, "beyond which our reason cannot go."[23]

His own words clearly define his position: "That the possibility of the fundamental forces should be made comprehensible is a wholly impossible demand; for they are called fundamental forces, precisely because they can be derived from no others, that is, cannot be comprehended (*begriffen*)."[24]

If the fundamental forces cannot themselves be comprehended or explained, if they are each the source of an ultimate explanatory principle, and if the concept of them is used to construct the concept of matter, then the delicate problem arises: of what are these forces predicated? Is it a vicious circle to say they are forces *of* matter? Would it be more nearly correct to say that these forces *are* matter? This is not the same as asking for an explanation of the forces. Rather, accepting them as ultimate, we are asking the different question: to what do they belong, if anything? Boscovich answered this question by making forces ultimate in nature, but retaining as carriers of the forces a finite set of points of singularity. For Boscovich, forces are predicated of these points, which for him solves the question that we are now asking Kant. Kant eliminates all points of singularity in space which might serve as ultimate subjects of the forces. Empty space cannot be an object of experience, and every part, that is, every point, of filled space possesses forces of attraction and repulsion.

Now it is tempting to say that in abolishing all points of singularity and predicating forces of every point of space that can be experienced, Kant has unequivocally adopted a complete dynamical theory of matter and has asserted that forces are matter. There are passages in the Dynamics that lend definite support to this view. For instance, the General Remark on the Dynamics begins: "The universal principle of the dynamics of material nature is: that all reality of the objects of the external sense, which is not mere determination of space (place, extension and figure), must be regarded as moving force. . . ."[25] However, there does not seem to be a fully adequate case for this view. The discussion of substance in the *Critique* forms one of the chief blocks to such an interpretation. The first analogy of experience states the principle of the permanence of substance. This analogy is the rule corresponding to the category of inherence and subsistence. The principle states that in all changes of phenomena, substance is permanent and is neither decreased nor increased.[26] Substance is simply the substratum of all determinations in time, that is, of all changing phenomena. Kant's argument is that the bare succession of phenomena must have a permanent substratum as a necessary condition, for this substratum is "the condition of the possibility of all synthetical unity of perceptions, that is, of experience."[27] Without this substratum, the manifold of phenomena given in time could not be determined according to any rules, and could not be connected as objects enduring in time. Now the second analogy of experience, which corresponds to the category of causality, is that all changes take place according to the law of causality. For the moment, the important point of this is that changes must be changes in the determinations or states of the permanent substance, one state following another according to a given rule. The permanent substance provides the ground for the connection of successive states; in fact, if substance were created or destroyed, the universality of the law of causality would be violated.[28]

But what is the empirical criterion of substance? "Action . . . is a sufficient empirical criterion to prove substantiality, nor is it necessary that I should first establish its permanency by means of compared perceptions, which indeed would hardly be possible in this way, at least with that completeness which is required by the magnitude and strict universality of the concept."[29] Action directly implies the relation of the subject of causality (substance) to the effect. But for action there is needed the permanent substratum, for "actions are always the first ground of all change of phenomena, and cannot exist therefore in a subject that itself changes, because in that case other actions and another subject would be required to determine that change."[30] Actions, forces, cannot subsist by themselves but must be determinations of a permanent substratum. On the other hand, Kant says, substance "appearing in space," that is, matter, can only be known to us through the two fundamental forces of attraction and repulsion. Other properties of matter are unknown to us.[31]

Without going further into the systematic discussion of substance in the *Critique*, I believe we may now answer the question we asked about the fundamental forces. Matter, as spatial substance, as the ultimate subject of the science of physics, is not simply the two fundamental forces. It is true that the concepts of these two forces are precisely those which permit us to construct the concept of matter, that is, represent it in intuition; and simply as an object of intuition, matter is equivalent with them. However, matter as substance is also the permanent substratum of all spatial phenomena. The fundamental forces are not this permanent substratum, but rather it is "the amount of the fundamental forces" possessed by a given part of this substratum that determines its particular state. The mathematician or physicist, dealing as he does only with pure or empirical intuitions, might successfully equate the fundamental forces and matter; but the philosopher, probing at the foundations of the data of intuition, knows that the fundamental forces are not the ultimate subject in space, but are the specific determinations of that subject (the permanent substratum). And this conclusion is supported in the third division of the *Anfangsgruende*, where Kant specifically states that the quantity of substance in a matter, that is, the quantity of the permanent substratum, is not a function of the amount of the fundamental forces in that matter, but must be estimated mechanically, that is, by the amount of its motion.[32]

It seems to me that this discussion of force and matter in Kant—the delicate effort he makes to assign a fundamental place to force, and yet not eliminate an independent concept of matter—is still pertinent today. It is particularly relevant to the tangled problems of thinking about force, matter, and energy, in any conceptually clear way, in the context of contemporary nuclear physics. I don't mean to suggest that detailed answers for today's puzzles are to be found in reading Kant. I do think that some of the too-simple models we associate with the Cartesian and Newtonian tradition would be more easily rejected as inadequate on general philosophical grounds if we took seriously Kant's careful and discriminating analysis.

4. The simple ideas of atomism and Cartesian physics have played far too dominant a role in our thinking about the fundamental kinds of explanations we are willing to accept for physical phenomena. More clearly, I would say, than any other philosopher, Kant drew the lines in a nearly consistent fashion between mechanical and dynamical explanations

of nature. He stated the virtues and strengths of the dynamical approach more explicitly than any preceding philosopher, and what he has to say is of interest today for some of the reasons just stated.

In the seventeenth and eighteenth centuries, "mechanics" and its derivative words were not defined as generally as they are today, and there was considerable controversy over what should be counted as mechanical explanations and as part of the science of mechanics. The Cartesians were the great reductionists in this debate; for they insisted on restricting mechanics to kinematics, plus only one kind of force or action: the motion communicated by one body to another through direct contact. Newton tried to stay out of this controversy by insisting that he studied only the mathematical, not the physical properties of forces, that is, the causes of motion. Newton's followers, however, challenged the Cartesian view; Boscovich, for instance, insists that mechanics is not limited to the study of impulsive actions, but may include the study of any forces which produce motion and change of motion according to general laws. Boscovich does have certain reservations about committing himself on the ultimate "physical" modes of action. It is Kant who states the problem most clearly and faces the issues most directly. As Kant sees it, the only two ways to explain the specific phenomena of nature are the mechanical and the dynamical. Here we use the word "mechanical" in the limited Cartesian sense, not in the general way it is used today. As stated above, the (Cartesian) mechanical method of explanation limits itself to assuming that the non-uniform motion of a body is entirely due to the actual motions of other bodies communicated to it only by direct impulse; the introduction of any other cause of motion smacks of the occult qualities of the Scholastics. The dynamical method, on the other hand, assumes that the non-uniform motion of a body may also be due to the repulsive and attractive forces of other bodies, these forces being fundamental physical properties of the bodies, which are independent of their actual motions.

An examination of Kant's discussion of this mechanical-dynamical controversy affords an opportunity to present Kant's own evaluation of his construction of the concept of matter by original moving forces.[33] The genuine problem is not simply to account for matter filling space, but to account for the specific varieties of matter that fill space.[34] The mechanical method of explanation, Kant says, assumes that matter is composed of primal bodies (atoms) possessing the following properties: absolute impenetrability, absolute homogeneity, and absolute unconquerability (by any forces) of the cohesion of the matter of these primal bodies.[35] From primitive matter of this kind, the mechanical method attempts to deduce an explanation of the specific varieties of different matter found in the universe. In this deduction, the assumption most characteristic of the mechanical method is added: the assumption that the different densities of different matters can only be accounted for by the distribution of empty spaces between the homogeneous primal bodies. Since the primal bodies cannot themselves be observed, the validity of the mechanical method really hinges on the supposed necessity of this last assumption of interspersed empty spaces. To establish a dynamical mode of explanation, with its several advantages, it is thus required only to refute the supposed necessity of this assumption by showing how density differences can be conceived and explained in another way.[36] This is easily done. The theorems of the Dynamics have shown that matter may be conceived to fill its space, not by absolute impenetrability, but by a repulsive force. The definite degree of this filling is a function of the balance of the repulsive and attractive forces. The attractive force is regulated by the quantity of matter considered, but the repulsive force may vary in a continuous and unlimited fashion. Thus the different densities of two different matters are accounted for by a difference in the degree of their repulsive forces. In fact, Kant asserts, in this way one can conceive a matter such as the ether which wholly fills its space without any void, and yet has for a given volume a quantity of matter which is far less than that of any body we can subject to experiment. All we need do for a matter such as the ether is to conceive its repulsive force as incomparably greater than its attractive force.[37] In general, therefore, there is no question that the supposed necessity for the assumption of empty spaces is directly refuted.

With this out of the way, we may examine the comparative advantages of the dynamical method. The largest critical or negative advantage of the dynamical method is that natural science is relieved of the burden of manufacturing a world "from fullness and emptiness according to fancy."[38] This negative advantage results from having got rid of the necessity for assuming empty space, which can never be an object of experience nor therefore of any possible experiments. The positive advantage of this method is the extension of the field of the scientific investigator to the proper, fundamental forces of matter itself. Traditional mechanical theories, from Democritus to Descartes, have denied such forces and thereby unduly limited the concepts available to the scientist. However, it must be carefully noted, Kant asserts, that this positive advantage cannot be extended to the construction of the specific varieties of matter, but only to the concept of matter in general. The specific determinations of the fundamental forces cannot be constructed on a priori grounds, and consequently the specific varieties of matter can never be deduced in an a priori manner.[39] In fact, on a priori grounds, the mathematico-mechanical method can go further than the metaphysico-dynamical method; for the distribution of ultimate parts of matter of given figure and size can easily be represented in intuition, which permits the construction of specific matters. But, as has been noted, the mechanical method pays for this single advantage at a high price. It makes fundamental the empty concept of absolute impenetrability, which is nothing else than a *qualitas occulta*: it must use the concept of empty space, it gives up all the proper forces of matter, and in general it must give more free reign to fancy and imagination than is consistent with the caution necessary in science and philosophy.[40] Kant sums up this evaluation by saying that the most that metaphysical research can hope to do is to lead natural science to the dynamical method of explanation, which alone is capable of definite laws lying within actual experience and cohering in a rational manner.[41] Metaphysics can carry us no further than the general framework of the theorems of the *Anfangsgruende*; for besides these, "no law whatever of the attractive and repulsive forces may be ventured on a priori conjectures, but everything, even the universal attraction as cause of gravity must, together with its law, be inferred from the data of experience."[42]

This final passage may serve as a warning as to how cautious we must be in interpreting the range of Kant's commitment to an a priori physics. He emphasizes in this passage as elsewhere that even so fundamental a law as the law of universal gravitational attraction cannot be derived from the concept of motion subsumed under the categories, but must itself be inferred from the data of experience. Randall's own emphasis on Kant's deep respect for the facts—all the facts—of experience is indeed one of the excellent features of his analysis of Kant's philosophy of science.

N O T E S

1. References are to the first edition (Riga, 1786). In the two other editions of this work, 1787 and 1800, published during Kant's lifetime, no changes were made in the text. Use has also been made of Belford Bax's translation, *Metaphysical Foundations of Natural Science* (London, 1900), but this translation is not very satisfactory. I am responsible for the few translations given in this article. Translations of short passages from *The Critique of Pure Reason* are taken from the Muller translation, 2nd edition, revised (New York, 1949).

2. *Anfangsgruende*, p. VIII.

3. *Critique*, A720-1, B748-9.

4. *Ibid.*, A161, B200. The table of principles, derived from the table of categories, provides all the fundamental principles of the pure understanding, insofar as the actual representations given in intuition are disregarded. Once these are considered, we derive from this table the principles of mathematics and of general physical dynamics. Cf. A162, B201-02.

5. For statements on this, see *ibid.*, A13-14, A81-82, B27-28, B107-08.

6. *Ibid.*, A848, B876.

7. *Anfangsgruende*, p. VIII.

8. *Ibid.*, p. XIV.

9. "Denn mehr giebt es nicht rein Verstandesbegriffe, die die Natur der Dinge betreffen koennen" (*ibid.*, pp. XV-XVI).

10. *Ibid.*, p. VII.

11. *Ibid.*, pp. 116-7; see also *Critique*, B224-5.

12. *Anfangsgruende*, p. XII.

13. *Critique*, A847, B875, footnote.

14. *Ibid.*, A172, B214; *Anfangsgruende*, 81-83, 105, 145-158.

15. *Anfangsgruende*, p. VIII.

16. Kant does not actually speak of "physical" possibility. It might be better to use "real possibility," meaning "capable of being presented in intuition." The deviation from Kantian terminology is merely in the interest of clearer exposition.

17. *Ibid.*, p. IX.

18. *Ibid.*, p. XX. Stadler's comment on this passage: "Warum musste sie das sein? Woher stammt die behauptete Notwendigkeit? Wer lehrt uns, dass die Sinne allein durch Bewegung afficirt werden koenen? Wenn eine Grundbestimmung eingefuehrt wird, so koennen wir uns doch nicht bei der blossen Thatsache beruhigen, sondern muessen eine Legitimation verlangen. Allein es findet sich kein Wort der Erklaerung." *Kants Theorie der Materie* (Leipzig, 1883), p. 6.

19. Cf. also *Anfangsgruende*, p. 4.

20. This statement is legitimate, for Kant dismisses the possibility of empirical psychology being a proper natural science. This leaves only physics. See *ibid.*, p. X-XI.

21. *Ibid.*, p. XXI.

22. *The Career of Philosophy*, Vol. II, p. 140.

23. "Denn es ist ueberhaupt ueber den Gesichtskreis unserer Vernunft gelegen, urspruengliche Kraefte a priori ihrer Moeglichkeit nach einzusehen, vielmehr besteht alle Naturphilosophie in der Zurueckfuehrung gegebener, dem Anscheine nach verschiedener Kraefte auf eine geringere Zahl Kraefte und Vermoegen, die zu Erklaerung der Wirkungen der ersten zulangen, welche Reduktion aber nur bis zu Grundkraeften fortgeht, ueber die unsere Vernunft nicht hinaus kann." *Anfangsgruende*, p. 104.

24. *Ibid.*, Lehrsatz VII, *Anmerkung* 1, p. 61.

25. *Ibid.*, p. 81.

26. *Critique*, B224.

27. *Ibid.*, A183, B226-27.

28. *Ibid.*, B232-33.

29. *Ibid.*, A205, B250-51.

30. *Ibid.*, A205, B250.

31. *Ibid.*, A265, B321.

32. *Anfangsgruende*, Drittes Haupstueck, Lehrsatz I, *Anmerkung*, pp. 114-115. In this passage Kant practically concedes the empirical point again—that is, that the

only properties of matter known to us are the fundamental forces (and that which is derived from them). For he admits that in determining the quantity of matter by the standard procedure of weighing it, we are dependent on the fundamental force of attraction, and thus determine it mechanically only indirectly.

33. The relevant remarks are primarily to be found in the "Allgemeine Anmerkung zur Dynamik," *Anfangsgruende*, pp. 81-105.

34. *Ibid.*, p. 100.

35. *Ibid.*, pp. 100-01.

36. *Ibid.*, p. 102.

37. *Ibid.*, pp. 102-03.

38. *Ibid.*, p. 83.

39. *Ibid.*, pp. 83-84.

40. *Ibid.*, pp. 84-85.

41. *Ibid.*, pp. 104-05.

42. *Ibid.*, pp. 103-04.

J. GLENN GRAY
Colorado College

Randall on German Idealism

The first thing to remark about Professor Randall's writings on German philosophy is the generous quality of his interpretation. In the second volume of *The Career of Philosophy*, he devotes over four hundred pages to "Building the German Tradition." Moreover, these pages contain some of the most eloquent writing which he has ever achieved. They reflect his great appreciation for the contributions of the Germans to Western civilization and to contemporary American culture.

Very early the reader becomes aware that Randall is not a prisoner of the anti-idealistic tendencies of recent Anglo-American thought. Nor is he inclined to blame the aberrations of German politics and social reactionism on German philosophers—in this respect being very unlike his admired predecessors John Dewey and George Santayana. Instead, his energies are centered on tracing the roots of German philosophy back to classic Greek thinking and Christian theology, and to showing how successfully that tradition contributes to present-day philosophic naturalism.

This second volume follows the development of German thought from Leibniz through Karl Marx and Friedrich Engels, leaving to the concluding one of the *Career* the events of the last hundred years. Its eighteen chapters are aptly apportioned among those devoted to the broad outlines of that development: "The German *Aufklärung*," "The Romantic Appeal to Experience," "Romantic Idealism," etc., and those treating in detail major and minor figures within these movements. A just balance between these two necessary tasks is not easy to maintain. In my judgment Randall has achieved it far better than his predecessors among historians of philosophy. This alone should make his book of enduring worth to generations of students. Though disagreement with many of his generalizations is inevitable, the value of his compact summaries and judicious quotations of key passages from individual thinkers can hardly be disputed. Hence, the second thing to remark about Randall's interpretation is its achievement of both inclusiveness and proportion.

Let me now suggest in summary fashion a few of the main considerations governing his analysis of this tradition. For him German thought has been characterized by a "sense of the multiplicity of human values, the intense need for some all-embracing scheme that would afford an intelligible reconciliation of them all, moral, esthetic, and religious, as well as purely scientific" (pp. 3, 4).* This passion for inclusiveness and reconciliation of everything originated with Leibniz, Germany's first great philosopher. And it continued to govern the aspirations of Enlightenment and Romantic thinkers throughout the enormously productive period of German culture from about 1770 to 1830.

In their insistence on taking into account man's total experience, Germans opposed the reductive analyses made fashionable by Descartes and Hobbes, a reductionism that seemed to follow from the atomistic and mathematical science of the sixteenth and seventeenth centuries. Such a narrow scientific ideal tended to make human values unintelligible, or at least to make them merely subjective. The Germans strenuously resisted this dominant trend of western European thought. As Randall puts it, "Germans at no time felt that natural science explained everything, or that its methods were alone valid" (p. 53). Rather, they tried to see things whole, to recover the ancient Greek vision of an intelligible world, in which man's artistic, moral, and religious possessions had as secure a place as his scientific knowledge.

> German rationalism was at bottom teleological and moral, not scientific; it meant, not a new and radical science of human nature and society, but God, freedom, and immortality. When rationalistic materialism and empirical scepticism, the two "scientific" philosophies of the late eighteenth century, developed into open hostility to the religious world-view, it was science and not religion that was curbed and put in its proper and subordinate place. And hence it was that the reaction against the complete adequacy of the method and the "reason" of the eighteenth-century scientific enterprise, started in Germany (pp. 54, 55).

Kant, whom Randall has no hesitation in naming "without question the most influential modern philosopher" (p. 106) despite the usual American preference for Hume, followed in the path of the intellectual tradition stemming from Leibniz and popular convictions as well. Randall seeks to explicate Kant's problems and his solutions from the perspective of his German heritage, in contrast to the usual historian's practice of deriving him from Hume and the empiricist-rationalist controversy. This means that *The Critique of Pure Reason* does not monopolize attention to anything like the extent it usually has. Putting Kant in the larger framework of his own culture as well as of Europe enables Randall to devote

---

* All quotations are from Volume II of *The Career of Philosophy*.

one chapter to his pre-critical writings, and other chapters to the frequently neglected *Critique of Judgment* and to his brief but first-rate works on politics and history. Randall's approach is here much more reminiscent of Continental practice than of the Anglo-American.

That Randall is much more than a chronicler of philosophic doctrines and influences, that he is a penetrating critic of culture and a philosopher in his own right, becomes particularly evident in these chapters devoted to Kant. To illustrate, perhaps I may be permitted to sketch the substance of Kant's problems as Randall sets them forth. First, Kant was concerned to vindicate the reality of science as synthesized by Newton and to establish its claims to truth and certainty against the attacks of radical empiricism on the one hand and religious orthodoxy on the other. His critical epistemology was designed to do justice to the warring claims of English empiricists and Continental rationalists, but above all, to establish the fact that man does possess scientific truth about his world. However, Kant does not stop here. Man is also a moral being, and the authority of rational ideals over his conduct is as truly compelling as scientific demonstration. Moerover, there is the fact of artistic creation, product of man's imaginative powers, and it too must be taken fully into account if we are to do justice to total experience.

> In all this, Kant stands with many of his contemporaries as a critic of the inadequacy of the exclusively and narrowly scientific ideal of the Age of Reason, which set up scientific principles and values as the norm to which all else must conform. He is calling men back to experience again; he is insisting on the autonomy of those other and nonscientific areas of human living, where truth and demonstration are not the primary values aimed at, although they may be treated and organized by scientific methods—by "reason." His is a philosophy of experience far more profound and penetrating then the so-called "empiricism" of the eighteenth century which had arrogated to itself that name.
>
> But in addition to this deep humility before the facts of man's living experience, Kant had also a profound passion for intelligibility. . . . In this, Kant stands as the heir of the philosophic enterprises of the ages from the Greeks, down, committed to the faith that the universe must be ultimately "rational," that is, intelligible or "noumenal"—Kant preferred the Greek term—even though that perfect rationality be not completely accessible to the imperfect mind of man (pp. 108, 109).

So conceived, it is possible for the reader to view Kant as a conservative of the best of the past and also as a forerunner of the radical Romantic revolt to come. By some he was thought to be the destroyer of every religious certainty; by others, the preserver of religion and science. In these pages he is seen to be close to the center of scientific, moral, and religious crosscurrents of the Enlightenment, and yet a source and inspiration for the critics that were preparing a new age. We are, in short, not simply told that Kant is the most influential modern philosopher, but given ample demonstration why he has been so influential. For Randall the reason lies more in his clear perceptions of the crucial issues of his time than in the solutions he attained.

This brings me to the second mainspring of Randall's interpretation, namely, to the central role that is assigned to creative imagination in this tradition. For the Germans, *Verstand* (analytic reason) stands in conflict with *Vernunft* (intuitive reason), and the latter is philosophy's ultimate resource against science, "common sense," and religious orthodoxy. As the highest human capacity, this intuitive reason, or intellectual intuition, served the Germans variously. Randall, who calls it "the central idea of German philosophy" (p. 99), likens it to *Nous* of the Greeks and considers it the instrument Germans used to appeal beyond a calculative, distinction-making, and separating intellect to a reason suffused with feeling and sentiment. For all of them the mind is active and creative, not simply receptive and analytical. As its highest capacity, imagination is spontaneous, synthesizing, and able to overcome the dualisms of sense and analytic reason. Imagination unites nature and culture, thereby transcending the artificial boundaries that divide the various disciplines.

The centrality of *Vernunft*, however, makes German idealism hard for an outsider to grasp and treat in scholarly terms. For better or worse, German thought in its classic period is an amalgam of art, religion, and philosophy, and it is impossible either to separate them clearly or to treat one or the other in isolation. Not only did artists, theologians, and philosophers study each other's books, also each endeavored to incorporate into his own sphere the insights and strength of the other field. For example, to interpret Hegel adequately, it is requisite to grasp not merely the systems of Leibniz and Kant but the intuitions of Goethe, Schiller, Hölderlin, and a long line of theologians, too. It is often difficult to say whether Herder, Lessing, and Schiller are primarily literary men or philosophers. Hegel's philosophy of religion and philosophy of art show him to be as profoundly at home in these areas as he is in metaphysics and the history of philosophy.

Hence, Randall finds it necessary to devote chapters to "Aesthetic Idealism," treating figures like Schlegel, Hölderlin, Novalis, and Schleiermacher, and to "Romantic Reinterpretations of Religion," where once again he takes up Hegel and Schleiermacher and adds Ritschl. Likewise, in his discussion of the German Forty-Eighters, he is compelled to deal with men like D. F. Strauss, Bruno Bauer, and Feuerbach from both the point of view of their contributions to religious criticism, and of their influence on the rise of Marxism. It is even hard to characterize Marx and Engels. Like so many of the others they are hardly "pure" philosophers, literary men, or theologians, and they have some pretensions to being social scientists.

Randall's long study of religion enables him to view this complex feature of the German scene in the eighteenth and nineteenth centuries more knowledgeably and sympathetically than most American scholars can. I am not aware of other histories of philosophic thought in English which contain anything similar to his careful study of the epistemological claims for religious experience of such thinkers.

More important than this erasing of boundaries, the higher function of *Vernunft* gave rise to that "fascinating, productive, and withal strange episode in the history of human thought" (p. 192) which we inadequately call Romanticism. Randall believes that the attempt to understand this disposition of mind forms a crucial challenge for anyone trying to come to grips with German thought. Though the movement was initiated in some sense by Kant's third critique, with his emphasis in that work on the place of creative imagination, the cautious Kant of the first critique became "an almost unmitigated curse" (p. 202) to the Romantic idealists. Why? Kant's reverence for facts, his unquestioned competence in the science of the age, his scepticism about man's capacity finally to know the highest truths, are a striking contrast to the confidence of this "host of fools who rushed in where Kant himself feared to tread—poetic, imaginative, and inspired fools, to be sure!" (p. 110)

What is the clue to understanding the essence of this Romantic idealism? Again and again Randall tries more or less successfully to capture it in language as he recurs to the theme throughout the chapters from Fichte to the Forty-Eighters. He is persuaded that even Marx and Engels are Romantics, that what we call today dialectical materialism is really a late version of idealism. Here is one of Randall's more successful efforts which I prefer to quote at some length.

> Romanticism as a temper and attitude is proudly multifarious and inconsistent; the most imposing philosophy that emerged from its conflicting tendencies makes contradiction a necessary element in all genuine thought. This was but natural in a movement whose one bond of union was the desire to escape the restrictions of a neatly articulated system of rational concepts. But viewed positively rather than as merely negative and emancipating, Romantic thought stands out as another stage in that never-ending process of criticism which we have already seen oscillating between the appeal to reason and the appeal to experience.   (p. 196)

And so Romanticism burst asunder the tight little world of Newtonian science. It called men back to experiences, facts, and values forgotten in the first enthusiasm for the mathematical interpretation of nature and of human life. Physics might be a marvellous tool: the Romanticists were only too glad to allow it to do its own work in its own field. But it was not the whole of life, nor did it provide the scheme whereby the important issues of human living could be understood. It failed to understand man and his eternal interests, art, religion, moral striving, and aspiration; and it had ended by failing to understand even itself. The very activity of scientific investigation, the very fact of the existence of science, grew unintelligible in the world it purported to describe.

The scientific ideal of the Age of Reason fell into disrepute, not because its beliefs were not "true" and "sound," though in many ways they were enlarged and made more adequate for their own purposes, but because the ideal of life it offered men was thin and flat and meager, because the values by which men live are not exhausted in the endeavor to be "scientific." The great idealistic traditions, those of Plato and Aristotle, of Thomas and Dante, of Goethe and Hegel, are incomparably richer in the values they include. They are far more adequate expressions of human nature, with all its wealth of symbol and value. . . . The Idealists, indeed, are the only thinkers of modern times to attempt a formulation of the Good Life that shall include all the facts and all the values. Theirs are the only ideals worthy of comparison with those of the Greeks or the Medievalists; they are the only modern philosophers, until this century, who have really cared about wisdom.   (pp. 198, 199)

Perhaps the decisive word in this interpretation of the idealists is experience, which Randall, like Dewey before him, cherishes as a near-absolute in the philosophic enterprise. The German trust in *Vernunft* and productive imagination (the two are not very different) impresses Randall as a way to overcome the dualisms that have plagued the French and British traditions in their preoccupation with rationalism and empiricism and the consequent overemphasis on *how* we know. German thought—and particularly Romanticism which culminated but did not end with Hegel—has been centered on the idea of Truth as the whole. It was Hegel who insisted that only the totality of any entity seen in its widest relationships is concrete; anything short of that is bound to be abstract, one-sided, and hence not fully real.

It is this basic insight of Hegel's that most impresses Randall, who in his omnivorous reading, erudition, and breadth of interest somewhat resembles Hegel. Truth as the whole, as the Concrete Universal, is a concept which provides Randall with his wide sympathies for the Renaissance man, for him to whom poetry is as crucial as science, religion as central as politics, and who is ever on the search for the sweeping generalization which will unite all. One of Randall's deepest motivations is a dislike for all reductionist analyses. Put more affirmatively, it is a conviction that only that interpretation can be sound which strives to leave nothing out of account which men can possibly experience. The more breadth and depth an interpretation has, the more concrete and true it will be.

To some of us, former students of his, it seems clear that Randall's own position can best be characterized as Romantic pragmatism, a position he has come to as a consequence of his long study of Greek and German thought, beginning in his youth, under Dewey, Woodbridge, and other American naturalists. He owes relatively little to the British or French heritage.

There is something troubling about the pragmatism of this position of his. Despite his assurance that nineteenth-century idealism recovered the Greek vision and transmitted it to us of the present day to be worked up into humanistic and naturalistic philosophies, one is tempted to wonder how much has been lost. Before I proceed with this *caveat*, let me quote Randall's account of the final significance of Romantic idealism:

> Broadly speaking, such an idealism is true, as Platonism is "true" or as the Christian philosophy is "true": each is a true interpretation of human experience, a wise exploring of the possibilities of human life. . . . It is an imaginative and symbolic rendering of life, illuminating its possibilities rather than describing its actual limitations. Romantic Idealists like Fichte make no claim to the possession of literal truth: Kant had banished for them that illusion. What they proclaim is rather a faith, a faith that will give meaning to life. It is the claim of the Idealists that science is not the literal truth either, that all renderings of experience are symbolic interpretations, that all discourse and all knowledge is a metaphor. That is what they learned from Kant; and whether it be learned from Kant or not, it is certainly "so." Idealism, that is, is not science, but imagination, poetry, and art—and so is science!   (pp. 202, 203)

Randall proceeds to designate all of these systems as "mythologies," to be judged in terms of the kind of life they lead to. They are not susceptible of proof except in the pragmatic sense of whether they enable one to make sense of experience and to create a fruitful existence. He is quite ready to concede that the world of science is "as anthropomorphic as any other; it is a human interpretation of a single part of our experience" (p. 205). Though the idealists were partial and one-sided in the facts they used to interpret the nature of reality, science is not less so in choosing other kinds of facts. Again and again Randall recurs to this basic pragmatism of his and assures us that "the Romantic Idealists were in one sense all pragmatists" (p. 204).

What is one to say of this? When I first heard it twenty years ago in Randall's course at Columbia, I found it greatly liberating. And I confess

I still find it appealing. But as the years pass, doubts have crept in. Let me try to formulate one or two of them. First, there appears to be a want of final seriousness about this position. If all men's philosophies are simply mythologies and the sole criterion is whether they are good or poor ones in terms of the kind of life they offer us, how are we to be rescued from an ultimate scepticism about truth? For a divine being such a view might not be paralyzing of effort, but only because such a being would possess the whole.

To Randall's assertion that the idealists were in one sense all pragmatists, I would reply, Yes, but not in the most important sense; not, that is, about the priority of truth. In the foreword to Volume II where he gives credit to his colleague, Albert Hofstadter, he comments wryly: "His sympathies with philosophic Idealism and with German philosophy make him hesitate to deny 'Truth' to that Idealism, and to see in it the perhaps higher function of imaginative symbolism." I wonder how one is to justify imaginative symbolism finally other than on the grounds of truth. It seems to me, in short, that a pragmatic position like this fails to take truth seriously enough. There lurks in it at bottom a sort of mocking scepticism which is somewhat alien both to our classic Greek and to our German inheritance.

Secondly, and perhaps more basically, this view suffers from a subjectivity that makes man too central in the scheme of things. It is one thing to grant that all our philosophies are human, only too human; it is quite another to make a virtue of it. If the price of making Romanticism relevant is to make the comprehensive visions of its protagonists mythological, then I think the price is too high. However tempting such a position is in our age when all principles have become uncertain, it will hardly aid us in overcoming today's widespread feeling of the irrelevance of anything philosophic.

Moreover, subjectivism in philosophy and its close ally scepticism are hardly the proper lesson to draw from the drama of German thought, despite our twentieth-century infections. The Romantics did not revolt against the inadequate scientific ideal of the Enlightenment, and seek to take man's moral, artistic, and religious experience into account as equally revelatory of the nature of things—in search of mythologies. They were very much in earnest not only about the good life but about the vision of truth, too. And their impulse was always away from the personal and the anthropomorphic. Randall knows this well, for he frequently cites it, even in the case of Fichte, who perhaps came closest to being a subjective idealist.

It was precisely their emphasis on experience that saved them from separating man from the world of nature. German idealism is monistic in metaphysics in several senses. First, man's mind is not apart from but a part of the larger mind that is exhibited in the order and structure of nature. In this idealism *Geist* comprehends both man and nature, and is alike operative in physical processes and in human history. Secondly, and as a consequence, moral and esthetic values are as objective as are the phenomena studied by natural science. The Germans insisted that there can be a science of ethics and of esthetics as truly as there can be a science of physics or geology. Third, by means of intellectual intuition or *Vernunft* they avoided the disjunction of reason and feeling and sought the unity of religion and science by appealing to the sameness of their goals, or by a genetic analysis of their past, or by differentiating them in terms of their function in experience. In every case the drive was not only away from dualisms but also against a merely subjective interpretation of experience.

In his chapters on Schelling and Hegel—superbly conceived and worked out, in my judgment—Randall himself demonstrates that the urge for inclusiveness and comprehensiveness on the part of the best of the Romanticists led inexorably away from the Self and from anthropocentrism in general. Schelling made artistic productivity (in contrast with esthetic sensibility) the pathway of escape from the Ego and its presumed overemphasis in the Fichtean philosophy. Of Schelling, Randall writes that he took Kant's *Critique of Judgment* far more seriously than its author did:

> In the process of artistic creation is to be found that fundamental activity of the Self of which knowledge and will are partial and opposed expressions. Indeed, in art the human Self becomes one with the productive process of Nature, and is conscious of the cosmic creative energy working through its own free acts. In art the very goal of the universe is attained: in the artist's experience the Absolute becomes aware of itself at last as productive activity, and man's conscious creation of beauty is thus the ultimate reason for all existence.   (p. 260)

> In the artistic attitude lies the fulfillment of the philosopher's long search, the ultimate metaphysical key to reconciling all oppositions in a final synthesis—necessity and freedom, the real and the ideal, the unconscious and the conscious, nature and thought. . . . This use of the process of artistic creation as the all-inclusive context within which the classic metaphysical oppositions of contingency and necessity, activity and structure, are seen as functional distinctions, is a foreshadowing of much present-day thought: these pages might almost have been written by John Dewey.   (p. 261)

For Hegel, of course, even this Schellingian stance was too egocentric. His philosophizing begins from the totality of human history; he seeks the truth in institutions, in the rise and fall of peoples, and even more in the phenomenologies of art, religion, and philosophy which have appeared in the course of ages. All such appearances are transient because they contain inner contradictions, partial truths, and must give way to more inclusive visions into which the positive elements of the former are absorbed.

Hegel heaped scorn on Romantic "feeling," on his predecessors over-estimation of the role of the private, single person in contrast to the grand sweep of history. For him what mattered really was what gets itself incorporated in the objective forms of culture. Though he sought to be just to the essential values of individuality—so dear to many of his fellow idealists—Hegel's vision is directed outward, toward larger wholes. His individual is forever turning into a universal, hence the massive reaction of Existentialism of the last century, which he did so much to originate.

Randall is appreciative of this "realism" of the greatest of the ideal-ists; he cherishes particularly Hegel's social insights and the uncom-promising priority which he gives to the cultural and the institutional. But I am not convinced that Randall estimates correctly Hegel's tendency to place highest in his scale of the concrete and real, not this "objective spirit," but "absolute spirit," namely, the ideal realms of art, religion, and philosophy. In his rejection of the subjective spirit, Hegel pushed beyond the simply objective spirit of institutions and forms of culture to that spirit which subsumed them both in a higher unity, the residue of truth leavening man's ideas and organizations in his restless course through history.

Though many of us would unhesitatingly reject the pan-logism of Hegel's *Weltgeist*, we would tend to value more than Randall seems to, the fruits of Hegel's thought in this latter realm. Hegel's lectures on art, religion, and the history of philosophy seem, to me at least, to be richer in insights than most of what he says in the philosophies of history and law. They are still largely neglected because they are not as controversial or politically effective as the *Philosophy of Right*.

But the basic point I wish to reiterate is that the direction of Roman-ticism, in its philosophical formulations, seems to be away from the psychological and toward the ontological. Its philosophers were interested, I think, not primarily in the good, but in the true. That their visions frequently led to a recrudescence of Platonism and Augustinianism seems to Randall to be a misfortune. Their genius should have led them forward to present-day naturalism, not backward to a divine source and to an affirmation of God. As Randall puts it in the case of Hegel:

> But to view the Hegelian philosophy as essentially a bulwark of tradi-tional religious faith is quite unjustified, for all the traditional problems

of religion break out again with the same insistence within the Hegelian world; and in fact wherever it was adopted, the Hegelian position immediately proceeded to work itself out into a naturalistic metaphysics, in the Left-Wing Hegelians, in the British Hegelianism of Bradley, in the American Hegelianism of John Dewey. (p. 306)

This may be said to be the third major guideline of Randall's interpretation of the German tradition, that is, his reading it in naturalistic terms. But I wonder. First, there are other followers of Hegel than these, and the right-wingers and conservatives can find much aid and comfort in Hegel, too, particularly the religious variety. Having recently studied the concluding volume of Hegel's lectures in *The Philosophy of Religion*—lectures he continued till his death in Berlin—I am far from sure that those who read him in naturalistic terms are as conversant with his secrets as they seem. Today we want him to be a humanist, but that is different from what he considered himself to be in the 1820's, namely, a Christian philosopher. However strong the infusion of Hellenism and the Greek forerunners of Christian theology is in this final formulation, Hegel seems to come out in some specifiable sense as a theist. At all events, he is hardly the religious radical of the early writings.

However that may be, it appears to me mistaken to read philosophers like Fichte, Schelling, and Hegel as turning or returning to religious absolutes in order to give their systems of thought final authority. I think it truer to say that they found religious convictions more compelling than most philosophers today. Certainly they are not Christian apologists in any sense. Having worked so hard to overcome the sundering of man's unity in their German past, they were clearly not interested in a supernatural realm set over against the human and natural. Like the Aristotle of Book Lambda, the idea of God, or the Absolute (a term they preferred), was for them the culmination of a vision of the universe they had sought and found in their restless search to be all-inclusive. God is a Power and a Presence, not a person, the substance of that life they sensed to be regnant in both spirit and nature. The Absolute was the capstone on their various programs for reconciling Greek philosophy and Christian revelation.

Whatever the limitations of this Absolute, or God, it did prevent them from subjectivizing truth or viewing the world in exclusively human terms. Without the Absolute, later German philosophy was immediately threatened by subjectivism—and even nihilism, as in Schopenhauer, Nietzsche, and in certain forms of current Existentialism. We should hardly minimize this threat in our tormented times. Nor should we dismiss so lightly the function of the Absolute in these systems as a regulative, not a constitutive, idea and ideal.

I realize that Randall in characterizing these philosophies as good mythologies intends to praise them, and is not denying the truth to be found in mythological form. Yet I cannot help remembering the harsh words Hegel used against Plato's reliance on myths, and his preference for Aristotelian sobriety. But the larger issue here is whether Romantic idealism was, consciously or not, interpreting the world primarily in terms of human good, or in terms of truth, in which human beings participate, to be sure, but do not create. I feel they were doing the latter, but I look forward to reading other contributors to this volume on one of Professor Randall's chief philosophical tenets.

My own objection to Romantic idealism is curiously different from Randall's, and one his pages only occasionally imply. In their zeal to correct the inadequacies of Enlightenment thought in the British and French versions, the Romantic idealists went too far in surmise and speculation. In some sense, as Randall says, they were poetic, imaginative, and inspired fools, but fools nevertheless; though the term is too harsh for what I have in mind. Too often they transcended the sphere of legitimate experience in their endeavors at inclusiveness and comprehensiveness. Despite one's sympathies with Hegel (and many of the others, too) it is hard to avoid the conviction that there is a large measure of presumption and overweening pride in this confidence of "the Truth" at last attained. They could have used more than a measure of the caution of Kant, and called what they hastened to work out and designate as science and system a philosophical faith, as he did.

In short, I agree with Randall in his major emphasis that the idealists were seeking to take account of man's total experience, in their various ways. And their works are a treasure house of brilliant insights in theological, aesthetic, and metaphysical realms. But in reading them today, one must pick and choose and leave much behind that exceeds the bounds of what mortal man can possibly experience with any clarity or with assurance that he is not dreaming.

Despite these reservations about Randall's own faith—I use the word reservations intentionally—it must be said that his position affects his treatment of the German tradition very little. And the price one pays is trivial in contrast with the value received from reading this interpretation by a first-rate mind, rather than by a mere chronicler of past ideas. The emphases that he chooses and the values he finds in this rich heritage seem to me essential ones. If there were space, I could quarrel with minor slips and contradictions, but that would be captious.

Moreover, if I have managed to hit upon the leading threads of his account in Book Five of his monumental history, these are very far from being all of them. These eighteen chapters teem with vitality. They take account of contributory figures to the main stream which most American philosophers will hardly have heard of. Perhaps when all is said, Randall's scholarship is his most impressive feature. It is indeed hard to find anything comparable to *The Career of Philosophy* in English. It should quickly replace the histories of Windelband and Höffding, which seem very dated to American students. We can only fervently hope that Professor Randall will find the time and strength to complete the third and final volume of the *Career* and therewith consummate his long labor of teaching and research on the making of the modern mind.

JOSEPH L. BLAU
Columbia University

The North American as Philosopher

In an address before the Institute for Religious and Social Studies in New York City more than twenty years ago, John Herman Randall, Jr., whose lifelong study and contributions to philosophy we honor in this volume, spoke of "The Spirit of American Philosophy."[1] This was not a casual excursion into a field to which Randall had given no prior attention. He is a historian, consciously and explicitly aware of the indebtedness of each philosopher to a distinctive intellectual milieu as well as to his predecessors. For Randall, there is as much merit, and perhaps as much interest, in studying the ways in which this double background has led to the characteristic emphases with which Americans "do" philosophy as in restudying the same question for more "classic" philosophers.

In addition, as a sophisticated and original naturalistic philosopher of history, Randall has noted the need for each historical era to rework history, in the light of its own knowledge and its own problems. This need, at the very least, requires the historian of philosophy to re-examine the great philosophic contributions of the past in the light of the philosophical issues of his own time and place. For Randall himself, as a twentieth-century American philosopher, understanding of the distant and remote could come only as mediated through the immediate and near at hand.

Because of Randall's long-continued interest in this theme, illustrated from his early writings to his monumental history *The Career of Philosophy*, I am pleased to be asked to contribute to this volume and honored to be thought worthy to do so.

To attempt to fix a precise date, a particular book, or the work of an individual philosopher as the turning point from dependence to independence in North American philosophy is something of a specious enterprise. For if the philosopher be described as the spectator of all time and all existence, his searching mind cannot be limited to a region, a country, a nation, or a culture. Nothing less than a universe can be his range; and for many philosophers *one* universe is hardly enough. There is, it is true, a tendency among human beings (and most philosophers, too, are human) to accept the local and temporary institutions and conventions of their native cultures as universal and eternal conditions of Being as such, to generalize the habitual patterns of their own societies into permanent features of the structure of the universe. That philosophers and others do this is, perhaps, the consequence of a human dilemma: If our culture be thus transformed into the very pattern of the eternal verities, its authority over us is justified and our submission to its molding influence is vindicated, but we are forever without the hope of changing even an iota of its form. If, on the other hand, our culture is not so translated and universalized, it has less power over us, but we have more power over it; it comes, to a certain extent, under our control. We can hope to make a difference in the world of relative cultures as we cannot in a world of permanent and unchangeable structures. In their avidity for absolutes, philosophers have too often chosen to impale themselves on the first of these horns. Yet surely, of all humans, the philosophically minded should be the most likely to avoid the snare of particularistic and parochial generalizations, even if the loss of precious absolutes should be involved. Indeed, it would represent a defeat for philosophy if we were able to talk about the philosopher as American.

Another way of approach may prove more fruitful. Although the themes of philosophic speculation are universal and cosmic, the philosopher is provoked to speculation by irritating factors in his local and temporal environment. Philosophy in the human, like the pearl in the oyster, is evidence of unease, if not disease. Irksome elements in the cultural environment may serve a philosopher merely as a scaffolding on which to take his stand while he elaborates a philosophic structure which is independent of them. From a social view, a philosophy thus erected must be regarded as escapist. Alternatively, the factors of the philosopher's environment that stimulated his philosophizing may be more completely integrated into his thought, either as particular illustrations of the universal truths he seeks or, perhaps even more intimately, as his point of return as well as his point of departure. Some practical problem may well be the impetus to reflective thinking; the reflective thinking may be extended to the utmost in speculative outreach, and a systematic philosophy may emerge. If the philosopher then applies his general solution to the resolution of the particular problem that was his starting point, we may say with justice that he has linked his cultural environment most intimately with his cosmic speculation without falling into the trap of making his philosophy a mere generalization of the conditions pertaining to the place and time of his philosophizing. We shall explore, then, the way in which a philosophic enterprise has grown out of a concern for North American life, rather than seeking to show that North American life can be elevated into a philosophy. Instead of considering the philosopher as American, we shall have regard to the American as philosopher.

One more preliminary remark must be made before we can proceed to illustrate and to document this theme. James Edwin Creighton, head of the Sage School of Philosophy at Cornell University, in his Presidential Address at the first annual meeting of the American Philosophical Association in March, 1902, declared that "there is in any generation a main drift of problems within which we must work." He was thinking of technical philosophic problems. His comment is even more apposite if we are concerned with other problems in a culture that may give rise to philosophic speculation. It is unlikely to be the case that all aspects of a culture seem problematic at the same time, although some recent European literature indicates that there is a group for whom the present is such an unusual period. More usually, in one age it is the social aspects, in another the economic aspects, in a third the religious aspects, and so on, that seem ripe for reconstruction. The basis on which the reconstruction is founded also varies from age to age. It is, as G. H. Mead of the University of Chicago said, "the most secure knowledge of the age" that is used as a foundation. But what is regarded as "the most secure knowledge" fluctuates; for one age it is theology, and around theology all the aspects of culture are reconstructed. In another age physics or biology or astronomy or psychology or history is thought to be the best-established, the most secure, knowledge, and is therefore taken as fundamental to reconstruction. The relevance of this to our general theme will, I hope, appear more clearly in the sequel. For the moment we need only take note that it indicates the necessity for considering each illustration in its own historical context. If we look to the seventeenth or eighteenth century for philosophic contributions that are relevant to the main drift of twentieth-century problems or that attempt reconstruction in the light of those culture areas that represent "the most secure knowledge" of the twentieth century, we shall return from our quest for the emergence of the American as philosopher with nothing but an empty pack.

If, on the other hand, we are patient to unravel the threads of historical background, the quest is rewarding almost from the start. As early in North American intellectual history as the first part of the eighteenth century, in Jonathan Edwards, we find a genuinely philosophic inquiry emerging out of the peculiar religious problems of the American environment. The conclusions of Edwards' philosophic enterprise, applied to the religious problems of New England Congregationalism, served as the theological groundwork for a century of American religious history. The work of Edwards came at a time when the sense of what constituted secure knowledge had shifted radically. For more than a century, in

England, Holland, and North America, in the Puritan group out of which Edwards came, the theology of Calvinism, structured in the five points of the Synod of Dort, had seemed to utter ultimate truth about the inter-relations of God, man, and the universe. To New England colonists of the first two generations especially, it seemed clear that Calvin's statement of man's total dependence upon God was an accurate representation of their actual situation in the American wilderness. The theocracy instituted in Massachusetts by the well-known law of 1631 limited citizenship to mem-bers of the church, while membership in the church was (by the terms of the covenant version of Calvinism that the Puritans followed) restricted to those believed by their fellows to be "saints," that is, predestined to salvation.

For later generations, neither total dependence nor theocracy nor a fellowship of saints seemed adequate. Rightly or wrongly, before 1700, when conditions of life had become less rugged for New Englanders, the assertion of man's total dependence became more and more a merely formal expression. In many phases of their lives the colonists felt that they were well able to take care of themselves. Furthermore, especially on what was then the frontier, as in Northampton, where Jonathan Edwards joined his grandfather, Solomon Stoddard, as pastor of the church, the social pressures of egalitarianism had broken down the concept of the church as a fellowship of saints covenanted together and had produced a form of church organization more like the open-membership churches of today. Arminianism, with its insistence upon human freedom, theo-logically important as a counterweight to absolute predestination, was replacing true Calvinism. Jonathan Edwards faced the problem of restat-ing Calvinism in terms adequate to the newer cultural situation.

He did so by working out a philosophic system that was keen, original, and comprehensive, and that was based on the "most secure knowledge" of his age, the psychology of John Locke's *Essay Concerning Human Understanding* and the physics of Sir Isaac Newton's *Mathematical Prin-ciples of Natural Philosophy*. The ingenious application that Edwards made of the Newtonian principle that every event must have a cause was to destroy the Arminian doctrine of the uncaused decisions of the will—the freedom of the will. The application that Edwards made of the Lockeian psychology was twofold: First, it enabled him to transfer the battleground of the Lord from church polity to the individual soul, to psychologize theology, by his restatement of the doctrine of total depend-ence as the *sense* or *feeling* of total dependence. Thus the prosperity and the bustling activity of the community, while it might be used as a ground for denying *actual* dependence, was completely irrelevant to the sense of dependence. In the second place, out of Locke's sensationalistic theory of human knowledge, according to which nothing could be in the mind which had not previously been in the senses, Edwards derived a sensationalistic and empiricistic religious epistemology which reaffirmed the Calvinistic doctrine of predestination. Each predestined "saint" was granted by God's grace a "supernatural sense," supplementary to the five natural senses; by means of this graciously added sense the saint was able to "perceive" spiritual matters. The psychologized version of Calvinism that Jonathan Edwards built on this foundation was used by later religious leaders as the theoretical justification for the individualistic, evangelical Protestant Christianity that became the religion of the mid-western frontier. Even from this brief summary it is clear that philosophical theology appropriate to his age and clime emerged in North America in a mature fashion in the work of Edwards.

If we again turn to the early experiences of the American people and view them on their social and political side, we find that there were elements that differentiated these experiences from any that were possible to Europeans of the seventeenth and eighteenth centuries. One such important feature of the American experience North and South, was that each group of new settlers had to create a new community. The American colonist was a producer of societies, rather than a consumer of societies already in existence. Moreover, the settlers created these societies out of human materials that were comparatively undifferentiated. It would be an exaggeration to assert that all the American colonists were of the same social class. Yet the class distinctions that European society had inherited from the still-recent feudal era were virtually non-existent in America. In short, as nearly as possible the conditions that social thinkers of the Enlightenment summed up in the phrase "state of nature" actually existed in America. For European theorists of the "social contract" tradition, the individual might logically be prior to the social order, but experientially the social order was present to each individual at his birth. Men were born into the community even though theory asserted that the community was born out of men. Thus, theories of the origin of society which seem like mere armchair theorizing in the European cultural context come forth as vital programs for the creation of societies in the New World.

Needless to say, not all of these programs originated in America. It is not my contention here that there was a significant degree of creative social thought in America, but rather that the adaptations of older schemes that were made in America had a special sort of validity in terms of American conditions of life. Perhaps the most ancient of the adapted theories was the pattern of biblical theocracy that was stated as an ideal (though in the judgment of many scholars never actually achieved) in the Second Commonwealth period of Jewish history, and in North

America made into the constitutional basis of the social order in the Massachusetts Bay Colony. The relevant point is that this and other such patterns were tried out in America; whether or not they were made in America is irrelevant.

In the process of trial, some theories were found to work better than others. Even in those that worked best some inadequacies of formulation or problems in operation were revealed. In this situation many men in America began to speculate about society and government, and were led to the development of philosophic positions that were in turn reflected back into the actual day-to-day problems of organizing new communities and governing them. Toward the end of the eighteenth century, three men who had been involved in the task of producing a constitutional frame for the new federal government of the United States, Alexander Hamilton, John Jay, and James Madison, justified and defended this constitution to the citizens of New York in a remarkable series of essays: *The Federalist Papers*, one of the major contributions to political theory in the modern world. As recently as 1948, these papers constituted the only North American political document studied by Oxonians reading Comparative Institutions. Both Hamilton and Madison rise to the level of political philosophy in some of their contributions to *The Federalist Papers*; Madison's *Federalist* No. 10, on the causes and prevention of faction, has lasting value as a philosophical analysis of the relations between politics and economics.

It was not only in the creation of formal political philosophy that the results of the American experience of creating communities was seen. In the late eighteenth and early nineteenth centuries, two other important philosophic developments emerged concurrently, a theory of man and a theory of culture. That these two themes are closely related to each other and to political theory needs no demonstration. When Hector St. John de Crevecoeur, in his *Letters of an American Farmer*, asked, "What is this American, this new Man?" his question was echoed by many who saw, or thought they saw, that the traditional Christian doctrine of man no longer seemed an adequate description of the North American. No more accurate was the materialistic substitute for the Christian theory, the man-machine of the French Enlightenment. Central to the new concept of man emerging in the United States was his freedom; man was thought to be neither supernaturally nor mechanically determined in his actions. The Augustinian-Calvinistic tenet of man's inability was replaced by the Franklinian-Jeffersonian belief in man's ability. Today we criticize this Enlightenment view of the nature of man; we introduce new forms of determination that our predecessors neglected. We see how readily the shallowness of the doctrine yielded to vulgarization in the theory of "rugged individualism," to etherealization in the Emersonian doctrine of "self-reliance," and to mediocratization in the still-too-prevalent Jacksonian "spoils system." What we forget is that in its time the American doctrine of man was a bright ray of hope for the lowly of Europe. The new doctrine asserted that each individual was what he became, what he made of himself. His parentage, his heritage, did not give him place. His only advantages were those he made for himself by using the opportunities afforded him by society. When a statement of this sort was made by one of Maryland's Jeffersonian legislators in the course of a debate in the 1820's, his speech was translated into German and circulated as a pamphlet in Germany. At that time all Europe, but especially Germany, was interested in what was being created in the new society in North America. And this interest later proved a source of new stimulation to American intellectual life.

The theory of culture that developed *pari passu* with this new theory of man had many facets. The one to which I would call atention is that so well expressed by William Ellery Channing in his "Remarks on National Literature." The question to be asked about any culture—any society, Channing said—is what kind of man it produces. Society exists to afford all men, not just a favored few, the opportunity to make the most of their potentialities. If freedom to become oneself is the keynote of the doctrine of man, equality of opportunity to exercise this important freedom is the keynote of Channing's American democratic theory of culture.

Underlying these excursions into social and political philosophy, there was a basis of what was believed to be secure knowledge—knowledge that was regarded as unquestionably true; so true, in fact, that it needed only to be stated for its truth to be acknowledged. This knowledge was conceived on the analogy of what Newton called the "mathematical principles of natural philosophy," but it served social philosophy instead of natural. It is this body of knowledge that was set forth in some of the fundamental documents of the period, especially documents that Thomas Jefferson penned. In the Declaration of Independence, self-evidence is claimed for part of this body of knowledge: "We hold these truths to be self-evident. . . ." In the "Act Establishing Religious Freedom in Virginia, "also Jefferson's work, the claim is made in different words: "Well aware that Almighty God hath created the mind free. . . ." Doctrines thus expressed in terms of self-evidence or of universal awareness were the presumably secure foundations on which the reconstruction of social and political ideas was based.

It would be easy to exaggerate the influence of the philosophy of the American Enlightenment on European and, in particular, on French thought. Not only Jefferson and Paine but also lesser American thinkers like Joel Barlow were known in France, and both Paine and Barlow were personally involved in the stirring events of the French Revolution. As in so many other matters, however, the telling point is not the large notice of American ideas but the small. More revelatory of the interest that some Europeans took in American ideas than the world-shaking events in France is a footnote at the end of Moses Mendelssohn's *Jerusalem*, published in Berlin in 1783. Mendelssohn's book is a discussion of the relations of civil and ecclesiastical power; its conclusion is a plea for the separation of these two forms of power. Here—and it must be remembered that the date is 1783, shortly after the end of the American Revolution—Mendelssohn adds in a footnote, "Leider! hören wir auch schon den Congress in Amerika das alte Lied anstimmen, und von einer herrschenden Religion sprechen" ("Alas! already we hear the Congress in America giving voice to the old song and talking of a dominant church"). What deep interest and close attention Europeans must have been giving to the course of affairs in American for so minor a point in congressional debate to have been noticed so promptly and with such dismay!

There is no need to multiply examples. I am content to have demonstrated that when, in the American cultural environment, problems arose that were susceptible of consideration in the broadest speculative context, there were Americans who had the ability to develop and expound a philosophic position within which these problems might be solved. In addition, I have tried to illustrate the point that there was a European interest in these American philosophic developments, and to show that American suggestions looking toward the solution of problems common to Western societies of the eighteenth century were taken more seriously and considered more carefully by Europeans of that age than they have been by later American scholars, who seem perpetually to feel the need to apologize for what philosophic Americans of that age did *not* do, instead of celebrating what they did.

In addition to the broad sense in which the term philosophy and its derivatives have been used thus far, there is another narrower and academically more conventional way. Here philosophy is a technical undertaking occupying itself with a special range of problems that are called philosophic to distinguish them from all other problems of men. I would not deplore the degree to which professional and academic philosophers are concerned with these problems, for they are truly fascinating exercises of speculative ingenuity. It is important for us to recognize, however, that the development of a corps of academic philosophers in the United States is a relatively recent matter. A concern for academic philosophy can be found only in the last hundred years; it would be absurd to expect the emergence of the American as philosopher in this technical sense before 1850. Properly to tell the story of this second emergence would require far more consideration than can be given here. We should have to indicate that, in a period of about one century, technical philosophy in America has given to the world more than a dozen first-rate philosophers, including perhaps six whose works seem likely to become part of the major philosophic canon from Plato to the present. In the scant century since the beginning of technical philosophy in the United States, a new chapter has been added to the epic history of Western philosophy. This second emergence of the American as philosopher cannot and should not be dismissed as trivial; it is no small emergence.

American technical philosophy received its first impetus from the nineteenth-century developments of sciences of change, notably geology and biology. Until that period "secure knowledge" had always been regarded as knowledge of the permanent and unchanging structure of reality. As far back in the history of thought as the Greek Parmenides our experience of change has been regarded as illusory. "That which is," said this early philosopher, "is; that which is not, is not." There was no way in which that which is not could become that which is, or that which is become that which is not. However we might experience the process of becoming, it was unthinkable and therefore unreal. Without entering the discussion of the metaphysical issue involved here, geologists, paleontologists, and biologists began to study change and to discover its regularities. The statement of these discovered regularities—the laws of change—did violence not only to traditional philosophic doctrines but also to traditional religious dogmas. In the attempt to resolve the conflict of science and religion, many Americans began to seek answers in philosophy.

The chief available lines of philosophic speculation were two: the empiricist philosophy developed especially by British thinkers which had no metaphysical prejudices against human experience as a source of knowledge but which led to a denial—or at least a doubt—of the objective reality of the gross objects of experience and to a completely subjective status for the relations between objects; and the rationalist philosophy developed especially by post-Kantian German thinkers, which granted—and even glorified—process, but which tended either to spin the universe as a web out of the subjective consciousness or to swallow up all variety, diversity, and plurality in an inclusive Absolute. Technical philosophy in America may be understood in terms of the combination of these two lines of thought, in varying proportions. The British empirical tradition has been a factor in North American intellectual life since the seventeenth century. The German tradition entered in three ways (1) Through the writings of certain Britons, notably Samuel Taylor Coleridge and Thomas

Carlyle, whose works were studied by the New England Transcendentalists; (2) through the large number of Germans, including a few well-educated liberals, who became Americans in the aftermath of the various revolutions of the first half of the nineteenth century, culminating in 1848—this influence was felt most deeply in the Midwest; and (3) through the increasing number of American students who went into the German universities for postgraduate studies.

From these sources and through these avenues there developed, first, a school of American idealism. It was dominant in the American colleges from 1880 to 1915. These idealisms tended to be more sympathetic to religion than to science; they differed most from the German systems on which they drew by being more interested in the multiplicity of individuals than in a single Absolute. Josiah Royce, who was born in pioneer California in 1855 and died in 1916 a respected member of the faculty of Harvard University, was a philosopher of world stature in this tradition. His philosophy ties in with earlier American thought in the centrality of his search for the meaning of community. His was a philosophy of harmony; he regarded our actions as moral in the degree to which we succeed in including the goals of as many individuals as possible in our own will to act. Other notable, though not as important, idealists were Borden Parker Bowne of Boston University, whose pluralistic personal idealism has been particularly influential in Latin America where to this day it is one of the chief alternatives to scholastic philosophy; George Holmes Howison of the University of California, who developed a similar position by adopting the monads of Leibniz as the ultimate basis of personal being; George Sylvester Morris of the University of Michigan, whose chief merit was to have emphasized the element of process in German philosophy; James Edwin Creighton of Cornell, whose insistence on the objectively rational structure of the universe led him to a position of greater sympathy with science in its search for objective rationality; Alfred Henry Lloyd of the University of Michigan, in whose thought the element of change is so strongly emphasized that his dynamic universe does not stand still long enough to be described; Felix Adler of Columbia University and the Ethical Culture movement, who worked out a subtle ethical idealism which provided for community by insisting that the highest flowering of the uniqueness of any individual consists in his drawing out the correlative uniqueness in other individuals; and Wilbur Marshall Urban of Yale University, who found in the objectivity of value and meaning a basis for both idealism and a transcendental realism in opposition to skepticism, relativism, and naturalism.

A second American school to have developed was that of pragmatism. In this philosophy there is a genuine blending of German and British elements, with a novel twist that gives the movement its distinctive character. Pragmatism finds the meaning of an idea in the way it functions in our experience. Its meaning is, therefore, always prospective; its reference is to future experience. An idea is true if it gives us accurate guidance in situations that arise in life. Thus both the coherence test of rationalist philosophies and the correspondence test of empiricist philosophies are subordinated to the pragmatic test of reliability in application. Charles Sanders Peirce first stated the pragmatic criterion as a test of meaning. The difficulty and the scattered character of his writings prevented recognition from coming to Peirce during his life, but in the past forty years he has come into his own and is now regarded as one of the seminal thinkers of the late nineteenth century. Peirce and his associates were among the first to realize that the experimental method as used by laboratory scientists had potentialities for philosophic use; his conception of pragmatic method is as a "laboratory logic" for philosophic analysis. His friend William James, professor at Harvard, made a more popular and more individualistic application of Peirce's pragmatism. Where Peirce's conception of the future consequences of any idea was limited to publicly demonstrable consequences, James was willing to admit any "agreeable leadings" for any individual, anywhere, as reasons for ascribing "truth value" to an idea. James moderated the extreme subjectivity to which this view of truth values would seem to lead by his affirmation that the consequences, though not necessarily public, were necessarily social, "leading away from excentricity and isolation." John Dewey, of Columbia University, combined an original idealist theory of the dynamic character of reality with a form of pragmatism that he called "instrumentalism." Dewey's thought was strongly influenced by Darwinian biology; he viewed ideas as instruments of control and adjustment in the interaction of an individual and his environment. Both James and Dewey refused to assign any eulogistic merit to mind as spiritual reality; both, but especially Dewey, considered mind to be merely a way of organic behavior. Dewey's interest in ideas as instrumental led him to consider the practical applications of pragmatism in education, art, politics, economics, and religion, so that he never strayed far from the problems of men. Other important contributions to pragmatism were made by George Herbert Mead of the University of Chicago, who developed a social psychology according to which mind was a remote emergent out of gesture, and a metaphysic that took greater account of twentieth-century advances in physics than did Dewey's; and by Clarence Irving Lewis of Harvard University, who has carried on pragmatist thought in the language and with the new methodological tools of recent philosophic analysis.

There have been other technical philosophies expounded by North

American philosophers, but I have mentioned enough to support my contention that we need make no apologies for the American as philosopher. He is part of the world history of philosophy; his problems are those of Western philosophers generally; his achievements, in Peirce, Royce, James, Dewey, Bowne, and Mead, and perhaps others, of more than local interest. Surely when we find books about these American philosophers written by English, German, French, Italian, and Latin American students of philosophy we are justified in claiming merit for the American as philosopher that cannot be dismissed as mere chauvinism.

But what is American about the American philosopher? His problems are not distinctively American; his methods are not uniquely American; his solutions are not characteristically American. Yet in spite of these denials, there is a flavor in the work of the American as philosopher that sets it off from the work of British or French or German philosophers. It would not be easy to characterize in a phrase or two what this flavor is. Certainly there is no "American" philosophy. But there are certain trends that reveal a prevailing temper, a mood, an outlook, a common sense of the overarching human problems. For one thing, philosophy as made in America is, in the best sense of the word, practical. It is thought out in order to make a difference in some institution, some activity, some aspect of life. There have been American "closet philosophers," but in general, philosophy in America has not been closet philosophy. A great deal of American philosophic speculation has been concerned with problems in the relation of the individual and society. It has reflected the attempt in American life to mediate between the absolute claims of the individual, the liberty that is license, and the absolute claims of society, *libertas obedientiae*. If there is any one statement to which almost all American philosophers would subscribe, it is that society exists to further the ends of individuals, not to frustrate them. Philosophy in America has been characteristically open-ended, receptive to novelties of thought and statement, as well as to the general sense that we live in an unfinished universe and can, therefore, produce no finished philosophy. Philosophy in America has been—if indeed such a distinction can properly be made—democratic rather than aristocratic; it has exemplified the belief that all men should have the chance to benefit from all advances in knowledge, and that all should have the chance to make whatever contributions they can to the ongoing processes of thought as well as to those of life. Philosophers in America have recognized in theory, and by their leadership in educational and social programs have aided in the attempt to realize, a human community of free men.

In all these ways, Randall stands as a major example of the North American as philosopher and historical critic of philosophy. His historical penetration has, perhaps, been taken as his chief contribution. Yet it must be realized that in these studies, too, he has been most deeply concerned with the question of relevance: what difference to our practical and theoretical understanding of our problems can a fresh reading of older philosophies make? He has been concerned throughout his career with the human and social consequences of philosophic beliefs. He has exemplified a conception of the philosopher as involved in his world, not the mere spectator of time and existence, so that his philosophy and its method have avoided the pitfall of abstract verbalism. Moreover, in Randall's own naturalistic metaphysics, we have a prime example of the way in which American philosophers can add "a new level to the long tradition of Western philosophical thought," by bringing "the lessons learned from American experience to all the lessons men had learned before and left for us in the embodied philosophical wisdom of the past."[2]

NOTES

1. Published in *Wellsprings of the American Spirit*, ed. F. Ernest Johnson (distributed by Harper & Brothers, New York, for the Institute for Religious and Social Studies, 1948), pp. 117-133.

2. Randall, "The Spirit of American Philosophy," *op. cit.*, p. 133.

PART TWO

PHILOSOPHICAL THEMES

VIRGIL C. ALDRICH
University of North Carolina

The Middle, the End, and the New Beginning

In his *An Essay on Nature*, Woodbridge wrote: "We speak and write in the same world as that in which we walk and breathe. No one, I imagine, would regard walking as an application of motion to Nature, or breathing as an application of respiration. Why, then, regard vocalization as such?"[1] This suggests, as Woodbridge points out elsewhere, that thinking is not something we first do "in the mind" or in the head and extrapolate afterwards. It is an exploration, a (starry) "consideration," through the realm of being. You can say "through the realm of mind" instead, if you like, since the realm of mind is identical with the realm of being in important respects. The universe of discourse is the universe; or, as Aristotle put it, anything that is or has been can be thought and discoursed about. Woodbridge also said something to the effect that our walking *with* our legs does not at all commit us to saying that we walk *in* our legs. Similarly, we may think with our brains—in collaboration with much else—without our thinking *in* our brains. Thinking is a way of going places in the realm of mind, *alias* the realm of being. It was sentiments such as these that put Woodbridge in line to contribute to the collaborative volume *The New Realism*, published in 1912. According to that philosophy, mind is not a subjective prison that confines thinking and prevents its direct access to the things in the independent realm of being outside. Rather, it coincides with portions of that realm. Thus, there is no epistemological problem of how to escape, and thus was metaphysics emancipated from epistemology, with Marvin framing the declaration of independence, and Perry showing the way out of the egocentric predicament.

Now, if a similar account is given of perceiving, including its imaginative and affective modes and its suggestions for volition and action, then a *Weltanschauung* takes shape—a shape that is the shape of things as I see them. I cannot only breathe in such a world. I live, move, and have my being in it, where much of that movement is not manipulatory but consists rather of my feeling my way through it in the articulate forms of perception and thought wherever that is feasible. Of course, I also walk in and through it, sometimes whistling in the dark. I then hear Nature speak to me in the words of inscription on the Temple of Isis: "I am all that is and that was and shall be, and no mortal hath lifted my veil." But it is not always night. When the day comes, I remember Nature's challenge and lift the veil and see her, thus casting off my mortality. It is in such moments that the realm even of *my* mind becomes conterminous with the realm of being, and self-consciousness becomes so expansive as to include the morning sun and the very Light of Nature, the light of light, all within the scope of the expanded field of consciousness. I then am prompted to say, "It thinks, It perceives, It feels"—this It using little me as an instrument in the process.

With such experiences and under such promptings, I could turn to Spinoza for the formulation if the mood is naturalistic, or to Royce if it is more personal. God-Substance-Nature, or the larger Self. Aristotle would be another worthy alternative, and Dewey yet another, these doing more justice to my pluralistic sentiments. Whitehead would also do—as he did for a while in my past—with the close-knit eclecticism that combined the above strands in the Extensive Continuum. This brings eternal objects into the picture, presented in immediate perception, providing the means for process to achieve thinghood or *re*-ality (Process *and* Reality, a synthetic conjunction not expressible in any analytic proposition). It was Santayana who influenced Whitehead on this count of "essences," and he would have applauded this part of the philosophy of organism.

·I have been speaking of *formulations* of world-views that do not restrict my philosophical respiration. If I may next distinguish the formulation from the philosophical vision or the world-view as the content of the formulation, I have grounds for saying that I am happiest of all with the way things look to Randall. That is the way I see them. (Or, that is the way It sees and thinks the nature of things when It is using Randall and me for its perceptual and conceptual purposes.) But Randall's formulation does a subtle violence to his vision. It is to a consideration of this that I now turn, fully realizing how delicate this job is that I assign myself. For, in the first place, any constructive metaphysics partially determines the content of the vision by the formulation, as the vision of Hamlet is nothing, or very much something else, without the literary form that Shakespeare gave it. Bosanquet and A. C. Bradley were so right about this sort of point. So one must be careful how he distinguishes content from form. A constructive metaphysics is rather like a work of literary art, in this respect. It makes things appear in a formulation that constitutes them that way, to put it in Kantian terms. Thus, if one likes the vision thus afforded, how can he find fault with its vehicle?

The answer is that the connection of content and form is not as strict

as all that, in constructive metaphysics. One can see what the metaphysician sees between the lines of the exposition, not only in them; as one
cannot in a good work of literary art. And, after all, Randall is not primarily trying to do what I am calling constructive metaphysics at all, the
sort that conjures up and captures what Montague would call a great
vision of philosophy. He is, in effect, aiming to achieve a reconstruction
in philosophy, a sort of reconstructive metaphysics that is more conscious
and critical of what has gone before in the great tradition. He has one
eye on this while with the other he looks at things. Thus he has a double
concern, the components of which tend, I shall argue, to militate against
one another. His fine historical grasp of what went before in the tradition
induces him to use the traditional language of metaphysics when he turns
from the history of philosophy to doing philosophy on his own, and what
gets thus formulated seems not to do justice to his own vision of the
nature of things, or to what Nature reveals in that rapport. To be sure,
"history and nature together offer the great challenge to the philosophic
mind," quoting Randall, but if it is the history of ideas he has in mind
here, then the philosophic mind will turn *finally* from this to the consideration of nature. Justice to the latter demands looking at her with
both eyes, and then using a more innocent language to make her more
articulate. (Only child-like people enter the kingdom of heaven; and,
believe it or not, philosophers are people.) That *some* distortion has occurred through failure to do this, is my impression; and my guess is that
it has distresed Randall himself. Of course no philosopher is privileged to
proceed in utter innocence of this kind, but all the great philosophers
have tried to have their own say in an idiom not too loaded with preconceptions bequeathed by the previous history of ideas, and this requires
binocular vision directed on things. Let me now single out some of the
threads in the cloth of this judgment of Randall's achievement.

First, just what is the content of his vision, freed as much as possible
from distortions of a borrowed *manière de parler* and the concepts it
carries with it? Well, there are things in situations. What characteristics
the things take on depends on their interrelationships and on the situation. The conditions involved in this are some general and some special.
It is innocent enough to call the former "categories." The characterization
of the *same* thing may differ in different situations, even within the same
situation, in some respects. The situations themselves are not interrelated
as the things in them are. That is, the notion of The Situation including
and determining all situations, as any situation includes and determines
the things in it, remains incorrigibly problematic. It is too "open-textured"
(Waismann) to be of any cognitive use. And, of course, the way in which
any situation "determines" the things in it is not the way in which these

things determine one another in that situation. The former, or the situational determination, is categorical, in the sense that features such general distinctions as those between "aesthetic," "religious," and "scientific." Finally, going along with the modes of characterization of things are appropriate modes of experience and thought, each sophisticated with the help of the appropriate language and all emerging out of the matrix of a basic rapport among things *simpliciter*. This submits such distinctions as "subject-object" to various adjustments, according to the situation and to the degree of sophistication of the mode of expression in perception, thought, and language.

This is Randall's naked vision, as stripped of what accrues to it in his explicit metaphysical formulation. I, for one, would say that anyone seeing things this way has 20-20 metaphysical vision. He then has in view the datum of philosophy or, if you prefer Aristotle, the starting point. I like to call this innocent and neutral awareness "phenomenological," though I do not care much about what term is to be used here. Unfortunately, the one I suggest reminds one of Hegel who was quite ruthless with starting points. They got *aufgehoben* at a breathtaking rate in his omnivorous sort of constructive metaphysics. I have never been able to breathe in that Bacchanalian revel of the *Weltgeist*, though what sanity there is in that madness is owing to even Hegel's incipient awareness of the above datum of philosophy which, as a potential for this or that interpretation, is certainly neither small nor unexciting. The datum may be to blame. It intoxicated Spinoza. Philosophical sanity might be defined as the mark of the philosopher who knows how to hold his liquor, after a deep draught of the datum of philosophy. That is, if he then proceeds to philosophize with respect for the starting point as the ultimate court of appeal. Dewey's denotative method was calculated to provide some such control, though he did not put it quite this way, owing to his own special sort of distrust of starting points in favor of outcomes. He never quite succeeded in exorcizing the World Spirit from his system because it too thoroughly spellbound him at the beginning. Yet, in his essay "Qualitative Thought," which appeared more than thirty years ago in the very first issue of the quarterly *The Symposium*, now defunct, he displayed considerable respect for a starting point of preanalytical, pervasive datum as the control. But as quality, not as the complex I have indicated above.

Nevertheless, it was at one point in this very essay that Dewey clearly exhibited the tendency of an inherited language of preconceptions to spoil what might otherwise have been a phenomenological portrayal of starting points. He wrote: "It is merely a linguistic peculiarity, not a logical fact, that we say 'that is red' instead of 'that reddens'." Dewey thereby rejected a natural way of speaking and a natural distinction it enables one to make, in favor of the metaphysical tradition gravitating around activity and process—thanks again to Hegel's influence and to Darwin metamorphosed into a metaphsyician. Now, in innocent or plain experience, and in plain talk about it, there is an indefeasible difference between, say, an apple's being red on the one hand, and its reddening on the other. I can *see* that it is red, and I *know* that it reddened as it ripened. But this change in color was too slow to be perceptible. I do not and cannot see that it reddens, as I *can* see water in a basin redden as a bleeding wound is washed in it. It is true, if you like, that the apple's red that I see is the outcome of process. But only a medieval Scholastic would say, if asked what process, "a process of reddening." The non-trivial answer is, "a process of ripening"; and this raises interesting scientific questions. (Even Aristotle would wince at the notion that qualities as such are processes or processed, though the substances they qualify certainly progress, and this is a kind of process; it is these that are produced, not the qualities).

I shall not be surprised if I get my face slapped for such a "childish misinterpretation" of functionalism. But, after turning the other cheek for the second slap—and getting it—I shall, without reddening, smile and say: "I know perfectly well that I indicated a sense of 'reddening' that was bypassed by the instrumentalistic account. But this is the best way to make my point. It is a critical one suggesting that the functional interpretation is loaded or saddled with something that requires it to put a crimp in plain appearances and plain talk about them. It is just another metaphysical invitation for people to see through such plain things to the alleged esoteric reality veiled by the appearances, and to be on guard against the 'linguistic peculiarities' of their natural language. Also, to construct an artificial language that does greater justice to reality. 'Reddens' instead of 'red.' Verbs and adverbs replacing adjectives. The presupposition in this heritage is that Logos is fundamentally a verb, ramifying into adverbs. "In the beginning was the *Verb*."

This line of my talk shocks even me because I was much impressed by Dewey's main intention to get beyond constructive metaphysics of the traditional sort, that makes ordinary things and experiences and manners of speaking look funny, into a reconstruction that makes methodological considerations central for philosophy. I remember reminding D. W. Prall of this in Berkeley, California, when he burst in to express his astonishment over Dewey's saying, in effect, that "quality" must be dropped from the vocabulary in favor of "qualification." If this is methodology, it is indeed hard to distinguish it from dubious epistemology and metaphysics. But Dewey was trying to do what needed to be done as a corrective for sense-datum theories such as those of Santayana and C. I. Lewis, theories that left *qualia*, as such, otiose and ineffable, to say nothing of tertiary qualities or values. It seemed to him that the only way out was to argue that, strictly speaking, there are no sense-data of this non-functional sort. Quality is what it does, so qualification replaces it as an operational concept with which we can work. Thus is quality brought under procedural controls. It becomes a construct, communicable and confirmable. Like "good."

Now I turn back, with pleasure, to be again with Randall in the ambit of the world of his metaphysical vision. But as I listen to his account of it, I see a crimp coming across the face of things. In the first place, I begin to understand why "vision" is perhaps the wrong word, and why he does not himself tend to consider metaphysics as a vision. This concept conjures up qualities of visual experience, and it is precisely these that resist most of all the dissolution into process. In the end I get the impression that he is saying, not what he sees, but what he thinks, and that in a way he realizes this, not caring very much about submitting to visual appearances. In fact, he says that the "universe of vision" is a mere appearance compared to the "universe of action." How things look, and how people talk about them, shouldn't matter too much therefore to a philosopher, he feels. The philosopher penetrates through such linguistic peculiarities to the logical and ontological facts. To formulate what he conceives—not perceives—in this vein requires special categories which, in turn, demand just that formulation. Thus does a constructive metaphysics function like a religion, though with the air of being secular and factual. One simply must think thus-and-so, never mind how things look or what people say. One thinks with the learned even while he speaks with the vulgar in their ordinary language.

Quality is not among Randall's categories, and he is on the defensive about this. In a long and able essay[2] he tries to justify the omission by showing that a quality is an operation or a way of operating of a kind of power. These are his categories: operations (verbs), ways of operating (adverbs), powers (nouns), kinds of power (adjectives), and connectives (conjunctions). These are the five categorically different ways that the Situation or Substance has of functioning, and all kinds of qualities can be "adequately treated under some one of the five" ways of functioning. These are functional "ways of being" that things or "factors" in Substance or the Situation have, Substance or the Situation itself being a "co-operation of processes." The *same* thing or "factor" may come to be—or function—in any of these ways.

Let us see how this correlates with, and what it does to, the world of Randall's innocent 20-20 vision, as I presented it in the language of descriptive, not constructive or reconstructive, metaphysics.

Randall explicitly says that there is no over-all Situation including all situations. He says that we do have a notion of The Whole, but that this is mythic or imaginative, not belonging in the sort of analytical or "empirical" metaphysics he is doing. Dewey said something like this, and it is reminiscent of Kant on regulative ideas of Reason, not of Understanding. Now when Randall calls a *situation* a substance, instead of thinking of the things or "factors" in it as substances, he departs from Aristotle. That is, his pluralism of substances (situations) is less radical than Aristotle's (things in them), though it is more radical a pluralism than Aristotle's as an ultimate metaphysics or cosmology. Aristotle did think he could make sense of, and understand, The Whole. This sort of monism Randall denies, wisely.

My impression is that Randall calls the situation a substance because this more thoroughly activates or processes the things in it, making *them* look less substantial. But of course this does not make the *situation* any *more* substantial because, in such an application, the term "substance" can have only a theoretically fixed meaning. This, for Randall, is "process" or a "co-operation of processes" or a "co-operation of powers." He explicitly allows any one of these alternatives as the meaning of "substance."[3] I remember the interesting twist that the late J. A. Smith, who was under the spell of Gentile's *Teoria dello Spirito Come Atto Puro*, gave this idea in a conversation I had with him at Oxford in 1926. While agreeing with the thesis that reality is ultimately an activity or *energeia*, he was for throwing out the concept of substance altogether with its suggestion of a still more fundamental x of which energy is to be predicated. This was a recognition of the more usual or theoretically innocent use—for Smith a misleading one—of "substance"; and it is this that I had in mind when I mentioned the "theoretically fixed meaning" Randall gives it, in contrast. One thinks also of Cassirer's contrast between "substance" and "function." Why, then, doesn't Randall simply jettison "substance," replacing it with "process" or "power" or "operation," or with Dewey's "subject-matter" that takes on different forms and gets variously formulated?

A part of the answer draws attention to his fine, scholarly affection for Aristotle, the other part to Randall's basic philosophical sanity. We need something fundamental of which the categories, as predicables, can be predicated, and this is substance. To be sure, at times he speaks of substance as if it were identical with process; but his repect for Aristotle, and half consciously for the etiquette of the plain talk that Nature demands for the making of nice distinctions, makes him vacillate between the equation with process on the one hand, and Aristotle's own notion of substance on the other that makes process or power or action or energy *predicable of substance* "in the truest and primary and most definite sense of the word." Randall's word for substance in this truer-to-Nature sense is simply "thing" or "factor," namely, the things or factors that he finds in situations that are "substances" in his artificial sense. He repeatedly vacillates between the locutions "things that *are* processes or powers . . ." and "things that *have* powers . . ." and "powers in things," and the like. This subcategorical use of "things" as elemental substances of which power and even process can be predicated is necessary to sane talk about Nature, such that one commits an offense to the nature of things if they are simply *equated* with processes or powers. It is with a fine feel for this that Randall speaks of the "five different ways that the *same* thing or 'factor' can function," *within* the situation; and since power is one of these categorical ways, the thing that evinces is not itself simply a power. This is in effect to say that "power," "operation," and the other categories are predicable of things as substances that, as the butt of the predication, cannot be identical with the predicables. Aristotle himself was never guilty of such wholesale identification, and Randall's sanity is trying hard to save him from it. It was with such points in view that I distinguished his constructive metaphysical formulation from his innocent vision of the world. (I think the reason for his using "factor" as interchangeable with "thing" is that this suggests—though just barely—that things are closer to being processes than just "things"; and then this would be a nascent bit of reconstructive metaphysics, like Gentile's suggestion that "*fatto*" be replaced by "*farsi*," or Dewey's tendency to construe undergoings or outcomes in terms of the doings or constructive operations that go into their making.

But to get back to quality as not a category. If Randall is on the defensive about this, knowing that people are going to ask questions about that, why isn't he worried about, say, relation as, or as not, a category? Relation, too, seems to innocent people not to be sufficiently distinguished and recognized in the process philosophy. Randall will exclaim here that he is an objective relativist and surely that takes care of relations. Moreover, he has said much against philosophies of pure flux, in favor of structured process. But the critic has two things in view. He remembers the Bradleyan sort of metaphysics that got rid of relations by making their terms insubstantial—unreal parts of The Whole. The relations then easily devour the terms and themselves disappear in the solvent of The Whole. The impression is that something like this happens in a process philosophy that converts terms of relations into processes. Calling the latter substances does not help. The picture is of rivers without banks. Second, the questioner notices that the verbs *featured* in this philosophy of Logos-as-Verb do not include the static little verb "is." "Is red" is dropped in favor of "reddens," etc. And, since so many relations are most clearly expressed with the help of "is"—"is bigger than," "is younger than," "is red"—one is left with the impression that relations and qualities are in the same boat, according to the metaphysics that says that all things, including qualities and relations, are identical with what they do or what may be done with them. To be sure, it may take operations to "determine" them, but not in the sense that they are thereby reduced to operations—or ways of operating, or powers, or kinds of power, or connectives that themselves are construed as functionings. Woodbridge and Whitehead would know what I mean, without any belittling of process. The point in general is that besides process there is thinghood. The balanced account of Nature will recognize both her dynamics and her statics. Saying that process and structure go together is not enough, if it is further suggested that one side of this coin is basic by calling the whole coin "process" and then adding "substance." This tempts one into the opposite extreme, to then, like Goodman, write a book called *The Structure of Appearance*. Meanwhile, Nature watches and waits, abashed.

But, for all that, Randall is trying, like Dewey, to salvage quality from the doldrums that phenomenalist and intuitionist and introspective theories had put it in. (Think especially of Ayer and Santayana and C. I. Lewis.) In fact, one does not quite understand his whole philosophy until he sees this as among the main motives. A similar remark applies to Dewey's instrumentalism. Even "doubtful" does not mean for him an inner, introspected quality, a private datum of introverted attention. The *situation* is pervasively doubtful to the doubter, in a doubting transaction with the environment.

But we understand Randall better if we realize that he is concerned to redeem not just quality as *observable* property. Even C. I. Lewis made quality in that sense—red as a property of a physical object—communicable and knowable, or objective, in his theory of the non-terminating judgments that formulate it for confirmation by observations. Quality in that sense is not the individuating and "immediatizing" function that Randall had in mind. What bothers Randall is the injustice done to affective qualities, including what Lewis calls *qualia*. Let me generalize this into the notion of the "tonalities" of things. Even colors have tonalities and expressive powers overlooked in the mode of perception I referred to above as observation. Now it was quality in this impressionistic sense that Lewis, following the tradition of scientific empiricism in epistemology, made wholly subjective and ineffable in his *Mind and the World Order*. Such qualities certainly cry out for an up-to-date emancipation, as did metaphysics some fifty years ago cry to be let out of the confines of the egocentric predicament. Randall responds to the cry, with his fine set of aesthetic sensibilities rising to the occasion.

"Quality is indeed a mighty power," wrote Randall in his account of the aesthetic transaction mentioned above. In this general sense, quality is the pervasive sort that transfigures a whole situation *à la* Dewey, providing the hunches and controls for a kind of procedure, scientific, religious, or aesthetic. Randall spotlights a corollary of this, namely, that even science is a constructive transfiguration of the situation and is, on that count, not unlike myth or religion. It differs from myth by formulating things in a way that makes truth considerations relevant. But both religion and science are "objective" in being public and social functions. Whitehead was wrong in supposing that religion is what the individual does with his own solitariness.

Now when Randall goes on to say that it is in the experience of aesthetic qualification that the individual realizes his solitariness, not in religious experience, it may seem that he is moving back into the tradition of the subjectivity of tertiary qualities or values, in this case the aesthetic. But he is still meaning to attack that notion. Though "something happens to the individual participant in the aesthetic transaction," and though this is going to turn out to be the crucial consideration, yet "something happens to the situation as a whole . . . both it and the artistic object become qualified with new and 'aesthetic' qualities." If we add to this Randall's thesis that the productive operations—"arts, skills, and techniques"—play an integral part in such aesthetic qualifications, yielding as the outcome what Bernard Berenson called "ideated sensations" focussed in the work of art as aesthetic object, then we have a complete and a good picture of the "aesthetic situation." I, for one, am prepared to accept it.

But as it stands it is a sort of variable—"something" happens—calling for an interpretation that supplies a value for the variable. The value Randall supplies does not quite satisfy me. He says the something that happens to the individual participant is personalization. "In the aesthetic transaction . . . man at last finds his inmost self." Surely this is to overlook the impersonality, the depersonalization, even dehumanization, involved in great aesthetic achievement, the sort of point made by Eliot or Ortega y Gasset or the formalists generally; though this is not the whole truth either. Great art is not the occasion for a man to realize his person, but rather to shatter it in the presence of the work of art, as Yeats said. It requires a distancing of something that would otherwise be too personal, an objectifying, a contemplative detachment of *some* kind. Like science, it is impersonal, but in a different mode of perception[4] from observation. Personality and a personal rapport with nature, in which nature herself takes on a personal quality, are realized in religion, not in art. This is achieved in the company of the faithful. But Randall says he is not here attempting to fill in specific values for the variables "functioning aesthetically," beyond the threefold suggestion above. My feeling is that if he were to proceed to the fuller account, demurrers like this one would have less ground to stand on.

One more point about aesthetic experience. Randall says it is not "a unique kind of experience, distinct from all other kinds of experience, and possessing no continuity with them." But surely aesthetic experience can possess all the continuity one could wish with other kinds of experiences, even interpenetrating most of them, without losing its distinctiveness: as blue, for example, is a unique or distinctive color-component of white light. In such an amalgam I suppose one could say that it loses its distinctive character, but he must not interpret this as meaning that it then *is* another component color. The difference between kinds of colors must be maintained, despite the color-fusions of the various sorts that actually occur in common experience. And it is the job of the artist to arrange things in a way that abstractively isolates or purifies aesthetic experience of them, as the occasion for their appearance as aesthetic objects. Here again art is like science. Art also employs abstractive techniques, but for the sake of another sort of perceptual experience, distinct from observation which, when expurgated, presents things as physical objects. This differs from aesthetic perception as blue from red, though both are "continuous" with the matrix of common experience (white light) in which they are fused potentialities, until actualized under special conditions (red and blue). To suppose that aesthetic perception is the consummation of observation is like supposing that blue is the consummation of red. Rather, each may be a consummation in its own way, a distinctive percipitate (pure saturated red or blue) achieved out of the amalgam of common experience by the skillful use of exclusive techniques.

The art of making distinctions is a delicate one, yet deadly unless mastered. Look at how Descartes distinguished mind from matter, subject from object, at the dawn of the modern scientific era. And see what this did to Berkeley, who thought that the only way out of the resulting insoluble problems was to take over just one of the discriminata, namely, mind, as restricted by Descartes, and work out a whole philosophy with that as the fundamental—or "substance." After Hume had taken the starch out of the notion, Kant had to put it back into things by his theory of forms that categorized the field of experience. The resulting rigidity Hegel dissolved in the process of the evolution of the Absolute. Substance is replaced by Subject and its dialectic of oppositions. This, finally, had to be broken down into a less monolithic conception of process, more in accord with actual operational procedures in science, but with process retained as the fundamental, as a solvent for the logical atoms and sense-data of the recent realisms at the turn of the century, and as "subject matter" that accommodates the various expressions of Nature's face, as the "language" changes from the scientific to the religious or the aesthetic.

If this picture is deepened and darkened a bit with the colors of existentialism, it is complete. It then represents the end of philosophy, in one sense of "end" and of "philosophy." In that sense, the Cartesian period was the middle, characterized by major distinctions rigidly made. And we all know what the beginning was like, where the philosophical consciousness emerged to make literal sense of the massive distinctions and conflicts that myth had presented dramatically.

The end that philosophy has thus reached is its goal, its fulfillment, its consummation. Not a dead end. So live is it in this consummate maturity that it is spawning another conception of philosophy. The very same historical consciousness that affectionately comprehends philosophy in the old sense is now conceiving it in a new sense. This is a natural consequence of the philosophical sophistication realized at this stage of history.

The phenomenon of this consciousness of something new is quite widespread, not confined to philosophers. In philosophy itself, there is the new phenomenology. By that I mean not only what, say, Merleau-Ponty had in mind when he mentioned metaphysics beyond metaphysics as the next step, one that he was himself taking in his own way to get beyond existentialism. I think also of Wittgenstein, who, in his way, did philosophy beyond philosophy. Even Austin suggested that "phenomenology," not "analysis," is the best word for this. In the religious field, we have Bultmann and Bonhoeffer doing religion beyond religion, with Tillich's ponderous and ambivalent support. And on the walls of the Museum of Modern Art there are beside some of the paintings inscriptions proclaiming art beyond art.

As Tillich in some respects straddles this great divide between the old and the new, so does Randall, though each tends to lean more heavily on the leg in the old tradition of making some one philosophical concept nuclear or fundamental to the rest ("Being," "Process"). Nevertheless, what John Anton said of Dewey's thought[5] may also be said of Randall's. It is in the gateway leading to future philosophy. Moreover, it is a new beginning, especially with respect to the content of the vision it formulates. While it is the consummatory end of an earlier beginning, it is also a portent of philosophy in the new sense.

NOTES

1. Quoted by Randall in, "The Art of Language and the Linguistic Situation: a Naturalistic Analysis," *Journal of Philosophy*, Vol. LX, No. 2 (January 17, 1963).
2. "Qualities, Qualification, and the Aesthetic Transaction," in his *Nature and His-*

torical Experience, chap. x.

3. See also his "The Nature of Metaphysics," in *Nature and Historical Experience*, p. 130.

4. I have dealt with this in my *Philosophy of Art* (Englewood Cliffs, N.J.: Prentice-Hall, Inc., 1963) especially pp. 19-27. Randall himself is uneasy about calling it a mode of "imagination" (*Nature and Historical Experience*, p. 291).

5. John P. Anton, "John Dewey's Place in American Thought and Life," *The Humanist*, Vol. XXIII, No. 5 (September-October, 1963).

JUSTUS BUCHLER
Columbia University

Ontological Parity*

"For the meditating philosopher," says Husserl, "the world is only something that claims being."[1] Just what the world would amount to (for the meditating philosopher) if it lost its claim, is bewildering. Presumably it would still be tolerated, and allowed a role of some kind somehow, whether it were degraded, forgotten, or renamed. In any case, a metaphysics of natural complexes requires a quite different keynote. According to Randall,

> "Reality" means either everything whatsoever—as we are here taking it—or else that a distinction of relative importance has been made. In any other than an evaluative sense, to say that only the Good is "real," only Matter is "real," only Mind is "real," only Energy is "real," is to express a prejudice refuted by a child's first thought or by every smallest grain of sand. No, everything encountered in any way is somehow real. The significant question is, not whether anything is "real" or not, but how and in what sense it is real, and how it is related to and functions among other reals. To take "the real" as in fundamental contrast to what appears to us, is to identify it with "the Good." . . . Such identification seems to have resulted invariably in confusions and insoluble contradictions.[2]

Now along with the notion of a complex as "unreal" we must discard the notion of some complexes as "less" and other complexes as "more" real. Let us contrast a principle of ontological priority—which has flourished from Parmenides to Whitehead and Heidegger, and which continues to flourish in unsuspected ways—with a principle of ontological parity. In terms of the latter, whatever is discriminated in any way (whether it is "encountered" or produced or otherwise related to) is a natural complex, and no complex is more "real," more "natural," more

---

* An earlier version of this piece was one of the papers presented to Professor Randall on his sixty-fifth birthday anniversary. The present version is reprinted, by permission of Columbia University Press, from Professor Buchler's book *Metaphysics of Natural Complexes* (New York and London, copyright 1966).

"genuine," or more "ultimate" than any other. There is no ground, except perhaps a short-range rhetorical one, for a distinction between the real and the "really real," between being and "true being." Among the favorite perennial candidates for the honor of "being" more truly or more completely than anything else is "primary substance" or "primary being." It has been the standing historical comfort of "tough-minded" philosophers, preserving their confidence in the solid concreteness of the spatiotemporal individual.

No discriminanda can be consigned to "non-being," on pain of contradiction; for they have the being that enables them to be discriminated. This being may consist in the being of a picture in a book; of an image or a fantasy; of a plan private to one man or common to many men; of a verbal expression; of a pain, a dream, a habit, a fear, an error, a tradition, a bond among persons. Some discriminanda strike us as deserving no further attention; others, as requiring clarification, action, or portrayal. Sometimes it is *said* that a discrimination has been made, even though people cannot ascertain that it has. Sometimes there is common agreement that a word or chain of words has not succeeded in achieving a discrimination other than the pattern of its own verbal being. Some philosophers think that action, in contrast to thought, does not function to discriminate. But when there is a discriminandum, of whatever kind or status, *its* being has neither more nor less of being than the being of any other.[3]

The principle of ontological parity scarcely implies that there are no differences among natural complexes. On the contrary, it presupposes that no two complexes, in whatever order and however discriminated, are similar in all respects. Their discriminability forces us to preserve their integrity, or better, to acknowledge it. Natural complexes, moreover, differ in both kind and scope. Difference is so basic that every distinction good and bad, every opinion shallow or deep, every fiction, hallucination, or deception, every product social or individual, is recognized as a natural complex. Nor are distinctions of degree abolished; on the contrary, they are preserved. What is abolished is any inference, from A's being less courageous than B or more skillful than B, that something is more or less real, of greater or lesser being, than something else. Little courage is not a lesser reality than great courage. The preservation of degree actually requires the principle of parity. Just as the principle does not warrant the attribution of higher reality to that which exemplifies a trait in higher degree, so it does not justify the attribution of lesser reality or unreality to that which exemplifies a trait in lower degree.

No distinction, then, is dismissed. It only awaits its analysis—the interpretation of "how and in what sense it is real." All complexes are equally "authentic" as complexes, distressing as this may be to certain points of view whose metaphysical orientation actually damages an ethical purpose which it is believed to support. The natural parity of all complexes, their ontological integrity, is what reveals all differences and makes it possible to ascertain them. The principle of parity obliges us to receive and accept all discriminanda. The conception of ontological priority, on the other hand, makes all ascertainable differences suspect, and instead of interpreting their relative character and ordinal location, always stands ready to efface them.

There are many possible ways of trying to justify the principle of ontological priority. It is a principle which seems to reflect a deep, standing need, and it lends itself to gratuitous affirmation and reaffirmation regardless of argument. We shall try to formulate a number of grounds for it, all different, and to show the untenable consequences which they entail. More important, perhaps, will be the concomitant opportunity to develop, by contrast, additional properties and distinctions in the theory of natural complexes.

1. Complex B, it might be held, is "more real" than complex A when A is dependent upon B, but B is not dependent upon A. The forms of "dependency" are of course various. We may assume that causal dependency, in the strong sense of a complex having been produced by another which is its necessary and sufficient condition, is as persuasive as any other form. Causes, then, must be more real than their effects. Now since B, as cause of A, is itself the effect of a cause, and this in turn the effect of a prior cause . . . and since A, as effect of B, is also cause of a further effect . . . there seems to be only one major conclusion consistent with the initial supposition: that remoter causes are more real than proximate causes. Each complex is more real than its posterity but less real than its ancestry. And from this it follows that the universe of actualities, to speak of no other, is becoming less and less real. The ensuing eschatology is grotesque. All the reality lost would have to be restored by an ontological resurrection if the Last Judgment were to be dramatically potent. Even an interpretation that would construe greater reality to mean greater goodness would fail dismally by this "dependency" criterion. Nothing is more obvious in the experience of men than the truth that an effect may be more admirable, more salutary, more encouraging morally than its cause; or the truth that human products are often much more important to mankind than their producers are.

2. Complex B, it might be held, is "more real" than complex A when A is [merely] a component of B, for B may contain not only A but other components. But as in the preceding position, an innocent-sounding assumption leads to stultifying results. If A is a component of B, and B a component of a still larger whole C, then B in turn is less real than C;

and so on "upwards" (or "outwards"), so that only a universe or grand totality is truly real, while its most "minute" components or elements are least real. One ironic consequence is that what is putatively "indivisible" or "simple" emerges here as least real, instead of being an "ultimate." When the position is stated not in terms of wholes and components but in terms of wholes and parts, it is equally weak. All components would seem to be parts, but not all parts components. A man who is part of a religious movement is not a component of the movement in the sense that a wall or a joist is a component of a house. In one respect, a man is part of a corporation; in another, the corporation is part of his life. In neither of these or various other senses of "part" is the part a component. If, without qualification, wholes are said to be more real than parts, the corporation must be more real than the man who is part of it; and at the same time the corporation must be less real than the life of the man who is part of that corporation. (It will be recalled that the generic term embracing "parts" and "components," as well as any other sub-complexes, is "constituents.")

3. Complex B, it might be held, is "more real" than complex A when the scope of B is greater or wider or more far-reaching than the scope of A. It is necessary to examine the idea of scope, with the purpose of showing that there are well-grounded distinctions in the scope of natural complexes, but that these distinctions actually render "degree of reality" an unsatisfactory and dispensable concept.

(a) B is greater in scope than A if it is more comprehensive or more generic than A. One complex is more comprehensive than another if it is not always a manifestation of the other but the other is always a manifestation of it. Juvenile crime is, let us say, a manifestation of the more comprehensive condition of social confusion and violence. Here the less comprehensive complex would also typically be called a "part" of the more comprehensive one. Being a sister is a manifestation of being a sibling: being a sibling is more comprehensive than being a sister. But in this case it is the more comprehensive complex that would most typically be called a "part" of the less comprehensive: being a sibling is part of what being a sister is or means. In each of the two examples it is possible, if less typical, to see the "part" in reverse. There is a sense in which social confusion is "part" of a juvenile crime; and there is a sense in which being a sister is "part" of what it can mean to be a sibling. The contrasting senses correspond to two of the senses which Aristotle enumerates for "in": the species, in one sense, is in the genus; the genus, in another sense, is in the species. If we consider once more the case of being a sibling as more comprehensive than and yet part of being a sister, we observe that the generic trait is part of a specific trait but not part of a "whole" in any obvious respect. To show it as part of a whole, we should have to frame and discriminate a natural complex that is somewhat different, and say that in another order the generic trait is part of the "whole structure of traits" which constitutes the specific trait.

(b) B is greater in scope than A if it is more pervasive than A. One complex is more pervasive than another if it is recurrent under more various conditions, or more widespread in its presence, or more extensive in its influence, or more diverse in its ramifications, than the other. A nation is a more pervasive complex than a stone in a cave, an ocean more pervasive than a swamp in a field. Being more comprehensive entails being more pervasive, at least in some respects. The class of physical bodies, which is more comprehensive than the class of sentient bodies, is also more pervasive in the spatial distribution of its members. (It is less pervasive, for instance, in the communicative powers of its members.) Being a sibling, which is more generic or comprehensive than being a sister, is also more pervasive because its occurrence is more frequent and widespread. But although greater comprehensiveness entails greater pervasiveness, the converse is not true. Nations are more pervasive than stones in caves, but neither more nor less comprehensive. To the extent that these are unrelated complexes, their comparative comprehensiveness might appear to be decidable not in terms of either as comprehended or embraced by the other but in terms of their respective divisibility, as kinds or types, into less comprehensive complexes. By this standard, however, there can be as many species of stones lying in caves as there are species of nations. The sense of overwhelmingly different magnitude that arises in a comparison of this kind, the sense that one of the two complexes "includes" far more than the other, boils down to a sense of relative pervasiveness. Although relative pervasiveness is often difficult to ascertain, this is a question of degree. In gross terms, if two complexes were selected at random, it probably would make sense to say that one was more pervasive than the other. In the matter of comprehensiveness, on the other hand, there is as likely as not to be an incommensurability of two randomly selected complexes, making the question of their relative comprehensiveness impossible to answer.

To vary the illustrations: in human affairs wastefulness may be more pervasive than planning, dullness more pervasive than imaginativeness. Even where two complexes, one of which is more pervasive than the other, are causally related, neither is necessarily more comprehensive than the other. Thus misunderstanding is a cause of divorce; it is a more pervasive human complex than divorce, but not necessarily more comprehensive, for divorce is not always a manifestation of misunderstanding.

Does the problem of incommensurability cast doubt upon the metaphysical goal of seeking to discriminate generic complexes that have the widest possible scope? No; the complexes sought by philosophy are deliberately selected for their commensurateness and applicability. Their comprehensiveness must be exhibited as a relation that they bear to numerous and diverse other complexes.

Thus comprehensiveness and pervasiveness are two forms of scope in natural complexes. There is no reason to believe that the kind of difference each represents gives any comfort to the doctrine of ontological priority. The scope of a complex is one of the factors in its contour or province. Lesser scope does not diminish the "naturalness" of a complex, nor does greater scope increase it. Nor is there any ethical significance in the idea of scope as such. Only when the ethical significance of a complex has already been established can greater or lesser scope be ethically relevant.

One impulse which motivates the doctrine of priority expresses itself in the concern that gradations in nature should be recognized. Herein lurks the deceptiveness of the doctrine. For to "recognize" gradation by seeing one extreme of a scale as the realm of the ultimately real, and the other extreme as the realm of the unreal or least real, is in effect to drive attention away from one of the extremes. For what is unreal is either impossible of query or unworthy of it. Consider the fatuity of a newly identified, newly located "unreality." Query, by its products, multiplies the complexes of nature. Can there be a more ludicrous idea than invention through the methodic discrimination of unrealities?

The scope of a complex, its pervasiveness and comprehensiveness, may also be regarded as its "inclusiveness." The latter notion has an unmistakable value, despite its somewhat indefinite character. There is much advantage to thinking of any natural complex as "including" traits or sub-complexes, or of an order of complexes as including complexes that are discriminable also in another order. Something like "inclusiveness" is pertinent to the understanding of what is meant by a natural complex. Every complex is inclusive, regardless of the way in which it is inclusive. Stated in the manner that has here been formalized, every complex has scope, no matter what the degree of its pervasiveness or the mode of its comprehensiveness.

4. Complex B, it might be held, is "more real" than complex A when B is more "determinate" than A. It is easy to see, at the very outset, that if the notion of determinateness varies, contrary conceptions can be made equally plausible. For example, where the "determinate" suggests the fixed and the eternal, forms are held to be more real than facts. Where the "determinate" suggests the concrete and the particular, forms are held to be less real than facts.

In a discussion of determinateness, the notions of actuality and possibility are inevitable. Most people accept the twinship or correlation of the two in the sense that if one talks of actuality one must talk of possibility and vice versa. Nevertheless, philosophers are less worried about actuality than about possibility. After all, they feel, actuality is—well, actuality; but just what is possibility? It does not occur to them that the familiar presence of actual "things" does not clarify the concept of actuality. They are content with the plain man's impression that the actual is near and accessible, the possible remote and insubstantial. No matter how primitive their metaphysics of actuality, philosophers seldom hesitate to talk of possibility as if it were illegitimately claiming to rival actuality in rank. They warn against the danger of ascribing to possibility the same status as actuality, but the typical questions they themselves raise, about the "kind of thing" possibilities are, and about where possibilities could be, violate the warning in the most serious way. Philosophers are wary of what some of them have called "possible entities." It is worth observing that we can hardly do without speaking of possibilities, but can very easily do without speaking of "entities." This term tends to obstruct, not only an adequate approach to the conception of possibility, but an adequate approach to the conception of actuality. The relevant considerations at the moment, then, are that the difficulties in the understanding of possibility do not justify abstention from thought about the relation between the possible and the actual; that the question, What is the nature of possibility? does not interfere with the recognition of possibilities and their significance; and that the question, What is the nature of actuality? is not less difficult than the preceding question.

Let us state five conceptions of "the determinate":

 I. That which is stable or constant.
 II. That which is active and motive.
 III. That which is not merely active but individual, or individually active.
 IV. That which is "complete."
 V. That upon which other complexes are more "dependent" than it is upon them.

And let us consider each of these separately.

I. This view of the determinate can serve as the basis of a contention—altogether opposed to the dominant one, according to which "determinate" at the very least means "actual"—that possibilities are more determinate than actualities. Thus: Some actualities are more stable or constant than others, but no actuality is as stable as a possibility can be. Actualities are subject to modification. Possibilities, on the contrary, are not; they remain intact, whether they are exemplified or not.

But in response to this contention: possibilities are mortal and modifiable, even as actualities are. The possibility of all Americans being literate by 1960 has ceased to obtain. Possibilities can be modified in their relation to actualities. In order to have a status that would remain perfectly intact, in order to be perfectly exempt from any kind of modification, a possibility would have to be totally unrelated, insulated from all actualities and all other possibilities. This means that it could not be located in any order whatever, and therefore could not have been discriminated as that possibility.

Are all actualities "subject to modification"? When the latter phrase is used and it is contended that they are, there is surely a certain model of actuality that is presupposed and that governs the answer. The question will have to be dealt with later in a number of contexts, along with the question whether any possibility is *not* "subject to modification." Answers will emerge, but not without the aid of additional categories.

II. This view can serve as the basis for a contention that actualities are more determinate than possibilities. For are not actualities agential and efficacious, and are not possibilities inert and non-efficacious?

But against this contention it can be argued that our ordinary notion of agency and efficacy is based on our disposition to think of one conspicuous type of efficacy associated with one conspicuous type of actuality. If a possibility merely as such cannot be said to yield a "result," neither can an actuality merely as such. Every actuality has limits. These represent "its" possibilities; in familiar cases they are sometimes called "powers" or "potentialities." Any "result" involves both an antecedent actuality and the possibilities resident in that actuality.

III. This view implies that, among actualities, individuals are "most fully" determinate. Since "societies," for instance, are constituted by individuals, and not the other way round, individuals are the "ultimate" agents.

But although societies cannot attain results that individuals can, they can attain results, and results that individuals cannot. Basically this is a commonplace of everyday belief, but it is also more than defensible metaphysically. For we cannot entertain the notion of a society, or even of a mere grouping, without taking seriously the relations that obtain among the individuals said to constitute the society or group. Nor can we recognize any complex as a society without recognizing the difference between an organization of individuals and an abstract number of individuals. A social complex is differently agential but not less truly agential than an individual.

And *are* societies constituted by individuals but not the other way round? If "constituted by" meant "composed of," the answer might be, yes. But to be a "constituent," as we have seen, does not necessarily mean to be a "component." What it means, more generally, is to be a trait that is relevant. The society of which an individual is member may enter into the complex that constitutes an individual, just as an individual may enter into the complex that constitutes a society. Indeed, so far as an individual at random is concerned, a society may be relevant to its integrity in a far more fundamental way than that individual is to the integrity of the society.

In the consideration of this point we have proceeded as if "actualities" comprised only individuals and societies (recurrently identifiable groups) of individuals. If relations and structures, for example, may be regarded as actual, then the question whether individuals are the "most" determinate actualities is even farther from resolution—or even more artificial and ill-founded than we are thus far in a position to indicate.

IV. This view can lend itself *(a)* to a claim that possibilities are more determinate than actualities, since they are "complete" just as they are, without actualization, whereas actualities "become" complete and may cease to be complete; *(b)* to a claim that actualities are more determinate than possibilities, since they are the "fulfillments" of possibilities, which as such are "unfulfilled" and hence incomplete; *(c)* to a claim that societies are more determinate than individuals, having the completeness of a whole which transcends any part; *(d)* to a claim that individuals are more determinate than societies, having the completeness that consists in indivisibility, as contrasted with the divisibility of societies.

Each of these senses of "complete," *(a)*-*(d)*, is a mixture of plausibility and speciousness. Each is of very limited significance. It seems far more significant to note that whatever is discriminable as a complex is fully as much a complex as any other; that any complex, whether possibility or actuality, is "complete" in so far as it [inherently] has an integrity.

Nevertheless, it is desirable to continue the dialectic of comment on each of the conflicting claims, the further to prepare for theoretical reorientation. *(a)* What it means for an actuality to "become complete" or cease to be complete is itself a nice question, and so is the allied question, at just what point an actuality may justifiably be deemed complete. *(b)* Every possibility is of course subject to actualization, but actualization does not complete it *as* a possibility. As a *possibility*, it is complete whether it is actualized or not. If, moreover, an actuality is the "fulfillment" of a possibility, this does not necessarily imply that an actuality it itself "fulfilled" or complete. *(c)* Why should a whole be more complete than a part? It is complete *as* a whole, and the part is complete *as* a part. There is undoubtedly an everyday sense in which, by a quantitative criterion, completeness is achieved when a vessel is filled or when pieces are assembled into a whole. But in these instances, the presence of a project waiting to be completed does not prove the point. For another project may be compelted only when a vessel is emptied or when a whole is dismembered and separated into pieces. *(d)* There is no reason for that which is (allegedly) indivisible to be considered more complete than that which is divisible. The integrity of neither is a model for the integrity of the other. Neither relates to the other on a scale of degrees. And if a scale were constructed, it could be constructed to show the relative completeness and incompleteness of either.

V. This view can encourage a chaos of claims. *(a)* Possibilities are less dependent upon actualities than actualities upon them. For possibilities are what they are whether actualized or not, whereas actualities are what they are in virtue of the possibilities that there are. *(b)* Actualities are less dependent upon possibilities than possibilities upon them. For actualities are dependent upon other actualities: merely because they exemplify possibilities does not mean that they are products or effects of possibilities. *(c)* Societies are less dependent upon individuals than individuals upon them. For a society endures though each individual in it eventually perishes, whereas individuals never exist in isolation. A society is dependent only upon some present collectivity of individuals—but not on any given individual, not on any specific number of individuals, and not on the same collectivity. *(d)* Individuals are less dependent upon societies than societies upon them. For individuals are irreducible and societies are not. The same individual can be in either or both of two societies.

All the foregoing claims in V, *(a)-(d)*, are invalid unless severely qualified. All the "dependencies" are co-dependencies. *(a)* It is true that specific possibilities do not require, for their being, actualization or eventual actualities: but in one or another sense they do presuppose correlative actualities, which precede them or are their contemporaries. Possibilities are "for" and "of" actualities. They are (to speak roughly until we come to Chapter IV) "conditions" for actualities and "natural definitions" of the boundaries or limits of actualities—however familiar or however bizarre these boundaries might appear to be. *(b)* Actualities are always actualizations of possibilities. If there were an exception to this, it would have to be an actuality which arose or prevailed regardless of any or all possibilities—whatever that might mean. An actuality is not the product merely of possibilities; but neither is it the product merely of actualities *as* such and unqualifiedly. It is a product of those actualities which provide the conditions or possibilities for it—that is, which make it possible, which (as we may say in some cases) have the power to produce it. *(c)* A society in which individuals simply "participate" is presumably like a box which continues in its identity though continually filled with new individual articles, or like a ship indifferent to the personnel of crew and passengers. But even a box cannot contain *any* number or *any* kind of articles, nor can a ship have *any* number or *any* kind of personnel if it *is* to be a ship. A society is more than a multiplicity of individuals, but not more than an order of individuals. The nature and continuation of the order is dependent at all times upon the traits of individuals and upon the relations among individuals which arise and which expire. *(d)* Individuals are inherently social or associational; no individual is without some mode of relation to other individuals. For as a natural complex it bears traits imposed by nature upon all complexes. It is related to those complexes which are conditions for its integrity, and in turn it has a sphere of domination or influence, which likewise presupposes association, or typical relatedness to other complexes. Finally, each individual, as a natural complex, is an order of traits. It is a society of subaltern complexes. It is no more and no less "irreducible" than any other complex.

Thus "dependence" is meaningful in various ways. But lesser dependence as a criterion of greater determinateness is reminiscent of the untenable versions of "substance" (if indeed the notion permits any tenable versions at all)—substance as less dependent than anything else: as the bearer of traits that it itself unanalyzable into traits, as the subject of predications that is itself not predicable of anything, as that which "is in itself" and is not in anything else.

The monstrous commitment facing such views is a notion of the fully determinate as that which is independent of traits. But philosophers never have been deterred from seeking a blend of the notion of determinateness with the notions of independence and completeness. Accordingly, that which is "in itself" is metamorphosed (for example, by Spinoza and Hegel) from that which is independent of traits to that which is the bearer of *all* traits and is therefore alone "truly" in itself.

But other philosophers have been unwilling to veer to this extreme and to identfiy the fully determinate with one basic order of traits, fearing that the notion of individuality is thereby eliminated. They have preferred to retain but to reinterpret the conception of a plurality of entities ("substances") each of which is complete. Completeness is thus held to belong not to the "ultimacy" of a universal order but to the "ultimacy" of its parts—to genuine "atoms" of reality. The completeness of each of these atoms or individuals lies, however, not in its "independence" but in its being uniquely "a system of all things" (for example, Leibniz and Whitehead). Traitlessness is banished. Completeness is reconciled with finitude. An individual or atom, though finite, is fully determinate, because unique relatedness to everything else is basic to its being.

According to Whitehead, these ultimate atoms ("actual entities") are "the final real things of which the world is made up. There is no going behind actual entities to find anything more real." These "final realities" are also described as "devoid of all indetermination," as "complete" (or "completely real"), and as "devoid of all indecision." They are not individual in a mere loose or rhetorical sense. Unlike what one might wish to identify, for instance, as an individual culture or nation, they have "absolute individuality." And as such, they have "an absolute reality." Actual entities are construed as "activities" and "processes." In so far as they are "grouped" into one or another kind of "nexus" or order, such as a "society," they compose a reality which alone has the property of "enduring." Societies, however, must not be confused with these "completely real things" of which they are composed. The actual entities or ultimate processes are themselves "composite" and "analyzable," and in "an indefinite number of ways." They have their own "component elements," of as many kinds as there are modes of analysis. Nevertheless, to *these* component elements "complete actuality" does not belong; they are "subordinate elements" only.[4]

It turns out, then, in Whitehead, that (1) the atomic actualities always have component elements; and that (2) the atomic actualities are always components in an order or nexus of actualities. Yet somehow the former kind of components, considered as realities, are less real, less "ultimate," than the latter kind of components. An atomic actuality is more real than its components, but an order of such actualities is less real than *its* components. Both that which goes to constitute an atom and that which an atom goes to constitute are less real than the atom. All this, curiously, in spite of the fact that the atoms are as inconceivable without their components as the components are without them; and in spite of the fact that these atoms are as inconceivable apart from an order as an order is apart from them.

It turns out, also, that (3) the atoms or "final realities" are actualities; so that actualities are more real than possibilities. This in spite of the fact that the atomic actualities do not endure but only become and perish, while "pure" possibilities ("eternal objects") neither become nor perish; and in spite of the fact that actualities are dependent, for their being, upon possibilities getting realized in them, while these pure possibilities are not dependent, for their being, upon any actualities—they are "the same for all actual entities."

It turns out, finally, that (4) possibility is "deficiently actual." Why this makes it less than "really real" is a puzzle; for by the same token, actuality should be "deficiently possible" or "deficiently eternal." Just what can be meant by a complex being deficient in that with which it is essentially contrasted, or to which it is essentially correlated, is problematical, to say the least. Is a male "deficiently female" and a female "deficiently male"? Is a society "deficiently individual"? If so, should an individual not be considered "deficiently social"?

An atomic theory of "ultimate actualities" is a type of metaphysical theory stressing the crucial role of "components." To be sure, Whitehead's components, as "processes," are a far cry from the tendency to think of building blocks as the model type of component. But not all natural complexes can be interpreted in terms of components, and especially not in terms of a single type. Whitehead conceives of his "ultimate actualities" as processes containing a phase in which they achieve "full determinateness." The view of determinateness that is implied is an unnecessarily restricted one. There is certainly a sense in which each phase of a process is no less determinate than either the process as a whole or its consummatory phase. Ontological atoms, like their more familiar namesakes, can be relatively final in a functional capacity; that is, as explanatory or exhibitive devices accomplishing an envisaged aim in a particular perspective. That atoms of actuality should be unqualifiedly construed as the "really real things" proves only that there is an aesthetic or methodological bias, or an underlying predisposition of common sense, the absolutist cravings of which are appeased by the notion of actuality and not by the notion of possibility.

No natural complex can be a metaphysical atom, unless we wish to hold that whatever is discriminable is "atomic" in some respect, whether it is actual or possible, individual or social. Perhaps each is "atomic" in the sense that there is an order to the nature of which it contributes. Its own integrity is dependent on this order, within which it is located. But at bottom, metaphysical atomism does not belong and cannot survive in a theory of natural complexes. The required stretching of the notion of atom, to the point of abandoning the analogical traits that lend it whatever value it should have, serves no purpose. Since every complex includes and is included in a complex, all atoms would have to include and be included in atoms. All complexes would have equal claim; and if all complexes are atoms, none is.

NOTES

1. Edmund Husserl, *Cartesian Meditations*, trans. Dorion Cairns (The Hague, 1960),

p. 18.

2. J. H. Randall, Jr., *Nature and Historical Experience* (New York, 1958), p. 131.

3. Not only "being" but "existence" and "actuality" have been said to allow of degrees. And degree is sometimes expressed by specific kinds of "more" and "less." Thus: "Intuition not only exists, but is the most intense form of existence." George Santayana, *The Realm of Spirit* (New York, 1940), p. 94. Or to quote a more recent position: "What is actual *is* in a more intensive sense than what is

merely possible or potential." Albert Hofstadter, "Truth of Being," *Journal of Philosophy*, 1965, p. 171. What it means to *exist* more or less "intensely," or to *be* in a more and a less "intensive sense," does not emerge satisfactorily, if at all, from the context of the statements quoted.

4. According to Whitehead, "a coordinate division of an actual occasion . . . can *be conceived* as an actual occasion with its own actual world . . ." Such conception is described as "hypothetical" and as "potential." Whitehead says that "just as for some purposes, one atomic actuality can be treated *as though* it were many co-ordinate actualities, in the same way, for other purposes, a nexus of many actualities can be treated *as though* it were one actuality." Otherwise stated: ". . . In addition to the merely potential subdivisions of a satisfaction into coordinate feelings, there is the merely potential aggregation of actual entities into a super-actuality in respect to which the *true actualities* play the part of coordinate divisions" (italics added). See A. N. Whitehead, *Process and Reality* (New York, 1929), p. 439.

PAUL KURTZ

State University of New York at Buffalo

Meta-Metaphysics, the Categories, and Naturalism

Professor Randall's interest in metaphysics is a constant theme of his philosophical work; and it is an aspect of his position that distinguishes him from the age. For at a time when metaphysical inquiry has been in eclipse, Randall has pursued a basically metaphysical interest in philosophy. As a former student of Randall, stimulated by his bold and provocative lectures, I am in a quandary similar to that faced by Aristotle when he felt called upon to analyze the theory of the Forms of his teacher. Aristotle noted that the Forms had been introduced by his friends, but he asked whether his devotion should be to truth or to his friends—and he concluded that, while both are dear, piety required that truth should be honored above his friends. I take it that Professor Randall would want me to make the same choice and that he would prefer that I submit his metaphysics to detailed critical analysis rather than polite compliment. It is incumbent on naturalists interested in metaphysics to conduct their inquiries with caution. Although I am impressed by the sweep of Randall's philosophical net, I am concerned with its lack of precision on key points, which I think are in need of clarification by someone sympathetic to his general naturalistic approach. Moreover, I am troubled by what I detect to be a modest deviation from an empirical and scientific naturalism.

I. RANDALL'S META-METAPHYSICS

In an early paper[1] and again in *Nature and Historical Experience*[2] Randall provides an account of the nature of metaphysics, as he views it. Metaphysical inquiry has been in disrepute in modern thought; and Randall agrees that certain kinds of metaphysics in the Western tradition deserve their bad reputations. Thus, he argued quite effectively that the quest for "Being" as "Totality" or as a "Whole," or the attempt by metaphysicians to provide an overall unification of knowledge, is mistaken. Empirical thinkers have judged these claims premature, presumptuous, and to have employed mythical means to achieve supposed unities. Moreover, he also shows that the search for "True Being" or "Reality" as distinct from "Appearances" is illegitimate, for nature is irreducibly plural and the so-called theories of "Reality" are generally masks for underlying moral biases in terms of which metaphysicians seek to exclude parts of nature as "unreal." Everything which can be encountered is in some sense real, says Randall, and to denigrate or exclude part of the world is to impose one's value judgments upon what one finds.

There is another conception of metaphysics, the Aristotelian, which Randall does mean to defend as meaningful and legitimate. Indeed, he believes that metaphysics, as the "science of existence," is one science among many, distinguished not by its methods but by its own specific subject matter. According to Randall, the goal of Aristotle's metaphysics is to analyze "the 'generic traits' manifested by existences of any kind, the distinctions . . . in any universe of discourse drawn from existence" or exhibited in any "existential subject-matter."[3] And Randall maintains that present-day empirical naturalists concur in this inquiry. Such a metaphysics, for Randall, is "empirical" because the "primacy of the subject matter" is its basic principle, and the beginning of any "sound" metaphysical inquiry is the world "as initially encountered." However, this empirical inquiry is not to be merely identified with the findings of the sciences, as so many other contemporary empirical naturalists have attempted to do. Metaphysics is, for Randall, as we shall see, much broader in scope.

Metaphysics, says Randall, is also "analytic"; though his use of the term "analytic" is specialized and distinct from the prevailing view, which considers analyses to be of terms, concepts, propositions, their meanings and logic, and not of things in the world, where descriptive or synthetic statements more appropriately apply. Metaphysical inquiry, for Randall, is "analytic of natural existence" in that "it lays bare those generic traits and distinctions which terms can formulate."[4] It is "analytic" in the "further sense that it seeks to disclose the traits of existence and to trace their implications."[5] According to Randall, although metaphysical reflection of the world as intellectually experienced begins with existence formulated and expressed in language and discourse, it soon leads beyond this to the world as directly or immediately experienced. The metaphysical analysis of any specific subject matter is for Randall the "critical analysis of the distinctive traits of that subject matter, of the intellectual instruments, the concepts and distinctions for dealing with it and of its implications for the nature of experience."[6]

Many philosophers today might agree with Randall's critique of those abstract metaphysical systems which seek "Reality" or the "Whole" of existence. They also might agree that a limited kind of metaphysics is possible. Randall's metaphysics, however, does not appear to be "empirical" or "analytic" in the usual sense of those terms; it seems to go beyond what most other twentieth century descriptive metaphysicians are willing to do.

For example, Randall maintains that his "empirical" and "analytic" metaphysics inquires into science and language, their methods, concepts, and implications; but he claims that it also includes "an analysis of other types of human experience besides those primarily cognitive."[7] Without "the religious dimension of experience" accounted for, says Randall, metaphysics is incomplete and hardly "imaginative and comprehensive." Moreover, metaphysics for him must include an account of art, morality, and other basic types of human activity, which are all responses "to the generic traits of existence." Such responses, he maintains, "have metaphysical implications for the nature of the world that generates and sustains them."[8] Each, according to Randall, can be analyzed in itself, and can be seen "as revealing the traits of existence that call it forth."[9] Philosophical theories of religion, art, and morality thus lead to our "seeing" them in their contexts. These "theories" enable metaphysics "to serve" as "a method or instrument of criticism and clarification."[10] But they also provide a form of "intelligibility" and "understanding." Thus, although metaphysics has a critical function—it is a "critique of abstractions"—it also has a theoretical function, for it enables us to see things in their widest range of relationships, and as such seems to provide a form of "synoptic vision."

Randall also seems to share the view widely held today that metaphysical analysis entails the introduction of "categories," at least this is one interpretation that Randall lends himself to. Thus Randall is interested in presenting a list of "ontological" categories or "predicates," which he calls different "ways of being" or "ways of functioning." These categories, he says, do not denote different kinds of things, but rather, "different ways in which the same thing (or factor) can function."[11] " 'To be' anything means to function, and hence to be, in one of these . . . ways."[12] Thus it is the task of metaphysics to provide a set of highly general intellectual concepts that apply to *any* existential subject matter, thing, or factor. Although the quest for "categories" is not the whole of Randall's metaphysics, nonetheless it seems in some way to be an important part of it—as it was in Aristotle, which Randall draws upon so heavily. And it is that aspect of his metaphysics which is perhaps most open to criticism, for Randall does not provide us with a detailed account of what he conceives the categories to be.*

---

* In a letter received from Professor Randall in response to this paper, after it was in press he replies that he completely rejects the notion of "categories" and that any analysis which attributes such a theory to him is mistaken (though he has not written up this part of his thought as yet.) Inasmuch as this paper is based upon Randall's published writings, and since the concept "categories," or something similar to it, has brooked large in the literature on metaphysics and the metaphysics of

II. What Are the Categories?

There have been many lists of categories in the history of thought. Most frequently these have been based on an interpretation of the sciences of the day. For Aristotle the categories presented both a logical and ontological distinction about the nature of existence and of our manner of thinking about it. The categories were predicates, one or other of which must be affirmed of any subject, if we inquire as to what it is in itself. These state the mode of essential being of any subject that exists. For Aristotle, the ultimate subject of predication or primary existence was substance and the other categories ("quantity," "quality," "relation," "place," "time," "position," "state," "action," or "affection") were secondary and predicables of this. The important point was that there was nothing which was not either a substance or some other category, and that the categories cannot be further reduced. It is important to see, however, that Aristotle's categories were not definitory of the whole of Aristotle's metaphysics, for metaphysics involved a quest for the first principles and causes of being, and Aristotle introduced many other important concepts: the four causes, matter and form, potentiality and actuality. Moreover, to the list of categories he later added five other key predicables: *genus, species, differentia, proprium, accidens.*

Kant adapted Aristotle's doctrine of the categories to his own use in the *Critique.* He was not interested in "the metaphysics of being," but in

---

naturalism, I have decided to publish this paper substantially in its original form, in the hope that it may help to clarify the concept "categories." If one examines Randall's writings one can find quotations which support the claim that he has a theory of "categories." Thus he writes:

"Now since these five "ways" are five different ways in which factors can be *said* to function, or *said* to be, they might be called five "predicables" or five "categories.". . . In terms of the functional realism of the present analysis, there would be no objection to calling them "categories," since that position implies that ontologically, they are ways of functioning in Substance before they are formulated as ways of stating: they are definitely ontological or metaphysical categories." (*Nature and Historical Experience,* p. 177)

"This analysis has so far been led to distinguish five fundamental ways in which factors can function in Substance, or the Situation. . . . Since these are five ways in which factors can be *said* to function, or *said* to be, they might be called five "predicables" or categories. But since the ways of functioning are prior to the ways of stating them, they are ontological categories." (*Ibid.,* p. 271)

In any case, Professor Randall may not *now* wish to employ the term "category" because it is misleading and confusing; nevertheless, he still talks of "ways of functioning," "ways of being," or "traits of existence"—and I believe that much of my criticism would continue to apply to those concepts no matter how they are designated.

"the metaphysics of experience." He asked, what are the modes of synthesis on the part of the mind through which objects are apprehended and known? The categories, he claimed, were *a priori* and presupposed in all thinking. Kant's twelve categories were deduced from a study of logic, and were based upon a fourfold structure: "quality," "quantity," "relation," and "modality." The point was that the categories denominated the conceptual characteristics which *any* object must possess to be thought, much the same as the forms of intuition, space and time, denominated the *a priori* and necessary characteristics which any object must possess to be experienced.

P. F. Strawson, in his influential work, *Individuals: An Essay In Descriptive Metaphysics*, has recently provided a categorial scheme.[13] "Descriptive metaphysics" for Strawson is supposed "to describe the actual structure of our thought about the world" and "to lay bare the most general features of our conceptual structure."[14] And Strawson focusses on "particulars," "material bodies," and "persons." However, his analysis is based more upon ordinary language than upon contemporary science, and it is distinguished from what he calls "revisionary metaphysics" in that it simply describes our concepts embedded in language, and does not propose a radically new way of looking at the world.

There is obviously a confusion in the literature on metaphysics between different senses of "category." It has been used as a synonym for "predicable," "trait," "presupposition," "assumption," "invariant condition," "basic reality," "methodological principle," "first principle," "rule," etc. Some writers, for example, have interpreted materialism as providing a set of categories: "matter in motion," "mass," and "energy" are said to be fundamental in nature. But this is an extended conception of categories, and according to Randall's view, it presents a reductive account of basic "reality" rather than a categorial metaphysics. Whitehead's organismic metaphysics may seem to provide another list of categories. But this approach for Randall is a speculative metaphysical account of the whole of reality rather than a limited statement of key categories.

For a descriptive and categorial metaphysics not concerned with the "reality" or "totality" of being, at least six different interpretations of "category" seem to emerge.

I. In the so-called "metaphysics of being," (a) a "category" may be said to be that which applies to *any* object or subject matter that exists. This is the Aristotelian notion, and it is apparently what Randall means when he says that metaphysics is an inquiry into the characteristics that appear in every existential field of inquiry and in existences of any kind. These categories appear to be "universal" in the sense that they state the characteristics that *every* thing in the world which allegedly *is* possesses. This conception of metaphysical category is open to criticism by empirical metaphysicians, who wish to focus their inquiry on observable data, for universal assertions apply to analytic, not descriptive sentences. (b) Thus the term "category" has also been used to refer to "generic trait." Such categories are not universal assertions, but only probabilistic generalizations about some of the properties and characteristics that nature seems to manifest. They do not apply to any and everything, but only to many or most things, and they are drawn primarily from an interpretation of the data of the sciences.

II. In the so-called "metaphysics of experience," (c) a "category" may refer to the underlying presuppositions of experience and knowledge, such as the Kantian categories of the understanding and the forms of intuition. This interpretation again has been questioned by empiricists, who are dubious of absolute presuppositions that are said to apply to *all* experience and knowledge. (d) Empirical metaphysicians have transposed this inquiry into an inquiry into the categories of "transaction," i.e., an account of the generic (though not universal) characteristics and traits of human interaction as revealed by the biological and social sciences. Dewey's *Experience and Nature* would seem especially to fall under this interpretation, for it is a generalized account of human transactions within nature (though Dewey was no doubt also interested in "the generic traits of nature"). (e) The term "category" may refer to the basic methodological rules and principles which govern inquiry, or in Randall's language, the "ultimate intellectual instruments," "concepts" and "distinctions" for dealing with nature. Such an inquiry is an inquiry into the "logic of inquiry" and the basic criteria found to be most effective in empirical investigations in science and practical experience. (f) A "category" may refer to the key concepts uncovered in the "logical geography" of a language system, i.e., the key rules governing the uses of language. This apparently expresses Strawson's conception of descriptive metaphysics. It is similar to Kant's quest for presuppositions, but it is unlike Kant's, in that it is not a metaphysics of Mind or mental forms but of linguistic rules underlying usage.

In my judgment the interpretation of "category" as I (a) predicables of any object, and II (c) *a priori* presuppositions of experience, are most open to criticism, especially if these are construed in universal terms as applicable to *any* or *all* objects. For a descriptive metaphysics, only categories in sense I (b) generic traits of nature, and II (d) generic traits of human transactions are meaningful. "Category" as (e) methodological rules, is an extended sense of the "category," and perhaps the term "metaphysical" does not really apply here. I (b) and II (d) can only be based upon a close reading of the conceptual framework and conclusions of the sciences, and II (e), where investigated, upon the methods of the sciences.

II (f) the analysis of fundamental linguistic rules, is an important inquiry, which is based upon a careful analysis of the rules of use, primarily of our natural languages. I do not see how an examination of the concepts employed in ordinary language (Indo-European primarily) can be divorced entirely from an examination of those used in the sciences. A fuller analysis of Strawson's metaphysics, however, is an appropriate topic for another paper.

Now Randall's conception of category seems to involve I (a), (b), II (d), and (e). He appears critical of II (c), the Kantian approach, and II (f) of ordinary language unrelated to an ontological or instrumentalist framework. Randall however talks continuously of the metaphysics of experience in generic or universalistic terms, and he has a theory of language, so that although (c) and (f) are called into question by him, they are not necessarily excluded from his inquiry.

III. THE CATEGORIES OF RANDALL

I submit that aspects of Randall's meta-metaphysics and his categorial scheme as outlined above can be questioned, and on the following grounds: First, because it moves back and forth between, and identifies or equates, a metaphysics of being (I) and a metaphysics of experience (II), without recognizing the differences between them. Second, because it does not properly distinguish the different conceptions of the categories, and in particular blurs category I (a) and II (d). Third, because it does not actually employ the methods or conclusions of scientific observation and generalization in its account of the categories.

Randall's metaphysical position is in accord with the classical Aristotelian quest for the basic categories applicable to any subject matter I (a). Like Aristotle, Randall begins with "Substance" as "primary existence." However, he introduces an entirely new list of five categories or predicables: (1) "operations," (2) "powers," (3) "ways of operating," (4) "kinds of powers," and (5) "connectives."

"Substance" is first interpreted by Randall in (I) the Aristotelian language of being to mean (a) "the operation of powers" found in any existential subject matter. But Randall then extends the classical conception of "Substance" to (II) the language of experience. For although Substance refers to "the facts encountered," "the field inquired into," "the forces worked with," "the material manipulated,"[15] in the last analysis it applies to "the context of interaction" II (d). Randall finds that "Aristotle's analysis of Substance as the operation of powers, and Dewey's analysis of the situation, mutually illuminate each other."[16] It is Randall's extension of the concept "Substance" to Dewey's transactional situation, however, that is at once the most distinctive and yet most puzzling aspect of Randall's entire approach.

Randall refers to his theory as a kind of "functional realism," and he also says that it is a "behavioristic," "operational," and "contextual" view of being. But it is here that the most profound difficulty of Randall's metaphysics arises. His transition from a metaphysics of being (I) to a metaphysics of experience (II) has him talking in two ways. He says that "Substance is encountered as 'activities' or 'operations' taking place in various determinate ways—as acting and interacting with us and with other activities, as co-operating with us and each other, as doing things to us, as something to which we do things in return."[17] But it is not clear if he is interpreting Substance *entirely* as a transaction of man within a context (in the language of experience), or if Substance applies to "real things," in Aristotle's sense, independent and in their own terms (in the language of being).

Randall distinguishes Substance from Structure. The latter refers to "form," or that which linguistic or reflective experience formulates in the situation at the end of a process of inquiry. Structure is not apart from Substance, but within it. Substance includes both reflection, as the introduction of terms and distinctions in science, and experience, as a transactive co-operation of an agent in nature. Randall is no doubt intent on showing that metaphysics should be concerned, not merely with language or the world of intellectual formulations and discourse, but with the world as immediately encountered and directly experienced. He is saying that our contact with the world is active and dynamic, not merely passive. In this regard Randall's philosophical outlook is consonant with a theme pervading much of twentieth-century thought.

But Randall on the other hand claims that his is an *ontological* account of nature, not merely an account of human transaction. He states that his behavioristic and operational way of formulating the nature of primary existence is ontological, that "it applies to the behavior and operation of whatever is encountered, and not to human behavior and operations alone"[18]; and that Substance is encountered and known "as a complex of interacting and co-operating processes, each exhibiting its own determinate ways of co-operating, or Structure."[19] He illustrates the realistic and ontological foundations of his theory when he asks: "What is motion? What is electricity? What is light? What is energy?" And he answers that "the statement is always a formulation of how it 'works,' acts, co-operates, or behaves."[20]

But what does it mean to say that motion, electricity, light, or energy "behave," "work," "act," or "co-operate," or are "the operation of putting to work" of their powers, or the actualization of their potentialities? Or what does Randall mean when he says, "In an isolated system, like the planets, we can predict with complete success: we know exactly how all the masses will co-operate"?[21] One might reply that organisms can be said to "behave" and human beings to "co-operate," *not* natural objects.

The point is that Randall, like Woodbridge, is committed to a form of "natural teleology." If we examine what Randall has written in his book on Aristotle, concerning the relevance of Aristotelianism to contemporary science, we find Randall talking as if contemporary science has rediscovered Aristotle and virtually reinstated his teleology over the errors of Newtonianism:

> In the twentieth century, the physicists themselves found their billiards balls, the Newtonian mass-particles following the simple laws of motion of molar masses, dissolving into complex functional systems of radiant energy. They discovered that the subject matter of physics itself must be treated in functional and contextual terms, in terms of concepts appropriate to "the field." And what this means is that in his basic concepts the physicist himself must think like the biologist . . . Today, the concepts of Aristotle's physics, those notions involved in his analysis of process, have been driving those of Newton out of our theory. . . . Far from being obviously "wrong," it seems today far truer and sounder than the basic concepts of Newton. . . . This holds true of many of his analyses: his doctrine of natural teleology (etc.) . . .[22]

But Randall surely overstates the case. Although there has been a revolution in twentieth-century physics and Newtonian concepts have been modified in important ways, I do not see how this leaves room for the reintroduction of Aristotle's physics or of his teleology, however illuminating the study of Aristotle may be.

Randall also seems to overstate the case for teleology in modern biology. Although holistic and functional explanations are employed in the biological sciences, they are not sufficient in themselves, but are only among many kinds of explanatory devices used by modern biologists. Thus I think that Randall perhaps overemphasizes their use when he says: "Functional and teleological concepts are just the notions that modern biologists, no matter how 'mechanistic' their explanatory theory, actually have to employ in describing the subject matter they are attempting to explain."[23] Or again, it is very hard to claim that modern theories of evolution involve teleological assumptions, when the exact opposite seems to be the case:

> It is to be noted that for Aristotle the world is not a process of processes, it is not an "evolution." Aristotle is not thoroughgoing enough, he does not exhibit enough "natural teleology" in his conception of the world,

to satisfy our own present-day evolutionary thinking. Far from being too much of a teleologist, to a post-Darwinian Aristotle does not seem to have been enough of a teleologist.[24]

Randall thus seems to approve of Aristotle's reading of functional and teleological means-ends relations into nature; and he seems to accept without dissent Aristotle's analogy, which I find dubious, that nature behaves like art, and that in both, means-ends relations can be found:

> The teleology found in processes that take place by art is not radically different from the teleological order found in processes that take place by nature. There is no gulf between natural processes and processes of human production, but rather a continuity. Art is actually a cardinal illustration of natural processes . . .[25]

Randall's "natural teleology" raises a special problem in regard to value, and whether it too can be read into nature. He writes that:

> Substance . . . is shot through with "directions," "ends," "powers now coming into operation," "vectors" . . . (and) exhibits a great variety of functional and teleological structures, of relations . . . between power and their operatings . . . just because it is literally teeming with directions and ends, because it exhibits so much natural teleology, Substance is shot through and through with "values."[26]

Now if what Randall means by this is that *human beings* in their behavior presuppose ends or purposes, and in their inquiries institute operations and evaluate hypotheses in terms of them, I would have little difficulty in understanding what he is saying. Under this interpretation, Randall would simply be an instrumentalist in science, and his teleological concepts would apply to *man* and the goals he introduces in the course of inquiry, and not to nature independently. Randall's metaphysics could then be construed as providing an ontological basis for pragmatism. (Though I might add that such an interpretation of science as behavioral and operational is too general. While Dewey's instrumental philosophy of science does account for much experimental inquiry, it is hardly adequate for mathematical or theoretical physics.) However, the key point is that although the purposes of an inquirer are involved in any context of inquiry (second order) these purposes surely must be distinguished from the data under study (first order), and these purposes are *not* simply identifiable with the data. To say that Substance is "shot through and through with values" only confuses matters, for it is hard to see how values apply to interactions which are not human.

If Randall's metaphysics is to be construed solely as a metaphysics of human transactions, II (d), then in a sense it is primarily a theory of human behavior and not of nature. That human transactions are *in* and *of* nature, and not merely subjective, that they involve objects and factors in the environment, and that human beings introduce mean-ends relationships and values is an important point. But if this is what Randall is saying, then why the need for the language of Substance or of being? It is true that man is part of nature; but it only clouds the issue by talking in the language of being and interpreting the categories as an account of *any* subject matter, I (a), or even as an account of the generic traits of nature, I (b).

Randall's distinction between Substance as primary existence and the other five categories likewise presents some difficulties. Randall does not seem to talk, as far as I can determine, of Substance as a "category." Yet it is a key, and highly general, concept, and it may function as a "categorial type" in that it distinguishes common features of the world as experienced and known. Thus Randall should have at least six categories, not five. But what of his other five categories?

(1) "Operations," according to Randall, "are what we encounter directly in Substance or the Situation."[27] But in regard to the language of being or nature such a notion is dubious. Do we, in the natural and biological sciences, encounter "operations," or rather do we not observe processes of change, a far different matter? That operations are instituted in the course of inquiry as one experiments and tests, I am not disputing, but that operations are present in the data under observation is another matter. Randall rejects the language of "events" as phenomenalistic, yet "events" or "processes" seem more neutral to me than do "operations." The term "operations" seems to apply only to the language of transaction, but even here its use is not accurate, for many kinds of human behavioral transactions occur which can not be considered as "operations." Operations seem to involve conscious purpose, but many forms of human behavior are nonconscious.

(2) "Powers," for Randall, refers to the factors responsible for an operation, "the factors that are operating as means and mechanisms in the process."[28] "Powers" however is a vague term. If "powers" apply to the language of being, then they may invoke a whole closet of teleological ghosts. Randall seems to overlook the discussion of counterfactuals: merely to read "powers" into nature seems to provide little by way of explanation, particularly in view of Randall's recognition that "all knowledge of those powers is derived from operatings."[29] If "powers" apply to the metaphysics of transaction, then "dispositional properties" would perhaps raise fewer problems, i.e., under certain observed conditions certain things in interaction with men have certain observed properties.

Randall's categories (3) "ways of operating" and (4) "kinds of powers" are difficult to interpret precisely. "Ways" are defined by Randall as "functional structures, as something discriminated in concrete operations, and co-operations."[30] They refer to "how" things behave. "Operations" function as "particulars," and "ways of operating" function "universally." "Kinds" are "a different type of structure" on the generic level applicable to powers. Thus Randall implies that although the situation as encountered is particular, we do generalize; hence "ways of operating" and "kinds of powers" are introduced as ontological categories. But I fail to see why "ways" or "kinds" are not subsumable either under "powers" (i.e., "dispositional properties"), or under Randall's fifth category, "connectives," which I shall touch on shortly.

Randall's categories are also interpreted by him as methodological criteria or principles of explanation, II (e). He distinguishes the internal or "formal structure" from the "functional structure." And he suggests that in our inquiries, both a reductive structural and a functional explanation are used. He says that the functional structure of operations and behaviors can be formulated equally as the properties of powers, and he indicates that the same structure of behaving discriminated in processes "can be expressed equally as 'ways' of operating, or as 'properties' of 'kinds' of powers." Although it is the same structure, "it is that structure functioning in two quite different ways."[31] What Randall seems to be saying is this: functional explanations are necessary and useful to inquiry—but to say that is to refer to a methodological rule, not a fact of nature and least of all inanimate nature. We begin, according to him, with observed processes (functions), we read back structures (powers) as explanations of them.

Why does Randall choose this language? Because I suspect he is really intent in preserving the Aristotelian system of matter and form (the noun language), potentiality and actuality (the functional verb language), and of its teleological underpinning. But Aristotle's categories, even in the revised form that Randall gives them, and his use of teleological explanations do not provide an adequate account of present-day scientific inquiry. I restate my point: although functional explanations may have *some* use in biological and behavioral inquiries, they seem to have little relevance to inorganic or physical-chemical inquiries. Hence I believe that a list of categories so thoroughly based upon an Aristotelian foundation is today questionable.

But what is omitted from Randall's list of categories disturbs me more than what is included. *If* metaphysical analysis is supposed to uncover the chief traits of *any* subject matter, then there are surely two further categories that Randall seems to leave out. After comparing Randall's statements concerning the nature of "history" with his conception of a meta-

physical category in sense I (a) predicable and I (b) generic trait of
existence, one concludes that "history" certainly would qualify as a
category:

> Everything in our world has *a* history, and the man who wants to
> understand any particular thing or field is well advised to inquire into *its*
> history. Everything that is, is *historical* in character, and has an existence
> that can be measured in time. And this historical aspect which any
> particular thing has and possesses is an essential part of what it is. . . .
> History is not a "thing" at all, it is not a noun, a "substance." It is rather
> a character, an adjective, a predicate. . . . It is rather at once a trait of all
> subject matters.[32]

Similarly, Randall excludes mass, energy, and physical-chemical processes from his list of basic categories; yet it is difficult to see on what basis
one can do this, for physical-chemical structures seem to be present in
every process in some way. Randall himself is the best source for this view:

> This "internal" or "formal" structure of the means and materials of
> processes—the way in which they are put together—is ultimately "physical-
> chemical" . . . (and is) involved in all natural processes and actions. . . .
> Physical-chemical behaviors . . . are invariant through a range of contexts.[33]

If physical-chemical processes are invariant in the internal structure of
all things, then does this not qualify matter as a "generic trait of existence"
and hence as a fundamental category? I see no sense in attempting to
subsume history under "operations" (a genetic account is more than an
account of an operation), or to subsume matter under "powers." Both
"history" and "matter" seem to be "generic" in their own right. Moreover,
one can ask upon what grounds Randall excludes from his list of categories "function," "relation," "level," "continuity," and similar concepts
which seem to have a kind of "generality."

This leads me to consider the last category of Randall, which I find
to be the most puzzling, (5) "connectives" or "conjunctions." Randall
defines "connectives" as "factors functioning in Substance," and he includes under it not only all the linguistic signs and symbols of language
but also the symbols of mathematics, logic, theology, *all* the hypotheses
and theories of science, moral and legal codes, human and social ideals,
and metaphysical and historical myths. Connectives, he says, are "operations functioning in Substance," organizing and unifying them. Although
nature is plural, according to Randall, it is "a fundamental metaphysical
fact that Nature can *become* unified in human vision."[34] Connectives are
"functionally real," though they are "not operative or 'actual' in the absence of the participation of *human* activities."[35] There is no ultimate
Substance or context for Randall: what we encounter is a particular

Substance or situation; however, we do try to relate, connect, and fuse together our various experiences into unified perspectives. Nature itself is not so unified, but she lends herself to human unification. However, such unifications in the last analysis are "myths." This does not mean that they are meaningless, says Randall, for they have a definite function, they have deep roots in human demands, and they provide meaning to life. Although such connective myths are objective facts about the human condition, they make no truth claims about the universe.

My basic concern about "connectives" is similar to that which I have raised in regard to the other metaphysical categories. It is still unclear to me whether "connectives" apply both to (I) a metaphysics of being, and to (II) a metaphysics of human transaction. If it applies to (II), as would appear to be the case, then many issues can be raised. "Connectives" would hardly qualify as a category, for they are not universal factors functioning in Substance, and they are not present in any and every subject matter. They only seem to come into play when certainly highly sophisticated and cultural human interests are operating, and they are not present in all behavioral transactions. Furthermore, there would appear to be, using Randall's own terminology, other highly generic characteristics, which seem to be present in most human contexts. For example, "value" and "purpose," according to Randall himself, seem to be invariant in every transactional situation. Why are these not "categories"?

If, on the contrary, the category "connectives" is construed as applicable primarily to (I) the nature of being, then it would be a mistake to consider scientific "connectives" in the same way as other connectives, such as religious myths. Although it is the case that attempts at unified physical theories or comprehensive biological or overall social theories have been open to question in the history of science, yet surely there are integrating conceptual hypotheses on lower levels that "connect" explanations from various ranges of data. Thus it is an overstatement to interpret as "myths," for example, micro-bacterial explanations of disease in biology, electromagnetic theory in physics, or S-R theories of learning in psychology. Although scientific theories do not provide total unifications, they do provide "unifications" of sorts on a lower order. However, many scientific hypotheses and theories seem to function more like "ways" or "kinds," in Randall's terms, than like "connectives."

It is of course the case that human language, art, religion, morality, and science all have instrumental functions within human experience—as Randall has astutely pointed out. But I should insist that their functions differ. Cognitive "connectives" within science are of a different logical order than noncognitive ones; they tell us more about the world than do the others, for they are testable in terms of the data. That Randall does not emphasize sufficiently the *differences* between scientific "connectives" and other connectives weakens the claim that his general philosophical orientation is thoroughly naturalistic; for naturalists insist upon the priority of scientific method in the area of knowledge.

This is no place to enter into a detailed analysis of Randall's theory of noncognitive aesthetic and religious symbols. But I would like to indicate that I am somewhat hesitant about an aspect of his treatment because I think that it may deviate again from empirical naturalism. Although Randall maintains—correctly I would urge—that noncognitive symbols do not provide a form of knowledge, as do cognitive symbols, nonetheless, he also indicates that they

> Can be said to "disclose or "reveal" something about the world in which they function. . . . This revelation can be called "knowledge" or "truth" only in the sense that it is equivocal or metaphorical . . . it resembles what we call "insight" or "vision." Such religious symbols do not "tell" us anything that is verifiably so; they rather make us "see" something about our human experience in the world.[36]

Randall further explains his conception of the function of religious symbols in his book *The Role of Knowledge in Western Religion*.[37] Here he maintains that what religious symbols "disclose" can best be seen analogically by analyzing "insight" into the character and nature of another human personality. He agrees that external observation of a human being's behavior is useful, but he also says: "Intimate acquaintance with another human personality acquired through a long experience of friendship or of love, can give us an 'insight' into the essence of the man that cannot be won by any merely external observations of his behavior."[38]

Randall, unlike most other naturalists, does not appear to be fully committed to the behavioristic scientific program. Indeed, Randall maintains that a man is not exhausted in his behavior, but rather in the "possibilities and powers latent in his nature"—and that these are known by a kind of *verstehen*. Randall generalizes from this analogy of personality to the "Divine"—thus increasing his distance from empirical naturalism. He claims "that a religious symbol unifies and sums up and brings to a focus men's long and intimate experience of their universe and of what it offers to human life."[39] Thus he claims that religious symbols disclose or reveal powers and possibilities "inherent in the nature of things," and that they serve as instruments of insight and vision. Now perhaps I am overemphasizing one aspect of Randall's theory. For he does stress the pragmatic and functional side of religion and he is thoroughly naturalistic in focus here. Moreover, he also indicates that the "Divine" is a symbol of human value, an ideal. But I am somewhat concerned about the aspect of "vision" that he seems to add.

For Randall, religious symbols enable men to discern "Perfection shining through the world's imperfections in a dimly reflected splendor."[40] Thus, although religion involves practical commitment and know-how, it also provides a "vision of the Divine" and of the "order of splendor."[41]

In his discussion Randall suggests that scientific hypotheses and theories are no longer "true" in modern science, but merely "warranted" or "tested." If this is so, he asks, then how adjudicate the claims of religion and science? Religious symbols are tested by their adequacy—even though they cannot be confused with the warranted knowledge of science. Perhaps, he says, "it is now the visions of the unified possibilities of the world—of the Divine, of the 'order of splendor'—that we are once more permitted to call 'true.' "[42]

These latter remarks of Randall should bring to a head what has been implicit in my discussion thus far, and what is in a sense my major reservation about Randall's metaphysics. He transgresses from what I consider to be a basic methodological principle of philosophic naturalism, i.e., the commitment to the methods of science. This principle, fundamental of course to Dewey's naturalistic metaphysics, is a key assumption of the collected volume *Naturalism and the Human Spirit*, where Randall recognizes this commitment when, in the Epilogue, he says the "insistence on the universal and unrestricted application of 'scientific method' is a theme pervading every one of these essays."[43]

If one asks, How does one judge or appraise Randall's metaphysics? an answer seems to emerge. Here is a kind of "vision," a "seeing," a "perspective," which Randall has and which he is attempting to communicate. Randall's categories perhaps thus function, to use his own language, as unifying "connectives" or "myths." These may provide a kind of "insight" in Randall's sense much the same as all other metaphysical theories; but they seem incompatible at times with contemporary science—even though he may not intend such to be the case. Thus, in the last analysis, I am forced to conclude that Randall's categories are not an entirely reliable guide of what a naturalistic metaphysics should include. Randall's categories appear to function as a generalized account of "human transactions" (*sans* the behavioral sciences); they do not say enough about the "generic traits of nature" or of the world as viewed by contemporary science.

IV. THE CATEGORIES AND NATURALISM

What of meta-metaphysics and the search for the categories from the standpoint of naturalistic metaphysics? My own position should by now be clear. I reject the Aristotelian notion that metaphysics is a "science of existence" with a distinctive subject matter of its own. And this involves a rejection of other aspects of the Aristotelian program which Randall fortunately also rejects—the view that metaphysics gives us a "special" kind of knowledge that we could not possibly get in any other way, or that it gives us knowledge of Being independent from beings in concrete contexts. I also reject the search for categories which are universal, I (a) in the language of being, or the Kantian search for universal and *a priori* presuppositions, II (c) in the language of experience; for I do not know how one would go about testing such categories by empirical observation and generalization. The whole notion of a universal category which applies to *any* subject matter or of a universal presupposition violates the principle of verification, so essential to an empirical naturalism. Universal statements are analytic, not synthetic; they are based upon logical analysis, not empirical observation. And an appeal to the synthetic *a priori* is surely not an option for an empiricist.

Does this mean that I consider all metaphysical inquiry nonsense? *No.* For I think that metaphysicians have a useful job to perform, though on a *limited* scale. Empirical metaphysicians can, as I see it, bring to light various sets of general concepts which function in different subject matters and areas of inquiry; they can thus uncover the categories of "the middle range" (to borrow a term from the social sciences). A generalization based upon probabilities is not the same as a universal statement. In this more modest sense, metaphysicians can examine II (b) "the generic traits of nature," if this inquiry is construed as a distillation of the assumptions and conclusions of the natural and biological sciences. Aristotle's categories are, in the last analysis, a reflection of the scientific view of his day, much the same as Kant's categories bring out the presuppositions of the Newtonian world-view. A categorical analysis which is not related first and foremost to the philosophy of science hardly has a claim to our attention. This, however, should be viewed in historical terms, as Collingwood points out, for our presuppositions are constantly being modified. In any one age, we can help to interpret how the sciences approach nature, and we can help to interpret and sum up what they are saying about the cosmos; we can generalize and take inventory. The metaphysician in this sense is a "middleman." Although he does not himself engage in an experimental test of his concepts, he does seek to analyze, explicate, and clarify the key concepts and hypotheses which are used by the sciences of nature and have been tested. A category would be a generalization from our tested theories; it would not itself be a scientific theory or law or a substitute for it. Moreover, a metaphysical category would not be equivalent to any and every law, theory, or concept used in the sciences; but it would rather refer to the most fundamental concepts which seem to play a key role in the body of our knowledge at any one time in human history. Unlike Aristotle and Kant, I would say meta-physicians of the "middle range" seek categories based upon cognate concepts and generalizations from several sciences, but they do not necessarily apply to *all* the sciences. Thus, for example, similar concepts are today used in physics, chemistry, and the natural sciences: "mass," "energy," "particle," and "field." It is important to interpret their meaning and function. Difficulties emerge however when such categories are simply stretched by the metaphysician or universalized as applicable to all the sciences. I am not saying that "universal" or generic categories are logically impossible, only that they depend upon the development of a unified scientific theory which we do not have at present. Metaphysicians do leap ahead of scientific theories, and they find clusters of concepts that bear "family resemblances," which they label "categories." The danger in metaphysics is always that such categories may be extended so far that they become simply "root metaphors," analogical, and equivocal, and that in the process they lose their precise cognitive significance.

Metaphysicians of course should not restrict their inquiries to the natural or life sciences. They can also investigate II (d) the generic traits of human transactions; they can provide generalized conceptual accounts of the sciences of human behavior, i.e., summary statements of what we do and do not know about man from the standpoint of the biological, behavioral, and social sciences. Although drawing of analogies between I (b) and II (d) is useful, these inquiries should not be equated or confused. Nor does this imply that man is bifurcated from or not a part of nature. In regard to II (d) the generic traits of human transaction, there are a great number of concepts that may be fruitfully investigated: "behavior," "function," "intention," "value," "decision," "evolution," "culture," "society," etc. The quest for a single set of categorial concepts which is either universal, exhaustive, or complete, hardly seems to do justice to the wide range of data and knowledge that we have about human beings. We are far from a unified theory of human behavior, and thus any categorial scheme of human interaction would be incomplete.

In dealing with human behavior, we must surely take into account all of the varieties of human experience; and philosophers need to develop conceptual analyses appropriate to the special subject-matters of art, religion, and morality, among others. However, I should say that the moral, religious, and aesthetic dimensions of human experience are *not* candidates for truth in any special way—surely not about nature and perhaps not even about man—but, rather, that they provide us with *data to be explained by the sciences*. They are not sources for generic metaphysical categories. The key principle of naturalism should not be compromised here: all claims to truth must be examined by the same responsible methods of empirical observation and test; and intuitive "insight" or "vision," whether from art, religion, or morality, is no substitute for experimental verification.

In metaphysical contexts, the term "category," as we have seen, has also been applied to (e) methodological principles of inquiry and (f) linguistic rules of use. Methodological investigations and analyses of the logical grammar of our language are both vital and necessary to philosophy. An analysis of the methodological principles and criteria that are employed in scientific inquiry, and of the language that is used in ordinary life, may shed further light about the nature I (b) of the world, and II (d) of human beings. These analyses however, while significant in themselves, can be carried on without a primary "metaphysical" interest or concern. They are not distinctively nor peculiarly "metaphysical"; for they are presupposed in all philosophical investigations of art, morality, religion, politics, education, history, science, etc. Thus, to stretch the term "metaphysics" so that it applies in some special way to (e) and (f) invites either the charge that "metaphysics" is here being used in an equivocal and metaphorical sense, or that it has become a kind of superphilosophical inquiry involving virtually the whole of philosophy.

The chief conclusion that I wish to draw here is that, for descriptive and empirical metaphysics, the term "category" may be applied fruitfully, in the qualified way that I have suggested, to an account of (b) the generic traits of nature, and (d) the generic traits of human transaction. Insofar as Professor Randall's metaphysical interest does this, I think that his work deserves serious attention and that he has made a *notable* contribution to metaphysics, particularly at a time when many other philosophers have forsaken her. But insofar as there is an attempt to introduce, under the heading of "category," other inquiries, then I think that we perhaps need further clarification of the nature of this enterprise by Professor Randall and by Randallians, present and future.

NOTES

1. "The Nature of Metaphysics: Its Function, Criteria, and Method," *Journal of Philosophy*, XLIII (1946), 401-12.

2. *Nature and Historical Experience* (New York: Columbia University Press, 1958), Chap. V.

3. *Nature and Historical Experience*, p. 124.

4. *Ibid.*, p. 144.

5. *Ibid.*, p. 144.

6. *Ibid.*, p. 137.

7. *Ibid.*, p. 135.

8. *Ibid.*, p. 135.

9. *Ibid.*, p. 136.

10. *Ibid.*, p. 137.

11. *Ibid.*, p. 177.

12. *Ibid.*, p. 176.

13. London: Methuen, 1959.

14. *Ibid.*, p. 9.

15. *Ibid.*, p. 147.

16. *Ibid.*, p. 148-9.

17. *Ibid.*, p. 150.

18. *Ibid.*, p. 152.

19. *Ibid.*, p. 152.

20. *Ibid.*, p. 151.

21. *Ibid.*, p. 175.

22. *Aristotle* (New York: Columbia University Press, 1960), pp. 166-68.

23. *Ibid.*, p. 229.

24. *Ibid.*, p. 129.

25. *Ibid.*, p. 188.

26. *Nature and Historical Experience*, p. 155.

27. *Ibid.*, p. 177.

28. *Ibid.*, p. 183.

29. *Ibid.*, p. 186.

30. *Ibid.*, p. 177.

31. *Ibid.*, p. 187.

32. *Ibid.*, p. 27-28.

33. *Ibid.*, pp. 164, 174.

34. *Ibid.*, p. 195.

35. *Ibid.*, p. 197.

36. *Ibid.*, pp. 265-66.

37. *The Role of Knowledge in Western Religion*, Boston: Starr King Press, 1958.

38. *Ibid.*, p. 116.

39. *Ibid.*, p. 117.

40. *Ibid.*,p. 118.

41. *Ibid.*, p. 121.

42. *Ibid.*, p. 134.

43. *"The Nature of Naturalism,"* in Y. H. Kirkorian, ed., (New York: Columbia University Press, 1944), p. 358.

ARTHUR C. DANTO

Columbia University

Reflections upon Randall's Theory of Language

I shall make no effort here to summarize Randall's views on language.* Instead I mean to offer some elucidations which will serve those who undertake to read him in finding their way about, and which will provide Randall himself with a mirror in which he may somewhat better make out what he has accomplished. For I believe he does not have a clear view of his own achievement. In part this is the fault of his own language, which is heavily instrumentalistic. It has led him to profounder matters than are dealt with by most contemporary linguisticians, but has, perhaps ironically, obscured the nature of his occupation, suggesting an account of language which is only superficially in harmony with "the functional aspects of the analysis of language in other present-day philosophies" (29 n). Because concern with language, especially along instrumentalist lines, is much in the philosophical vogue, Randall's rather recent effort to deal with language might appear a somewhat perfunctory bid at time-liness. But it is none of this, and the seeming overlap of descriptive vocabularies between his treatment and that of others is merely misleading. They scarcely are addressed to the same issues.

I

Wittgenstein, too, spoke much of the *use* of words. The proposal that the meaning of a sentence should be its use rather than its mode of verification marked not only a deflection in the history of his thought; in view of the wholesale endorsement accorded this proposal, it bespoke an historical shift of a more appreciable dimension. I see it as a departure from a deeply embedded, almost neurotically compelled, philosophical propensity to collapse knowledge and understanding together in such a way that meaning and truth can hardly be prized apart; to make knowability

---

* Randall's views on language are primarily contained in his "The Art of Language and the Linguistic Situation," *Journal of Philosophy*, LX, No. 2. (Jan., 1963), 29-56. Page references in my text are to this paper.

a precondition for intelligibility; and to restrict the offices of language primarily to the expression or exhibition of what we know, so that every non-cognitive use of language counts as nonsense, more or less thinly disguised. But this, in turn, reflects a rather less covert prejudice in favor of depicting human beings essentially as *res cogitans*, distracted by somatic preoccupations from their higher and proper calling, which is to achieve clear and distinct perceptions of, and *a fortiori* attain to cognitive insight into, the way the world is. So the broadening of the concept of language went together with a widening of the concept of human nature, and Wittgenstein's almost paranoiac anti-cartesianism must be taken together with a belated recognition (not uniquely his, of course) that human beings engage more variously with the world than as mere cognizors of it, and employ language to other ends than the concededly important one of articulating knowledge. In the end, I believe, the energizing contest was really over the question of what man is, though it was masked even from the antagonists, perhaps, by the question of what is meaning. And the disguise was probably providential, for what emerges with increasing distinctness in contemporary philosophy is the view that our nature is a logical amalgam of flesh and word, our essence that of *res loquens.*

Whatever may have been the submerged, ulterior philosophical concerns, it is a fact, I think, that a more sensitive appreciation of linguistic phenomena has proved sufficiently absorbing to the recent philosophical generation that philosophy itself has come dangerously close to a socio-lexicographical enterprise, exercised in an ill-defined territory vaguely bounded by social psychology and structural linguistics. In part this conversion of philosophical energy must be attributed to a curious reluctance on Wittgenstein's part to allow that there should be any specifically *philosophical* uses of language. Here he exceeded the rather more charitable verificationists, who left for philosophy the task of providing *definitions in use.* But Wittgenstein, even in his latter, liberal phase (which I regard as a philosophical decline), held that philosophy begins when language goes on holiday, and his broadened conception of language had a perplexingly dour and utilitarian—not to say Stakhanovite—tone: philosophical use is *ab*use: one can be properly concerned with philosophy only therapeutically, since it belongs only to the pathology of speech. Therapy was to consist in recalling to the homely contexts of use the wayward sentences of philosophers, and forcing them to do the work they fled. Beginning, thus, with a quest for *the* use of a sentence, these therapeutic aims subsided as sentences provided to be immensely more versatile than had been anticipated, the identical phrase serving often a vast and heterogeneous range of uses, varying with often only the slightest variation in context. The exploitation of this was perhaps the chief final contribution of Austin and his school, and the sheer fascination in registering subtle sentential variations, together with the never utterly abandoned suspicion that philosophy was in its traditional practices nonsense after all, produced an atmosphere in which what came to be called philosophy just *was* the study of language. But now the question had to arise whether those who practiced it were anything other than amateur linguists, who might not do the more honest thing by acquiring the disciplines demanded for work of this sort at the professional level. With this, philosophy would have undergone its final transformation. The heretofore unredeemed remnant, left over since physics, psychology, logic, and the other disciplines, which once were part of philosophy, attained their majority and independence, will prove to have been only inchoate linguistics. The history of philosophy would be ended.

What I particularly admire in Randall's discussion of language, is its utter resistance against this liquidation, its refusal, despite Randall's instrumentalistic rhetoric, to tolerate the sea change into something plain and useful. What he offers really is a philosophy of language, not an exercise in linguistic philosophy, and in doing so, raises those ultimate, unwieldly questions *about* language which cannot be answered, but only evaded, by scrutinizing, however fastidiously and with whatever delicacy of wit, the mere convoluted surfaces of usage. Philosophical utterance has no place in the domestic economy of ordinary speech; it has a region of its own. But we can, since the mere *words* are often the same, have entered it unawares, and so will locate ourselves wrongly. We cannot respond to Randall's queries without adjusting our focus to accommodate wider philosophical horizons than the ones within which we have latterly been confined. We will have chic, obvious answers to questions which only *resemble* the ones he has put, or will take *him* to be giving flat, standard answers to questions from the putting of which we long since have graduated.

Consider only the way in which he speaks of language as an instrument. It is not at all primarily to the fact that sentences are used as instruments of communication and expression in contexts of social interchange that Randall refers here, though he also *notices* that fact about sentences. It is, rather, the idea that language, just as such, is an instrument for the manufacture of sentential tools which interests him, given that once they have been produced, they may be put to what use they will. Indeed, much as we have learned to think of philosophy as an activity rather than a set of doctrines (though of course an activity concerned in part with the production of doctrines), here we are invited to think of language as an activity rather than a set of sentences—though of course an activity concerned with the production of sentences. To identify philosophy with the doctrines it generates is not only to confuse an activity with its results: it is to take the task of philosophy to be the study and clarification of doctrines, which is scholarship, after all, rather than philosophy. Philosophy is something to be engaged in and not merely studied. It cannot be mastered in a non-participant manner, and the mere mastery of philosophical doctrine does not qualify one as a philosopher at all. There is in analogy to this an important sense in which to be master of a language consists in having internalized the grammar of it so that one is able to produce appropriate sentences and not merely to have an external competence with respect to the sentences of that language. To be sure, there is a phase of grammatical, or linguistic, study which is concerned with the syntactical structure of the language as such; and it has been this sort of formal reconstruction of language, with meaning postulates, formation and transformation rules, and the like, which has been, until relatively recent times, the dominating preoccupation of "philosophy of language." But this structural, formal discipline—as well as that aspect of language which it is concerned with—must be distinguished, on the one side, from the use to which sentences are put, and, on the other, from questions of the generation of sentences. One might indeed speak of three regions of linguistic study: the syntactical middle region, concerned merely with the formal shape of language, which is the province of Carnap and logisticians generally; the socio-linguistic region, which is concerned with the situational matrices of linguistic use, which has been the province of the later Wittgenstein and the philosophers of Ordinary Language; and the region which is investigated by those who think of language as the activity of making sentences, and not merely applying sentences already made, as it were. It is this latter territory which Randall is concerned with, though he has things to say regarding all three of them, as well as their interconnections. He is concerned with language as the activity of shaping sentences forth, language virtually as a force of nature, generating sentences 'out of the raw material of the world. It is this which gives his discussion so exceptional a philosophical interest.

The generation of sentences, which I take to be Randall's main topic, is very remote from the painstaking sort of inquiry into "what we say when" which was Austin's chosen province, and which, as it were, takes language for granted. Perhaps it is felt in general that the question of generation is not of philosophical concern—as though, from the fact that there are genetic fallacies, it follows that philosophical preoccupation with genesis is inherently fallacious. This may have distracted us from the problems which Randall finds important; and the fact is that his investigation is carried on in the shadow of immense metaphysical considerations, which brood like forbidden, unacknowledged Himalayas on the horizons of even the most mincing bits of linguistic analysis—considerations which dominate our investigations whether or not we recognize them. The linguistic activity, as Randall is concerned with it, is one of primordial conversion and transformation: he sees language as almost literally transforming things into words, as though sentences were merely final products from a manufacturing process, the raw material of which consists of the brute world, language being just the shaping of this rude stuff into sentential form. Or, to use the sort of Aristotelian distinctions which surely are always in Randall's philosophical unconscious, sentences are formal causes and the world is material cause (natively unshaped *materia prima*), and language, as an activity, is efficient cause (stamping form on matter), and communication is final cause. The *metaphysical* questions to which I allude, and which stand whether we tolerate this Aristotelian orientation or not, are, how must the world be if it is to be "put into words," and how must language be if it is to capture the world sentientially? And who, since the great days of Logical Atomism, has so much as *raised* these questions?

II

Something like the same analysis I have been sketching might be made in the philosophy of science. Here, too, we might be concerned with three regions of inquiry. There is a middle region, concerned with "the language of science," and its rational reconstruction into formal edifices. This takes scientific theories as *faits accomplis*, it being taken as the task of philosophy only to ascertain and exhibit their "logic." There is the region of application, where we take philosophy of science to be the study of "what scientists say when." And then we might take the generative analogue to Randall's concern as the study of what recently has become termed "patterns of discovery," which was a salutary recognition that certain issues, relegated to the history and psychology of science, had impressive philosophical importance. But we would not fully have specified the analogue to Randallian investigation unless we thought philosophy of science to be concerned with how the world must be if it is to be put into theories, and how theories must be if they are to represent the world. And we would not have gotten out Randall's view of the matter unless we thought of science as a shaping activity, transforming the raw stuff of the world into theories. The word "transform" would have to be taken literally, e.g., in much the same way in which we use it in such remarks as "the chemical industry transforms coal into synthetic textiles." And a metaphysics of the chemical industry would be concerned with how coal must be if it is to be "put into threads," and how fabrics must be if they are to become transforms of coal. A Randallian philosophy of science would see theories as transforms of reality, as a Randallian philosophy of language sees sentences as transforms of the world.

Galileo was concerned with at least the sort of metaphysical question Randall poses. He said that the world consists of mathematical entities. Seventeenth-century scientists (of whom Arthur Eddington was perhaps the last) said that the world was made of primary qualities. We all, I think, know the genre of such answers. And we all must find something disturbingly primitivist about them. They suppose that in order for a sentence truly to describe what it is about it must share some common feature with its subject matter. And so the deep, misguided theorist proceeds to deduce the ultimate features of reality from the manifest, striking features of the idiom we use to talk about reality. Thus we speak mathematically about the world. But how, this mentality insists, could we do so if the world were not already, in essence, mathematical? Or, certain terms seem "primitive" in certain theories. So the features of the world which these stand for must be primitive in the world. And so the metaphysics one adopts tends to be a projection of one's language onto the surface of reality, which is then reeled back as how the world must be if our language is to suit it. The shadow cast by language is taken for the ultimate substance of the screen upon which it is cast. Philosophers seem curiously susceptible to this essentially Neanderthal manner of thinking. And philosophy itself is in large measure little more than the products of this way of thought.

I do not believe Randall is altogether immune to this primitivism. He takes language to be an instrument. How then must the world be if language *is* an instrument? The answer almost falls out automatically. If language is an instrument, it must relate to the world in the sense of *acting upon* it, that is, the way any tool acts upon the material it transforms. But after all, one wants to say, there are tools and tools, and they act differently upon their material. The paradigm tool for Randall seems to be the cutting or penetrating instrument. Well, this could be an enlightening model for appreciating language "in action." Suppose language acted on the world in something like the way in which augers act upon planks. Then it might be peculiarly ingenuous to wonder at the amazing congruency between language and the world, since the world would show the precise marks of the tools which acted upon it. There is a nice harmony between the diameter of bits and bores, an almost perfect exactitude of fit. But of course it is not as though the plank were unaltered by the drilling through of it. It is different afterwards than it was before. Tools co-operate, as it were, with planks to produce new entities. Language, as an instrument, is a "natural process" co-operating with other natural processes to produce new entities. Language transforms the world it acts upon into a new, sententialized, articulated, grammaticized world, different afterwards than it was before.

As a metaphor, this is not a bad one. But does it perhaps not beg a question? There are, as we said, tools and tools. Suppose we take as our paradigm instrument, not a gouge or drill, but some sort of recording gear, like a photographic device, say? This simply provides simulacra of antecedent structures without causally interacting with the structures it reproduces. Between photographs and their subjects there is a relation of resemblance, an isomorphic parity of structure. And why should not the relationship between language and the world be that way? And the activity of language be like the making of pictures, rather than like the making of—well, birdhouses out of planks, for example? Drills do not reproduce antecedent structures. They penetrate reality, tunnel out hollow spaces, open up, make possible joinings and articulations which would have been impossible without them. They enter into and make reality over. But cameras are not like that. They are essentially "outside" the processes they reproduce, and are successful to the degree that they do not interfere with or distort what they are meant to show forth. For photography, the world is given. It is only required to "take" it. It has a structure which remains unaltered on either side of the moment of its reproduction. Is language then to be "in the world" or "outside the world"? Randall's views are, of course, the strenuous ones. Language is a force amongst forces. It linguicizes a world not antecedently articulate. It wrestles into verbality a reality not initially intelligible. It makes the world over, and does not merely give back a structure already there. The task of language is not to get more and more refined and congruent with a prior, given structure, but to make something out of a dumb, uncouth, uncultivated stuff. And put in these terms, one suddenly begins to see, behind the instrumentalistic disguise, the Idealist which *in petto* Randall all along has been. Language is Spirit redeeming Nature, spiritualizing its metaphysical opposite number to the end of a higher synthesis in which the Word is made Flesh and the Flesh is made Word. Who any longer talks this way? No one respectable. But that almost irrepressible and devious Hegelian manner of thought finds *personae* of respectability through which to place its message before the world. And it is perhaps not enough to keep unmasking an idea which will only find another facade of respectability through which it will seek insidiously to bewitch our thoughts. So why not try, for once, to see if there is not something there?

III

Let us put aside our metaphors. The question concerns the relation between language and the world. On the one side we have the view that language is outside the world, and ideally reproduces it. On the other, language is in the world, contributing to the final shape the world is to have, a shaping rather than a duplicative instrument. Which of these ways of thinking of the relationship is correct cannot be determined within the limits of either.

Wittgenstein thought once that language was outside the world, and ideally gives its picture. But he discovered that this, if so, could not be said in an ideal language. For the relationship could not be shown. You cannot put into a picture the relationship between it and what it depicts, since the picturing relationship is at right angles, so to speak, to the surface upon which subjects are projected. Philosophy, being concerned with nothing but the unpicturable space between language and the world could not be housed in the picture it created. Correctness or adequacy of depiction could only be raised about, but not *within* an ideal language, and in the perfected, tractarian idiom, epistemological queries, much less skeptical doubts, could not be intelligibly raised. "Whereof you cannot speak, thereof you must be silent." If the representationalistic account of the relationship between language and the world were correct, it could not be said. Or, if it could be said, the correctness of what we said could not be a matter of mere representation. So the theory turns back upon itself with the promise of a paradox.

But after all, nothing very different emerges from the Hegelian-Randallian account. For we could not speak of the relationship between language and reality as it really is unless we assumed one invariant, antecedent, correctly described relationship with which language does not interfere, namely, the connection between language and the world. So the instrumentalist account cannot be generally true, in that it leaves no place for any statement of itself. The Randallian metalanguage has, indeed, to employ a notion of truth, and a concept of correspondence with a fixed, antecedent fact which it is a negative feature of his theory to impugn. And this is a comparable irony to that of which Wittgenstein was victim, in that in his metalanguage he employed a set of terms and concepts which it was the explicit purpose of his enterprise to render unintelligible.

We often, in such topics, find ourselves in dialectical coils, forced to employ the very terms in the formulation of a theory which that theory is intended to invalidate. Perhaps it is too much to expect the same criteria of adequacy to be satisfied by a metalanguage which specifies that criterion of adequacy for the language it describes. But then it is at least an interesting fact that on a sufficiently weakened notion of correspondence, that is, correspondence without (pictorial) congruence, we can get just the same relationship to hold between the metalanguage and its language, as the former specifies as holding between language and the world. That is to say, it at least thinks of some sort of matching relation between sentences and situations which they describe, and it, in turn, matches in much the same way the situation *it* describes. I shall later say a few words on the sort of matching I have in mind, but I am aware that, however weakened a notion or correspondence it is that I shall be advocating, it will bring upon me a charge of begging the truly fundamental question with which Randall is dealing. For any notion of correspondence seems to suppose some matching up of sentences with antecedent structures in the world, it being the task of language merely to describe, or note, what is the case, without entering causally in the constitution of what is the case. But this is *not*, of course, to deny that words and even sentences have causal efficacy in the processes of the world. In an obvious but not terribly interesting sense, they do have. I use the words "Shut the door!" and, via the intermediary mechanisms of understanding and translation of words into action, my compliant hearer shuts the door. So my words were causally involved in the shutting of the door. Who could deny that language is causal in such and in similar ways? But this sort of modication of the world is *not at all* what I take Randall to have been talking about in his instrumentalist idealist discussion. I take him to have been after something deeper by far. He thought of language as the making over of the raw unstructured matter of the world into sentences. It is strictly *that* process which touches the metaphysical depths in which I think of him as dwelling. That once constructed, sentences should be used for all variety of purposes is hardly even interesting philosophically. That is an insight which belongs to the socio-linguistic studies of language of which Austin was master. It provides no evidence at all for the thesis Randall wants to advance; although I think Randall himself has failed to keep the two sets of considerations apart, and often has allowed the obvious but uninteresting facts which encourage an instrumentalist account of sentential *use*, to dominate and obscure the covert but fascinating account of sentential *generation*. Concerning merely use, he is in harmony with the later Wittgenstein, with Austin, and with all the minute linguisticians of contemporary philosophy. Concerning generation and semantics, he is in a space left virtually vacant by contemporary philosophers. His peers there are the early Wittgenstein, Dewey in his metaphysical phases, Hegel, and some others of like stature.

IV

Whatever theory we may hold concerning the ultimate, deep connection between language and the world, there are at least two features of natural languages with which such a theory must at least be compatible. To think of language as an activity captures one of these features. To think of it as the *sort* of activity which Randall does is to come dangerously near to being incompatible with the other one. I shall designate these features as, respectively, *Linguistic Creativity* and *Semantical Indifference*. Each of them requires some comment.

A. *Linguistic Creativity*. A natural language cannot consist in a set of sentences. A *book* consists in a set of sentences, but not a language. If there were, moreover, a process which permitted only the production in principle of a finite number of sentences, that would not be a natural language. A language must be distinguished from the sentences produced within it. Insofar as he thinks of language as an activity distinct from but concerned with the production of sentences, Randall's account is compatible with this feature of the natural languages.

One can distinguish the sentences of a language from the rules in conformity with which these sentences are produced, and then identify the language with just these rules. The rules permit the formation of sentences in the language. But these rules of generative grammar must, I should think, be distinguished from the normative rules of *correct* speech. The latter stand to sentential output in roughly the relationship the rules of a game stand to the playing of a game. The rules tell us which are the permitted moves. But they do not tell us which are the strategic, the best, the clever, moves to make. They tell us how to play a correct game, not a good one. Grammatical rules are weaker. An incorrect play isn't really a play at all, though a bad play is. But incorrect sentences will remain sentences. A child or foreigner will typically be understood however badly he may have gotten his grammar. We absorb his maimed phraseology in a compensating system which tolerates immense variation from the norm, communication proceeding smoothly nevertheless.

Due principally to a stunning insight of Wittgenstein's, the concepts of language and of games have recently been conflated, with a concomitant emphasis upon rules. But philosophical concern with rules has curiously become concentrated on the notion of *rectitude*, of "correct usage," of "what we [ought to] say when." And this in turn has led to severe mistrust of "deviant" usage, of which—naturally—philosophical language has been the alleged worst offender. Hence some specially schooled tribe of linguistic vigilantes is required to keep the games honest and to protect native speakers. But quite apart from confusing here the difference between a non-move (a would-be move which breaks a rule) and an incorrect sentence, attention has been drawn away from those other aspects of game playing where the emphasis is not so much on *moves* as on *plays*, where style and strategy and talent and, finally, creativity are exhibited. Mere rectitude is taken for granted here, but the important stress is on an ability to respond in novel and unpredictable ways in familiar situations, or intelligently and tactically in novel situations. A man, that is, may be master of all the moves in chess, but not of all the *plays*. And comparably in language. To be master of a language cannot consist in knowing all the sentences for, no more than in connection with the plays of chess, can there be a limited set of these to master. Playing, like speaking, is in this respect a creative activity. A play in chess must be understood as part of a game, much, I suppose, as a sentence must be understood in terms of a conversation, playing a different role depending upon its location in a system of mutually involved sentences. There demonstrably cannot be a list of "all the chess games," any more than there could be a list of "all the conversations." (Or an invitation to play chess would require one to say "which game one would like to play"—and what would be the point of that, since it already is known how it comes out, and one would only idly—and obviously not even for purposes of learning—follow the description of the games like a script. Perhaps one could get graceful at moving pieces, but then chess would become a curiously performative art, e.g., like ballet).

A volume could not be compiled of "all the sentences of the language," e.g., a *phrasikon*, as, ideally, it is at least possible that a complete lexicon could be made for all the *words*. Linguistic creativity does not consist in the power to add to the vocabulary of a language. For all speakers of a language must be creative, in the sense I am concerned, and very few add words. Moreover, even dead languages retain the creative aspect I am stressing. A man can add a new and useful word, e.g., "nymphet." But he cannot in the same way add a new and useful sentence. In part this is because there is no set of "old" sentences to augment. But chiefly it is because *anyone* who has internalized the language at all will be making new sentences all the time, and yet be understood by other speakers of the language. But were we to introduce new words with that frequency, the language would collapse of its own weight into a set of private tongues. Perhaps a constant vocabulary is a precondition for sentential flexibility, but there are deep reasons against the inscription of a *phrasikon*.

I suppose one could imagine a society in which life has been arranged and almost ceremonialized, so that all who are masters of its form of life would be masters of "what [sentence] to say when." You could master the language of that society as you would a religious service, e.g., "responsive prayer." Wittgenstein suggested that to imagine a language is to imagine a form of life. What he meant, perhaps, was to imagine a language-*game* is to imagine a form of life which consists in the playing of it (though no room for comment upon the game *within* the game itself). But there is no room here for linguistic creativity. One could, on such a view, add a sentence to a language: it would involve modification of a form of life; it would, like adding a new piece to chess (e.g., a gryphon), be to *change the game*. But while not meaning to deny that there is a certain etiquette of speech, where certain sentences are just the things to say in certain repeated situations, the fact is that our life is so linguistic that the situations in which we speak are partially determined by what has already been said there, and to be master of a language is to be able to produce a new and apposite sentence to fit such holes. And all of us have this power. Perhaps every sentence in this paper is, in this respect, a new sentence. It is this spontaneity of language, the voicing of new sentences in the confidence that they will be caught on the wing by one's fellow speakers and responded to with equal agility, which makes language so much a pleasure, and almost like a game. Pleasure in talk is a mark of civilization, if not humanity: silence is *inhuman*.

So a language cannot be memorized, but can only—in a manner far from clear even to those linguists who have, in the past few years, become impressed with the concept of a generative grammar—be internalized. It cannot be memorized because it is inconsistent with the concept of language that it should be committed to memory. Foreigners, perhaps, memorize sentences. But imagine having had to memorize all the sentences which come up in the normal day's speaking; *it would be like not having a language at all.* It would be like walking through the painful means of deliberately flexing, one by one, all the right muscles. And that is not walking, as we understand such an activity.

B. *Semantical Indifference.* The rules in conformity with which sentences are minted make it no less easy to form false sentences than true ones, and the grammar will never be written which would permit us to read off the structural surface of a sentence what its truth-value must be. So the generative grammar of language entails that our linguistic reach exceeds our grasp upon the world, however that grasping is to be characterized. It follows that the semantical aspects of language cannot be *part* of language, nor truth (or falsity) properties of sentences as such. Comparably, and for reasons significant in the history of epistemology, it cannot be determined from an exhaustive scrutiny of the surface of a picture whether there exists something, independently, *of* which it *is* a picture. It was this semantical anonymity of pictures which, for example, so plagued Descartes who thought his ideas were like pictures—*"comme des tableaux et des peintures"*—and despaired, in a dark moment of the *First Meditation*, of breaking out of the private gallery of the mind into the world beyond, or of even knowing whether there were, outside the gallery, a world beyond at all.

Since it is commonly thought to be determined by external factors alone whether a sentence which comes up to the mark so far as meaningfulness goes is true or false, it must always be possible, given the rules of meaningfulness, to produce false sentences; for there would otherwise be an external limitation upon linguistic creativity. Hence, whichever model we may decide is correct for appreciating the relationship between language and the world, it must, if it is consonant with the linguistic creativity of language, be consonant as well with the semantical indifference of language, so that nothing internal or grammatical marks the true sentence from the false.

V

The Picture Theory of Language very easily satisfies the requirement of Semantical Indifference. It was, indeed, exactly in terms of a picture theory of *thinking* that the concept of semantical indifference first arose in philosophy in the guise of skepticism. For one could be supposed to have just the same ideas one does have, whether or not they rightly represented the world outside, or whether they represented any world since; for all we know, they could be just as they were though there were no world external to them. Imaginary landscapes, imaginary portraits, are distinguished from "real" ones externally, and through the chance accordance between pictures and scenes or faces in the world itself. The Picture Theory of Language goes with a Correspondence Theory of Truth (or a Representationalist Theory of Perception), and it actually entails Semantical Indifference. For it very naturally excludes pictures from the world, so far as what once was called their "objective reality"—their representative capacity—is concerned.

But how may a "natural process" (as Randall thinks of language) produce something false? If one natural process induces changes in another, in accordance with the laws of nature, then these changes will be facts of nature no less than any other. And what are or could be false changes? Processes, to be sure, can miscarry. But thwartings are relative, one must think, only to human norms and expectancies, and so far as the face of nature is concerned, are—so naturalists have told us since Spinoza—as natural as anything else. A miscarried sentence would be equally natural, I suppose, but the question I am pressing is how we should think of that failure of connection between language and the world (which is a metaphorical way of speaking of falsehood) if language is a natural process amongst natural processes? It was, to take a comparable case elsewhere, precisely the incapacity to assimilate semantical connections to mere facts of nature which made neutral monism philosophically indigestible to such critics of it as Russell.

If we think of sentences as tools, I suppose we have an appropriate idiom: we speak of a saw not cutting true, and "to true" is a verb which covers such orthogonal activities as straightening, lining up, adhering to verticals, bringing into position, and the like. And of course a saw might be regarded as semantically indifferent, since the very same saw, in different hands, can cut true or cut false, there being nothing in the saw which guarantees against false cuts—or in the piccolo which guarantees against false notes. But then there is nothing unnatural about a false note, or a false cut, and the laws of nature are equally well observed by a saw which cuts true to the line as by one which takes off obliquely through a mahogany slab. We might, of course, say that there was a failure here on the part of him who blows or saws. But no comparable failure, surely, is involved in the production of a false sentence! A man is equally master of language whether his sentences are true or false; and since, strictly speaking, the mass of our great literature consists of sentences which are false, the very highest exercise of linguistic skill is compatible with the production of false sentences. It is no defect of language, but an intrinsic requirement of its generative grammars, that false sentences should be produced as easily as true ones. It is, to be sure, only when we undertake to apply language, to *assert* sentences, and hence in connection with the use (and not the mere generation) of sentences, that questions of truth and falsity seriously arise; and hence only when we seek to establish connections between language and the world. But the connection is, in a way, evidence of an intrinsic gap which naturally exists between language and the world (as between pictures and their subjects), a gap which the semantical relations are supposed to reach across. And to say, from the beginning, that language is a natural process amongst natural processes is to overlook the logical inescapability of that gap which has so crucial a position in the structure of philosophy, being the habitat of skepticism and the empty corridor which brings bitterness to the hearts of those who quest for certainty.

Now I do not say that you cannot work out an instrumentalist account of falsehood. But, to apply it, you must withdraw from nature, and superimpose upon its face a system of human aims and norms. Opening up a distance now between language and the world, we can let the terms "succeed" and "fail" go instrumentalist proxy for the old terms "true" and "false." A "true" sentence now will be merely a sentence correctly used (according to a norm), e.g., as a saw is "correctly used" when it cuts true. A "false sentence" will be a failure, deviant from the norm. Sentences, like saws, may be used "correctly" or "incorrectly." So we restore semantical indifference, and hence an instrumentalist theory of language will work out as far as compatibility with our two criteria of natural languages are concerned.

But none of this, I think, will help Randall with his deep idea. I mean, it will not work and, by instrumentalist criteria, fails (= is false). The reason is this. A saw has one main use. It may be misused or abused, i.e., misused when used "falsely," abused when used for something other than cutting. But sentences have many uses, and hence many misuses. *But only one specific sort of misuse corresponds to semantical failure.* Randall, like Austin, is much concerned to denounce the descriptivist emphasis of linguistic philosophers, and has heavily underscored the versatility of sentences to subserve multifarious purposes other than mere description. "Language," he writes, "is in fact a veritable toolbox of varied specific tools: sentences, statements, ejaculations, prayers, wishes, promises, questions, and the rest" (p. 42). And, in an echo of an Austinian sniff at the "Descriptivist Fallacy," he adds, 'Traditionally, far too great an emphasis has been placed on 'statements' as the normative tools of language." Well, this may be. But for each of these uses, there is an equal and opposite misuse, and hence many ways in which language can go wrong. To call all of these by the name of "falsehood" is precisely to obliterate the multifariousness which is being insisted upon. Rather, falsehood only arises, really, in connection with "statements" and with that primitive, crucial point of contact between sentences and the world which, after all, it is Randall's high purpose to illuminate. So we may concede, and then dismiss as irrelevant, the fact that language does more than describe. It is only the descriptive aspect which really has philosophical importance. And when Randall himself speaks of what he terms the "proximate" function of language—which he characterizes as "grasping" or "rearranging"—it is specifically with the descriptive dimension of language that he is concerned. The other uses really do not much matter so far as concerns the question of how the world and language must be if the latter is to put the former into words.

But this serves to deflect a certain criticism which has often been leveled against the picture theory of language. Language, the critics of that theory have tirelessly insisted, is more than descriptive, and as users of it we are concerned with things other than mere exhibition of the world through true pictographical phrases. And nothing could be more true. Language is indeed a dexterous, flexible, multifunctional instrument. But what a farce of a criticism this is in being utterly irrelevant to the questions of truth and falsity and descriptive meaningfulness which it was the purpose of that theory to illuminate! Not only is the criticism misguided, but it has done a further damage in distracting philosophical attention away from the vast questions which were being wrestled with by the founder of the theory.

Of course, the pictographical language can produce true sentences only if the world itself is picturable, and truth is congruence of shape between picture and fact. So construed, a picture would be a "re-arrangement" of the fact pictured. It would be that, not in the sense of "rearrange" which means merely redistributing the same elements in a different order (as when a woman rearranges her parlor), but in the somewhat idiosyncratic sense where different elements are arranged in the *same* order, so that there is parity of form without identity of elements. In this respect, a map of Europe is a "re-arrangement" of Europe. Such a notion of rearrangement comes close to what Randall means by rearrangement, which involves the preservation of something, albeit in another medium. Actually, his thought is more unusual than even this suggests. He wants to say that language is an activity which releases the potentially sentential powers of the world, and actualizes them in sentences. This is linguistic philosophy in a grand manner, and a thesis of virtually pre-Socratic dimension. Small wonder that in thinking it out he lost sight of the semantical factors—which, after all, come in pairs—and scanted a serious discussion of truth and falsehood. And this is not a mere remediable defect or oversight. I am not sure I can say what of his theory can be salvaged once we undertake to accommodate it to a semantical theory.

VI

Unlike stones and sticks, words fall too lightly upon the surface of the world to modify its convolutions, save as they might be amplified by linguistically sensitive receivers who convert words into actions: insulted, they destroy towers; touched, they raise churches. But all of that is irrelevant to the semantical aspects of language, where concern is with descriptions which are true or false, depending, ultimately, upon how the world already is. Some philosophers have taken truth and falsity to be a matter of congruence or discongruence, the *true* sentence being a portrait of a fact. For natural language, at least, this is implausible, and some sentences of the natural languages are, presumably, true. And it is hard to suppose that two sentences which fail to resemble one another—as, say, a Turkish and an English sentence—can be thought to resemble the same fact. And moreover, there are important limits to picturability of a sort which are not, I believe, coincident with the limits of truth. If the picture theory

itself is wrong, if sentences show no obvious similarity to whatever allegedly would make them true, then, thinking this to be a deep failure,
philosophers have thought there can be no fit connection at all between
language and the world, and have concluded that language cannot capture
reality at all. But this, in its own way, is bred of the same superstitious
mentality which finds it impossible that there should be any connection
between *res cogitans* and *res extensas*, the former being too refined for
interaction with the latter's crassness. It is against both these views that
Randall's position is worked out. The world, for him, is worked upon
by language, and made over in the image of a sentence, language being
the instrument of transformation. But he, in his turn, succumbs to the
same uncriticized assumption—as I shall in a moment show—that in
order for there to be a connection between two things, there must be some
community between them, either of form (as in the picture theory) or of
matter (as in a kind of *panlogos* theory).

Suppose, however, that the skein of sentences stood to the world in the
manner of the system of latitudes and longitudes? By means of these, we
locate ourselves upon a globe which is not in any real sense scored by the
grid of geodesics we impose upon its surface. The seas toss freely, uncon-
strained by the great arcs projected by geodesy. Were some madly literal-
minded king to decide, for the ease of his navigators, to have stripes
painted upon our sphere, the question could arise where to lay them;
and this would presuppose command of a system which never before had
required physical striping of the earth's flanks. We navigate the seas successfully by means of (after all) conventional, arbitrary lines. But to enter
that system, we need some mechanism of dead reckoning, some means of
co-ordinating grid points with world points. Thereafter we may strike out
on the open seas with impunity. All that is required is that the world
have sufficient stability from moment to moment, that the system of grids
satisfy certain minimal formal properties, and that there be some suitable
semantics, viz., co-ordinating devices which intermediate between the
world and the grids. Perhaps the connection between language and the
world is like this!

But aside from these highly general factors, there is no one way the
world must be, and no one way language must be, for us to use the one to
get around with in the other. Language need not resemble the world, and
need be no more part of it than the curves of Mercator. But it is crucial
that we must have means of ascent and descent, from the world to language and back, or else language is empty and the world uncharted. So
truth might be represented as the set of ordered couples, consisting of bits
of language paired with bits of the world. But the truth of a sentence is no

more part of the sentence than, for the matter, it is part of the world. It is only the ordered connection between the two. But this is to suggest some version or other of the Correspondence Theory of Truth, and upon those minimal metaphysical notions which go with it, namely, that there be some fixed and antecedent realities, some fixedness in the world, which will be our points of dead reckoning. Thereafter, there may be what instabilities one will, and language may be as instrumental in modifying the world as you wish. But it cannot serve its navigational purposes if it is construed as always modifying what it is about.

Randall, who wishes the world to be merely plastic, merely a set of powers to be articulated, is, as we saw, an idealist in disguise. Part of his disguise is his Naturalism, which insists that language be part of nature, one force interacting with the others. As though merely declaring the relation between language and the world to be "natural" really makes it like every other connection! "Nature," he writes, "displays certain 'passive powers' or potentialities of being shaped into linguistic form" (p. 49). Otherwise, he says, "Language and communication would then be left hanging, suspended above nature, as an incomprehensible addition to its processes" (p. 50). So he has marked in his thought a place for a connection, and hence for a Correspondence Theory after all. But in place of recognizing this, he slides, as though driven by the unacknowledged logic of the problem, into an answer of precisely the same sort as motivates both the picture theory, and the theory that dispairs of ever getting the world into language since language and the world are so "different." He insists that the world, as it were, is *linguistic already*. For "nothing could be applied to any material if it were really of a different order than the material, that is, if it were not a manipulation of something originally 'abstracted' or 'isolated' from it" (p. 49). And it is his view, more or less, that the world is frozen language, as language is fluid world.

There may be poetry in this. But it scarcely serves to mitigate a fallacy as old as philosophy. The fallacy is one we mentioned, namely, that in order for there to be any connection between things, they must be "the same" in some essential regard. Thus bodies and souls, like language and reality, must be of the "same order." And Naturalism merely insists that "everything is of the same order" in order that there should be the connections we hold. But what business has a naturalist to speak of different orders anyway? And what have we added to the fact that connections hold by saying that their terms are "of the same order"? It is a metaphysical superstition which serves, as it did in the humdrum days of Naturalism, to conceal and blur distinctions which are philosophically crucial. The distinction between language and the world, and the nature of their connection, are matters ill served by attempting to assimilate them to anything else, or to dash roughshod over them by declaring them to be "natural."

VII

Yet I do not want to end things just here, and I believe that something like a naturalistic theory of truth could be worked out. In these last few pages, I offer a sketch of a fragment of such a theory.

I am concerned only with descriptive sentences now. The meaning of such sentences will be that situation associated with them by members of that linguistic community for whom these are sentences. When sentences in different languages are associated with the same (sorts of) situations by members of different language communities, these sentences are *translates* of one another. If members of the language community L recognize a situation z associated with a sentence s of L, and members of another language community L' do not, then s has no translate in L'. The notion of *association* I wish to have appreciated in precisely the way in which Hume thought of it in connection with the conception of causality. That is to say, there is a constant conjunction *(ceteris paribus)* within the language community L, of sentences with situations, for a large and important class of sentences; and to master the language of L, I submit, one must learn which situations are associated with which sentences. Since the situations of L are the form of life of the members of L, to master L is to master a form of life. In many essential respects, forms of life are invariant from language community to language community, which is what makes translation possible. But of course forms of life vary enough so translation is seldom perfect.

If we think of the primitive relationship between sentences and situations merely as association, we are spared the temptation of supposing that a sentence and its associated situation must "resemble" one another, or be of the same nature; nor need we worry that sentences are so awfully different from situations that situations must be indescribable. Any two things can be associated, and it will be an important association if there is a constant enough conjunction between them. The taste of quinine is associated with a certain white pill: but what less resembles a certain white pill than the taste of quinine? The sort of association I am proposing is, by and large, inductive. And to master a language is, in effect, to master a complex set of inductive signs for situations signaled by the speakers of the language. Thus "Dinner is ready" is an inductive sign that dinner is ready, just as any appropriate set of cooking odors is an inductive sign of the same situation. True, sentences are conventional and culture-dependent. But so, for the matter, are dinners; and for a culture which takes its meals cold, cooking odors are an unreliable sign for the readiness of meals. The smell of noodle soup in China is a sign of breakfast, not a sign that they have dinner in the morning. In general, however, the mastering of language can be handled, within certain easily specified limits, along just the same lines as the mastery of any bit of inductive behavior. Of course, there is always the matter of stipulation: a sentence s can be stipulated to mean the situation z. But henceforward, if the stipulation is accepted, s remains an inductive sign for z.

Out of this, I think, we can get a theory of truth. Roughly, and restricting ourselves to present-tense sentences, we must take the primary use of sentences as situational signals. Then s is true in L if the situation z, associated with s by the members of L, is present. That is, if a man m understands s and, accordingly, *expects z*, then m is not disappointed. Now there are almost always ways of neutralizing the signaling function of sentences, making room for other uses: crossed fingers, quotation marks, stage paraphernalia, and the like, which put our inductive expectancies out of gear. However, we know the meaning of the sentence as that situation for which it would be, in the normal context, an inductive sign. Only here it is not either true nor false, since it in fact is not being used inductively. Truth, of course, is commonly independent of meaning, but I am suggesting that you could not naturally learn a language by means of false sentences.

Having a language, of course, is more than a matter of taking sentences as inductive signs of associated situations. It also is a matter of being able to *produce* the apposite sentence at the appropriate moment. When a hostess says, "Dinner is ready," her so saying is not an inductive sign for *her* that dinner is ready. This fact has some philosophical importance. It sometimes is said that we do not infer what our own mental states are from our behavior. I do not infer, thus, that I am in pain from my saying that I am in pain. But the fact is I very seldom infer from any sentence I utter that whatever situation is associated with it holds. What I say may be a signal to others without being a signal for myself, which is an intelligible assymmetry only because another neutralizing assymmetry holds, namely, that the very same sentences, produced and hence not inductive signs for them, are so for me.

The inductive theory of meaning, and the correspondence theory of truth which goes with it, will work, I think, only for certain crucial classes of sentences. But these will be those sentences which make, as it were, the immediate contacts with reality, at those points where language touches the world. It is a theory which satisfies the criterion of semantical indifference, and is at least compatible with linguistic creativity. It is natural—in a way which I should like to hope satisfies Randall—in that it makes the building up of one's language very like one's building up of any bit of natural or inductive knowledge. It even gives some support to his view that language serves to structure the world. For it is after all with situations that we associate these lowest-order sentences of our languages, and situations are not merely *things*. They are near-relatives to what not long ago were called facts, in which things were but constituents. But all of these are topics which lie outside the immediate horizons of this paper. I present them, and the problems which go with them, to John Herman Randall, Jr., whose theories on language I have been examining here, and which I have found so immensely stimulating. In gathering gifts for a philosopher, we seldom need worry that he "has everything." The better the philosopher, the more he needs. Good philosophers are philosophers with problems.

EMMANUEL G. MESTHENE
Harvard University

Nature Functioning Aesthetically:
In Discovery of Randall's Philosophy of Art

THE ARTIST IN RANDALL

Its subtitle marks this essay as heuristic. Among the listings in Randall's bibliography, there is not a "Philosophy of Art" nor an "Aesthetics." With only one, albeit significant, exception, moreover, such words as "art," "artistic," and "aesthetic" never appear in the titles of any book or article.[1]

Yet I think that Randall approaches the world with the soul of an artist. He is in this respect a Platonist, as his own chosen Greek hero, Aristotle, was also in this respect a Platonist. Randall himself comes closest to recognizing his commitment to art when he discusses its first cousin, religion: "I have discovered that whenever in my thinking I take religion as one art among many others, and begin to consider it in terms appropriate to the other arts or *technai*, things at once begin to happen for me intellectually."[2]

Important things have been happening intellectually for Randall—and for his students—for forty years. His thinking has illuminated not only religion but also history, metaphysics, Aristotle, and the grand traditions of epistemology and the philosophy of science. He has, to be sure, not written a "Philosophy of Art," but there is just as surely a philosophy of art in what he has written. I have set myself the task here of showing Randall's reader where it is and what it looks like.

Indeed, the attempt has been invited. At the end of *Nature and Historical Experience*, Randall approaches more explicitly than anywhere an analysis, as the chapter heading (but not the book's title) puts it, of "Qualities, Qualification, and the Aesthetic Transaction": "It is clear that any responsible metaphysical analysis has got to do something about 'quality' [and] I am here at last attempting to face up to this obligation." He does so, he tells us, *peirastikōs*, strictly as "work in progress." He neither offers nor defends a developed position. "What I should most appreciate is suggestion and help."[3] No student grateful for so much suggestion and help received in earlier years can resist the pleasure of taking this request as an obligation.

THE AESTHETICS IN RANDALL

The passages most revealing of Randall's view of art and aesthetic experience are in the three works already cited. The most important of these are pages 124-134 of *The Role of Knowledge in Western Religion* (Religion), the last chapter of *Nature and Historical Experience* (NHE), and the whole of "The Art of Language, etc." (Language). The latter at no point deals directly with the creation of art works or with their appreciation. It does see and deal with language as an art in the more generic meaning of the term, and is thus in one sense the most complete statement about art that we have from Randall.[4]

This is so, however, only by analogy and inference, which must be principal instruments for extracting the aesthetics from Randall's writing. It would be difficult to do even that if we did not have the two explicit discussions in Religion and NHE, but these remain partial and insufficient. Randall's aesthetics is rooted in, and grows out of, his metaphysics and epistemology, as did Dewey's, and Aristotle's, and Plato's, and as must any aesthetics that would make art and its functioning intelligible.[5] Whatever else it might be construed to be, art is after all at least a functioning in the world, and understanding it depends on the instruments by which we understand the world.[6]

Randall's discussion of art, therefore, must be understood in the context of the categories he sees in existence—particularly the category he calls "Connectives"—and of his conception of knowing, especially of the role of language in knowing. Randall himself testifies to the importance of this context to understanding what he says explicitly about art—and about religion, which he tirelessly likens to art. After recalling his early concern to understand history, he says:

> I undertook also a similar metaphysical analysis of language and communication [leading to] a set of more general metaphysical distinctions [that] I have been led to elaborate, because I have found them helpful in clarifying the analysis of various other subject-matters, including art and religion. . . .   (NHE, p. 143)

What emerges from the relevant passages taken together, and from the thinking and its history that are their context, is a view of art as one among many ways of acting upon and experiencing the world, i.e., as a particular form of the interaction between man and nature: art is continuous with other ways in which man and the world co-operate; but it is also distinct in serving its own particular purposes, and in thus complementing—even "completing"—those other ways. For example, both art and science discover and communicate, but they differ in the what, the how, the by which, and the for what that they discover and communicate. Perhaps most important, Randall's philosophy of art shows the way out of a problem that has bedeviled aestheticians: that of explaining the interaction and continuity between artistic activity and aesthetic experience.

What these statements import, and that they hang together, will hopefully emerge in what follows.

Encountering and Unifying

"Substance," says Randall, "the existing world, is what is encountered in all types of experience. . . . This is the fundamental principle of all sound metaphysics, the primacy of the subject-matter encountered, which cannot be intelligibly called into question" (NHE, p. 150). The world, in other words, is there, wherever and however we turn. "To this insistence our world is forever forcing us back" (NHE, p. 17). We can affect the world, suffer it, act upon and change it, but we cannot think it either out of or into existence, because thinking is a way of experiencing and therefore a way of encountering the world. This does not mean that existence is prior to experience, except in a straightforward temporal sense. Logically, it is neither prior to it, nor its product, nor intelligible apart from it. "Substance [existence, the world] *is* what it is encountered *as*, in all these [different] ways [of experiencing]" (NHE, p. 150).

"Experience," thus, names the ways in which men interact with (and encounter) nature (including men) in the world. It is not separate from, other than, above or below existence, because existence is encountered only *as* experienced. But if experience cannot be transcended to achieve some vision of pure existence (since transcending and having visions are ways of experiencing), it is nevertheless possible to differentiate among experiences. There are many ways of encountering the world, many "types of experience": there are knowing, manipulating, enhancing and appreciating, sharing, worshiping and transcending.

Now, that the world is experienced and that there are all these ways of experiencing it says something about the world. It says that it is an experienceable world, and that it is experienceable in different ways. What kind of world is such a world? In the traditional form of the question, is it one or many? Randall's answer is unequivocal:

> If we start with the world as a *unity*, it is impossible to get from that unity to the encountered plurality of things, which remains therefore a mystery. . . . But if we start with the encountered plurality, there is nothing to prevent us from tracing as much of *unification* as we may.
> (NHE, p. 214)

The world, then, is encountered as many, plural, and is therefore neither an absolute *nor* a flux; for a flux, structurelessness, is also one: "No, Nature cannot be taken as a flux, Time is not a flux. Substance, existence, is shot through with 'importances for,' with 'significances for,' with 'meanings for'—'for' the directions and ends it itself generates" (NHE, p. 156).

The plurality, in short, is a plurality of unities, structures, meanings, that are first encountered, and then "traced," discriminated, combined, sundered, or brought about—above all "brought about," as we shall see. How do we know the world is so? We know, because we experience it so. It behaves one way when we know it, reacts in another when we manipulate it, takes yet a third stance when we enhance it. Its unities are as the plurality of stops on an organ that will respond differentially according to the different intentions of the player who is skilled in the art of registration. (The analogy might be extended. For example, no organist sitting for the first time before an unfamiliar organ will find it either a unity, having but a single voice, or a flux, i.e., unregistrable. He will encounter it as structured, at least by the previous organist, and will then seek a new constellation of unities, according to its possibilities and his inspiration.)

These unities, meanings, "stops," are *histories* for Randall, dynamic structures. He sees nature as interacting histories, as a co-operation of processes:

> Galaxies and stars, mountain-ranges and forests, as well as human societies, institutions, and ideas, are all what they are because of their respective pasts. They are "concretions" and "cumulative conservations" of the co-operations of processes into which they have previously entered.
>
> (NHE, p. 210)

Some of these unities, histories, or eventuations—e.g., galaxies, stars, mountain ranges, and forests—do not require human intervention in the course of their actualization. Others—the human societies, institutions, ideas—eventuate from processes that do require the co-operation of man, so that they exist only potentially in advance of that co-operation. They are stops on the organ that have yet to feel the hand of the player.[7] But they are there waiting for the hand, otherwise there would be nothing for the player to play on: ". . . it is not man alone who connects and unifies: it is existence co-operating with men. And the powers of existence to connect and be connected, to unify and become unified in vision, are essential to the character of existence" (NHE, p. 213). In other words, a world that is encountered as a plurality of unities lends itself to further unification, or to unifications of different sorts, by the deliberate intervention of man. These further unifications are a particular subset of the unifications that characterize nature generally; they are the subset of "connections," of "human unifications in knowledge or vision" (NHE, p. 210).[8] It is because they would not occur except for deliberate human intervention that they can be spoken of as brought about—"made," in the traditional idiom; "created," in the artistic one.

CONNECTIVES

These "bringings about" by man of new unifications in the encountered world are the stuff of human experience. Like all unifications, they are processes, histories. Unlike unifications that are not "connections," however, these are *technai*, arts, processes of human making or creating. As arts, they require instruments by which the "artist" may work upon his "material"—more neutrally, by which man and nature may co-operate to connect and be connected in new ways. Randall calls these instruments "Connectives." Connectives are agents in processes "of connecting and unifying by means of an instrument, the Connective proper" (NHE, p. 261). "They serve in general as instruments of relating" (*ibid.*, p. 258). Just as "connections" are a subset of "unifications," however, so are Connectives "instruments" in a narrower sense than "agents" in any process whatever. Connectives are elements only in those of nature's processes of unification in which men participate: ". . . the functioning of Connectives involves a human co-operation with other operations: Connectives do not function without man's activities participating in Substance" (NHE, p. 259).

What kinds of things are these instruments called 'Connectives'?

> . . . they include not only such complex constellations of linguistic signs and symbols as the greatest Connective of all, language and discourse itself, and such elaborations of symbols as mathematics, logic, and theology. They include also all the hypotheses and theories of the several sciences, and all systems of spatial and temporal measurement; all legal systems and human moral and social ideals, all artistic symbols and religious symbols; and all myths, both historical and metaphysical. All such Connectives are symbols or manipulations of symbols and symbol systems.
> (NHE, p. 258)

Connectives are of these many and varied types, because, as Randall has noted, there are many and various ways of experiencing the world. Each different type of Connective is an instrument appropriate to a particular way of experiencing: language to knowing, religion to worshiping, law to co-operating, science to manipulating, art to enhancing and appreciating, theology and myth to transcending. Collectively, they are the "orchestra" of instruments necessary to the occurrence of human experience.

Randall emphasizes that Connectives are symbols and symbol systems. They are not signs:

> . . . it is necessary to draw a sharp distinction between a "symbol" and a "sign." A "sign" we have defined as something which provokes the same response as some other thing, for which it can stand as a kind of surrogate or substitute. A "sign" hence "stands for" or "represents" something other than itself: it is always the "sign of" something else, and can hence serve as evidence for that other thing. In contrast, a "symbol" is in no sense representative: it never stands for or takes the place of anything other than itself. Rather, a "symbol" *does* something in its own right: it operates in its own characteristic way.   (NHE, p. 263)

Symbol-Connectives then, to the extent that they *do* something, are themselves processes, with their own distinctive structures, capable of operating as agents in other processes, i.e., in processes of connecting. Consider language, for example, the "greatest Connective of all," about which Randall talks more frequently than any other:

> It is these nonrepresentative "symbolic" factors in connected discourse that make impossible any naive, nonfunctional, "iconic" or picture "realism" as to the relation of language to its subject matter. They make any language system what is metaphysically a "myth" or "connective," and render it impossible for any "sentence" to "mirror" or literally "describe" existence.   (Language, p. 34)

There is no direct, one-for-one, isomorphic correspondence, in other words, between talking and what is talked about. That is what gives language its freedom of manipulation, its possibility of transformation into innumerable mathematical or logical "artificial" languages, and its heuristic power. A collection of verbal *signs* yields nothing but a vocabulary, a dictionary. Its symbolic dimension over and above the signs is what makes a language, i.e., a process in its own right, that has its own laws and ways of operating, and that can therefore genuinely interact with other natural processes to make the connections, the new unifications that are sought.

The Art of Language

How does language interact with other processes to yield new unifications? What, in other words, does language as a symbol-system *do*?

> Language, employing as it were a "tool box" of varied instruments in the practice of its art, first *selects* from the linguistic situation . . . the

particular materials that will serve as the subject matter of its discourse. It then proceeds to *manipulate* and *reorganize* those selected materials, *reconstructing* them into a linguistic form that will be able to do a further job. . . . Language can thus be said to "grasp" and "convey" some feature of the structure of the situation, by constructing, in accordance with its own institutionalized rules, a new linguistic instrument, some "sentence" or piece of discourse, some connected series of words, that will serve as a vehicle by which that feature can be borne or "conveyed."

(Language, pp. 38-39)

Clearly, a language that "manipulates," "reorganizes," and "reconstructs" its subject matter is more than a passive reflection or representation of the world. It has a structure of its own by which it does something new to the world. In the case of scientific languages, for example, the structure is that of postulate-theorem that recent generations of logicians have explored. The symbolic (as distinct from representative) character of such languages is testified to by the possibility of constructing wholly artificial types whose meaning is exhausted in their structure, with no reference whatever to existence. These are the languages of pure mathematics, quasi-aesthetic objects to those who revel in them.

The more useful scientific languages—such as those, if one wish, of applied mathematics—have the same structure, but a different origin. They are chosen for what they can do in the world, rather than born of a sophisticated play instinct. They start out by formulating some feature of the world, selected for its significance, and they end by saying something about that same world, usually something new. "Communication as a natural process is continuous with other natural processes: . . . it arises out of a prior active situation or 'universe of action,' and it normally leads to further activities that are not merely talking" (Language, p. 32). But between their starting and their ending they are as freely manipulable as the purest of abstract languages, and no less subject to the laws (axioms, rules) that define them as languages and govern their own internal structures. In that interim, they are entirely free of any requirement to "represent" or "picture" or "say" anything about the world. "The square root of minus one," as many have noted, certainly represents nothing in the world. It is a pure symbol, in no sense a sign. It is pure possibility and derives its meaning wholly from the rules of the language in which it appears.

The "square root of minus one," or "velocity at an instant," to use Randall's example (NHE, p. 263), will never picture anything in the world, but yet can be a necessary link between a preceding proposition that formulates something known about the world and a subsequent one that discovers something about it that was not previously known. The disciplined realm of pure possibility in a language that is typified by such propositions as the "square root of minus one" is the workshop in which the material that language "selects" is "manipulated," "reorganized," and "restructured" to issue in something new. It is a necessary condition to the creation of new unifications.[9]

Another necessary condition, as I have noted, is that the world, Substance, be subject to new unification, i.e., to reorganization and restructuring:

> . . . in any process of art, the fundamental relation between the instrument and the material it works with is the possession of what can be called "correlative" or "cognate" active and passive powers. The instrument must possess the active power of being able to work upon and shape the material; the material must have the passive power of being worked upon and shaped by the instrument. Each, that is, must have a structure and such properties that both are capable of interacting in a joint and common functioning or cooperation.　　(Language, p. 46)

The art of language works upon and shapes its material because its axiomatic structure gives it the property of free manipulability of a realm of pure possibility. Its material, i.e., the world, is worked upon and shaped by language, in turn, because its structure of a plurality of processes in co-operation gives it the correlative property of movement and change that allow of direction. In different words, the relevant property of the world is the potentiality to be different from what it is. Its different potential issues, moreover, are at least as many as the processes in it that are heading for their issues, and are probably many more than that, since the processes of the world (or any number of them) may, in their co-operation, reinforce, neutralize, transform, destroy, or otherwise combine with each other to yield a whole new range of potential issues.

It is from these myriad potentialities that language selects those that may serve a contemplated function "in action, social co-operation, inquiry, or [in] enhancing immediate enjoyment" (Language, p. 33). It will take them "within itself"—"the initial function of language seems to be to 'grasp' certain selected structures" (ibid., p. 36)—and treat them, for a time, not as the potentialities that they are, but as pure possibilities that can be manipulated, twisted this way and that, combined and recombined, in temporary freedom from material constraint. In this process, some particular constellation of possibilities, some idea, some novel structure will suggest itself that promises to yield the end in action, social co-operation, inquiry, or immediate enjoyment that was but contemplated in the beginning. If it does, it has revealed, and at the same time actualized, potentialities in the world that were previously not actual and that might never have been except for the intervention of language. It has brought about new unifications. It has connected the previously un-connected.[10]

> . . . "grasping" and "conveying," as an art, displays not only [the] first phase of selecting its material. It then goes on to "manipulate" it, to reorganize it, or arrange and order it to serve its various functions. It does this by means of a complex instrument or tool, some specific language, which is in fact a veritable tool box of varied specific tools: sentences, statements, ejaculations, prayers, wishes, promises, questions, and the rest.   (Language, p. 42)

THE LANGUAGE OF ART

"What can be said about language after a careful metaphysical analysis of communication," Randall tells us, "could be generalized to apply to all Connectives" (NHE, p. 258). . . . "there is no reason to suspect that scientific Connectives—or languages and symbol-systems—enjoy any different ontological status from poetic and religious Connectives" (*ibid.*, p. 226).

Artistic, religious, social Connectives, then, are like languages. Randall comes close to calling them so, "in a broad sense," at one point (NHE, p. 258), but shies away for fear of the confusion potential in an outright identification (NHE, p. 266).

Knowing, we have seen, is the art of using language to reveal new powers or potentialities and to achieve new unifications in the world. Since knowing is but one of many ways of experiencing, the potentialities it reveals and the unifications it makes are not all there are. They are restricted to those that are "capable of generalization, which can hence serve as *means* to the production of values [i.e., to achievement of further goals] in the widest range of circumstances. [Science] does not select and formulate the 'immediate values' of the scientist's own personal situation. . . . It aims at 'impartiality,' at a 'theoretical character,' in what it selects" (Language, p. 41). The work of the scientist tells us about the world in objective, public, instrumental propositions that are derived from the possibilities revealed in the symbolic operations of language. It teaches what we call scientific truth that has consequences in the "universe of action."

But art also reveals and teaches—" 'artistic truth,' we sometimes call it" (Religion, p. 127):

> The work of the painter, the musician, the poet, teaches us how to use our eyes, our ears, our minds, and our feelings with greater power and skill. It teaches us how to become more aware both of what is and of what might be, in the world that offers itself to our sensitive receptivity. It shows us how it discern unsuspected qualities in the world encountered, latent powers and possibilities there resident. Still more, it

makes us see the new qualities with which that world, in cooperation with the spirit of man, can clothe itself. For art is an enterprise in which the world and man are most genuinely cooperative, and in which the working together of natural materials and powers and of human techniques and vision is most clearly creative of new qualities and powers.

(Religion, p. 128)

Art too, then, reveals potentialities, unsuspected powers in the world, and "is most clearly creative of new qualities," new unifications. It, too, in some sense "explains" the world, not "in the sense of accounting for it . . . [but] in the sense of making plain its features" (Religion, p. 127).

Art and knowing remain different ways of experiencing, to be sure. There are differences in their respective objectives. Art, for example, *does* go after "immediate values." The artist's selection of his materials, unlike the scientist's, "must *include* the human reaction to them" (Language, p. 41):

> Thus, the language of lyric and dramatic poetry concentrates in its selection upon the human interaction, the actor-speaker himself. It grasps and conveys his feelings and reactions, the qualities of his private experience, . . . it then proceeds to manipulate them, doubtless in distinctive and important ways that call for much inquiry. It clearly "intensifies" them and "clarifies" them, so that they are then sharable by those less sensitive. (Language, pp. 40-41)

The function of the language in art remains that of the art of language generally: to select, to grasp, to manipulate, to reorganize and reconstruct (cf. also NHE, p. 283). The identity of ontological status is unaffected by differences in vocabulary and material worked upon.

Yet, as one might expect, the difference in way of experiencing entails a difference in the operation of the language-Connective in each case. Randall anticipates it in the distinction between the "mediating" (cognitive) and "immediatizing" (specifically artistic) functions of language (NHE, p. 279), and elaborates it as follows: ". . . a language system includes both representative *signs* and non-representative *symbols*" (NHE, p. 262, n10), whereas "the arts, including religion, do not significantly employ 'signs' of anything else. . . . They resemble language to the extent that it employs *symbols*, not to the extent that it uses *signs*" (*ibid.*, p. 268).

This distinction between mixed linguistic systems and nonrepresentative symbols is fixed in a table at NHE, p. 262, yet we find, just six pages later, that "one of the main problems in the analysis of the arts is to inquire in detail just how they manage to transform the signs they use into symbols" (*ibid.*, p. 268).

Do the arts use signs, then, or do they not? The operative word in the passage at NHE, p. 268 is "significantly": "the arts . . . do not *significantly* employ 'signs'" (emphasis added). They clearly do employ representations: a drawing of a pear, a flute sounding like a bird, a sculpture of an angel. But these do not function as signs and still function artistically: "no matter how extensive its employment of signs, . . . that is not the art's primary function" (NHE, p. 268), otherwise it would in no way differ from the passport photograph.

This distinction between the uses of language in knowing and in art is one of the most difficult in Randall. The key to it, I think, is that, in its cognitive uses, language employs signs at the points where it "arises out of" and "leads to" the universe of action, i.e., at the limits of the interim period of free manipulation of symbols (cf., Language, p. 32). In its specifically *artistic* uses also, language arises out of the encountered universe, just as scientific language does, and does to that extent use signs. But, unlike scientific language, its symbolic operations are not undertaken *as a means* to getting back to new signs directive of further practical operations in the universe of action. It is not "mediating."

The natural end of the language of art is the "symbolic universe" itself. Its total function is to reveal possibility as such, to "immediatize" experience. It is at the *end* of the process, thus, that the arts resemble language "only to the extent that it employs *symbols* [and] not to the extent that it uses *signs*."

Enhancing and Appreciating

The world enhanced and appreciated in the experience of art is not a different world from that which is known. It is the same Substance that is encountered:

> Any set of factors can be involved in functioning aesthetically, and can serve as powers to cooperate aesthetically. There is no one type of material that alone possesses aesthetic powers, or qualities. There is no one type of experience that alone possesses aesthetic powers.   (NHE, p. 287)

The powers that are revealed are different in each case, however. The powers, potentialities, revealed in knowing are the powers to do and to act. Those revealed in art, including religion, are the powers "of seeing and of being seen" (NHE, p. 283). There are no inherently "aesthetic" materials, because materials become aesthetic—become "qualified," Randall calls it—as they co-operate with man in aesthetic experience, in the "aesthetic transaction" (cf. NHE, p. 284). The same material that can be "worked upon and shaped" by the instrument of science possesses equally the "correlative" or "cognate" power to be worked upon and shaped—for different ends—by the instrument or language of art.

The language of art, to be sure, employs a different vocabulary. Its "tool kit" includes such things as line and color, sound and time, mass and shape. Even in the case of the language of poetry, where the tool kit appears the same as in scientific language—i.e., letters of the alphabet in combination—the tools themselves are different: verse, rhyme, simile, and onomatopoeia have replaced the sentence, the statement, and the proposition.

But we have seen that a language functions, not according to the particular vocabulary in its "dictionary," but by virtue of possessing a structure of its own. The essence of scientific language, as we have seen, lies in that interlude of free manipulation of symbols that its axiomatic structure makes possible. In the languages of art, "free manipulation of symbols" is no longer an interlude, but an *end*: "they resemble language to the extent that it employs *symbols,* not to the extent that it uses *signs.*" In its cognitive uses, in other words, the structure of language remains instrumental in the sense of mediative, even in its apparently most abstract symbolic operations. In its artistic uses, the structure is elaborated for its own sake. It is instrumental only to the exploration of its own possibilities. It has no other end than to be. It has become the aesthetic element of form: "The aesthetic qualities we make out of the composer's musical qualities teach us how to hear sounds better, how they can be put together, how they can illustrate a pattern of musical logic and dialectic, how they can create a world of pure and unalloyed form" (NHE, p. 290).

Similarly with the materials formed: the vocabulary itself becomes enriched and thus conveys more of the unsuspected richness of the world. We "hear sound better." The poet teaches us "the music . . . of language, the feel of words" (NHE, p. 290). The color green that in its practical function may mean no more than "go" or "we have arrived at the park" can, in the artist's hands, reveal unsuspected qualities of color as such. It becomes aesthetic matter:

> The aesthetically sensitive painter or poet can "notice" further features, in the seeing of grass, for instance, than the mere "green" that suffices for most practical purposes. He brings to the visual transaction an experience, a skill, a trained art of perceiving, that enables him to qualify it in new ways; and he can "communicate" these new "qualities" in his particular "language" or medium. He can thus reveal unsuspected powers of being seen, unsuspected "qualities," in grass. Chinese and Japanese painters are notoriously good at this; so, in very different ways, are the Impressionists and Van Gogh.   (NHE, pp. 281-282)

This revealing of the possibilities of form and enriching of the world's materials "is not the kind of thing that can be put into words and statements. . . . It is not the aesthetician with his books, but the painter who by his *painting* teaches us how to 'see' the world" (NHE, p. 282). The qualities that the artist detects, captures, and conveys "seem to be literally 'ineffable': they cannot be stated or expressed directly, but they can be communicated, and thus 'shared,' only by suggestion" (NHE, p. 273). The suggestion is contained in the artistic qualities that the artist puts into his work of enhancing the world. It is that work of enhancement, in turn, that occasions the heightened appreciation of the world that is communicated to the "seer" or "hearer" or "reader" who enters into aesthetic transaction with it (cf., NHE, p. 285).

"We have no word in the English language that unambiguously includes what is signified by the two words 'artistic' and 'esthetic'," Dewey once complained, and he went on to deplore the separation of the act of creation or production from that of perception and enjoyment that was encouraged thereby.[11] The distinction in Randall is between the "artistic transaction" and the "aesthetic transaction," and the relation he sees between these is such as to minimize the danger that Dewey feared.

The *artistic* transaction, the "situation functioning artistically," issues in the production of a work of art, "in the painting of a picture, the making of a poem, the composing of music" (NHE, p. 284). It is the situation in which nature co-operates with man *qua* artist. In the *aesthetic* transaction, by contrast, nature co-operates with man *qua* "seer," "reader," "hearer." The work of art is a factor in the aesthetic transaction, serving "to qualify the situation aesthetically" (NHE, p. 285). But it is only a factor. " 'Qualifying,' producing aesthetic qualities, is far from being the only way in which things can function aesthetically" (*loc. cit.*). It is not only the picture, poem, or symphony that is seen, read, or heard. It is also the world that is "seen" by means of the work of art, just as it is the world that is known by means of the scientific theory:

> . . . as a discoverer of new powers and possibilities the painter has much in common with the scientist. What he does with and makes out of what forces itself upon his attention and what he sees, by selecting from it, manipulating it, reorganizing and reconstructing it by means of his distinctive art, is very much like what the experimentation of the scientist effects.   (Religion, p. 131)

The artist does not create *ex nihilo*, in other words. He creates out of his own aesthetic experience:

> . . . at every stage of the artistic transaction the artist finds himself also in an aesthetic situation—he is qualifying what he is doing aesthetically, and these aesthetic qualities are important, even controlling factors in his artistic activity.   (NHE, p. 285)

The Chinese painter has qualified his grass aesthetically through his sensitive perception before he begins to select and manipulate with his brush.
                                                                    (*Ibid.*, p.284)

It is that, in the end, which enables the artist to share what he sees, and to communicate it. And it is that which guarantees the continuity of the artistic and the aesthetic in experience, of the activities of enhancing and appreciating the world. It is so, because it is the world as it is encountered that governs in the end, and all experience, whatever distinctions we might make in it along the way, is but a celebration of that encountering.

"This is the fundamental principle of all sound metaphysics," Randall has said, "the primacy of the subject-matter encountered, which cannot be intelligibly called into question." It is also the fundamental principle, if I read Randall right, of a sound philosophy of art.

NOTES

1. The exception is "The Art of Language and the Linguistic Situation: A Naturalistic Analysis," *Journal of Philosophy*, Vol. LX, No. 2 (January 17, 1963). This article will be cited frequently below and will henceforth be abbreviated "Language."

2. *The Role of Knowledge in Western Religion* (Boston: Star King Press, 1958), p. 124. Further references to this work below will employ the abbreviation "Religion."

3. The quotations are from pages 272 and 273 of *Nature and Historical Experience* (New York: Columbia University Press, 1958). This work will henceforth be abbreviated "NHE."

4. This article is more than an occasional piece. It takes up the entire issue (pp. 29-56) of *Journal of Philosophy* in which it appears (see n.1 above), and Randall tells us in a footnote to its title that it should properly have been included in NHE. It was indeed promised at NHE, p. 262, n.10.

5. I am asserting a *logical* connection, which does not preclude Randall's having *arrived* at his metaphysics and theory of knowledge in part from a fundamentally artistic temperament, as I have suggested. Compare p. 29 n. of Language, where Randall says that his general metaphysical position grew (historically) out of his analysis of language. The parallel is not strict, because there is no analogous analysis of art, but it is another instance of "things happening intellectually" for Randall when he thinks in terms appropriate to art (as, e.g., language).

6. My use of the concept "art and its functioning" is an attempt to overcome a lack to which Dewey called attention: "We have no word in the English language that unambiguously includes what is signified by the two words 'artistic' and 'esthetic' " (*Art as Experience* [New York: 1934], p. 46).

7. Mountain ranges too, of course, can co-operate with men, e.g., as partners in skiing, in an engineering project, or as objects of a geological inquiry. They are then potential in new eventuations, however actual *as* eventuations. One organist's melody may be another's noise.

8. "Such human unifications in knowledge or vision are but a pushing further of Nature's *own* unifying powers," the passage continues (*loc. cit.*, emphasis added). There is nothing at all subjective about them. As the analysis below will show, the unifications first occur imaginatively "in knowledge or vision" and then have consequences in the world in which man is as natural an interacting factor as any other.

Conversely, of course, there are presumably unifications in the achievement of which men serve as occasions rather than as partners, as perhaps in the working out of a Greek tragedy. But then men are rather more like mountain ranges than distinctively men, and such unifications are in the end indistinguishable from that more general set which occur without human co-operation in any intelligible or intelligent sense.

9. The three preceding paragraphs may be too compressed for the reader unfamiliar with the ideas and the terms in which they are couched. It has not been possible, in this short treatment designed for another purpose, to deal extensively with the philosophy that serves them as context. I have done so, however, in E. G. Mesthene, *How Language Makes Us Know* (The Hague: Martinus Nijhoff, 1964), to which the attention of the interested reader is invited.

10. See Mesthene, *op. cit.*, chap. iii, pp. 99ff. and *passim* for a detailed hypothesis about how language thus operates on its material.

11. See n.6 above.

WILLARD E. ARNETT
Chatham College

Are the Arts and Religions Cognitive?

I

One of the most interesting as well as one of the most crucial aspects of John H. Randall's philosophic naturalism is his novel, sympathetic, and provocative treatment of the arts and religions. As he himself would no doubt readily admit, it is probably not too much to claim that the ultimate adequacy of naturalism as a philosophic framework must depend greatly on its success in reconciling the enormous experiential significance of the arts and religions with its fundamental principles. For whatever naturalism may affirm about the order of efficacy among various substances and complexes or about the "executive order" of nature and the primacy of scientific categories and methodologies in the achievement of genuine knowledge, the arts and religions will presumably remain among the dominant features—qualifying and in some sense accounting for a host of highly important and complex activities, products, and tendencies—in any world in which man delights, suffers, and loves and which he may approach and modify in various ways. Thus a philosophy that fails to recognize and include artistic and religious "facts" and "values" can hardly remain an adequate or acceptable framework for the analysis and understanding of experience or the conceptual envisagement of the most pervasive and significant traits of existence.

Randall is indeed profoundly aware that philosophy must take careful—if not a special—account of the arts and religions. He has said emphatically that "metaphysics cannot arrive at any valid conclusions which would leave the fact of religion unintelligible. Like every other activity of men in their world—botany, art, physics, politics, and all the rest—religion is part of the subject matter of existence which metaphysics must understand."[1] His treatment of religion especially is accordingly marked by an informed sensitivity and concern that are altogether rare among contemporary secular philosophers, matched in America perhaps only by George Santayana and Alfred North Whitehead. Thus the questions at issue are not about his basic evaluation, attitude, or outlook in regard to the philosophic importance of the arts and religions, but only about the adequacy of his analysis in certain important respects.

II

Although he has given no systematic or extended account of the arts as such, there are numerous references and passages in Randall's writings which explicitly compare or contrast the character and functions of the arts with the elements of religion, science, and philosophy. Consequently there is no fundamental difficulty in determining the general nature of the arts as conceived in this version of naturalistic metaphysics. Briefly, as Randall conceives them, there is in fact no great or basic difference between the character and functions of the arts and the religions. And although he sometimes suggests that science also may be in some respects most appropriately regarded as an art, his more persistent thesis is that the arts and religions in contrast to the sciences belong fundamentally to "the world *for* knowledge" or "to the subject matter to be understood" and not—or at least not basically or significantly—to the methods and instruments by or through which the world may be known or understood.

Yet Randall also claims that the artist "has much in common with the scientist":

> What he does with, and makes out of, what he sees—selecting it, manipulating it, reorganizing and reconstructing it, by means of the instrument of his distinctive art, his "language" or medium—is very much like the "experimentation" of the scientist. Both the scientist and the artist, by revealing new powers and pushing back the limits in things, enlarge our horizons, increase our knowledge, and extend our power. . . . And dare I add that the activities of the prophet and the saint also resemble the "experimentation" of the scientist, and are subject to the same conditions?[2]

The answer to his own question is, in a later work, explicit and affirmative. The prophet and the saint do "teach us something, about our world and about ourselves":

> They teach us how to see what man's life in the world is, and what it might be. They teach us how to discern what human nature can make out of its natural conditions and materials. They reveal latent powers and possibilities not previously noticed. They make us receptive to qualities of the world encountered; and they open our hearts to the new qualities with which that world, in co-operation with the spirit of man, can clothe itself. They enable us to see and feel the religious dimension of our world better, the "order of splendor," and of man's experience with it. They teach us to find the Divine; they show us visions of God.[3]

Yet Randall is profoundly reluctant to call the "teachings" of any art or religion "true," or to suggest that either may result in genuine knowledge. His reluctance is apparently due in part at least to the fact that "the arts, including religion, do not significantly employ 'signs' of anything else. Their resemblance to language lies not in their 'expressive' function; it lies in their 'impressive' function."[4] Art and religion do not express the truth about things but record the impressions that things make on us. The function of art or the artistic use of language is "to create certain 'impressions' ";[5] and the aim of religion "is not to give 'knowledge' but rather 'salvation'—it is to express, strengthen, enhance, and clarify a practical commitment, to one's 'ultimate concern.' . . ."[6] Or in terms Randall has perhaps used most consistently, the artist and the prophet and the saint teach *how*, and not *that*. "The painter shows us *how to see* the visible world better—how to see grass. Even so, the prophet and the saint show us *how to see* the Divine better—*how to see* God."[7]

But *knowing how*, according to Randall, is fundamentally different from *knowing that*; and it is the function of science to teach *that* certain things are so. Thus he concludes that the arts and religions should be said to belong to the class of "non-cognitive symbols" which "do not have as their function to participate in activities that eventuate in knowledge and truth." Their function is to " 'symbolize' not some external thing that can be indicated apart from their operation—they are not evidence— but rather what they themselves do, their proper functions."[8] So although the arts and religions may be said to "disclose" or "reveal" certain features of the world or of experience, they cannot, he suggests, be said to provide "understanding" or "knowledge" of anything at all.

III

Now obviously the question whether the arts and religions are cognitive turns in some measure, as Randall recognizes, on the meaning attached to such terms as "cognitive," "knowledge," and "understanding." In what is perhaps his most stringent definition of "understanding," which is apparently employed at least almost synonymously with the others, he claims: "We 'understand' when we can formulate in exact—at best, in mathematical—terms, the way in which a thing will interact or co-operate with other things under specified conditions."[9] He also suggests that to understand is to be able to "explain" events and processes in terms of their causes and consequences.[10] Thus the arts and religions are not cognitive, he explains, because: "The knowledge so taught is not an explanation or account of anything. It is not something that can be formulated as a set of rationally demonstrated conclusions. It cannot even be warranted by any precise method of experimental confirmation, though it clearly has its own standards of adequacy."[11] For Randall, the method of physics is obviously the paradigm of cognitive activity or of knowledge and understanding.

No doubt this approach belongs squarely in what is by now a long and distinguished tradition. The tradition may be said to have been inspired in its modern and most rigorous forms by the methodological assumption of the early modern scientists that only primary or measurable (mathematical) qualities are ultimately real and truly comprehensible, while secondary qualities are unreal and incomprehensible in themselves, but completely dependent upon and knowable only in terms of the primary qualities. This approach to religion in particular has presumably been thoroughly justified in the minds of many by the critical work of such men as David Hume, Immanuel Kant, Karl Marx, and Sigmund Freud, each of whom has demonstrated—at least to the satisfaction of a band of faithful followers—that religion especially (but also the arts) can be understood in scientific or non-religious terms—as "sophistry and illusion," or "the recognition of duties as divine commands," or "the opiate of the people" suffering from economic inequities, or "the survival into maturity of the wishes and needs of childhood." Each of these is presumably the basic element in an "explanation" or account of the causes and consequences of religious experience and activity. But surely they are not equally *true*, if true at all. And apparently each is reductive in the sense that it attempts to "understand" religions on the assumption that existence may be ultimately, if not completely, described and understood without the use of religious language.

Now Randall is of course much too candid, and much too aware of the errors and dangers, to be guilty of the reductive fallacy in the simple form it took, for example, in Schopenhauer and Nietzsche or in Marx and Freud. He is clearly convinced that there are no simple formulae in terms of which all art or all religion may be understood. Indeed, his great confidence in the scientific method, as he sees it, is obviously due largely to the conviction that this method is precisely a way of taking account of the complexities of existence without oversimplification. There is, nonetheless, a reductive character, similar to that of Hume or Kant, in his exposition of the claim that the arts and religions can be understood scientifically, which suggests that his pluralistic naturalism, although perhaps basically sound, is not as penetrating and sympathetic in relation to the arts and religions as it sometimes seems. For surely it is not only possible but even necessary for those who have experienced the apparent cogency of the arts and religions to doubt that a scientific account of them—whether in the name of physics, history, sociology, or psychology—is ever either as possible or as relevant as Randall claims.

Under what circumstances could religious symbols, according to Randall, be regarded as *cognitive* or as *true* in a sense comparable to that of *truth* in science? The standard form of cognitive claims, he says, is "formulated assertions or propositions capable of being tested by evidence and of being judged true. As thus susceptible to verification, they are commonly agreed to constitute 'knowledge'; they include both descriptions of fact and explanations of those facts, for both take the form of statements *that* such and such is the case."[12] This definition of "knowledge," together with themes to be developed presently, suggests the conclusion that, according to Randall, religion or religious symbols could be significantly cognitive only if traditional rational theology should turn out to be "susceptible to verification" or "warranted" by evidence. A true religion, he is apparently convinced, would necessarily make "verifiable" or "warranted" assertions about the existence of God, the requirements of morality, and the immortality of the soul. Convinced that claims about these matters are not subject to proof or disproof, he therefore concludes that religion must be symbolic and non-cognitive, or radically different from the symbols of the various sciences in their implications for the nature of existence. Under such circumstances, religious phenomena, including claims about the existence of God, morality, and immortality, must be regarded as "impressive symbols" of "the most important concerns of living" which can and must be understood scientifically and philosophically.

The correctness of this account of Randall's view of the conditions under which religion might be regarded as cognitive is confirmed by certain aspects of *The Role of Knowledge in Western Religion*. One of these is his treatment of the different approaches of Thomas Aquinas and Immanuel Kant to the problem of knowledge. He asserts that "Thomas Aquinas was more successful and sounder than Kant in his solution" of the problem of knowledge. And Kant's chief failure in this respect, he obviously believes, was in "making science only relatively true" or in claiming that science "does not describe 'things in themselves,' things as they really are." Thus Aquinas "was more successful and sounder" because for him "such a way out was impossible: he was too much a rationalist and a scientist, too impressed by the Aristotelian conviction that the real world is intelligible. For him science is absolutely true, and so is faith, for both alike come from God."[13] If we follow the spirit of Randall's treatment of the theme, Aquinas was mistaken only in making the assumption that there are things which can be known only by faith or religiously. He is sounder than Kant only because Kant denied that science is completely reliable on all matters.

Now surely one need not affirm the "literal" truth of rational theology or deny that religious claims and practices are essentially symbolic in order to suggest that Kant's claims about "things in themselves" and the limits of science, although perhaps romantic and thoroughly unjustified, are not essentially more dubious than the claim that "science is absolutely true." He was apparently on the trail of an important truth, even though he may have exaggerated both its remoteness from ordinary experience and its ultimate implications for man's conduct and destiny. He saw, it may be suggested, that there are aspects of experience and existence which apparently cannot be expressed or understood either scientifically or philosophically, but which one may, at least in some sense, come to grips with through the arts and religions. At least Santayana, Cassirer, and Whitehead, among others, have argued with considerable cogency that artistic and religious symbols may be said to reveal certain "dimensions" or "features" of experience or existence as truly as the sciences reveal others. If this is indeed the case then surely it is ill-advised to suggest that the arts and religions are noncognitive, if only because Santayana was apparently right in observing that "if all other intellectual possessions save strictly experimental science are denied the title of knowledge, we may suspect that, even if admitted as forms of feeling or of poetry, they will be rather despised."[14] Unless the aim is to discredit the arts and religions completely—and apparently nothing is more remote from Randall's basic purpose—greater care in language at least is evidently demanded.

A second (but closely related) feature of *The Role of Knowledge in Western Religion* that confirms the above account of the conditions under which Randall would be willing to regard religion as genuinely cognitive is his treatment of the possibilities in regard to religious knowledge. There are, he suggests, only three possibilities:

1) A "special and privileged religious knowledge."
2) A "consistently rational philosophical theology," which would show that "religious 'truth' must agree with man's best knowledge of the world."
3) Acceptance "that there is no theoretical 'truth' at all in religion."[15]

Assuming that scientific inquiry has discredited the various claims to "special and privileged religious knowledge," and that rational theology was demolished by the critiques of Hume and Kant, Randall concludes that the only defensible claim is "that there is no theoretical 'truth' at all in religion." And from this it presumably follows that religious symbols must be regarded as non-cognitive, or that there is a radical difference between the intellectual status and power of scientific and religious symbols, and that consequently "it is well to keep 'truth' for the knowledge that is science, with all its complex procedures and criteria for verifying propositions that can be stated in words."[56]

Now, no doubt Randall is thoroughly justified in protesting the fact that when Christianity was conceived as "rational," with science as the paradigm of rationality, "the wealth of aspiration, feeling, emotion, expression, symbolism and poetry of the great Christian tradition" was abandoned or ignored and "men looked to it for the two things it had never pretended to give: scientific truth and the pattern of business success."[17] Furthermore, he is no doubt right when he claims that science and religion "cannot be brought together in harmony by trying to found religion on scientific beliefs."[18] But it is nonetheless doubtful that there is more hope for harmony between them in the assumption that religion provides "material for knowledge," while science is the method of securing genuine knowledge. The failure in Randall's account, however, is not his claim that religion does not provide the same sort of knowledge as science, but his claim that there is a clear and immense difference between the cognitive status and function of the religions and the sciences, so that the results of the religions are never appropriately called "knowledge." This failure is evident in the fact that he appeals to Santayana's "modern interpretation" of religious beliefs as "symbols" rather than "literal knowledge" in support of his own claim that the religions are non-cognitive. So far as the words are concerned this appeal is of course quite accurate. But it nonetheless ignores the very important fact that Santayana also regarded science as "symbolic" and religion as "a form of reason." "No physics can be adequate," Santayana wrote,

> and just as one sense gives us one idea, say colour, and another sense another idea, say hot or cold, so one science may give us a classification into the genera and species and another science a mechanism of a geometrical or atomic kind. . . . They will be theories, just as our experience will be ideas or sensations. And both science and experience are only *languages* in which, for human purposes, nature may at times be described.[19]

All our ideas, he insists, are expressive, symptomatic, and symbolic, "superficial lights on a great dark ocean of existence." There is then no great difference between the cognitive powers of science and religion or art. They are all obviously, according to Santayana, cognitive in different degrees. Consequently, although Santayana shares Randall's view that the religions are not "literally" true, he by no means agrees that there is an absolute, or even a significant, difference between the religions and the sciences in this respect.

IV

To suppose that science and religion are ultimately in conflict, or that the method and validity of the one imply that the other is completely irrelevant and mistaken, is surely not justified by anything in the contemporary situation. Randall would clearly agree with this claim. But to suppose that, in order to be cognitively significant, religion must provide knowledge in propositional form about such matters as the existence of God, standards of conduct, and immortality seems equally mistaken, or at least confuses a particular set of religious doctrines with religion itself. Religion is not theology; and it is neither fortunetelling nor ethics. The religious person may be as ignorant of such ultimate matters as anyone else—though his beliefs about them *may* indeed differ radically in some respects from the beliefs of the non-religious. But surely the diversity of religious practices and beliefs suggests, with little room for doubt, that religion as such is quite compatible with enormously different claims in regard to the ultimate nature of existence and human destiny. It seems indeed almost beyond dispute that no specific claim or set of claims is indispensable to religion.

Instead, religion even as science and philosophy is apparently, in the phrase (if not the meaning) of Santayana, "an invitation to think after a certain fashion." And the fashion itself evidently has no very definite limits and is never wholly inseparable from its current claims and particular forms. Religion, free of superstition and irrational hopes, is most obviously an attitude towards the conditions of existence—an attitude that may be partly formulated as the conviction that one most appropriate response to existence is worship, or praise, or adoration. The claims of the religions are essentially the records of the experiences and hypotheses which have seemed to justify the attitude and particular forms of worship. And no doubt to many existence may seem demonic rather than divine unless certain irrational hopes and demands promise to be finally fulfilled. But surely the fact that such irrational hopes have inspired—and been inspired by—religious experiences and doctrines by no means implies that an essentially "rational" religion is completely inconceivable and impossible. The fact that unrealistic aims have both inspired and resulted from genuine scientific investigation and understanding detracts little, if at all, from the actual power and beneficence of the sciences.

But should religious symbols be called cognitive? Or do the arts and religions teach only *how* to do certain things and never *that* certain things are true? No doubt there is much to be said in favor of Randall's claim that the arts and religions are primarily ways of learning or knowing *how and* not ways of knowing *that*. At least this approach emphasizes in its own manner that the doctrines of religion, which have inspired so much disagreement and fanaticism, are not nearly as important as they have often seemed. But on the other hand, to deny that the arts and religions are cognitive while asserting that the sciences are so seems both to underestimate the powers of the arts and religions and perhaps to overestimate the "understanding" and the "certainty" that are possible through the sciences. Science too, although it is often much more, is surely sometimes itself only a way of teaching or learning *how* to do certain things. Very often in science the understanding *that*, is apparently quite inseparable from knowing *how* to produce certain results. Yet science does appear to demonstrate *that* such and such is the case with a clarity and certainty never attained in any other way. And just as obviously, religion is unable to teach many of the things it has often professed to teach. It seems nonetheless unjustified, however, to make the sharp and radical distinction suggested by labeling the one *cognitive* and the other *noncognitive*.

Do the arts ever teach that certain things are so—things which could not be learned in other ways? It seems to me impossible to deny that they do, even though I should also want to insist that one cannot say just what is learned from the arts without the artistic medium and style involved. Yet the person who does not know the works of Shakespeare, for example, is not only ignorant of Shakespeare's art, of the poetic forms and styles he employed to such great advantage, but evidently remains unaware that the world contains (or may contain) many things—qualities, characters, relations, meanings—which, through such art, he might come to know and appreciate. We discover through Shakespeare's art—or through the art of Milton, Beethoven, or El Greco—that the world contains complexities and relations, that it exhibits qualities and meanings which are precisely *this* or *that*, none of which we would otherwise know. We learn from literature, in the words of J. Bronowski, "an enlargement and a sharpening of our sympathy. . . . We know better what it feels like to be cowed, perverse, in love, to be embarrassed and to blush for someone else."[20] Surely our cognitive powers are involved in such knowledge and in the judgments which, as a result, we make about the character and value of education.

Very similar things may be said *mutatis mutandis* about the knowledge gained from any profound religious perspective or from the symbols and practices of the religious life. Religion teaches that a life of reverence and worship is possible, that existence contains qualitative possibilities which may be apprehended and expressed in the singular languages and symbols of piety and aspiration, that our lives are such that no merely logical or mathematical account of them is sufficient or can signify the elements that are important beyond estimate. If the arts can teach that the world contains certain qualities, characters, relations, and meanings, the religions teach that there are still others which our lives may embody or exemplify. As Whitehead has said, we find in religion the best rendering of the 'integral experience" of both actuality and possibility. And the truth of religion so regarded does not depend upon either "a special and privileged" form of religious knowledge or on "a consistently rational philosophical theology," but simply on the apparent fact that the religious aspects of experience are as undeniable and inescapable, as cogent and dependable, if we do not demand too much of them, as the sensory and logical features of experience. Religious sensitivity and symbols—the dialectic sustained by the sense of the presence of the holy—no less than logical powers and observations, evidently reveal dimensions of existence—unless existence is defined so stringently that even the sciences must be regarded as either more or less than knowledge of existence.

Of course, and this must be carefully noted, Randall does not propose that religion should be treated only as "material *for* knowledge" or a subject to be understood scientifically. Religion is also experienced, shared, and enjoyed. Indeed, he notes that "religion is doubtless culturally more necessary than science, for few cultures, until very recently, have ever developed any science, while none has been without religion."[21] Religion, he suggests, performs "a complex group of functions" which are "indispensable for any society." For "religion is a practical commitment to certain values," religious symbols "reveal the powers and possibilities latent in the nature of things" and "unify men's experience" as well as sustain "the awareness of 'the order of splendor.' "[22] But all this, it may be maintained, only suggests that his treatment of the arts and religions would have been sounder and more consistent if he had taken more seriously the comment he himself made about the independence of the different aspects of experience and judgment. Commenting on the limitations of the natural sciences in dealing with cultural and spiritual experiences and products, he wrote that "a real understanding of the moral life, of human society, of art and poetry, and of religion, is an understanding which in each case must stand on its own feet."[23] This implies, not that the arts and religions are "material for knowledge" or understandable in terms of "more adequate schemes of intelligibility" modeled after the methods of the natural sciences, as he goes on to suggest, but rather that they are independent forms of judgment which reveal and communicate in their own terms—and perhaps as unequivocally as the sciences—certain aspects of the many-dimensioned "order of splendor." If he had thus taken more seriously the independence of the arts and religions, he might also have taken more seriously his observation, near the end of *The Role of Knowledge in Western Religion*, that "there still seems to remain something unsatisfactory about the complete denial of all cognitive values to religious beliefs."[24] For if the religions and the arts (like the sciences) sometimes mislead us or generate unwarranted enthusiasms and false expectations, this is presumably a function of both their unparalleled powers of revelation (or discovery) and the necessarily selective vision of finite man in an infinite but pluralistic world—a world as yet so unfathomable that even the obviously limited powers and potentialities of man are still largely unknown and undetermined.

NOTES

1. John H. Randall, Jr., *Nature and Historical Experience: Essays in Naturalism and in The Theory of History* (New York: Columbia University Press, 1958), pp. 127-128. Complete bibliographical information is given only in the first reference to a text.

2. *Ibid.*, p. 283.

3. John H. Randall, Jr., *The Role of Knowledge in Western Religion* (Boston: Starr King Press, 1958), pp. 128-129.

4. *Nature and Historical Experience*, p. 268.

5. *Ibid.*, p. 267.

6. *Ibid.*, p. 269.

7. *Ibid.*, p. 282.

8. *Ibid.*, pp. 263-264.

9. *Ibid.*, p. 232.

10. *Ibid.*, p. 40. Randall's claim that religion is not cognitive because it does not explain anything is examined in my book *Religion and Judgment: An Essay on the Method and Meaning of Religion* (New York: Appleton-Century-Crofts, 1966); cf. pp. 258-270.

11. *The Role of Knowledge in Western Religion*, p. 129.

12. *Ibid.*, p. 103.

13. *Ibid.*, p. 52.

14. George Santayana, *The Idler and His Works*, ed. Daniel Cory (New York: George Braziller, Inc., 1957), p. 46.

15. *The Role of Knowledge in Western Religion*, pp. 8-9, 57.

16. *Ibid.*, p. 133.

17. *Ibid.*, p. 68.

18. *Ibid.*, p. 62.

19. *The Letters of George Santayana*, ed. Daniel Cory (New York: Charles Scribner's Sons, 1955), p. 330.

20. J. Bronowski, *The Identity of Man* (Garden City: The Natural History Press, 1965), p. 86.

21. *The Role of Knowledge in Western Religion*, p. 5.

22. *Ibid.*, pp. 121-122.

23. *Ibid.*, p. 75.

24. *Ibid.*, p. 122.

HORACE L. FRIESS
Columbia University

A Naturalistic View of "Functioning Religiously"

John Dewey admitted to some of his students that he had not been able to free himself from a negative association of the word "religion" with cramped, sectarian views and attitudes that he knew during his youth. To think of organized religions as generous, constructive forces in building a freed, humane life went much against the grain of his personal experience. Yet Dewey recognized that human actions and persons could become sustainingly "religious" in quality through the unifying of ideal and actual factors in the process of life. The line thus drawn between religious quality emerging in existence, and religions as distinctly instituted social entities, has become a familiar and much employed contrast in current discussions of the subject.

In a brief review of Dewey's book, *A Common Faith* (1934), where this distinction is made, Professor Randall ventured several criticisms. He remarked that an emphasis on living religious quality, freed from sectarian clothing, could for all its spontaneity tend to encourage another kind of provincialism of the immediate here and now. He commented that the art and wisdom in a long-gathered heritage of religious traditions might suffer undue neglect as a consequence. "To free the religious attitude from institutional embodiment in a religion," said Randall, "sounds suspiciously like freeing art from any particular work of art."[1]

Soon thereafter, Randall came to the conclusion that a theory of the nature of religion might well be developed in an adverbial mode, rather than in either a substantive or adjectival one. It is more normal in Western thought, he noted, to view religion in terms of its object of devotion, whether that be God or gods, spirits, ancestors, a sacred community, the Ideal or an ideal order. All these nouns, as "divine names," serve to focus thought upon final objects that religious practices intend or have in view. An adjectival emphasis on "religious" quality, such as Dewey proposed, could serve to focus on conditions of persons or of behavior, regarded as essential or as consummate for what Dewey called "the human abode of the religious function."[2] Randall does not deny the validity of either a substantive or an adjectival approach, depending upon the interest and aim of inquiry. But he suggests that other important questions for a theory of religion to explore might be most fruitfully met, if the subject-matter of inquiry were defined in this adverbial focus: *"how do situations function religiously?"*[3]

By making this question central, Randall says the nature of religion is identified with what it does. Inquiry becomes concerned with what is going on and with what consequences, when situations function religiously. It is important to note that the noun remaining in this formulation is "situations" and not "men" or "people." Randall intends thereby to stress that he means not to construe religious functioning as an operation of human nature alone, but rather as a co-operation of powers in man and in the world. His interpretation will not be a psychologizing of religion, insofar as that makes exclusive or abstracted reference to human traits as sufficient to acount for religion. His theory of religion will be naturalistic rather than radically or merely humanistic. It may be added that the noun "situations" as a general term is one that Randall has used in metaphysical discourse as virtually equivalent to "substance" viewed as primary subject-matter.[4]

If we ask next what then is going on when situations function religiously, Randall wants the theory of religion to recognize amply the variety, the multiple functions, that may be genuinely and significantly realized. The range of this variety may be suggested, in one of its aspects, by considering the great contrast in human moods that religion exhibits, from extreme humility to triumphant confidence. One finds, says Randall, "a mood of dependence and self-abnegation, a bitter realization of frustration and failure, in which man's confidence oozes to nothingness and he feels himself the plaything of forces which he cannot pretend to comprehend; and there is another mood involving the triumphant apotheosis of man, the creator and builder."[5] Another way of suggesting the range of human attitudes that can be involved in different cases of religious functioning is by the polarity of detachment and commitment. And in this connection I am repeatedly reminded of a striking statement by the fifteenth century Indian poet and religious teacher Kabir. Taking the confluence of the sacred rivers Ganges and Jumna as a symbol, Kabir says: "The devout seeker is he who mingles in his heart the double currents of love and detachment, like the mingling of the streams of Ganges and Jumna. In his heart the sacred water flows day and night."[6]

Professor Randall does not want to slant his general theory of religion toward commitment or toward detachment; he wants it to be competent to recognize and to explore the whole range of religious possibilities. With this inclusive intention, he suggests that the whole "family of religions," the whole range of situations functioning religiously, may be identified by three general marks. (1) "Something happens to the individual" for whom a situation so functions. What happens may be a strengthening of his faith, a conviction of sin, a conversion, or some other reassessment of his condition. (2) A social matrix is involved. There are consequences for society in the cultivation of community through observances and sentiments that "confirm and clarify shared values." (3) Situations that function religiously are also identified by the arts and techniques of symbolic expression which they employ.[7]

It is in respect to this third aspect of religious functioning, through arts of symbolic expression, that Randall has chiefly developed his theory by considering the functions and the standards that pertain. Do religious symbols convey knowledge that we cannot otherwise have? This question has for a long time occupied a central place in philosophical discussions of religion. But before analyzing Randall's treatment of this question, it will be useful to note that he regards the societal matrix as primarily generative and the individual's religious experience, however deviant and original, as a special variation or development within some social context. Another way of putting this point would be to say that he takes William James's contributions to a dynamic psychology of behavior as more fundamental for theory of religion than the special interest of James in varieties of individualized mysticism. What social situations do to form individual religiousness accounts, generally speaking, for more than what individuals make of religion in their solitariness.

Randall's view of the nature and work of religious symbols, however, turns his theory of religion away from being a sociologically reductive one. He does not interpret religious symbols as simply standing for, or as being just representations of, social conditions and relations. In fact, he rejects the view that religious symbols are in character essentially representative of anything, whether on earth or in heaven. Instead, he regards them as *connective* and *organizing* agents or instruments. According to Professor Randall, the identifiable referent of a religious symbol, what it actually points to, is not some holy object or being per se, but rather the whole celebrative activity or plenary process that the symbol is serving to focus.[8] Connecting society, the individual, and encompassing natural and ideal regions, built up through an interplay of many powers and relations, religious symbols serve to organize responses that convey a more or less full and devout meaning gathered toward a world. A Buddha image or a Crucifix, although it may be taken to stand for or even pictorially to represent a specific person or event, does not function as a religious symbol except by serving as a vehicle of some Buddha or Christ-focussed response.

Such a functional view of religious symbols sees them as dynamically related to features of experience and of the world. The problem is how to discriminate these relations, to see what religious discourse and symbol characteristically do and what they do not do. To deal with this problem critically Randall says we have to observe the functioning of language and symbol in specifically religious activity, and we have also to compare this with language and construction as they function in other kinds of activity, e.g., poetry, science, and metaphysics. It is the comparison, he adds, which makes the investigation genuinely philosophical. By using this method of comparing how different kinds of language function, Randall has advanced several pronounced conclusions. Religious discourse and symbol do not add to our "knowledge," in the modern sense of verifiably explaining how things happen. This is a function reserved for the kind of activity that is more and more perfected in experimental science. In contrast, what religious discourse and symbol can do is to express "vision of powers and possibilities." What is so revealed (as by artistic productions also) does not suffice to explain how things happen, but it does inform interpretation of the meaning of what happens. If religious visions and interpretations are little suited to provide "independent knowledge," they can function to focus and to consecrate "long trains of experience."[9]

They can do so, but they succeed variously. That is to say, not everything is equally apt; there are standards pertaining to religious vision and interpretation, though they are not the same as the norms of scientific activity. In religious vision, what counts is living relevance, a kindled light, and moving effect. Such qualities, I judge, are included in what Randall means when he says "for religious vision the requirement is that it be authentic." As to religious interpretations, he holds it more possible and fitting to estimate them as more or less adequate—in terms of inclusive range and fruitfulness—rather than as true or false.[10] "True" and "false" are norms that he prefers to reserve for judgments that concern the accomplishments of exact scientific activity.

In an article on "The Art of Language and the Linguistic Situation," Professor Randall points out that every kind of language selects materials appropriate to its distinctive aims.[11] He then illustrates this by comparing the selections made in the language of science, of lyric poetry, of metaphysics, and of religion. Scientific language abstracts from the observer and selects its materials to bring out specific structures in delimited fields of observation. Lyric, metaphysical, and religious languages all include the inquirer and his environment, in their fields of discourse. Randall sees their differences as follows. While metaphysical discourse selects materials suited to expound the general structures that contain man-in-his-world, lyric poetry chooses materials to express feelings arising for the poet through aspects or qualities of life in his experience. The materials found in religious language are characteristically expressive both of structures and of feelings. It talks both of the way the world is and how we feel about it; it combines a lyrical and a metaphysical bent. Hence, religious discourse can be most richly complicated, and by the same token is often especially puzzling and confused in its deliverances. Referring to Martin Buber's stress on "I-Thou dialogue," Randall at one point characterizes religious language as attempting "We-You-All" communication.

Thus, the examination of religious language in comparison with other kinds of discourse leads Randall to identify "visions," more or less luminous and moving, and "interpretations," more or less capacious and adequate, as central effective factors in "functioning religiously." He takes it as historically and experientially evident that such visions and interpretations ("seemingly infinite in variety even within a single religion") authentically "reveal" a dimension of life, which he has referred to as the "order of splendor"—indeed, a "splendor of the Divine."[12] Their revelations, however, are symbolic rather than representative, interpretative rather than cognitive in a modern exact sense. That is to say, they do not represent the Divine Splendor as an unconditional reality in itself, nor do they explain it scientifically; but they organize responses, form activity, in which the Splendor figures as genuinely constitutive of life and the world.

Professor Randall holds further that religious discourse, however philosophical it may become, still remains symbolic in its functional character. There is a familiar contrast between the "God of worship," addressed as a person or in any case as a living being (a father, shepherd, king, etc.), and the "God of the philosophers" (called e.g., first cause, infinite substance, principle of concretion, being, etc., in various intellectual contexts.) Randall's point is that these two very different kinds of discourse serve to connect, to organize, the religious response within two different contexts—the first, a context of social worship and conduct, and the second, a context of several theoretic attempts at comprehensive or philosophical understanding. The discourse of the first context aims at enabling personal communication, that of the second, at intellectual consistency of the religious concept, or of theology, with other current ways of construing the world. Without prejudging the success achieved in any particular case in either context, Randall is saying that these two kinds of discourse need not be construed as presupposing two unrelated Gods, two separate orders of Splendor. They do serve to organize two different sets of components in human behavior, the one set more practical, the other more theoretic. Randall proposes no doctrine of double truth here, but rather of twofold action. Philosophical theology, insofar as it participates in functioning religiously, remains symbolic; it does not detach itself (though it may seem to make the attempt) from the human inquirer and thereby arrive at some purely scientific knowledge of Divinity.[13]

In the remainder of this essay I wish to leave the course of exposition which has been followed up to this point, and digress a little into some freer channels of comment and reflection. Since 1955, when Paul Tillich left Union Theological Seminary, I have several times joined Professor Randall in giving a half-year course on "the nature and theory of religion." Before that, Randall had more than once joined in conducting a class with Tillich, and he acknowledges a benefit to his thinking about symbols from that collaboration. We both, however, find problems in certain of Tillich's formulations, for instance, in his use of the term "ultimate." The designation of religion as "ultimate concern" definitely caught on. Nevertheless, the term "ultimate" is ambiguous, and also is in several ways obnoxious to a naturalistic theory that would employ experientially controllable concepts, as far as possible. As to ambiguity, "ultimate concern" may mean an eschatological concern for the last things, the end of destiny, or it may mean a concern calling for complete commitment, as in the command "to love the Lord Thy God with all thy heart, strength, and mind." In either case two questions arise: (1) Do we want to say that religious functioning universally implies ultimate concern in either or both of these senses? And furthermore, (2) how will we reliably identify ultimacy of concern in either sense?

As an alternative to Tillich's formula Randall has sometimes suggested that religious functioning involves a "central organizing" concern. And on my part I have said it involves identifying with what is regarded as inalienable, not to be set aside (e.g., God and the neighbor in biblical religion.)[14] In making these suggestions we see, not just semantic niceties, but issues of method, of effective inquiry, to be involved. Of course, whether our specific formulations actually have methodological advantage can only be proved through their use.

But the matter reaches further to a large and fundamental question about the aims of inquiry for which a theory of religion is constructed. The term "ultimate" has a note of finality about it, which is doubtless intended in Tillich's choice of it. For all the breadth of his interests, the familiar claim of Judaic and Christian and Muslim religion to absolute finality seems to be regarded by Tillich as a claim essential to the very nature of high religion, without which it would not be fully genuine. Can such a judgment be taken into a naturalistic view of religion without qualification? In fullness of commitment most devotees (if not all) will claim to find for themselves an utter finality in the religion they espouse. Such conditioned finality is available to a genuine faith. But can the symbolic validity in such faith ever be a knowing that the whole range and power of the Divine, the "order of splendor," has been completely expressed or represented in a final "Absolute Religion" once and for all?

In respect to this point Professor Randall and I have shared a strong, if not an identical, persuasion in favor of religious pluralism.[15] We believe that it is not only the accidents of history but also the rich variety of life that will continue to evoke significant differences in authentic and profound vision as well as in relations and modes of attachment and detachment. We do not find that this kind of pluralism entails a flattening quality, any less sensitive and ardent response to the glory in life and the world. In fact, the opposite effect may be expected. For, as Randall has put it: "The Divine awakens our insight most of all in the vision of a fellow spirit kindling our own vision."[16] We both have noted that in the changes of history the religious traditions of different peoples have achieved a certain similarity of type by reason of responding to and dealing with similar conditions of society and culture in a given period of time. We may expect that the spread of new conditions and problems throughout today's world will engender this kind of a community of type, that is, of similar changes in the different religious traditions and ways of the world. But we would also expect that within such community a confrontation of distinctive visions and faiths will continue, and that it will bring not only some melting down but also a newly informed sense of relevant differences.

Whatever the future may show as to the validity of these expectations, Professor Randall and I feel a present need for theory of religion which is strongly focussed upon the diversity of the subject-matter, the variety of situations functioning religiously. We do not conceive such theory to have the character of a closed systematic construction that either upholds or denies the adequacy of some particular religion. We think of it rather as a continual seeing, and an interpreting with the time's best available intellectual lenses, of what goes on in the way of religious activity. It should be genuinely cognizant of authentic religious visions; it should help to interpret more adequately their relevant meaning for situations; it should build up a fabric of thought that will improve communication and understanding between people with different visions and faiths. Such aims appeal to us as particularly pertinent to the condition of mankind today.

As fellow students (already together in high school), Randall and I were introduced, in 1915 and after, to the kind of philosophic naturalism that prevailed at Columbia University in the department headed by Dewey and Woodbridge. Another teacher, with a special interest in religion and anthropology, who influenced us there was Wendell T. Bush, a co-founder with Woodbridge of the *Journal of Philosophy*. Bush wanted to get across the idea that religion should be studied "as an important part of the world of the imagination that functions socially."[17] And he held that such study, critically conducted, can make a vital contribution to the understanding of society and culture. We felt a forwarding power in this idea, and would be happy if we could claim to have done something to develop its potentials. I think that Randall's reflections on religious language and symbol do contribute to exploring how what Bush called "the world of the imagination" can function religiously. But while recognizing that this is rather basically, as Bush said, a "functioning socially," Randall has left close study of social dynamics to other investigators. And I have not helped him in this as much as he may have expected, or as I myself would have wished to be able to do. For we agree that understanding of social structure and social action is an integral part without which an interpreting of how "situations function religiously" can not be very reliable or full-bodied. What is called for is indeed a large and difficult order. Progress in it is being made, yet much more is needed in a world of massive and intricate organization with great increase of cross-cultural activity. Respect for wisdom and for differences of belief must prevail in the ways of unifying such a world if resort to sheer coercive power is not to be unimaginably destructive.

Now and then Randall has given his emphasis on religious symbols and vision, as compared with works and discipline, a religious explanation. At such times he may twit me with a charge of moralism, and will protest that men are "justified" much less by what they can do to please God than by what they can see and revere of the Divine glory. Whereupon he may add, "It is not for nothing, I guess, that my ancestors were Calvinists."[18]

I would not want to see his personal disposition changed in this respect. At the same time I do think that theory of religion needs to give more thorough attention to matters of religious discipline and conduct than Randall and I have so far managed to give. But in closing I wish to acknowledge that my indebtedness to J. H. Randall, Jr., includes a strong benefit from his moral fortitude, over many years, in circumstances of personal, academic, and public stress. I know also that he deeply shares the aspiration for a greater community of mankind, even while the range of his intellectual awareness advises me against absolutizing an overdone ethical version of it. Above all, his perseverance and integrity in the track of his intellectual calling have been for me, as for so many others, invaluable corrective and teaching influences.

A student in our joint course once asked Professor Randall, "Would you expect your theory of religion to be satisfactory to believers as well as to non-believers?" His answer was, "Yes . . ." and then after a noticeable pause, "that is, if they understand it."[19]

NOTES

1. J. H. Randall, Jr., "Art and Religion as Education," a review article in *Social Frontier*, II, No. 4 (January, 1936), p. 111.

2. John Dewey, *A Common Faith* (Yale University Press, 1934), chap. iii.

3. Columbia Lectures, 1963 & 1966, by J. H. Randall, Jr., on "The Nature and Theory of Religion," hereafter cited as Columbia Lectures.

4. Cf. John H. Randall, Jr., *Nature and Historical Experience* (New York: Columbia University Press, 1958), p. 148.

5. *The Standard*, April, 1951, p. 307. Cf. John Herman Randall, Jr. on "Naturalistic Humanism" in *Patterns of Faith in America Today*, ed. F. Ernest Johnson (New York: Harper & Bros., 1957), hereafter cited as *Patterns of Faith*.

6. *Songs of Kabir*, trans. R. Tagore (New York: Macmillan, 1915), p. 61.

7. Columbia Lectures, 1963 and 1966. Cf. also John Herman Randall, Jr., *The Role of Knowledge in Western Religion* (Boston: Starr King Press, 1958), p. 102, hereafter cited as *Role of Knowledge*.

8. Columbia Lectures, 1966. Cf. *Role of Knowledge*, pp. 114ff.; and *Patterns of Faith* p., 168.

9. Columbia Lectures, 1966. Cf. *Role of Knowledge*, p. 117.

10. *Ibid*. Cf. *Role of Knowledge*, pp. 109-118.

11. *Journal of Philosophy*, LX, No. 2 (January, 1963), pp. 29-56.

12. *Role of Knowledge*, pp. 118ff.

13. Columbia Lectures, 1966. Cf. *Role of Knowledge*, pp. 110-112; and *Patterns of Faith*, pp. 165-166.

14. Columbia Lectures, 1966.

15 *Patterns of Faith*, pp. 157ff.

16. *Role of Knowledge*, p. 121.

17. On Wendell T. Bush, cf. Horace L. Friess, "Growth of Study of Religion at Columbia University, 1924-1954," *Review of Religion*, XIX, Nos. 1 & 2 (November, 1954), p. 15.

18. Columbia Lectures, 1963. But cf. *Patterns of Faith*, p. 156.

19. *Ibid.*, 1963.

JOHN E. SMITH
Yale University

Randall's Interpretation of the Role of Knowledge in Religion

In *The Role of Knowledge in Western Religion*, Randall has raised in an original, learned, and engaging way an issue that has long been focal for Christianity and the Western religious tradition. That issue concerns, as the title indicates, the place of reason, of intelligence, of thought, of understanding, of knowledge within the religious life as envisaged by Christianity, Judaism, and Islam. The crucial nature of this issue has been determined by at least two principal factors: first, the interplay between the Western religions and the schools of Greek philosophy, and secondly, the exchange between these religions and the bodies of scientific knowledge they later helped inspire men to seek. The result is that the place of intellect has been discussed with an intensity in the Western religions not matched in the great religious systems of the Orient. One need only recall the discussions and debates that fall under the heading of "the relation between faith and reason" to become aware of how long and earnestly Western thinkers—philosophers and theologians alike—have struggled with the problem of understanding faith and of relating religious insight to secular knowledge. Randall has not only proposed an intelligible solution to the problem, a solution relevant for the present situation, but he hás illuminated both the problem and the solution by his brilliant account of religion's involvement with reason throughout the development of Western thought. Through the historical approach we are led to see the problem as it has persisted over many centuries and in various forms. I have the vivid impression that with this background in mind we are able to confront the problem in the present with greater confidence than we could otherwise muster, for we know that it is no passing issue raised for the first time by modern science or modern skepticism; it is an essential and unavoidable problem generated by the fact that man is both a *religious* and a *rational* animal. If man is to retain his integrity as a person and the unity of his life and his vision, these two aspects must be related in some rational way to each other. They must be related in a way that is relevant for the religious life as well. Randall has helped to clarify and resolve the problem through his vast historical knowledge and the philosophic insight that stems from rethinking the thoughts of the great knowers of the past.

Randall introduces the problem on the contemporary scene with the claim that we no longer assume the existence of a "conflict" between science and religion of the sort that figured in the great controversies of the nineteenth century, and that consequently there is no need for "reconciliations" between the two after the fashion of the great harmonizers. Although Randall makes this claim several times, he does not take it quite literally himself, since in the end he comes down on the side of the reconcilers and harmonizers. It appears that the main reason for his doubt and talk of reconciliation and harmonization between science and religion is that a conflict or competition is thus presupposed, and Randall rejects that way of setting up the problem. For him, religion does not compete with science because it contains no knowledge of the sort that science develops. In his view, a major contribution of "science"—understood in a sense broad enough to include the cultural sciences, anthropology, history, sociology—to religion in the modern world is to have taught us to understand religion in a new way so that "we have come to a very different conception of the role of knowledge of truth in religion"[1] from the one that prevailed in former periods, when it was believed that salvation depended on the espousal of fixed and certain truths concerning God, man, and the world. Randall's point is that a scientific understanding of the functioning of religion in the modern world leads us to abandon this intellectualistic conception in favor of a more practical and esthetic point of view placing greater emphasis on the function of religious symbols in consecrating life and in enabling us to celebrate the Divine in the midst of human experience. Another way of stating the distinction is to say that the old conflict between science and religion is to be translated into two different ways of understanding religion, a "traditional" way in which religious knowledge and belief were paramount in importance, and a "scientific" way in which this emphasis is replaced by moral, esthetic, and social functions performed by the intervention of religion into life.

This fundamental decision as to the standpoint from which religion is to be understood is so important that it deserves further comment. It is not clear to me that the important issues involved in the so-called "conflict between religion and science" can all be taken into account merely by exchanging the "traditional" view of religion for the "scientific." By the latter view, Randall means the "functional" understanding of religion as it manifests itself in the studies of the anthropologist, the historian, and the sociologist. Important as these studies are for disclosing the facts of the religious situation, the sciences in question are necessarily limited in their approach in at least two respects: first, they aim at discovering what religion shows itself to be actually, and they are unable to do justice to what religion ideally means to be in its own aim and self-understanding; and secondly, as Randall himself has made us abundantly aware, all sciences, especially cultural sciences, reflect the common sensical and philosophical assumptions of a period, which means that these sciences are not purely descriptive but are controlled by some conception of the nature of religion not uniquely derived from free inquiry. With regard to the first point, Randall criticizes Tillich[2] for resorting to what "religion itself" claims to be, and suggests that whereas Lutherans, for example, make claims about the nature of religious faith, "religion itself" makes no such claims. So stated, Randall's point is correct, but he may be overlooking an important feature to which Tillich's elliptical expression points, namely, that Christianity in particular has a form of *self-understanding* in its classic theological systems and does not discover itself *only* through so-called objective inquiry into what it has actually manifested of itself in the course of history. That Christianity can, and indeed must, learn to learn more of itself from the inquiry of the cultural sciences is a consideration of the utmost importance, but resort to this form of self-knowledge must not lead to a total neglect of the internal expression of what a religion means to be as reflected in its theologies, which are, after all, a form of self-expression.

With regard to the second limitation of the approach to religion through the cultural sciences, the idea of studying religion from a "functional" standpoint furnishes valuable insight into its nature; but we must not overlook the modern bias, philosophical and even scientific, that forms part at least of the meaning of "function," namely, that of being a technique or an instrument for realizing human goals. Important as it may be to understand what religion "is" by grasping what it "does," the fact remains that religion (and Christianity in particular) is not meant to be an instrument for gaining human ends. Magic means the attempt—no matter how ill-informed or superstitious—to manipulate and control; religion in its ideal form is distinguished from magic precisely in the point that it condemns the attitude and outlook of the manipulator.

The point of these criticisms at this juncture is not to minimize or discredit the importance of studying religion externally or objectively as a phenomenon or subject matter, but rather to call attention to the danger of neglecting *self-interpretation* in religion as furnished by the theologian. A complete picture demands that both sources of understanding be taken into account. On the other hand, Randall is opening up an important point when he says that according to the modern view of religion, in contrast to the traditional understanding, we no longer take religion to be *primarily* an affair of knowledge in the sense of furnishing a theoretical explanation or account of the world. The essence of the task contained in the question "What is the role of knowledge in religion?" becomes clear when we see that while religion may not be primarily a matter of knowledge, it clearly involves knowledge, and therefore the precise status and function of that knowledge becomes an unavoidable problem.

Randall's approach to the issue and its resolution is subtle in the extreme. First, he sets forth three major positions that have been proposed in the past and then proceeds, both by analysis and historical illustration, to show their dialectical interrelationship. Randall's own position is itself dialectical and not without an internal tension that brings it perilously close to inconsistency. On the one hand, he allies himself with the position which claims that religion contains or offers no independent knowledge, but is essentially practical or esthetic in character; on the other hand, he argues for "rational theology" and ends his book with a moving plea for more theology and an expression of the hope that men—especially theologians—will come to place more emphasis on "knowing" God. Since Randall seems to think that "reconciling" and "harmonizing" are, in his words, "tricks" that can be turned rather easily, he no doubts knows how to bring both views within the unity of a single vision, but on the surface a least they appear to be pulling in opposite directions.

As a widest possible framework within which to consider the entire issue, three fundamental positions are marked out. It is of great importance to notice that these positions, while retaining a certain integrity of their own, nevertheless overlap and qualify each other in essential ways. Following in the footsteps of Hegel, Randall starts with certain abstract formulations and then proceeds, if not with the "labor of the notion," then with the labor of historical knowledge and insight, to make these initial formulations concrete. In the process the initial abstractions take on life; they do not remain where they were at the outset, but are in fact revealed as abstractions because of the supplementation they require from each other.

I. *The Three Positions Concerning Knowledge in Religion*

1. According to the first view, Christianity embraces a revelation of religious truth or a set of beliefs contained in the Bible and elaborated in the historic Creeds and theologies. This knowledge or truth is said to be like other knowledge, except that it has its ground in revelation. Gradually, according to Randall, reinterpretation of the doctrine of revelation led to its being identified with "an acceptable philosophic scheme of understanding"[3] leading ultimately to the principle that truth in religion must

be in agreement with the best warranted knowledge we can obtain about reality from other than religious sources.

2. The second position holds that Christianity embraces a revelation of truth, but that the knowledge thus revealed is *not* like other knowledge, because it deals with a special "realm of grace" and includes truths not accessible to man's reason. This basic position is said to have several forms; in Aquinas it was represented by the delineation of the two spheres of faith and of reason; since Kant, the contrast has been between the realm of value and the realm of fact, or, more recently, between objective and theoretical knowledge on the one hand, and existential or participating understanding on the other. Common to all versions is the belief that the two spheres are distinct in kind even if it is said that they do not conflict.

3. The third position, generated for the most part through the effort to avoid the difficulties arising from the other two, holds that religion itself furnishes no knowledge of its own: "religion is a way of acting and feeling, not a way of knowing."[4] Theology then becomes a practical science dealing in symbols that are not intended to be cognitive, but rather to "clarify and strengthen a commitment."[5] Stated in the baldest possible form, this view means that there is no "truth" in religion and that religious beliefs are devoid of cognitive value.

Randall sees a certain superiority in the third position and he himself accepts what is "fundamentally a form of that view,"[6] although, as he is frank to admit, there are elements of truth in the other two positions which force any adherent of the third to formulate the position in a subtle and properly qualified fashion. Randall, in fact, appears to arrive at his initial conviction of the superiority of the third view as the result of an historically illustrated dialectic. The first position, he claims, inevitably leads to conflict between religion and each new body of scientific knowledge because of the belief that man is saved only insofar as he holds correct doctrine about God, man, and man's destiny. Randall's point is that by thus putting religious knowledge on the same level as other knowledge and by making adherence to correct doctrine a condition for salvation, conflict must result, or if not conflict, constant adjustment on the part of religion to the new knowledge or truth. The latter alternative has the consequence that the religious content is identified with some philosophical system which, of course, belongs to a particular time and place in history and is not likely to have the universal appeal claimed for the religious truth. It is the disadvantage of this involvement, and seeming reduction of religious belief to some secular standpoint, that Randall sees as the major factor in a move to the second position and the view that there is no "natural theology" based on secular knowledge, since all knowledge of God is unique and distinctive, being other than human and finite knowledge. The second position, since it involves two distinct and autonomous spheres, manages to preserve the religious content from dissolution into the secular or the natural; but, as Randall is entirely correct in pointing out, the solution of the second position is necessarily unstable. First, because the dividing lines never stay put; reason cannot be kept within the bounds or limits within which it is supposed to remain if conflict is to be avoided. Moreover, a wholesale decision made in advance which says that there can be in principle no conflict between religious truth and scientific knowledge seems incompatible with free and open inquiry. Secondly, in the two separate spheres solution, religion becomes identified with a wholly fixed set of "truths" authoritatively formulated in some classic past, and "reason" comes to be identified with the particular form of science or knowledge dominant at a given time. The Catholic tradition, for example, has found itself tied to the antiquated physics of Aristotle as the model of "reason," and the Protestant tradition, insofar as it has followed the line of Kant, has been forced to identify the pole of reason with Newtonian science. There is no *permanent* general formula that tells us in advance how to adjust the religious content to the results of continuing inquiry.

On the basis of the foregoing considerations, expanded and illustrated in greater historical detail than we need follow, Randall argues that the first and second solutions inevitably give way to the third, and that the third position indeed represents the direction in which modern thought has been tending. And yet we must ask some further questions both about Randall's view and the third position itself. Does Randall really accept the view that there is no truth or knowledge in religion? If so, can he reconcile this conclusion, first, with his acute analysis and presentation of the distinctive insight in religion in terms of "knowing how" to become aware of the religious dimension in existence, and secondly, with his conviction about the importance of *knowing* God that forms the basis of his eloquent Epilogue devoted to a justification of rational theology? At the root of these questions is the underlying question as to the adequacy with which the social sciences can treat the phenomena of religion: how can the properly philosophical and even theological element in religion be adequately understood from the standpoint of descriptive and explanatory sciences? If religion is not primarily either descriptive or explanatory in its essence—which is why it is said to contain no knowledge—then it must have a theological and philosophical (a mythical?) dimension. The question is, can we adequately understand this extra-scientific dimension in religion from a purely scientific standpoint? Randall is inclined to say that we can, except that he looks to new and more philosophically oriented cultural science to perform the task. He is prepared to admit, for example, that much of what we have been given thus far by the psychologists fails to do justice to the distinctive insight furnished by religion. In fact, for all of his emphasis on the practical and esthetic function of religion as disclosed in the inquiries of the cultural sciences, Randall does not himself believe that religion can be made intelligible without both philosophical and theological interpretation. For this reason he ultimately answers "yes" to the question about the existence of some form of "knowledge" in religion, and argues in behalf of rational theology.

II. *Randall's Solution to the Problem*

Randall allies himself, as we have seen, with the third position concerning the role of knowledge in religion. In accordance with this view, religion contains no new or independent knowledge, and the function of religion is not primarily any theoretical activity, but the clarifying and consecrating of moral ideals. In this regard, Randall follows Dewey in holding that science broadly conceived is the "final arbiter of all questions of fact and existence"; the knowledge with which religion does and must become involved is not a product of its own vision, but is furnished from beyond the religious consciousness. As an initial reaction to this view, anyone acquainted with the development of religion in the West must agree that religion generally, and Christianity in particular, are not primarily theoretical enterprises in which the drive to *explain* what is in terms of laws and theories is uppermost. Christianity has to do primarily with the vision of God—the Alpha and Omega of all things in the traditional symbol—with the quality of human life, and with the final purpose or destiny of man. As the quest for God and for redemption, as a celebration of the Divine, as the holy ordering of life, such religion is not at all to be understood in terms of the quest for facts and causes that characterizes the search for knowledge which we identify with modern science. Thus far, Randall is right. And yet, as he seems to be well aware, the apprehension of the initial and basic difference between religion and the avowedly theoretical enterprise, clear and well founded as it is, does not of itself answer the question about the role of knowledge in religion. Our task in the end is to understand religion in its full scope and dimensions. It does not follow that we are succeeding in our attempt merely because we are following the principle that religion, whatever it may turn out to be, must not contain a "knowledge" that is in competition with the knowledge that is science.[7] There are *ideas*, doctrines, interpretations, and they remain an integral part of religion no matter how much we interpret it in a "practical" or "esthetic" way. Where there are ideas and doctrines, moreover, the question of their validity, their adequacy, or, to use the holy but currently forbidden word, their "truth," is bound to arise. The *critical* question, in short, cannot be avoided; interpreting religion as a wholly practical affair does not avoid or resolve the issue, since there must be a better or a worse "art" or *techne* which religion is. Randall sees all this, which is why his view, like every sound one on this topic, is fraught with tension—on the one hand, there is no independent knowledge in religion when compared with science, and on the other, religion is said to be the "know how" of perceiving the Divine, and rational theology is dedicated to knowing God and unifying all that we know and think in one vision of the Divine.

As I understand Randall's view, it has three foci even if this fact is not stated as such. From Augustine comes the model for combining the knowledge of the thinker with the faith of the saint; from Dewey comes the concept of art as a metaphysical category to be used for making the "know how" of religion intelligible; from Spinoza comes the impulse to stress the *knowing* of God, which Randall regards—and rightly—as the lost dimension in contemporary religion. Of Augustine's philosophical theology, Randall says, "what he accomplished in his time can stand as the ideal, the very Platonic Idea, of the role of knowledge in the religious life."[8] Considered in the light of the entire discussion, this judgment brings out the truth in the first position, the truth in the idea of a philosophical theology in which the best thought and knowledge of the time are employed for interpreting and resolving the theological questions implicit in religious faith and life. The endorsement of Augustine's approach I take to be an acknowledgment of the need to qualify the third position in order to make room for the expression of faith by means of the knowledge that is contained in philosophy.[9]

Randall comes more closely to grips with the central question, Is there any properly religious knowledge? in his provocative and suggestive account of religion as an "art" and his interpretation of religious "knowledge" as the art of unifying all knowledge through the vision of God. Here room is made for the truth enshrined in the second position—the view that in addition to the knowledge contained in the sciences there is a specifically religious knowledge. "Is there," he asks, "any religious 'knowledge' significantly different from the verifiable and explanatory knowledge of scientific truths, so that the two never compete but rather supplement each other?"[10] In reply, he writes: "With proper and careful qualification, it seems that the facts do suggest to a sensitive and candid mind that the answer is, yes, there is."[11] The nature of religious knowledge is to be understood not in the way of science and propositional form, but after the fashion of art and the artistic vision. The artist and the prophet or saint have in common the capacity to discern or to "know how" to apprehend the powers and possibilities of things; in such apprehension we go beyond what we find in fact or actuality to a consideration and appreciation of the powers and tendencies manifested in things. The meaning of the Divine is found in a complex transaction between the world and the discerning human spirit; on the one hand, there is the capacity of the world to disclose its Divine character, and on the other there is the capacity of the discerner to apprehend or receive what is revealed or disclosed. Both sides of the transaction need to be stressed, the disclosing and the receiving; each belongs to reality or within reality. As I understand Randall, he is denying that the response or receptivity on the part of man is a merely "human" creation, and also that the "order of splendor," as he calls the world grasped religiously, is merely a human projection. An art is a transaction between man and world in which genuine qualities of the world are actually revealed and actually received by the one who "knows how" to see. Although both sides are equally "objective" in character, a certain difference in, a "variety of," religious experience results from stressing one side or the other. As Randall points out in comment on Tillich, if the receiving part is stressed, we have the "religious temper of humanism," and if the revealing side is emphasized, we have the religious temper of humility.

If we inquire more closely about the character assigned to the Divine—this aspect is surprisingly slighted by Randall because of his excursion into religious "epistemology"—we see that the Divine is essentially what it was for Dewey, a tension between the actual and its ideal possibilities for fulfillment. Randall is more of a "process" theologian than he is perhaps aware. From the side of man, religion means the capacity to see in a unified vision the unity of the world's possibilities. More than this we are not given; but this is perhaps as it should be, since Randall was not to furnish us with a theology, but rather to explain the "role of knowledge in religion."

Having said all this and having stressed again and again that the "know how" of the religious art of seeing God is not to be understood as a form of "knowledge" that could in any sense be compared with the propositional knowledge of the sciences, Randall still cannot give up his underlying conviction that knowledge is to be found *in* religion somewhere. His *Apologia* for rational theology shows how strong his conviction is. In the end Randall is on the side of the philosophical theologians, which means that no matter how hard he tries to identify himself with the third point of view, he keeps returning to the first. The need to understand and the need to have some assurance that the meaning expressed in the religious symbols is in accord with what is known of reality through both science and philosophy is a powerful need; Randall describes it as religious, and in this he is right. Job wanted to have the power to *withstand* his trials and his suffering, to be sure, but he sought the power to withstand in the possibility of *understanding*. Randall is right, the drive to understand is a religious drive and men will not long retain a religious faith that is devoid of intelligibility.

In the course of defending those who want religious symbols to have a grounding in our best thought and knowledge, Randall strikes a note that is of the utmost importance at the present time—the need to unify all the facets of religion in a knowing of God. He sees very clearly that the priest, the prophet, and the healer each represent an aspect of religion, but that no one of these aspects is exhaustive. The first sees religion as the shaping and consecrating of a form of life, the second sees it as the practical activity that will transform the earth into the kingdom of God, and the third sees it as the task of ministering "to a mind diseased." Each would identify the whole of religion with the facet he takes to be paramount. Randall's important word at this juncture is to call all three back to an understanding of the primacy of God—the theologian is the one who is needed, the one who knows God and who can show us how to unify the many aspects of religion. The failure of the theologian in the present situation, or rather of the priest, the prophet, and the healer to pay sufficient attention to theology and to the Divine vision, has had its fateful outcome in the "death of God" and in the dividing of the seamless robe of religion into lesser garments which by themselves can only represent less than the truth. "This is the life eternal, that they should know thee the only true God." In the end, this is Randall's fundamental text, and it is a very good one indeed, especially for those whose commitment is to the values of understanding, of insight, of vision.

NOTES

1. *The Role of Knowledge in Western Religion* (Boston:Star King Press, 1959), p. 3. All further citations in this paper are from this book.

2. P. 124, n. 4.

3. P. 8.

4. P. 9.

5. *Ibid.*

6. P. 13.

7. Randall seems not sufficiently aware of what might be called a reverse Thomism in his position. Thomas held the view that reason and faith *cannot* conflict because of their identical source in God; Randall likewise maintains that religion cannot compete or conflict with science, but since for him science alone is knowledge, religion cannot therefore embrace an independent knowledge of its own.

8. P. 42.

9. See p. 140 for a defense of those who try to bring religious belief into accord with philosophic truth; cf. p. 123.

10. *Ibid.*

11. *Ibid.*

FRANK TANNENBAUM
Columbia University

Group Responsibility[1]

After searching the history of the labor movement in the United States for an answer to the question of how to discover the means of group responsibility to society, Professor Randall found that "there is no solution." He qualified his generalization by saying that "no elaborate formula can be applied to the concrete material any more than there ever is a 'solution' to the complex human problem."[2] If there was no "solution," he saw that in an industrial society certain issues could not be avoided. Labor would somehow achieve a "reasonable equal status with minimum and possibly maximum" income arrived at through a graduated income tax. An industrial society must guarantee stability and security for the worker. Labor is determined to have a secure and equal position in society.[3]

There is a certain prophetic quality about this, it was written in 1922 or earlier, when American labor was weak and when the air was filled with recriminations between the A.F. of L., the I.W.W., the New Unionism, the Socialist Party. The author saw no Marxist "solution"; the American people would stand for no more "post offices."[4] In the United States, whatever was achieved would have to be by agreement with the owners of industry. There would have to be effective provisions against unemployment;[5] the industrial society must satisfy the chief aim of labor. Whatever was accomplished would be done slowly. We did not really know enough about the complexities of our society, and every undertaking would have to be of an experimental character. The chief value of the labor movement was its educational influence upon the development of group responsibility.[6] Education for "group responsibility" to society was "not a wholly impossible task." This was certainly a modest and conservative demand for a labor movement that had elements of brimstone and fire about it, and spokesmen who talked about the panacea of Whitley Councils, the miracles hidden in the "New Unionism," the utopianism of a Eugene Debs, and the Revolution of a "Big Bill" Haywood.

Forty years have now passed since these modest hopes for an education of "group responsibility to society" were written. How much evidence is there that the trade union movement has become more aware of its "group responsibility to society" or to itself? So many contradictory things have happened in our society since 1922 that it is more hopeless to seek for a "solution" now than it was then. The word "solution" suggests a prospect that is probably misleading when used in dealing with a social phenomenon. It assumes a degree of control over the consequences of our deliberate activities which, I think, lies beyond human reach. If the word "solution" is not useable, then perhaps "problem" ought to be discarded as well. If one has a "problem," then presumably there is a "solution" given in the formulation of what is called a problem.

The labor movement is a movement of labor, a process, a drift, a continuing change which may produce many specific issues, like demands for higher wages, shorter hours, better ventilation in the factories, or protective devices against machinery. But these are all specific things and can be dealt with in different ways. They are mere incidents in a movement, a process, a drift. To the drift itself there can be no "solution" because it is not a problem. The labor movement is a human response to a changing material universe. It is an effort to maintain a "society," a very human need among men in a mechanized world which as it grows destroys an older society organized about the house, the village green, the church, the handicraft—a society where men could feel "at home." "At home" here has the very specific meaning of feeling that you are master in your own house and control the tools you use.

It is this inherent desire to control the tool, the machine, that explains the labor movement. It is a reassertion of the superiority of mind over matter, of the dignity of man, of the power of the human being to convert the material environment to social ends. The labor movement is a continuing manifestation of this inherent desire for self-identity: to be part of a community, to have standing, to play a role, to be a recognized member of a society. The contrast between the older and the new society is not defined in these terms by either the proponents or the opponents of industrialism. They see the issues as good or bad, as desirable or undesirable, as legal or illegal, as moral or immoral. In fact, however, the changing community is all of these things at the same time—on occasion more moral, on others less so; on occasion visibly good, and on others visibly bad. A historical process of many generations involving millions of human beings (there are now nearly eighteen million members in the unions of the U.S.) of necessity has all of the characteristics of history itself—it is both good and evil.

If this is the character of the trade union movement, it is broader than any code, precept, rule, formula, theory, or educational doctrine. What has been happening in the industrialized parts of the world in the last two hundred years is comparable in scope to what occurred in Europe between the Renaissance and, say, the middle of the sixteenth century. Today, we in the Western world are living through a profound reconstruction of society in all of its phases. Urbanism and individualism go together in the Western world. So, too, do mechanization and unionism go together. They are but the opposite sides of the same coin. They are indivisible. The large corporation and the large union are kindred institutions that belong together and could not exist apart. The modern labor-leader and the modern corporation-manager look alike, dress alike, have approximately the same income, drive the same kind of a car, talk the same language, and have similar goals.

This is obviously an overstatement—only some labor leaders have arrived at this position. But give them time. That is where they are going and nothing will stop them—nothing, except a reversal of the centralization of industry. For the centralization of industry has made necessary the centralization of labor, and both of these, the centralization of government.

When we are talking about education for group responsibility we are speaking in the context of a highly fluid world. We are in the United States dealing with a population that in the last hundred years moved from the farm to the city. Farm labor is only about 10 per cent of that engaged in all other employment.

The matter of fitting into a city-wage-labor-factory-union relationship became a primary burden. Accommodating the farmer—with his independence, his individual self-management, his very special sense of value-ownership of his own farm, his love of his animals, his house, his equality with his neighbors, his sense of being "king of all he surveys"—to a small apartment on a narrow street, a factory job, and the factory whistle as the guideline of his daily existence, was a major complication in the movement from the farm to the trade union. The difficulty is still with us. But man must have a moral reason for his work; he must have some identity with it. That is what the union has provided. It has given him freedom and status within the factory, and therefore in the community at large. The union has given the farmer who became a wage-hand citizenship in the society of the factory. In that sense it has "educated" him to play his part in the large community—and provided him with a sense of "group responsibility to society," in so far as he has it. I say, in so far, because he obviously has it only partially. But one could ask the question of whether he has it in a lesser degree than other elements of the population.

No group, not even the church, stands outside of its own time, place, and milieu. To expect a labor movement that embraces many millions of human beings to rise above its own time is to ask for something that cannot be had. The trade union movement cannot be either much better or much worse than the totality of the society where it has its being. It is predictable that its members will have a full measure of both the good and the bad current among the men and women who are their brothers and sisters, uncles and aunts, teachers and foremen, employers and governors.

There is the additional fact that in the United States a large part of the labor force had to make the transition not only from rural to urban, but from foreign to American. The worker and his children, in millions of instances (we had some fifty million immigrants between 1820-1920), learned to accommodate to a new urban environment, a new language; new motives, values, and ideals. All of this is part of the story of why and how American trade unions came to be what they are. It is as characteristic of them as of any other mass phenomenon—pioneering, westward migration, the gold rush, prohibition, and gangsterism. Its history is part of all of these elements in the American scene—and more cannot really be asked of it than what the environment both offers and expects. The expectancies in the American environment are themselves elements of change and adaptation in our enormously fluid society.

The transformation over which the "machine," automatic or otherwise, has presided has no visible terminal ending. The direction of the drift is recognizable by the marks it has left, by the temporary goals it has set, and by the body of law it has given rise to. It has done this very much the way a river leaves bench marks along its banks, or the way an ocean tide shapes its beaches. I put it this way because what has happened in industrial society was necessary to its growth. An industrial society goes hand in hand with urbanization, with faster communications, more widespread schooling. It involves a breakdown of the family and the support it has given to the weak and fallible human being whom it has cherished, served, and protected. It also goes with the breakup of the face-to-face community. The stranger becomes your neighbor, your traveling companion, and working partner at your elbow.

This is what the industrial process does, has done, and continues to do on an increasing scale and with increasing speed. This is "natural." So, too, has the response to this sudden wrenching of the individual from his customary moorings been natural. At first, the individual did not understand what had happened to him and reacted rather slowly to the isolation in which he found himself. His response was slower, too, because he had no philosophy that fitted his new situation or explained his direction. Whatever philosophy there was seemed indifferent to his state of isolation and helplessness. It did not confront the reality in which he found himself, and had not been developed to explain his condition. The individual worker, the stranger among strangers, without a family to care for him in illness, or to bury him when he was dead, had no explanation for what had happened to him.

What had occurred was the coming of the machine and the cutting of the social roots that made life meaningful. The individual must belong to something, to someone; someone must belong to him. He must "own something"—something that defines him as a moral creature. The union was the unwitting response to this situation. I say unwitting, because the justification given for the efforts to organize the unions were of another order. They were for shorter hours, for higher wages, for more safety, for a grievance committee. True enough. These, however, were mere incidents in an effort to re-establish a moral universe, a place where man had a place recognized by all, a home among neighbors, a feeling of mastery over the tools he used to earn the bread he ate. These were the real though unspoken issues in the initial organization of the trade union and have mostly remained unchanged. Group responsibility to the community requires as a preliminary the adaptation of the individual to the industrial environment.

The gradual conversion of the original farmer to an industrial laborer has taken many forms. One of these is the drift towards egalitarianism. It is probably true that a monetary economy must of necessity be "hell bent" for equality. The emphasis upon money is an emphasis on consumption, and an industrial society operating for profits tends to emphasize the acquisition of gadgets. With or without trade unionism, increased wages would have been a prerequisite of a gadget-manufacturing society. Making "money" has only this route to travel. It must spread the product among those who produce it. The trade union, however, added something to this inherent drift. It added the idea of minimum standards, of equal pay for equal work, of limits on hours of labor, or a right to a voice in furthering the process, and of recognition to a right in the job.

Let's look at the egalitarianism which forced itself on the machine-made society. One effort has been to set minimum standards of income. This has been done in many ways. We now have a federal minimum hourly wage. Every trade union tries to set its own minimum. The bakers, hatmakers, bricklayers, teamsters, miners—they all have their minimum wage. The theory of a minimum has spread beyond the organized union. It has contributed to a growing egalitarianism in our society. What has been happening may be seen from a few figures.

The lowest 20 per cent of income-receiving families had an increase of 125 per cent between 1935-36 and 1956, while the upper 20 per cent had an increase of 32 per cent. The total share of all family income of the lowest group rose from 4.2 to 6.1 per cent, while that of the highest group fell from 51.5 to 43 per cent. These figures are pre-income-tax, which reduced the gap still more.[7]

The same tendency shows itself in other ways. The wage rate of the unskilled laborer has tended to rise faster than that of the skilled. The skilled craftsman falls in a bracket with some professionals. The two highest wage-brackets include telegraph operators, boilermakers, electricians, locomotive firemen, plumbers, structural metalworkers, brakemen, railroad conductors, compositors, locomotive engineers, printing craftsmen. They are classed with teachers, artists, professors, writers, and chemists.[8] This tendency toward a minimum wage, toward national standards, toward reduction of differentials between skilled and unskilled, between craftsmen and professionals, between lower-income groups and upper-income groups, is evident in industrial nations everywhere. It is part of the drift from the eighteenth to the twentieth century, wherever the machine has become the major tool employed by man. These changes include old-age pensions, sickness insurance, unemployment benefits, social security. Institutions established by the state, the trade unions, or corporations take on services that were performed through the ages by the family and the parish. The pensions and medical care now provided may be more "efficient," but psychologically and morally they are no substitute for the necessary identity within the community. The only alternative, though "inefficient," is the union.

Obviously, neither caprice nor the labor agitator has brought these millions of human beings together into unions, either here in the U.S. or in other industrial societies. Because we are a society recently constituted and not yet fully formed, this gathering of men into unions has special features. The fifty million immigrants that we absorbed between 1820 and 1920 are still short of complete involvement in the new society. How long will it be before the Irish, the Jews, the Spaniards, the Germans, the Italians, the Polish, have lost all recollection of where they came from and become so welded together as a people as to know and have memories only of the United States? Surely, this will not be in our generation nor the next. And as long as this is true, everything in the U.S., including the trade unions, will have the character of a culture in the process of self-identification. The trade union movement with its violence and corruption is after all part of the American scene.

Part of this scene is the fact that there are nearly eighteen million workers in trade unions. They have grown from between four and five million in the 1920's to their present place in American society, where they embrace over one-half of all the manual workers outside of agriculture. Of the 30.6 million classed as manual labor in 1956, slightly more than half were in unions, while of the nineteen million white-collar workers, only 13 per cent belonged to labor organizations.[9] Increase in union membership from white-collar workers and the service trades will probably be slower than it has been from blue-color occupations. White-color workers and intellectuals are less prone to organization in trade unions, but there is no reason to assume that they will remain unorganized. What has occurred in the aviation industry, in the theatre, among musicians, is likely to occur in other fields.

What is involved is the way of life in an urban society, where a worker earns his living by tending a machine, or by occupying a chair among a thousand draftsmen in an engineering firm. How does he acquire status, moral identity, in "a society" where he is known, or where he has rights and an opportunity to voice them? How and where does he acquire a sense of "ownership"—the feeling that this is "*my* job," "*my* factory"? The union, with all of its imperfections, is the only available institution which has, and the only one which probably can provide, this kind of feeling of "belonging," of having a "place," of being part of. To be able to say that this is "my job" is as important as it used to be to say this is "my home," "my family," "my town." If the individual is not to become completely vagrant, disillusioned and destructive, he must identify with something higher than himself. The only thing available to him in the machine-made world is "his job," and his job can only be "his" through an institution which belongs to him. The only one in sight is the union.

This is not the place to go into a lengthy discussion of the wider meaning of identity with the surrounding material and social environment. But one way of explaining the destructiveness of our teen-agers, the young people invited to a house party who demolish the house, is that they have no attachment to the world about them. They do not identify with it. It is not theirs. The union has helped save the worker from this complete isolation. At least the job is his. Seniority, featherbedding, and other devices have been devised to protect a man's security, status, and dignity in a world that machinewise is indifferent to human values. This is especially true when men confront automation and sudden industrial changes. Whether or not in the long run these changes really mean an ever-narrowing place in producing, distributing, and providing the material goods that satisfy man's needs for food, comfort, and pleasure, they do mean that many men will find their jobs gone.

A man without a job in an industrial society is a man without a reason for existence. He can no longer provide for himself and his family. Whatever footing he had found against the tide has been swept away. He has become a creature no longer needed among men. If he disappeared, he would not be missed. For most men brought up in the Western world— in the ethic of an individualistic society, in the belief that idleness and godlessness are synonymous and that a man is what he does—to do nothing is to be no one: not to exist. I submit that man reared in a world where hard work and ambition were major virtues will find this change unacceptable. Fortunately, these changes, though they may be sudden in the life of the individual, take much time before they envelop a whole society. It took a hundred years or more for the first industrial revolution to make its way in western Europe and the United States. It will take a long time for the second one, with cybernetics and automation, to make its way.

How many years will it take to replace the current equipment, to train people, to develop a sense of the necessary interdependence of resources, skills, suppliers, distributors, and users of the newer machinery to achieve a substitute for what we have now? Will it require a hundred years? Fifty? Surely, it cannot all get done in twenty-five years. Surely, the commitment to help industrialize the new nations will call for a great deal of effort, time, equipment, and capital. What I am trying to say is that automation cannot overtake us in a week, a month, or a year. We cannot know what alternative activities may be generated that will provide meaningful employment for many or most of the people who are being thrown out of jobs. Time is important, for we could not deal with the issue if it came like an earthquake. If the change arrives quickly, too quickly to accommodate our present institutions, then centralized government will become more centralized and men will be put on the payrolls as soldiers are—but with less meaning to their existence. But if the new industrial revolution comes slowly—twenty-five, fifty years—the union may prove a flexible-enough institution to make a meaningful readjustment for the individual. A feasible adaptation really means the provision of stability for the workers in an increasingly changing world. What the union have done about giving the worker a sense of security is a matter of record. A part of this effort has taken the form of developing pension funds.

These funds are a byproduct of the union's search for protection against those incidents in the life of man which in a non-industrial society were provided for by the family and the parish. Accident, sickness, old age, like birth and death, were looked after by relatives, friends, and neighbors. The individual's house was his hospital, his old people's home, his unemployment insurance, his childhood nursery, and his funeral home from which, when the time came, he was carried to the family grave. Only in an industrial society where men are hired for wages by the hour, the day, or the week could it be said that there was no place for the individual in his days of distress. In the new factory-dominated town no one had either a formal or moral responsibility for him. This is why first the union and then the pension funds were initiated. The funds were characteristically enough described as fringe benefits, something in addition to wages. They would pay for vacations, for a doctor, for unemployment benefits, for care in old age, and, finally, for a pension to the widow and children. These fringe benefits differ as widely as do the unions and employers.

There are broadly three kinds of funds. Those managed by trustees named by employers, those managed by employer-union committees, and those that are uninsured and managed by the union itself. In their origin, fringe benefits seemed like an innocent venture. John L. Lewis demanded and secured five cents on every ton of coal; more recently the International Longshoremen and Warehousemen's Union in San Francisco signed an agreement which would increase the contributions to the pension funds in proportion to the freight handled. Whatever the basis—and they differ from contract to contract—these payments have grown to massive funds set aside for the sole purpose of providing for various needs, including health, sickness, unemployment, and old-age benefits. They add up to many billions. The corporate funds, those managed by trustees appointed by management, have risen to fifty-five billion dollars and are described as the fastest growing capital accumulation in the country. The funds in the hands of employer-union groups and those managed by the union directly are much smaller, but growing. In addition, the unions have increasing sums accumulating from dues. The Teamsters Union alone has an income of some twenty million dollars a year from this source.

These funds set aside for various pensions, and derived from employer and employee contributions or union dues, deserve careful study. When set aside for pension purposes, the companies divest themselves of ownership in these monies. They no longer belong to the corporations. They do not belong to the workers. The latter are only entitled to specified fringe benefits provided in a contract. The funds do not belong to the banks where they are deposited, nor to the managing trustee, who is a hired employee of a fund. They belong to no one. Here is an increasing body of capital invested in industrial and government bonds to which no legal person stands as an owner. It is certainly predictable that the union will claim increasing participation in shaping the investment policy of funds set aside for the protection of their members.

The smaller sums managed by employer-union boards occupy the same legal position—it is money that belongs to no one. It is managed jointly, through a trustee paid for his services, and similarly invested. There are, in addition, the large and increasing amounts derived from union dues. The $20,000,000 of the Teamsters Union annual income make a hundred million within five years. How much in ten, twenty, fifty years?

The workers have become the beneficiaries of increasing amounts of invested capital, and the labor organizations are owners of large and growing investments managed by the union—a role the labor leader did not expect and is not prepared for. For the ordinary trade-unionist, capital and wealth have always been mysteries he did not understand and not infrequently considered tainted if not unholy.

Sudden wealth has given rise to occasional misuse, sometimes dishonesty, by labor leaders unprepared for the role of trustees of funds belonging to the corporate body. There were no rules because there had been no experience. The management of money on a large scale is not an art easily acquired.

The question raised by this new wealth is broader than this or that labor leader's integrity. Experience and the law will ultimately deal with dishonesty here as it has sought to deal with it in other areas of money management, as, for instance, in insurance. The more difficult matter is the impact this new role is going to have upon the labor leader, the union, the relation between them, and the relation of the unions to the industries in which their members are employed.

The labor leader brought up to be a soldier fighting a battle against his employer now finds that he has another role. He must be a banker, like the leader of the Amalgamated Clothing Workers, or the United Mine Workers of America. He must be an investor, and so the A.F. of L.-C.I.O. and the International Ladies Garment Workers Union appoint investment counselors. He must operate an insurance company, or sit on a board of such a company. He must decide whether to promote a housing project for his own members or put the union's money in mortgages in expensive hotels, or golf courses in Las Vegas. He must consider whether to place the union funds in government bonds at $2\frac{1}{2}$ per cent and then pay 6 per cent for money needed in a housing project, or decide to buy common stock that will yield him a better income. He must decide whether to buy the majority stock of a company to keep it from failing, as did the Hat Makers Union, who wanted to save the jobs of 325 of their members, or buy a block of stock in Montgomery Ward during a proxy fight, as the Teamsters Union did, and force a contract upon a non-union manager.

The labor leader is suddenly a businessman, a broker, a builder of a hospital, the organizer of an elaborate health and medical service. As the union has expanded and grown in membership and wealth, the labor leader has found himself in many public roles that hitherto belonged exclusively to the businessmen, bankers, political figures, and men of the highest public standing. The fact that David Beck, president of the Teamsters now serving a sentence in prison, could be named head of the Board of Regents of the University of Washington, is a revealing instance of what has occurred and is occurring on a widening scale in our community.

What happens to the relation between the leader and the rank and file under these circumstances? To the relations between the local union and the national union? To the character of the bargaining relationship between the union and the industry? Between them and the government, at the local, state, and national level? What happens to the ownership of property when corporate bodies of millions of workers are holding, through contractual rights in pension funds, or through direct ownership of common stock, mortgages, and government bonds, an increasing share of the active capital used in our economy? And what bearing have these and many similar developments upon the question of group responsibility to the community?

Clearly, what was hitherto a private interest has become a matter of public concern. The unions have ceased to be private institutions that could carry on in secret. In a way undreamt of fifty years ago they have become public institutions, not only because of their sizeable wealth, but also for reasons of public policy. The Wagner Act, the Taft-Hartley Law, and other legislation have not only given the unions rights they did not previously possess, but made them subject to public scrutiny. It is no accident that the United Automobile Workers set up a public review board to which an individual member, an officer, or the local can appeal against arbitrary treatment by the national executive board. Responsibility of the group to the community is here made manifest by the maintenance of civil rights inside of a large corporate body. When the unions become sufficiently powerful to effect public policy, their activities become a public concern. The question of public responsibility becoems more sharply defined and the direction discernible. It is not an easy matter, but neither is it a hopeless one. The growing practice of continuing consultation and negotiation between labor and management is a step in the right direction.

Questions of group responsibility may be difficult, but one need not be overly pessimistic in areas where public opinion can make itself felt. It is more doubtful where the labor leader has lost his bearing, his sense of direction. Is he a labor leader or banker? What is the role of the union leader in an affluent society, where most people graduate from high school and in increasing numbers from colleges? What is the language one uses to distinguish the separate roles of the employer, the worker, the labor leader, and the management? This perplexity could make itself felt, perhaps painfully so, in a situation where the management of an industry, whose majority stock is held by a trustee for a union pension fund, was bargaining for a new contract with its own employees. And such situations are likely to become ever more frequent. For the unions, through accumulated dues, through various pension funds, are increasing their stock ownership in American industry.

The process is a long one. But there is no hurry. Our largest corporations are only a little over half a century old. Give the unions another fifty years and they will, at the present rate of involvement, loom large among the owners of American industry. This is inevitable if we assume a continuation of the present norm in union-employer-government relations. The problem of responsibility cannot be worked out in a vacuum—a propertyless working class is a moral anomaly which in the long run is historically intolerable. The unions are destined to become larger owners of industrial shares. The visible outcome is joint responsibility of labor and management to the larger community. Public opinion would in the end set the standards and the expectancies.

What automation will do to this trend is hard to predict. One thing is clear. In the United States, whatever difficulties arise will be resolved in a manner conformable to the politically possible in the American milieu. And the poltically possible contains a substantial and growing element of "corporate" responsibility. It has already impressed itself upon our society in a measurable degree through the growth of the trade union movement.

NOTES

1. John Herman Randall, Jr., *The Problem of Group Responsibility to Society*, New York, 1922.
2. *Ibid.*, p. 269.
3. *Ibid.*, p. 224.
4. *Ibid.*, p. 263.
5. *Ibid.*, p. 264.
6. *Ibid.*, p. 250.
7. Lloyd G. Reynolds, *Labor Economics and Labor Relations* (New York, 1959), pp. 535-536.
8. *Ibid.*, pp. 482-483.
9. *Ibid.*, pp. 3-37.

PART THREE

TWO MEMOIRS
AND TRIBUTES

HARRY ELMER BARNES
Columbia University

John Herman Randall, Jr.: A Memoir and a Tribute

It is a pleasure and a privilege to pay a brief and rather specialized tribute to the intellectual traits and professional achievements of Professor John Herman Randall, Jr. I think it no exaggeration to say that there is no other person of whom I have seen so little personally and yet to whom I owe so much in the way of intellectual stimulation and assistance.

In the academic year 1917-1918 I was professionally engaged as a lecturer in history in Barnard College. I was too young and inconspicuous to refer to holding a "chair," but it did turn out that before the year ended I was occupying a "sofa," as Albion W. Small once referred to his first important academic post. I was originally chosen to handle the senior course in Modern European History at Barnard College, which had previously been given by Professor James T. Shotwell, who was then on leave of absence to assist the Colonel House Committee in preparing to negotiate peace at the end of the first World War.

I was just getting well adapted to dealing with this formidable challenge—all my previous college teaching having been in sociology and economics although I had majored heavily in history as a student—when Professor Carlton J. H. Hayes suggested to the Columbia history department that I be brought over to teach a section of the introductory European history course. He had no authority to do this, nor did the extra burden bring any added financial emolument; but beginners, if wise, are not choosers or resisters. Hayes wittily justified his action to me by stating that he had been subjected to similar servitude in his youthful teaching days by Professor William Milligan Sloane, who frankly announced that his motto or slogan for subordinates was *juniores sunt labores*.

Then, in a few weeks, I was asked to take over a new course on World Politics which was just being launched by Dr. Parker T. Moon. He also, was taking leave of absence to join the House Committee. Neither of us knew too much about the nature and objectives of the course, but it ultimately grew into Moon's famous work on *Imperialism and World Politics*, and my much more modest product: the long article on "World

Politics" in the *Encyclopedia Americana*. In January, 1918, Dr. Austin P.
Evans, who handled the Columbia College course on Medieval History,
left to join the House Committee, and I was saddled with this specialized
course for which I had no special professional preparation.

Overburdened and chagrined, I dropped in to see Professor William
Archibald Dunning, then chairman of the history department. I told him
of my plight and asked him if he thought I would ever have an opportunity to teach anything I had ever studied. With his usual quick and
cogent wit, Dunning replied, "My boy, you will be lucky if you ever get a
chance to study anything you have taught!"

Further to impress me with the relevance and scope of the Sloane
motto, Hayes demanded that I read the quiz papers and assigned reports
in his famous course on Modern Social Politics. Since a conflict with one
of my own courses prevented me from attending Hayes' lectures, he permitted me to use his lecture notes to assist me in grading the quiz papers.

When I read the first batch of these, I found there were a number of
students who showed superior ability and rated the grade of 'A." But
there was one completely perfect paper that stood out in a class by itself
for thoroughness of information, logical organization, clarity of expression, and maturity of perspective. Impressed and curious, I looked back
at the name on the paper and found it was that of John Herman Randall,
Jr. Although I was then a relatively young college-teacher, my experience
with quiz papers was disproportionately extensive. As a graduate-student
reader at Syracuse University back in 1913, my major professor sorely
needed to supplement his meager salary by frequent lecture engagements.
When any was in prospect he usually scheduled a quiz for one of his
heavily attended classes, leaving me with a lapful of blue books to read.
But in all my previous experience I had never read so perfect an examination paper as Randall's.

When there was an exact repetition of this perfection at the next examination, I became curious to see what manner of young man Mr. Randall
could be, and dropped him a note suggesting that he come by my office in
Hamilton Hall. He turned out to be a tall and handsome young man,
alert and friendly, but modest to the point of diffidence. I congratulated
him on his test papers, and we had a brief conversation relative to James
Harvey Robinson, intellectual history, and philosophy.

As I recall, the Columbia professor that he most admired, and to whom
he was professionally most akin, was Frederick J. E. Woodbridge
rather than John Dewey. This was not surprising in the light of Randall's
interest in the history of philosophy. I had only seen Woodbridge when
he signed some of my papers as dean of the graduate school, but I met
him a number of times later on when I took over an Amherst College

course that Dwight Morrow wished to have continued from the Meiklejohn regime. As a very active Amherst alumnus, Woodbridge was often on the Amherst campus during the years 1923-1925 when I taught there.

Upon my request, Randall showed me the notes that he had taken in the Hayes course, and I found them more complete, better organized, and often clearer than Hayes' own notes that the latter had let me have to grade the test papers, probably due to the fact that Hayes elaborated on his notes during his lectures. From this time onward, I borrowed Randall's notes immediately after each quiz and based my grading as much on them as on Hayes' notes. I repaid him in part by having his notes professionally typed, and I kept a carbon copy which proved very helpful to me in my own later lecturing. I gave Randall a grade of "A plus" and predicted for him a brilliant career in teaching and writing in the field of philosophy and the history of ideas.

In the autumn of 1918, I left Columbia to assume a professorship at Clark University, returning to New York for a year during the first full session of the New School of Social Research in 1919-1920. I then went back to New England for the whole decade of the 1920's, teaching at Clark, Smith, and Amherst. I may have seen Randall a few times on the campus of Columbia University or at professional meetings of mutual interest during that period, but if so they were such hasty and casual contacts that I do not remember any such occasions at the present time.

My first knowledge of his post-student activity which seemed to bear out my prediction as to his future career was the announcement of his prominent participation in the preparation of the famous Columbia College Syllabus on the *Introduction to Contemporary Civilization*, which was launchd in 1920. Next, I was both surprised and delighted by the appearance in 1926 of his *Making of the Modern Mind*, which was not only a notable contribution to the history of philosophy but also one of the most striking and useful books on European intellectual history that had appeared in this country. It admirably implemented the last half of James Harvey Robinson's famous course on the History of the Western European Mind. In fact, it was the first book to provide a substantial textual supplement to this course.

This volume was followed by a long series of learned and lucid articles and books on the history of philosophy, ideas, and religion, culminating in his monumental *The Career of Philosophy*, the first volume of which was published in 1962. With the second volume of this work now published (1965), it constitutes, in my opinion, the most impressive contribution to the history of philosophy and ideas since the height of the Middle Ages to be written by an American scholar, and a third volume is approaching completion. This magisterial enterprise will compensate for the failure of

Preserved Smith to complete his *History of Modern Culture*.

It has been said that Smith abandoned his promising project because of what he regarded as a devastating review of the second volume of his book by Randall. If so, Smith must have been over-sensitive. It appeared to me to be a discriminating and appreciative appraisal of the book. As compared with some of the reviews of my own books, I would have regarded it as a very favorable verdict.

While I had embraced very expansive hopes for Randall's intellectual and literary future back in 1917-1918, his actual achievements have far surpassed my predictions in those early days. Despite the magnitude and high quality of his accomplishments, Dr. Randall has retained the same modesty that he revealed when he first came to my office in Hamilton Hall in the autumn of 1917. When it became appropriate, I sent him a copy of my tribute to him which is being published herewith. Instead of telling me in slightly disguised phraseology how lucky I have been to have known him and exploited his knowledge and wisdom, which would have been all too true, he wrote me that he could not imagine how I could have learned anything from him; he had always thought of it as being the other way around and had on his desk at the moment a copy of my *History of Historical Writing* to assist him in dealing with a problem of historiography.

When my *Living in the Twentieth Century* appeared in 1928, I was pleased and honored to read a favorable review of the book by Professor Randall which concluded with the statement that "the volume as a whole is heartily to be commended as the best brief survey of the genesis of contemporary industrial civilization." It was about this time that I resumed personal contact with Professor Randall. This took the form of correspondence, and consisted mainly in my appeals to him for aid and criticism in the preparation of my books which touched in any extensive degree on the history of philosophy and ideas.

He and his father gave me many helpful suggestions in the preparation of my *Twilight of Christianity*, which appeared in 1929. These are noted and listed in the index to that book. I have always regarded as especially significant Professor Randall's article in *Current History* of June, 1929, in which he stressed the fact that the growth and intrusion of secular activities and interests in recent years, arising out of industrialism and urbanization of life, have done far more to subvert and diminish religious orthodoxy and its role in contemporary life than all the attacks of freethinkers and modern scientific theories combined.

Far more important and extensive was Professor Randall's assistance in the preparation of the sections on philosophy and intellectual history in my *History of Western Civilization* (1935). His aid to me in preparing and rewriting the comparable portions of my *Intellectual and Cultural History of the Western World* (1937) was so comprehensive and indispensable that I felt that it was not adequately indicated when I listed him first among those to whom I acknowledged substantial assistance on the book. The considerable praise given to some sections of the volume dealing with modern philosophy and ideas was more due to Professor Randall's aid than to my own efforts.

Although I made heavy inroads on Professor Randall's time, which was inadequate even to take care of his own busy career as a teacher and writer, his assistance was as prompt, gracious, and cheerful as it was competent and invaluable. Professor Randall never was entertained in my home but he will live in my books on the history of civilization, intellectual history, and historiography as long as they continue to exist and remain in use. My indebtedness to him could not be adequately conveyed in words.

Despite our years of intellectual contact, my first more than casual personal meeting with Professor Randall, following our contacts at Columbia College away back in 1917-1918, took place at the summer school at the University of California at Berkeley in 1941, where Randall was giving courses in philosophy and I was teaching sociology. We met only infrequently even then, the most extended and formal occasion being at a dinner party given for us preceding an anti-interventionist lecture I gave before the Woman's International League for Peace, in which Mrs. Randall was much interested.

Although it was a hotly debated question during this summer when President Roosevelt, for better or worse, adopted the economic and financial measures which made war with Japan inevitable, Professor Randall did not elaborate or wax eloquent with respect to his own views on intervention or isolation. But I got the definite impression, perhaps as a result of wishful thinking, that he shared the anti-interventionist ideas of Mrs. Randall and myself. I was most interested in a remark he made indicating that John Dewey had repudiated the rabid interventionism that had characterized his thoughts and actions relative to the first World War. Dewey had observed to Professor Randall that, "If I had not been so wrong about the last war I might have been 'wronger' about this one!"

This is the last time I have seen Professor Randall personally; our paths have not crossed since then. Soon after, the United States entered the Second World War, following the Pearl Harbor attack. My main interest and activities reverted for some years to the field of criminology and penology, especially in connection with federal government efforts to put the largely idle inmates of state prisons to work in producing war materials, and admitting patriotic and qualified convicts to the armed services. I had finished my publications in the realms in which Professor Randall was chiefly concerned, save for a couple of marginal books on the history of sociology and a condensation of the *History of Civilization*. Most of my professional interests and publications since 1950 have been in the field of international relations and diplomatic history, far removed from Professor Randall's absorption in his philosophic researches.

In his review of the first volume of *The Career of Philosophy*, contained in the *American Historical Review*, January, 1963, Dr. William Gerber wrote: "It takes full account of recent scholarship. While it is rich in detail and erudition, it does not bog down. It is lively, and even at times sprightly. Its insights are revealing and persuasive." Although these words were written about his book, no better characterization could be found of the intellectual traits of the author.

While the designation of a man as "a gentleman and a scholar" has long since become threadbare and hackneyed, it can be applied to John Herman Randall, Jr., with such precision, cogency, and accuracy as to revitalize it and give it new respectability. I shall always recall him with unalloyed respect and gratitude, and regret that it was not my privilege to enjoy personal association with him on a greater scale.

JAMES GUTMANN
Columbia University

John Herman Randall, Jr.: A Memoir of His Career at Columbia, 1915-1967

When Jack Randall and I, together with a half dozen of our classmates, were inducted into the Columbia College chapter of Phi Beta Kappa in the early spring of 1918, I received a warm note of congratulations from his parents. I had been their guest many times during the preceding three years at the Randall home on East 126th Street near Mt. Morris Church, where Dr. Randall was the minister, and I had come to know the family even more intimately during a visit at their summer home in Maine.

Replying to Dr. and Mrs. Randall's friendly congratulations, I wrote that although I had had many notable teachers in Columbia College none had taught me more than their son Jack. That, I still believe, was literally true. We had had a number of teachers who could justly be called great, some whose names stand high in the history of American education: John Dewey and John Erskine, Frederick J. E. Woodbridge and Felix Adler, Carl Van Doren and Charles A. Beard, and James Harvey Robinson. Others less renowned had meant much to Jack Randall and me, and to our friends Horace Friess, Albert G. Redpath, and Frank Tannenbaum. And, first and foremost for all five of us, there was John Jacob Coss. Yet what I wrote to Dr. and Mrs. Randall was true—none of these nor other excellent teachers had taught me more than had Jack Randall—and it has remained true, with increasing significance, through the more than half a century which has passed since we first met in September, 1915.

Randall's power as a teacher has, of course, grown and developed in the course of five decades. Even in the first of these decades, before he was twenty-five years old, he had written *The Making of the Modern Mind*, which alone would have won him a distinguished place as an historian and philosopher. The students in Columbia College for whom it was written recognized it at once as the keystone in the Introduction to Contemporary Civilization, which was the first of the famous orientation courses placed in the curriculum of the college after Herbert E. Hawkes became Dean, in 1917. Needless to say, no freshman learned as much in those courses as did those of us young instructors who plunged into teaching them. And none of the texts especially prepared for the Contemporary Civilization courses under the direction of John J. Coss and Harry Carman—Irwin Edman's "Human Traits and Their Social Significance," John Storck's "Man and Civilization," and a succession of historical studies—was more of a challenge to freshmen and freshmen teachers alike than was Randall's *Making of the Modern Mind*. We used it first in mimeographed folios, and the author, learning most of all from the experience, revised and recast it before giving the book to Houghton Mifflin for publication. It is still a widely used text in its enlarged, second edition, presumably unique among college textbooks in having been used as the central feature on a cover of the *New Yorker* magazine.

In the same years of the early 1920's, and also with John Coss's guidance, a group of philosophy instructors prepared the co-operative volume *An Introduction to Reflective Thinking*, as an alternative to traditional logic textbooks. Each of us wrote a chapter; only Randall wrote several.

As I have remarked, Randall's distinction as a teacher developed and matured through the years. In the first specialized course which he offered, he lectured on modern French Philosophy. The group which he taught was naturally not large, but the instructor prepared his notes with the same meticulous care that has been admired by generations of students since Randall took over the famous course in the General History of Philosophy from our teacher F. J. E. Woodbridge, in 1925. I recall passing down a corridor one semester in the early twenties and eavesdropping at a room in which the class on French Philosophy was meeting. I stood in the hall as Randall addressed a group of eight or ten students; and I was fascinated by his mastery of the subject he was presenting—I think it was Diderot and the Encyclopaedists—to that small group of students, who were recording the words of a scholar not many years, if any, older than themselves.

Certain characteristics were identifiable from the outset in Randall as a teacher. Enormous industry, an unexcelled memory and intellectual power, an ever-ready wit—these qualities have always marked his teaching, as well as his writing. None would wish to say that all his later wisdom and insight were equally evident at the beginning of his career; but there from the start were the elements which have reached fulfillment in the mature wit and wisdom exemplified in the first volume of *The Career of Philosophy*. I cite:

> The moral problems of medieval and modern philosophy have been essentially those of conciliating diverse values. The task was first to harmonize Christian ethics with those of Greek humanism, and then to adjust the fusion of both to the values of a scientific and industrial

world—an adjustment that is peculiarly our own problem of moral reconstruction. Western Europe started in its professed ideals, though never in fact, with a dualistic view of life as something to be saved from; that was the lesson set for it by Augustinian Christianity. Such a view was the natural expression of the decaying Hellenistic world in which it was formed. It was imposed from without on the barbarian Western peoples as an integral part of the only civilization they could know. But it was totally alien for their own experience. They were not decaying, they possessed an immense exuberance and vitality; they were already thirsting for power and prosperity, in love with the world and the flesh, and willing to go to the devil to get them—as they have. It was but natural that such men should be attracted by Greek thought and by the Roman philosophy of Power; though it was also natural that they should fail to understand Greek thought as an aesthetic vision of intelligibility, and should turn it into an instrument of power—Plato into a moral romanticism, and Aristotle into an amoral technology. But that the Europeans should have tried to be Christians—that passes all human comprehension. It is as incredible as that modern Americans should be able to convince themselves they ought to follow the teachings of Jesus, and sometimes even do so—which though quite a different thing is an equal miracle. . . .

Jack Randall's wit and humor, both in his writings and in casual utterance, sometimes have a cutting edge, and his colleagues, as well as his students, have occasionally felt the lash. I myself had the experience many times, including the years when, as chairman of the Columbia philosophy department and therefore in the most limited sense Randall's superior (as he liked to say, calling me his "boss"), I was most appropriately available as the victim of his most caustic utterances. But all of us came to realize that beneath the wit, and behind a facade of apparent withdrawn-ness, there is a warmth and gentle interest, extraordinary insight and understanding and generosity. Happily, I had been aware of this for many years before he attacked my deficiencies as an administrator, once in violent prose and once in verse. The latter, a satirical Christmas greeting, can be quoted in part:

> You're very democratic
> For one with so much power;
> You always tell us what you've done
> And argue by the hour. . . .
> You grant us perfect liberty;
> A "must" we never hear;
> A chore is not demanded—till
> You've made us volunteer.

Randall not only taught us, his friends and colleagues, he even taught us *how* to teach. When, in the early thirties, I undertook a difficult advanced course in the history of ideas and went to him in something of a panic, I saw for the first time chapters which have in recent years appeared in the successive volumes of *The Career of Philosophy*. The opportunity to read these chapters in their earliest form not only helped me through the course I gave for several years but ironically gained me inclusion in the list of those to whom the author expressed obligation in his prefaces. Never were obligations more inverted!

In the so-called Columbia University Seminar on the Renaissance, which he chaired for its first and formative years, Randall showed his talents for organization and administration. The influence of this group spread to the Renaissance Society of America and, indeed, has involved international relations in what Randall sometimes refers to as the Columbia-Padua axis. One recognition of his attainments in this domain was the award of an honorary doctorate by the University of Padua. Randall's editorship of the *Journal of Philosophy* and his chairmanship of the board of editors of the *Journal of the History of Ideas* represent other aspects of applied scholarship. It might be added that he has been no pure scholar, unsullied by the world: a youthful interest in the Labor movement, reflected in his doctoral dissertation, has persisted; a lifelong concern for international peace, shared with his parents during his youth, and with his wife in the Women's International League for Peace and Freedom, has been a *Leitmotif* of applied philosophy.

Giving co-operative seminars with Randall has been a source of continuing education for several of his colleagues, myself included. We have offered seminars on Spinoza and on Leibniz, for example; sometimes the teaching staff was a triumvirate with the addition of Paul Kristeller or Stuart Hampshire or Horace Friess. A seminar on social philosophy has occasionally had as many co-operating instructors as students—Frank Tannenbaum taking the lead, with Randall, Friess, Herbert Schneider, Charles Frankel, and myself all involved. In such and similar groups Randall is likely to keep long silence, but when he speaks all listen—and to advantage.

We have all learned from his many books and monographs and articles, which Professor Anton has listed in the Bibliography at the end of this volume. I have reason to cherish particularly the book entitled *Nature and Historical Experience*. The dedicatory lines are followed by a poem of Goethe's which Jack Randall and I first learned when we sat side by side in a sophomore course in German literature, and which now fifty years later I venture, to set down in inadequate but, I hope, essentially faithful translation:

> Blest is he who without hate
> Locks the world away

Holds a friend in his embrace
With him to assay
That which mortals seldom know,
Knowing lose from sight,
Through the heart's own labyrinth
Wanders in the night.

PART FOUR

A BIBLIOGRAPHY OF THE PUBLISHED WORKS
OF JOHN HERMAN RANDALL, JR.

Compiled by

JOHN P. ANTON

NOTE

This bibliography provides a comprehensive listing of the published works of John Herman Randall, Jr., from the year 1919 to 1966. The entries are arranged chronologically and sub-arranged by type of material. For example, under the year 1924 entries are arranged under three headings: Books, Articles, Reviews. These are the three primary categories of materials, although specific types of materials are also named: translations, abstracts, letters, forewords, introductions and so forth. There are 233 entries in four different categories: Books: 16, Articles: 109, Reviews: 83, Miscellaneous: 25.

It should be mentioned that book reviews which in the opinion of the editor appear to be more nearly articles than reviews have been placed under the category Articles.

J. P. A.

JOHN P. ANTON
State University of New York at Buffalo

A Bibliography of the Published Works
of John Herman Randall, Jr.

1919

Article "Instrumentalism and Mythology" (in) *Journal of Philosophy,* Vol. XVI, No. 12 (June 5, 1919): 309-24.

Review Troilo, E., *Figuri e Studii di storia della Filosofia,* Roma, "L'universelle" Imprimerie Polyglotte, 1918 (in) *Journal of Philosophy,* Vol. XVI, No. 18 (August 28, 1919): 501-2.

Thesis *Neokantian Social Philosophy in Germany and France: The Critical Method Applied to the Philosophy of Control,* [Manuscript in the Philosophy Library, Columbia University].

1920

Article "The Really Real" (in) *Journal of Philosophy,* Vol. XVII, No. 13 (June 17, 1920): 337-45.

Reviews Taylor, Henry O., *Prophets, Poets and Philosophers of the Ancient World,* New York, The Macmillan Co., 1919 (in) *Journal of Philosophy,* Vol. XVII, No. 18 (April 8, 1920): 220-2.

1921

Review Rignano, Eugenio, *Psychologie du Raisonnement,* Paris, 1920 (in) *Journal of Philosophy,* Vol. XVIII, No. 12 (June 9, 1921): 332-4.

Obituary "Theodore Flournoy" (in) *Journal of Philosophy,* Vol. XVIII, No. 4 (February 17, 1921): 110-2.

1922

Dissertation *The Problem of Group Responsibility to Society: An Interpretation of the History of American Labor,* Ph.D. Thesis, Columbia University, 269 p.

Obituary "Emile Boutroux" (in) *Journal of Philosophy,* Vol. XIX,

No. 1 (January 5, 1922): 26-28.

1923

Book   An Introduction to Reflective Thinking (with H. Schneider
                 and J. Gutmann) Boston, Houghton Mifflin, 351 p.

Reviews   Busson, Henri, Les sources et la développment du rational-
                 isme dans la littérature française de la renaissance (1533-
                 1601), Paris, Letouzey and Ane, 1922 (in) Journal of Phi-
                 losophy, Vol. XX, No. 25 (December 6, 1923): 697.

                 Josey, Charles C., The Social Philosophy of Instinct, New
                 York, Charles Scribner's Sons, 1922 (in) Journal of Philos-
                 ophy, Vol. XX, No. 18 (August 30, 1923): 494-7.

                 Luce, Arthur A., Bergson's Doctrine of Intuition, London,
                 Society for Promoting Christian Knowledge; New York,
                 Macmillan and Co., 1922; Nicolardot, Firmin, Un Pseu-
                 donyme Bergsonien?, Paris, Librairie philosophique Vrin,
                 1923 (in) Journal of Philosophy, Vol. XX, No. 26 (De-
                 cember 20, 1923): 718-9.

                 Malebranche, Nicolas, Dialogues on Metaphysics and Reli-
                 gion, trans. by Morris Ginsberg, London, G. Allen and
                 Unwin Ltd., 1923 (in) Journal of Philosophy, Vol. XX,
                 No. 25 (December 6, 1923): 696-7.

                 Tassy, Edme, La Philosophie Constructive, Paris, E. Chiron,
                 1922 (in) Journal of Philosophy, Vol. XX, No. 26 (Decem-
                 ber 20, 1923): 719.

1924

Book   The Western Mind: Its Origins and Development, 2 vols.,
                 New York, Columbia University Press, (also published
                 under the title The Making of the Modern Mind, Boston,
                 Houghton Mifflin, 1926).

Article   "The 23rd Annual Meeting of the Eastern Division of the
                 American Philosophical Association" (in) Journal of Phi-
                 losophy, Vol. XXI, No. 2 (January 17, 1924): 40-51.

Reviews   Maréchal, J., Le point de départ de la metaphysique,
                 Cahier I-II. Bruges: Charles Beyaert; Paris, Félix Alcan,
                 1922-1923 (in) Journal of Philosophy, Vol. XXI, No. 3
                 (January 31, 1924): 74-6.

                 Masson-Oursel, Paul, La Philosophie Comparée, Paris, Félix
                 Alcan, 1923 (in) Journal of Philosophy, Vol. XXI, No. 9
                 (April 24, 1924): 241-4.

1925

Articles   "American Labor—What of the Future" (in) The Standard,
                 Vol. XI, No. 6 (February, 1925): 182-186.

                 "Religio Mathematici: The Geometrical World of Malebranche" (in) *Studies in the History of Ideas*, Vol. II, New York, Columbia University Press, 1925: 183-218.

"Samuel Gompers—Business Unionist" (in) *The Standard*, Vol. XI, No. 5 (January, 1925): 140-143.

Review Cardozo, Benjamin, *The Growth of the Law*, New Haven, Yale University Press (in) *The Standard*, Vol. XII, No. 1 (July, 1925): 21-23, (under the title "Law and Ethics").

1926

Book *The Making of the Modern Mind: A Survey of the Intellectual Background of the Present Age,* Boston and New York, Houghton Mifflin Company, x, 653 p.

Article "The 25th Annual Meeting of the Eastern Division of the American Philosophical Association" (in) *Journal of Philosophy*, Vol. XXIII, No. 2 (January 21, 1926): 34-46.

Review Ward, Stephen, *Ethics: An Historical Introduction*, New York, Oxford University Press, 1924 (in) *The Standard*, Vol. XII, No. 7 (March, 1926): 229, (under the title "Gentlemanly Ethics").

1927

Articles "Education as Propaganda" (in) *Adult Education vs. Worker's Education*. Edited by a Committee of Local #189, American Federation of Teachers (Fourth Annual Conference, February 18-20, 1927), Brookwood, Katonah, New York, 1927: 77-83.

"The Public and It's Problems" (in) *World Unity,* New York, World Unity Publishing Corp., Vol. I, No. 2 (November, 1927): 129-133. (A discussion of John Dewey's *The Public and It's Problems*).

"The Science of Man" (in) *World Unity*, New York, World Unity Publishing Corp., Vol. I, No. 3 (December, 1927): 209-215.

Reviews Breasted, James, *The Conquest of Civilization*, New York, Harpers 1926; Robinson, James H., *The Ordeal of Civilization,* New York, Harpers, 1926 (in) *Survey Graphic* (February 1, 1927), (under the title "The Uses of History").

Riley, Woodbridge, *From Myth to Reason*, New York, Appleton & Co., 1927 (in) *The Saturday Review of Literature* (June 18, 1927), (under the title "Faith in Science").

Reading Lists "Reading List of Current Books on World Unity" (in) *World Unity* . . . Interpreting the Spirit of the New Age, Vols. 1-15 (October, 1927-March, 1935), New York, World Unity Publishing Corp.,, 1927-35. (Classified reading lists of books on world unity edited by J. H. Randall, Jr. in v.

1 and 6; world unity reading list; a classified index . . .).

1928

"The Cooperation of Europe" (in) *World Unity*, New York, World Unity Publishing Corp., Vol. II, No. 5 (August, 1928): 359-361. (A discussion of John Spencer Bassett's *The League of Nations*).

"The Future of Christianity" (in) *World Unity*, New York, World Unity Publishing Corp., Vol III, No. 1 (October, 1928): 67-73. (A discussion of Charles Guignebert's *Christianity Past and Present*).

"Nationalism and Economic World Unity" (in) *World Unity*, New York, World Unity Publishing Corp., Vol. I, No. 4 (January, 1928): 281-287. (A discussion of Francois Delaisi's *Political Myths and Economic Realities*).

"Peace—The Condition of Survival" (in) *World Unity*, New York, World Unity Publishing Corp., Vol. II, No. 2 (May, 1928): 135-140. (A discussion of Henry N. Brailsford's *Olives of Endless Age*).

"Philosophy for an Industrial Civilization" (in) *World Unity*, New York, World Unity Publishing Corp., Vol. III, No. 3 (December, 1928): 201-209. (A discussion of Charles A. Beard (ed.) *Whither Mankind?*).

"The Problems of Religion in the Modern World" (in) *World Unity*, New York, World Unity Publishing Corp., Vol. II, No. 4 (July, 1928): 285-291. (A discussion of Reinhold Niebuhr's *Does Civilization Need Religion?*").

"The Rainbow of Human Cultures" (in) *World Unity*, New York, World Unity Publishing Corp., Vol. II, No. 3 (June, 1928): 212-217. (A discussion of Roland Dixon's *The Building of Cultures* and Charles Ellwood's *Cultural Evolution*).

"Realpolitik and the Realistic Mind" (in) *World Unity*, New York, World Unity Publishing Corp., Vol. III, No 2 (November, 1928): 132-139. (A discussion of Herman Stegemann's *The Mirage of Versailles* and Alfred Fabre-Luce's *Locarno: The Reality*).

"Science and the Educated Man" (in) *The New Student* (New York), Vol. 7, No. 34 (May 23, 1928): 1 ff.

"Toward Pan-Europeanism" (in) *World Unity*, New York, World Unity Publishing Corp., Vol. II, No. 6 (September, 1928): 422-425. (A discussion of Count Herman Keyserling's *Europe*).

"The Unification of the Social Sciences" (in) *World Unity*,

New York, World Unity Publishing Corp., Vol. I, No. 5 (February, 1928): 354-358.

Book Note "Outstanding Books of the Season" (in) *World Unity*, New York, World Unity Publishing Corp., Vol. II, No. 1 (April, 1928): 65-71.

1929

Books *Our Changing Civilization, How Science and the Machine are Reconstructing Modern Life*, London, G. Allen & Unwin; New York, F. A. Stokes Company, vii, 362 p. (Also translated into German, Stuttgart, Germany, 1932).

Religion and the Modern World (co-author John H. Randall) New York, F. A. Stokes; London, William & Norgate, xii, 249 p.

Articles "Dualism in Metaphysics and Practical Philosophy" (in) *Essays in Honor of John Dewey on the Occasion of His Seventieth Birthday, October 20, 1929*, New York, Henry Holt and Company, 1929, xi, 425 p.: 306-323.

"The Meaning of the Pact of Paris" (in) *World Unity*, New York, World Unity Publishing Corp., Vol. IV, No. 2 (May, 1929): 150-155. (A discussion of James T. Shotwell's *War as an Instrument of National Policy*).

"The Ordeal of Liberalism" (in) *World Unity*, New York, World Unity Publishing Corp., Vol. V, No. 3 (December, 1929): 200-207. (A discussion of Gilbert Murray's *The Ordeal of this Generation*).

"The Reconstruction of Religious Thought" (in) *World Unity*, New York, World Unity Publishing Corp., Vol. III, No. 5 (February, 1929): 347-356. (A discussion of Gerald Smith's *Religious Thought in the Last Quarter-Century*, Harry Barnes' *Living in the Twentieth Century*, William Wallace's *The Scientific World View*, and Roy Sellars' *Religion Coming of Age*).

"Religion's Peril from the Machine Age" (in) *Current History*, Vol. XXX, No. 3 (June, 1929): 355-62.

"Science and the Educated Man" (in) *World Unity*, New York, World Unity Publishing Corp., Vol. V, No. 2 (November, 1929): 120-125.

Reviews Barnes, Harry Elmer, *Living in the Twentieth Century*, New York, R. R. Smith, 1928; Jones, Thomas Jesse, *Essentials of Civilization*, New York, Holt, 1929 ("Am. Social Science Series") (in) *Political Science Quarterly*, Vol. XLIV, No. 3 (September, 1929): 435-438.

Dewey, John, *Characters and Events: Popular Essays in*

Social and Political Philosophy, 2 vols., edited by Joseph Ratner, New York, Henry Holt and Company, 1929 (in) *New York Evening Post*, (May 18, 1929).

Ornstein, Martha (Mrs. Jacob Bronfenbrenner), *The Role of Scientific Societies in the Seventeenth Century*, Chicago, University of Chicago Press, 1928 (in) *American Historical Review*, Vol. 34 (January, 1929): 386.

Book Note

"Books on the New Civilization" (in) *World Unity*, New York, World Unity Publishing Corp., Vol. III, No. 4 (January, 1929): 274-276.

1930

Articles

"Copernicus" (in) *Encyclopedia of the Social Sciences*, Vol. IV, edited by Edwin R. A. Seligman, New York, The Macmillan Co., 1930: 400-401.

"The Forces That Are Destroying Traditional Beliefs" (in) *Current History Magazine* (June, 1930): 355-362. (Reprinted in *Readings in Contemporary Problems in the United States*, Vol. II, eds. Horace Taylor & Joseph McGolddrick, New York, Columbia University Press, 1930: 690-700).

"Individuality Through Social Unity" (in) *World Unity*, New York, World Publishing Corp., Vol. VII, No. 3 (December, 1930): 193-201. (A discussion of John Dewey's *Individualism Old and New*).

"Pacifism in the Modern World" (in) *World Unity*, New York, World Unity Publishing Corp., Vol. V, No. 4 (January, 1930): 276-283. (A discussion of Devere Allen's (ed.) *Pacifism in the Modern World*).

"Personal Liberty and Social Control" (in) *Federal Council Bulletin* (September, 1930): 9-10.

"The Role of Science in Modern Life: What Must Religion Learn from It?" (in) *Religious Education*, Vol. XXV, No. 2 (February, 1930): 107-115.

"Science and Human Imagination" (in) *World Unity*, New York, World Unity Publishing Corp., Vol. VII, No. 2 (November, 1930): 133-139. (A discussion of John Langdon-Davies' *Man and His Universe*).

"Some Major Characteristics of Our Changing Civilization" (in) *Religious Education*, Vol XXV, No. 6 (June, 1930): 507-15.

Reviews

Brownell, Baker, ed. *Man and His World: Northwestern University Essays in Contemporary Thought*, 12 vols., New York, Van Nostrand Co., 1929 (in) *Saturday Review of*

Literature (February 8, 1930), (under the title "Scientific Journalism").

Calverton, Victor Francis and Schmalhausen, Samuel D., eds., *The New Generation*, Introduction by B. Russell, New York, The Macaulay Co., 1930 (in) *Current History*, Vol. 32 (August, 1930): 1028.

Book Note

"A Budget of Books" (in) *World Unity*, New York, World Unity Publishing Corp., Vol. V, No. 6 (March, 1930): 419-423. (A discussion of Alfred Zimmern's *America and Europe*, Bernard Joseph's *Nationality, Its Nature and Problems*, Jackson Ralston's *International Arbitration from Athens to Locarno*, and John Donaldson's *International Economic Relations: A Treatise on World Economy and World Politics*).

1931

Articles

"Deism" (in) *Encyclopedia of the Social Sciences*, Vol. V, edited by Edwin R. A. Seligman, New York, The Macmillan Co., 1931: 61-63.

"Elements of a World Culture" (in) *World Unity*, New York, World Unity Publishing Corp., Vol. VIII, No. 1 (April, 1931): 38-49.

"Equality as Equalizing" (in) *World Unity*, New York, World Unity Publishing Corp., Vol. VIII, No. 3 (June, 1931): 209-215. (A discussion of R. H. Tawney's *Equality*).

"Humanism and Humility" (in) *The New Humanist*, Vol. IV, No. 6 (September-October, 1931): 1-9.

"Humanized Religion" (in) *World Unity*, New York, World Unity Publishing Corp., Vol. VII, No. 6 (March, 1931): 428-438. (A discussion of Nathaniel Schmidt's *The Coming Religion* and Abby Hillel Silver's *Religion in a Changing World*).

"The Latent Idealism of a Materialist: A Review of Santayana's *Realm of Matter*" (in) *Journal of Philosophy*, Vol. XXVIII, No. 24, (November 19, 1931): 645-60.

"The Living God—A Power or an Ideal?" (in) *The Christian Century*, Vol. XLVIII, No. 45 (November, 11, 1931): 1418-1421.

"Religions of the World" (in) *World Unity*, New York, World Unity Publishing Corp., Vol. VIII, No. 2 (May, 1931): 137-140. (A discussion of Carl Clemen (ed.) *Religions of the World*).

"The Stages of Nationalism" (in) *World Unity*, New York, World Unity Publishing Corp., Vol. VIII, No. 5 (August,

1931): 353-360.

"The United States of Europe" (in) *World Unity*, New York, World Unity Publishing Corp., Vol. VII, No. 4 (January, 1931) 293-299. (A discussion of Edouard Herriot's *The United States of Europe*).

"The Value of Science" (in) *World Unity*, New York, World Unity Publishing Corp., Vol. IX, No. 3 (December, 1931): 187-197. (A discussion of Bertrand Russell's *The Scientific Outlook* and John Dewey's *Philosophy and Civilization*).

1932

Articles   "Nationalism and Reason" (in) *World Unity*, New York, World Unity Publishing Corp., Vol. IX, No. 6 (March, 1932): 414-421. (A discussion of Norman Angell's *The Unseen Assassins*).

"On the Humanity of Scientists" (in) *World Unity*, New York, World Unity Publishing Corp., Vol. X, No. 1 (April, 1932): 56-63. (A discussion of T. Swann Harding's *The Degradation of Science*).

"So Says" (in) *Columbia Spectator* (September 7, 1932).

"The Stupidity of the Sword" (in) *World Unity*, New York, World Unity Publishing Corp., Vol. IX, No. 5 (February, 1932): 324-331. (A discussion of Esme Wingfield-Stratford's *They That Take the Sword*.).

Review   Burns, Cecil, *Modern Civilization on Trial*, New York, The Macmillan Co., 1931 (in) *The International Journal of Ethics*, Vol. XLII, No. 2 (January, 1932): 213-215.

1935

Articles   "Historical Naturalism" (in) *American Philosophy Today and Tomorrow*, ed. by H. M. Kallen & S. Hook, New York, Lee Furman, Inc., 1935: 411-432. (Reprinted as the "Prologue" in *Nature and Historical Experience*, 1-19).

"Liberalism as Faith in Intelligence" (in) *Journal of Philosophy*, Vol. XXXII, No. 10 (May 9, 1935): 253-64.

Review   Cooper, Lane, *Aristotle, Galileo, and The Tower of Pisa*, Ithaca, New York, Cornell University Press, 1934 (in) *Journal of Philosophy*, Vol. XXXII, No. 21 (October 10, 1935): 583-4.

1936

Articles   "Art and Religion as Education" (in) *The Social Frontier*, Vol. II, No. 4 (January, 1936): 109-113.

"This So-Called Revolt against Reason" (in) *American*

Scholar, Vol. 5 (Summer, 1936): 347-360.

Reviews   Heidel, William Arthur, *The Heroic Age of Science*, Baltimore, Williams & Wilkins, 1933 (Carnegie Inst. of Wash. Pub. #44), (in) *Philosophical Review*, Vol. XLV, No. 2 (March, 1936): 215-217.

Russell, Bertrand, *Religion and Science*, New York, Holt, 1935; McDougall, William, *Religion and the Sciences of Life*, Durham, North Carolina, Duke University Press, 1935 (in) *Christendom* (Spring, 1936): 551-555.

1937

Reviews   Edman, Irwin, *Four Ways of Philosophy*, New York, Holt, 1937 (Amherst College, H. W. Beecher Lectures, 1936 (in) *New York Herald Tribune Books* (December 26, 1937): 2.

Hartshorne, Charles, *Beyond Humanism, Essays in the New Philosophy of Nature*, Chicago, Willett, Clark and Co., 1937 (in) *Journal of Philosophy*, Vol. XXXIV, No. 25 (December 9, 1937): 691-3.

Hertzler, Joyce, *The Social Thought of the Ancient Civilizations*, New York, McGraw-Hill Book Co., 1936 (in) *American Historical Review*, Vol. 43, No. 1 (October, 1937): 81-82.

Lippmann, Walter, *Inquiry into the Principles of the Good Society*, Boston, Little, Brown & Co., 1938 (Atlantic Monthly Press Book), (in) *The New York Teacher*, Vol. III, No. 2 (November, 1937): 26.

Santayana, George, *The Philosophy of Santayana: Selections from the Works of George Santayana*, ed. by Irwin Edman, New York, Scribner's, 1936 (in) *The Social Frontier*, Vol. IV, No. 28 (October, 1937): 33 (under the title "The Perfection of Rottenness").

Science and Society: A Marxian Quarterly, Spring, 1937 (in) *The New York Teacher* (teachers union of the City of New York), (June, 1937): 31-32.

1938

Article   "On the Importance of Being Unprincipled" (in) *American Scholar*, Vol. 7, No. 2 (Spring, 1938): 131-43.

Reviews   Augustine, St., *Concerning the Teacher (De Magistro) and On the Immortality of the Soul (De Immortalitae animae)*, tr. by G. G. Leckie, New York, Appleton-Century Co., 1938 (in) *Journal of Philosophy*, Vol. XXXV, No. 1 (May 26, 1938): 302-3.

Campanella, Tommaso, *The Defense of Galileo*, ed. and trans. by Grant McColley, Northampton, Mass., Department of History of Smith College, 1937 (in) *Journal of Philosophy*, Vol. XXXV, No. 26 (December 22, 1938): 720.

Hart, Joseph K., *Mind in Transition*, New York, Covici-Friede, 1938 (in) *Journal of Philosophy*, Vol. XXXV, No. 18 (September 1, 1938): 497.

Hogben, Lancelot, T., *Retreat from Reason*, New York, Random House, 1938 (in) *Journal of Philosophy*, Vol. XXXV, No. 2 (January 20, 1938): 51-3.

Hönigswald, Richard, *Denker der italienischen Renaissance: Gestalten und Probleme*, Basel, Haus zum Falken, 1938 (in) *Journal of Philosophy*, Vol. XXXV, No. 10 (May 12, 1938): 378.

Leander, Folke, *Humanism and Naturalism: A Comparative Study of Ernest Seilliere, Irving Babbitt and Paul Elmer More*, (Goteborgs Hogskblas Aarsskriet XLIII, 1937:1) Goteborg: Elanders Boktry cker: Aktiebolag, 1937 (in) *Journal of Philosophy*, Vol. XXXV, No. 18 (September 1, 1938): 490-1.

Lovejoy, Arthur O., *The Great Chain of Being, A Study of the History of an Idea*, Cambridge, Mass., Harvard University Press, 1936 (in) *Philosophical Review*, Vol. XLVII, No. 2 (March, 1938): 214-18.

Lovejoy, Arthur O., *The Great Chain of Being, A Study of the History of an Idea*, Cambridge, Mass., Harvard University Press, 1936 (in) *Review of Religion*, Vol. II, No. 3 (March, 1938): 343-53.

Oesterle, Friedrich, *Die Anthropologie des Paracelsus* (Neue Deutsche Forschungen, Abteilung Charakterologie, Psychologische und Philosophische Anthropologie, Bd. 5) Berlin, Junker und Dunnhaupt, 1937 (in) *Journal of Philosophy*, Vol. XXXV, No. 18 (September 1, 1938): 488.

Roberts, Michael, *The Modern Mind*, New York, The Macmillan Co., 1937 (in) *Journal of Philosophy*, Vol. XXXV, No. 4 (February 17, 1938): 104-6.

Abstract

"On Understanding the History of Philosophy" (in) *Journal of Philosophy*, Vol. XXXV, No. 25 (December 8, 1938): 681-3. (Abstract of a paper presented December 28-30, 1938).

Comment

"On Professor Hartshorne's Reply to J. H. Randall's Review of Hartshorne's *Beyond Humanism* (in) *Journal of Philosophy*, Vol. XXXV, No. 5 (March 3, 1938): 132-3.

1939

Articles

"Dewey's Interpretation of the History of Philosophy" (in) *The Philosophy of John Dewey*, ed. by P. A. Schilpp,

Evanston, Northwestern University, 1939. (The Library of Living Philosophers): 77-102.

"On Understanding the History of Philosophy" (in) *Journal of Philosophy*, Vol. XXXVI, No. 17 (August 17, 1939): 460-74. (Reprinted in *Nature and Historical Experience*, as part of Ch. 2, esp. pp. 46-62).

"The Paradox of Intellectual Freedom" (in) *American Scholar*, Vol. I, No. 1 (Winter, 1939-40): 5-18.

"The Paradox of Intellectual Freedom" (in) *The Key Reporter, The Phi Beta Kappa News Magazine*, Vol. V, No. 1 (Winter, 1939-40): 1; 4-5. ("Excerpt of an article which will appear in the Winter 1939-40 issue of *The American Scholar*").

Reviews   Durkheim, Emile, *L'évolution Pédagogique en France*, Tome I-II, Paris, Félix Alcan, 1938 (in) *Journal of Philosophy*, Vol. XXXVI, No. 5 (March 2, 1939): 135-6.

Gilson, Etienne, *Reason and Revelation in the Middle Ages* (The Richards Lectures in the University of Virginia) New York, Charles Scribner's Sons, 1938 (in) *Journal of Philosophy*, Vol. XXXVI, No. 18 (August 31, 1939): 495-6.

Mandlebaum, Maurice, *The Problem of Historical Knowledge, An Answer to Relativism*, New York, Liveright Publishing Corp., 1938 (in) *Journal of Philosophy*, Vol. XXXVI, No. 18 (August 31, 1939): 442-6.

Comment   Reply to G. McColley's note on the review of his edition of Campanella's *Defense of Galileo* (in) *Journal of Philosophy*, Vol. XXXVI, No. 6 (March 16, 1939): 158.

1940

Book   *The Making of the Modern Mind: A Survey of the Intellectual Background of the Present Age*, rev. ed., New York, Houghton Mifflin Co., xii, 696. (Also translated into: Spanish, Buenos Aires, 1952; Arabic, Cairo, Egypt, 1956; Urdu, Lahore, Pakistan, 1965).

Articles   "Dean Woodbridge" (in) *Columbia University Quarterly*, Vol. 32, No. 4 (December, 1940): 324-31.

"The Religion of Shared Experience" (in) *The Philosopher of the Common Man: Essays in Honor of John Dewey to Celebrate His Eightieth Birthday*, New York, G. P. Putnam's Sons, 1940: 106-145.

"The Development of Scientific Method in the School of Padua" (in) *Journal of the History of Ideas*, Vol. I (1940): 177-206. (Reprinted in part in *Roots of Scientific*

Thought, ed. by Philip P. Wiener & Aaron Noland, New York, Basic Books Publishers, 1957: 139-146; Reprinted in *School of Padua,* 1961, with extensive Latin foonotes added.)

1941

Articles   "The Study of the Philosophies of the Renaissance" (with Paul O. Kristeller), (in) *Journal of the History of Ideas,* Vol. 2, No. 4 (October, 1941): 449-496.

"Unifying Factors in the Development of Modern Ideas" (in) *Studies in Civilization,* Philadelphia, University of Pennsylvania Press, 1941: 105-118.

Review   Mannheim, Karl, *Man and Society in an Age of Reconstruction: Studies in Modern Social Structure,* New York, Harcourt Brace and Co., 1940 (in) *Journal of the History of Ideas,* Vol. 2, No. 3 (June, 1941): 372-381.

1942

Book   *Philosophy: An Introduction* (with Justus Buchler), New York, Barnes & Noble (College Outline Series): xiii, 302 p.

Article   "Newton's Natural Philosophy: Its Problems and Consequences" (in) *Philosophical Essays in Honor of Edgar Arthur Singer, Jr.,* ed. by F. P Clarke and M. C. Nahm, Philadelphia, University of Pennsylvania Press, 1942: 335-357.

Review   Gittler, Joseph P., *Social Thought Among the Early Greeks,* pref. by W. F. Ogburn, Athens, The University of Georgia Press, 1941 (in) *American Historical Review,* Vol. 48, No. 1 (October, 1942): 170-171.

1943

Article   "Human Destiny—Reinhold Niebuhr, A Symposium" (Contributors: Paul Lehmann, Edwin E. Aubrey, John Herman Randall, Jr., John C. Bennett), (in) *The Union Review,* Vol. IV, No. 2 (March, 1943): 18-26.

Reviews   Barzun, Jacques, *Romanticism and the Modern Ego,* Boston, Little, Brown and Co., 1943 (in) *Journal of Philosophy,* Vol. XL, No. 23 (November 11, 1943): 635-9.

Hook, Sidney, *The Hero in History,* New York, The John Day Co., 1943 (in) *Journal of Philosophy,* Vol. XL, No. 21 (October 14, 1943): 575-80.

Maritain, Jacques, *Education at the Crossroads* (The Terry Lectures) New Haven, Yale University Press, 1943 (in) *Journal of Philosophy,* Vol. XL, No. 22 (October 28, 1943): 609-14.

Nef, John V., *The United States and Civilization*, Chicago, The University of Chicago Press, 1942 (in) *American Historical Review*, Vol. 48, No. 2 (January, 1943): 346-348.

Solmsen, Friedrich, *Plato's Theology*, Ithaca, New York, Cornell University Press, 1942 (Cornell Studies in Classical Philology, Vol. 27), (in) *Review of Religion*, Vol. VII, No. 4 (May, 1943): 384-389.

1944

Articles "The Nature of Naturalism" (in) *Naturalism and the Human Spirit*, ed. by Y. K. Krikorian, New York, Columbia University Press, 1944: 354-382. (Reprinted 1945, 1946).

"Which Are the Liberating Arts?" (in) *American Scholar*, Vol. 13, No. 2 (April, 1944): 135-148.

Review Schilpp, Paul Arthur, *The Philosophy of G. E. Moore*, Evanston, Northwestern University Press, 1942, pp. xvi, 717, (in) *The Standard*, Vol. XXX, No. 6 (March, 1944): 172-3 (under the title "The Ethics of Good Usage").

1945

Translation Cassirer, Ernst, *Rousseau, Kant, Goethe: Two Essays by Ernst Cassirer*, translated from the German by James Gutmann, Paul Oscar Kristeller, and John Herman Randall, Jr., Princeton, Princeton University Press, 1945: 98 p.

1946

Books *Preface to Philosophy*: Textbook, New York, The Macmillan Co. (co-authors W. E. Hocking, B. Blanshard, and C. W. Hendel; Randall's contribution Part IV, "The Meaning of Religion for Man," pp. 297-410; many reprints): x, 508 p.

Readings in Philosophy, edited with J. Buchler and E. Shirk, New York, Barnes & Noble (College Outline Series): viii, 389 p.

Articles "Controlling Assumptions in the Practice of American Historians," with George Haines IV (in) *Theory and Practice in Historical Study: A Report of the Committee on Historiography*, Bulletin 54,, New York, Social Science Research Council. Reprinted as part of Sec. I, Ch. 2 in *Nature and Historical Experience*, pp. 37-46).

"Metaphysics: Its Function, Consequences, and Criteria" (in) *Journal of Philosophy*, Vol. XLIII, No. 15 (July 18, 1946): 401-12. (Reprinted in *Nature and Historical Experience* as Sections I-III, Ch. 5.)

"A Note on Mr. Sheldon's Mind" (in) *Journal of Phi-*

losophy, Vol. XLIII, No. 8 (April 11, 1946): 209-14.

"To Win Out, Must Humanists Embrace Sin?" (in) *The Humanist*, Vol. VI, No. 1 (1946): 20-27.

Pamphlet   *Emily Greene Balch of New England, Citizen of the World*, Washington, D.C., Women's International League for Peace and Freedom, 12 p.

Abstract   "Metaphysics, Its Function, Consequences, and Criteria," a symposium with W. E. Hocking and S. P. Lamprecht (in) *Journal of Philosophy*, Vol. XLIII, No. 3 (January 31, 1946): 62-7.

1947

Articles   "David Hume: Radical Empiricist and Pragmatist" (in) *Freedom and Experience: Essays Presented to Horace M. Kallen*, ed. by S. Hook and M. R. Konvitz, Ithaca, New York, Cornell University Press, 1947: 289-312.

"Emily Greene Balch" (in) *The Nation*, Vol. 164 (January 4, 1947): 14-15.

1948

Book   *The Renaissance Philosophy of Man*, edited with Ernst Cassirer, Paul Oskar Kristeller, Chicago, University of Chicago Press (Parts reprinted in *School of Padua*, 1961): viii, 404 p.

Articles   "The Churches and the Liberal Tradition" (in) *Bibliography for Annual American Academy*, The Annals of the American Academy of Political and Social Science, Vol. 256 (March, 1948): 148-164.

"The Spirit of American Philosophy" (in) *Wellsprings of the American Spirit*, ed. by F. Ernest Johnson, New York, Institute for Religious and Social Studies (Distributed by Harper Bros., 1948; Religion and Civilization Series): 117-133.

1949

Articles   "Cassirer's Theory of History as Illustrated in His Treatment of Renaissance Thought" (in) *The Philosophy of Ernst Cassirer*, ed. by P. A. Schilpp, Evanston, Northwestern University, 1949 (Library of Living Philosophers): 689-728.

"Salute to John Dewey" (in) *Survey*, Vol LXXXV, No. 10 (October, 1949): 508-10.

Reviews   Anderson, Fulton H., *The Philosophy of Francis Bacon*, Chicago, University of Chicago Press, 1948 (in) *University of Toronto Quarterly*, Vol. XIX, No. 1 (October, 1949): 99-103.

Cohen, Morris R., *The Meaning of Human History*, La-Salle, Ill., Open Court Publishing Co., 1947 (in) *Journal of the History of Ideas*, Vol. 10 (April, 1949): 305-12.

Strauss, Leo, *On Tyranny*, Chicago, Free Press, 1948 (in) *New York Times Book Review* (May 1, 1949): 14.

1950

Reviews

Cassirer, Ernst, *The Problem of Knowledge*, trans. by W. H. Woglom and C. W. Hendel, New Haven, Yale University Press, 1950 (in) *New York Times Book Review* (September 10, 1950): 27.

Freeman, Kathleen, *Greek City-States*, New York, W. W. Norton, 1950 (in) *New York Times Book Review* (December 17, 1950): 6.

Haydn, Hiram, *The Counter-Renaissance*, New York, Scribner's, 1950 (in) *Saturday Review of Literature*, Vol. XXXIII, No. 25 (June 24, 1950): 21.

Lovejoy, Arthur O., *Essays in the History of Ideas*, Baltimore, Johns Hopkins Press, 1948 (in) *The Kenyon Review*, Vol. XII, No. 1 (Winter, 1950): 156-161.

Nicolas von Cues: Texte seiner philosophischen schriften nach der Ausgabe von Paris 1514, sowie nach der Drucklegung von Basel 1565, Band I, Herausgegeben von Alfred Petzelt, Stuttgart, W. Kohlhammer, 1949 (in) *Journal of Philosophy*, Vol. XLVII, No. 16 (August 3, 1950): 472-3.

1951

Article

"History and the Social Sciences" (in) *Freedom and Reason*, ed. by S. W. Baron e.a., Glencoe, Ill., Free Press, 1951. (Reprinted in *Nature and Historical Experience* as Sec. I, Ch. I, pp. 23-8).

Review

Brinton, Crane, *Ideas and Men: The Story of Western Thought*, New York, Prentice-Hall, 1950 (in) *American Historical Review*, Vol. 57, No. 1 (October, 1951): 91-94.

Letter

"Some Observations on Contemporary Historical Theory" (with Merle Curti, Bert James Lowenberg, Harold Taylor) a letter to the editor of the *American Historical Review* concerning C. M. Destler (in) *American Historical Review*, Vol. 56, No. 2 (January, 1951): 450-452.

1952

Articles

"The Ontology of Paul Tillich" (in) *The Theology of Paul Tillich*, ed. by Charles W. Kegley and Robert W. Bretall, New York, Macmillan Co. (The Library of Living Theology, Vol. 1): 132-61.

"Philosophy: The Seminal Thoughts" (in) *Saturday Re-*

view, Vol. 35 (September 20, 1952): 19-20.

1953

Articles
"John Dewey, 1859-1952" (in) *Journal of Philosophy,* Vol. L, No. 1 (January 1, 1953): 5-13.

"On Being Rejected" (in) *Journal of Philosophy*, Vol. L, No. 26 (December 17, 1953): 797-805. (Reprinted in *Nature and Historical Experience*, as Sec. IV, Ch. 5).

"Statement Commenting on the Humanist Manifesto" (in) *The Humanist*, Vol. XIII, No. 2 (1953): 68:

"The Place of Leonardo da Vinci in the Emergence of Modern Science" (in) *Journal of the History of Ideas*, Vol. XIV, No. 2 (April, 1953): 191-202. Reprinted in *Roots of Scientific Thought*, ed. by Philip P. Wiener and Aaron Noland, New York, Basic Books, 1957: 207-18; also reprinted with Italian texts in *The School of Padua and the Emergence of Modern Science*, Padua, 1961: 117-38).

Reviews
Artz, Frederick B., *The Mind of the Middle Ages A.D. 200-1500: A Historical Survey*, New York, Knopf, 1953 (in) *New York Times Book Review* (May 31, 1953): 16.

Walsh, William H., *An Introduction to Philosophy of History*, London, Hutchinson's University Library, 1951 (in) *American Historical Review*, Vol. 58, No. 2 (January, 1953): 328-9.

Introduction
"What Isaac Newton Started," Introduction to *Newton's Philosophy of Nature*, edited and arranged with notes by H. S. Thayer, New York, Hafner Publishing Co., The Hafner Library of Classics, No. 16: ix-xvi.

1954

Articles
"George Santayana—Naturalizing the Imagination" (in) *Journal of Philosophy*, Vol. LI, No. 2 (January 21, 1954): 50-2. (Read at Santayana Memorial Meeting at Columbia University, May 12, 1953).

"The Wrong and the Bad" (in) *Journal of Philosophy*, Vol. LI, No. 24 (November 25, 1954): 764-75. (Presented as a Symposium paper at the 51st meeting of the American Philosophical Association Eastern Division, Goucher College, December 28-30, 1954).

Reviews
Cohen, Morris R., *Reason and Nature*, rev. ed., Glencoe, Ill., Free Press, 1953 (and) Santayana, George, *The Life of Reason*, rev. in collab. with Daniel Cory, New York, Charles Scribner's Sons, 1954 (in) *Journal of Philosophy,* Vol. LI, No. 13 (June 24, 1954): 391-93.

Plato, *The Dialogues of Plato*, 4 vols., trans. with analyses and introductions by B. Jowett, Oxford, Clarendon Press; New York, Oxford University Press, 1953 (in) *Journal of Philosophy*, Vol. LI, No. 2 (January 21, 1954): 64-9.

Romanell, Patrick, *Verso un Naturalismo Critico: Riflessioni Sulla Recente Filosofia Americana*, Prefazioni di Nicola Abbagnano, Torino, Taylor, 1953 (Collezione di Filosofia, No. 11), (in) *Journal of Philosophy*, Vol. LI, No. 13 (June 24, 1954): 389-90.

Rousseau, J. J., *Political Writings*, trans. and ed. by Frederick Watkins, New York, Edinburgh, Nelson, 1953; Plato, *Socratic Dialogues*, trans. and ed. by W. D. Woodhead, with an intro. by G. C. Field, New York, Edinburgh, Nelson, 1953 (in) *Journal of Philosophy*, Vol. LI, No. 13 (June 24, 1954): 393.

Foreword

Peery, William (ed.), *Studies in the Renaissance*, Austin, Texas, University of Texas Press, 1954 (Publications of the Renaissance Society of America, Vol. I).

Symposium
Paper

"Symposium: Are Religious Dogmas Cognitive and Meaningful?" (in) *Journal of Philosophy*, Vol. LI, No. 5 (March 4, 1954): 145-72. (Randall's contribution, pp. 158-63; presented at the meetings of the Eastern Division of the American Philosophical Association, Rochester, N. Y., December 30, 1953.

1955

Article

"The World to be Unified" (in) *The Unity of Knowledge*, ed. by Lewis Leary, Garden City, New York, Doubleday and Co., Inc., 1955: 63-76. (Address to the Bicentennial Celebration, Columbia University, October 27-30, 1954; reprinted as the "Epilogue" in *Nature and Historical Experience*, 1958).

Reviews

Aristotle, *The Ethics of Aristotle*, trans. by J.A.K. Thompson, London, George Allen & Unwin; New York, The Macmillan Co., (and) *Aristotle's Ethics for English Readers*, rendered from the Greek by H. Rackhan, New York, Barnes and Noble, 1943, 1952 (in) *Journal of Philosophy*, Vol. LII, No. 13 (June 23, 1955): 360-64.

Aristotle, *The Works of Aristotle*, ed. by D. Ross, Vol. XII, Select Fragments, trans. by Ross, Oxford, Clarendon Press, 1952; and D. J. Allen, *The Philosophy of Aristotle*, London, Oxford University Press, 1952 (in) *Journal of Philosophy*, Vol. LII. No. 13 (June 23, 1955): 358-60.

Berkeley, G. *Philosophical Writings*, ed. by T. E. Jessop, Edinburgh, Nelson, 1952; Hume, D. *Theory of Knowledge,* ed. by D. C. Yalden-Thomson, Edinburgh, Nelson, 1951;

and Hume, D., *Theory of Politics*, ed. by F. Watkins, Edinburgh, Nelson, 1951 (in) *Journal of Philosophy*, Vol. LII, No. 9 (April 28, 1955): 248-49.

Cohen, Morris, R. *American Thought: A Critical Sketch*, ed. with a critical foreword by Felix S. Cohen, Glencoe, Illinois, The Free Press, 1954 (in) *Jewish Social Studies*, Vol. XVII, No. 1 (January, 1955): 76-78.

Whitehead, A. N., *Alfred North Whitehead: An Anthology*, selected by F. S. C. Northrop and M. W. Gross, New York, The Macmillan Co., 1953 (in) *Journal of Philosophy*, Vol. LII, No. 12 (June 9, 1955): 333-4.

1956

Article

"Talking and Looking" (in) *Proceedings and Addresses of the American Philosophical Association*, 1956-57, Vol. XXX, Yellow Springs, Ohio, The Antioch Press, 1956: 5-24. (Presidential Address delivered before the Fifty-third Annual Meeting of the Eastern Division of the American Philosophical Association, University of Pennsylvania, December 27-29, 1956).

Reviews

DeWitt, Norman W., *Epicurus and His Philosophy*, Minneapolis, University of Minnesota Press, 1954 (in) *Journal of Philosophy*, Vol. LIII, No. 5 (March 1, 1956): 201-2.

Lamprecht, Sterling P., *Our Philosophical Traditions: A Brief History of Philosophy in Western Civilization*, New York, Appleton-Century Crofts, 1955 (in) *Journal of Philosophy*, Vol. LII, No. 4 (February 16, 1956): 168-74.

1957

Articles

"Introduction" (and) Chapter III: "The Department of Philosophy" (in) *The Faculty of Philosophy: The Bicentennial History of Columbia University*, New York, Columbia University Press, 1957: 3-57; 102-145.

"Naturalistic Humanism," Chapter V (in) *Patterns of Faith in America Today*, ed. by F. Ernest Johnson, New York, Harpers, 1957.

"Substance as Process" (in) *The Review of Metaphysics*, Vol. X, No. 4 (June, 1957): 580-601. (Reprinted as a portion of Ch. 6 in *Nature and Historical Experience*, pp. 143 ff).

1958

Books

Nature and Historical Experience: Essays in Naturalism and in the Theory of History, New York, Columbia University Press, viii, 336 p.

The Role of Knowledge in Western Religion, Boston, Starr

King Press (Mead-Swing Lectures given at Oberlin College in 1955-56): x, 147 p.

Articles

"Padua Aristotelianism: An Appraisal" (in) *Proceedings of the Twelfth International Congress of Philosophy* (Address to the Plenary Session held in Liviano, Università di Padova, September 18, 1958). Firenze, Sansoni, 1958-61, 12 vols.

Reviews

Boas, George, *Dominant Themes of Modern Philosophy: A History*, New York, Ronald Press Company, 1957 (in) *American Historical Review*, Vol. 63, No. 2 (January, 1958): 371-372.

"The Mirror of USSR Philosophizing," review of Reports and Papers of Representatives of Soviet Philosophical Science at the XII International Congress of Philosophy (Venice, September 12-18, 1958) Moscow, USSR Academy of Sciences, Philosophical Institute, 1958 (in) *Journal of Philosophy*, Vol. LV, No. 23 (November 6, 1958): 1019-28.

1959

Articles

"The Ethical Challenge of a Pluralistic Society" (in) *The Ethical Outlook*, Vol. XLV, No. 4 (July-August, 1959): 133 ff. (The Felix Adler Memorial Lecture, 1959).

"The Future of John Dewey's Philosophy" (in) *Journal of Philosophy*, Vol. LVI, No. 26 (December 17, 1959): 1005-10. (Read at a dinner on John Dewey's Hundredth birthday, October 20, 1959, at Columbia University).

"John Dewey's Contribution to Scientific Humanism" (in) *The Humanist*, Vol. XIX, No. 3 (June, 1959): 134-138.

Symposia

Dialogue on John Dewey, ed. by Corliss Lamont, New York, Horizon Press, 1959. (John H. Randall, a participant in this informal discussion on Dewey's life and philosophy).

"A Humanist Symposium on Metaphysics" (in) *Journal of Philosophy*, Vol. LVI, No. 2 (January 15, 1959): 45-64. (Randall's contribution, No. 6 "Epilogue" pp. 55-62).

Letter

"To Control TV Advertising," a letter to the editor of the *New York Times*, November 11, 1959.

Foreword

Dewey, John, *Dictionary of Education*, ed. by Ralph Winn with a foreword by John Herman Randall, Jr., New York, Philosophical Library, 1959: x, 150 p.

1960

Book

Aristotle, New York, Columbia University Press, xv, 309 p.

Review

Runes, Dagobert D., *Pictorial History of Philosophy*, New York, Philosophical Library, 1959; Russell, Bertrand, *Wisdom of the West*, ed. by Paul Foulkes, Garden City, New

York, Doubleday & Co., 1959 (in) *Journal of Philosophy*, Vol. LVII, No. 11 (May 26, 1960): 365-68.

1961

Articles　　*The School of Padua and the Emergence of Modern Science*: Series *Saggi e Testi* of Il Centro per la Storia della Tradizione Aristotelica nel Veneto of the University of Padua and the Columbia University Seminar on the Renaissance, Vol. 1, Padua, Editrice Antenore, 1961: 141 p.

"The Changing Impact of Darwin on Philosophy" (in) *Journal of the History of Ideas*, Vol. XXII, No. 7 (October-December, 1961): 435-62.

Foreword　　Aristotle, *Aristotle's Physics*, newly translated by Richard Hope, foreword by John Herman Randall, Jr., Lincoln, University of Nebraska Press, 1961: v-viii.

1962

Book　　*The Career of Philosophy: From the Middle Ages to the Enlightenment*, New York, Columbia University Press: xiv, 993 p.

Article　　"Religious Language," Written in response to a letter from the editor of *The Humanist* (in) *The Humanist*, Vol. 22, No. 6: 186.

Reviews　　Cassirer, Ernst, *The Logic of the Humanities*, translated by Clarence S. Howe, New Haven, Yale University Press, 1961 (in) *History and Theory*, Vol. II, No. 1 (1962): 66-74.

Ramsey, Paul, *Nine Modern Moralists*, Englewood Cliffs, New Jersey, Prentice-Hall, (in) *New York Herald Tribune Book Section*, December 11, 1962 (under the title "Justice, Mercy, Love, Ethics").

Solmsen, Friedrich, *Aristotle's System of the Physical World: A Comparison with His Predecessors*, Ithaca, New York, Cornell University Press, 1960 (in) *Philosophical Review*, Vol. LXXI, No. 4 (October, 1962): 520-23.

1963

Book　　*How Philosophy Uses Its Past*, New York and London, Columbia University Press, (Machette Lectures, No. 14): xiv, 106 p.

Articles　　"The Art of Language and the Linguistic Situation: A Naturalistic Analysis" (in) *Journal of Philosophy*, Vol. LX, No. 2 (January 17, 1963): 29-56.

"Arthur O. Lovejoy and the History of Ideas" (in) *Philosophy and Phenomenological Research*, Vol. XXIII, No. 4 (June, 1963): 475-79.

"Philosophy and Religion" (in) *The Great Ideas Today*,

edited by R. M. Hutchins and M. J. Adler, Chicago, Encyclopaedia Britannica, Inc., 1963: 227-277.

"Romantic Reinterpretations of Religion" (in) *Studies in Romanticism*, Vol. II, No. 4 (Summer, 1963): 189-212. (Note at bottom of p. 189 by Randall: "Some of the materials in this essay, which are taken from Book V, Vol. II of *The Career of Philosophy in Modern Times*, were first set in my *Role of Knowledge in Western Religion*, 1958: 78-93").

1964

Article
"John H. Randall's Shelf" (in) *New York Herald Tribune Book Week*, January 12, 1964: 32.

Review
Aristotle, *The Philosophy of Aristotle*, ed. by Renford Bambrough, New York, New American Library; Grene, Marjorie, *A Portrait of Aristotle*, Chicago, University of Chicago Press; Oats, Whitney, *Aristotle and the Problem of Value*, Princeton, Princeton University Press; Ross, Sir David, *Aristotle*, New York, Barnes and Noble; Walsh, James J., *Aristotle's Conception of Moral Weakness*, New York, Columbia University Press (in) *The Humanist*, Vol. 24, No. 6 (November-December, 1964): 196-7.

Foreword
Mesthene, Emmanuel G., *How Language Makes Us Know: Some Views about the Nature of Intelligibility*, foreword by J. H. Randall, Jr., The Hague, Martinus Nijhoff, 1964: vii-ix.

1965

Book
The Career of Philosophy: Volume Two: From the German Enlightenment to the Age of Darwin, New York, Columbia University Press, xii, 675 p.

Articles
"John Stuart Mill and the Working out of Empiricism" (in) *Journal of the History of Ideas*, Vol. XXVI, No. 1 (January-March, 1965): 59-88. (Reprinted in Randall's *The Career of Philosophy*, Vol. II).

"The University Seminar as a Source of Spiritual Power" (in) *American Scholar*, Vol. XXXIV, No. 3 (1965): 452-7. (Also reprinted in *A Community of Scholars*, the university seminars at Columbia, edited by Frank Tennenbaum, New York, Praeger, 1965: 46-52).

Review
Aristote et les problèmes de méthode, Papers presented at the symposium Aristotelicum, Louvain, 1960; Louvain and Paris, Éditions Nauwelaerts, 1961 (in) *Philosophical Review*, Vol. LXXIV, No. 2 (April, 1965): 244-251.

Introduction
Woodbridge, F. J. E., *Aristotle's Vision of Nature*, edited

with an introduction by J. H. Randall, Jr. with the assistance of Charles H. Kahn and H. A. Larrabee, New York, Columbia University Press, 1965, pp. xxii, 169.

1966

Articles

"Idealistic Social Philosophy and Bernard Bosanquet" (in) *Philosophy and Phenomenological Research*, Vol. XXVI, No. 4 (June, 1966): 473-502.

"Josiah Royce and American Idealism" (in) *Journal of Philosophy*, Vol. LXIII, No. 3 (February 3, 1966): 57-83.

"T. H. Green: The Development of English Thought from J. S. Mill to F. H. Bradley" (in) *Journal of the History of Ideas*, Vol. XXVII, No. 2 (April-June, 1966): 217-244.

Reviews

Niebuhr, Reinhold, *Man's Nature and His Communities: Essays on the Dynamics and Enigmas of Man's Personal and Social Existence*, New York, Scribner's, 1965 (in) *Journal of Philosophy*, Vol. LXIII, No. 2 (January 20, 1966): 46-53.

Richter, Melvin, *The Politics of Conscience: T. H. Green and His Age*, Cambridge, Mass., Harvard University Press, 1964 (in) *Journal of Philosophy*, Vol. LXIII, No. 16 (September 1, 1966): 476-478.

Wolff, Robert Paul, et al., *A Critique of Pure Tolerance*, Boston, Beacon Press, 1965 (in) *Journal of Philosophy*, Vol. LXIII, No. 16 (September 1, 1966): 457-465.

Contributors

VIRGIL C. ALDRICH
Professor of philosophy, University of North Carolina: author of *Philosophy of Art*.

JOHN P. ANTON
Professor of philosophy at the State University of New York at Buffalo; author of *Aristotle's Theory of Contrariety*.

WILLARD E. ARNETT
Professor of philosophy at Chatham College; has written *Santayana and the Sense of Beauty* and *Religion and Judgment*.

HARRY ELMER BARNES
Emeritus professor, Columbia University; author of *Sociology and Political Theory* and *Intellectual and Cultural History of the Western World*.

JACQUES BARZUN
Provost of Columbia University and author of *Classic, Romantic and Modern*, and *The House of Intellect*; a member of the editorial board of *The American Scholar*.

JOSEPH L. BLAU
Professor of religion and philosophy at Columbia University; has written *Men and Movements in American Philosophy* and *Cornerstones of Religious Freedom in America*.

JUSTUS BUCHLER
Professor and Chairman of the department of philosophy at Columbia University; among his books are *Nature and Judgment* and *The Concept of Method*.

ARTHUR C. DANTO
Professor of philosophy at Columbia University; author of *Nietzsche* and *Analytical Philosophy of History*, and one of the editors of the *Journal of Philosophy*.

WILLIAM F. EDWARDS
Associate professor of philosophy at the State University of New York at Buffalo, a member of the Center for Aristotelian Studies at Padua and assistant editor of *The Metaphysics of Naturalism*.

HORACE L. FRIESS

Emeritus professor of philosophy and religion at Columbia University; co-author of *Religion in Various Cultures* and editor of the *Review of Religion*.

NEAL W. GILBERT

Professor of philosophy at the University of California, Davis; author of *Renaissance Concepts of Method* and member of the editorial board of the *Journal of the History of Philosophy*.

J. GLENN GRAY

Professor and chairman of the department of philosophy, Colorado College; author of *Hegel's Hellenic Ideal* and co-author of *Continental Philosophy Today*.

JAMES GUTMANN

Emeritus professor of philosophy, Columbia University; author of *Shelling* and editor of Spinoza's *Ethics*; member of the advisory board of *Studies in Romanticism*.

GEORGE L. KLINE

Professor of philosophy at Bryn Mawr College; author of *Spinoza in Soviet Philosophy* and editor of *A. N. Whitehead: Essays on His Philosophy* and *European Philosophy Today*.

PAUL OSKAR KRISTELLER

Professor of philosophy at Columbia University; his books include *The Philosophy of Marsilio Ficino* and *Studies in Renaissance Thought and Letters*.

PAUL KURTZ

Professor of philosophy at the State University of New York at Buffalo; author of *Decision and the Condition of Man*; he has edited two volumes, *American Thought Before 1900* and *American Philosophy in the 20th Century*; he is U.S. Director of the *Bibliography of Philosophy*.

EMMANUEL G. MESTHENE

Executive Director of the University Program on Technology and Society, Harvard University, and a member of the Faculty of the Harvard School of Public Administration; author of *How Language Makes Us Know*.

RICHARD H. POPKIN

Professor and chairman of the department of philosophy at the University of California, San Diego; author of *History of Scepticism from Erasmus to Descartes* and editor of the *Journal of the History of Philosophy*.

JOHN E. SMITH

Professor of philosophy at Yale University; he has written *Royce's Social Infinite, Reason and God* and *The Spirit of American Philosophy*.

PATRICK SUPPES

Professor of philosophy and director of the Institute for Mathematical

Studies in the Social Sciences, Stanford University; author of *Axiomatic Set Theory* and *Decision Making: An Experimental Approach.*

FRANK TANNENBAUM

Director of University Seminars at Columbia University; among his books are *Crime and Community, The American Tradition in Foreign Policy* and *Ten Keys to Latin America.*

H. STANDISH THAYER

Professor of philosophy at the City University of New York; author of *The Logic of Pragmatism* and editor of *Newton's Philosophy of Nature.*

Index